Cambridge Urban and Architectural Studies

Energy, Environment and Building

A report to the Academy of Natural Sciences of Philadelphia
(19th Street and the Parkway, Philadelphia, Pennsylvania)

Cambridge Urban and Architectural Studies

General Editors: Leslie Martin
                     Emeritus Professor of Architecture, University of Cambridge

                     Lionel March
                     Professor, Department of Systems Design, University of Waterloo,
                     Ontario, and University Lecturer, Department of Architecture,
                     University of Cambridge

Volumes in this series: 1. Urban Space and Structures, edited by Leslie Martin and
                            Lionel March

                            2. Energy, Environment and Building, by Philip Steadman

                            3. Urban Modelling, by Michael Batty

                            4. The Architecture of Form, edited by Lionel March

Energy, Environment and Building

Philip Steadman
Assistant Lecturer in the Department of Architecture,
University of Cambridge

Cambridge University Press

Cambridge

London · New York · Melbourne

Published by the Syndics of the Cambridge University Press
The Pitt Building, Trumpington Street, Cambridge CB2 1RP
Bentley House, 200 Euston Road, London NW1 2DB
32 East 57th Street, New York, NY 10022, USA
296 Beaconsfield Parade, Middle Park, Melbourne 3206, Australia

Library of Congress Catalogue Card Number: 74 - 29352

ISBN: 0 521 20694 4, hard covers
ISBN: 0 521 09926 9, paperback

First published 1975
Reprinted 1975

Printed in the United States of America

Contents/Index

collectors, solar engines (74), work of Shuman (75), work
of Harrington, Willsie, Boyle, Abbott, Russian work (76),
Association for Applied Solar Energy, work of Tabor (77),
Trombe and solar furnaces, current U.S. solar research
(78), work of NASA, Glaser satellite proposal, Meinel
'solar farm' (79), selective coatings, Meinel 'planar'
collector, NSF support (80), work by commercial firms (81)
Applications of solar energy in buildings (81), radiation
reaching earth's surface, variation with seasons (82),
passage through atmosphere (83), tilt and orientation of
solar collectors, diffuse radiation (84), numbers of consecutive cloudy days, albedo, night sky radiation, meteorological data (89), solar heating and climate, map by
Siple (86), maps of solar radiation in U.S. (87), Löf
climate index, Telkes map of degree days/sunshine hour,
performance of flat-plate collectors (88), tilt of collector,
architectural incorporation, collector walls, variation in
orientation (90), cover sheets, glass and plastic covers,
design of absorbing surface (91), heat transfer, insulation of
collector, selective blacks, work of Seraphin (93), materials
of absorbers, efficiency, collector costs (94), solar water
heaters, standards of hot water consumption, water circulation (95), auxiliary heating, solar water heating in Japan
(96), costs of solar water heaters (97)

Heat storage, proposal of Schönholzer (100), required heat
storage capacity, 100% solar heated buildings, area of
collector (101), Löf 'heating design index', 'design adequacy index', materials for heat storage, water, rocks (102),
position of heat storage reservoir, latent heat storage (103),
Glauber's salt, work of Telkes, Dover house, buildings
using latent heat storage (104), University of Pennsylvania
work, storage of 'cold' for air conditioning, combination
of collector with heat storage, Hay 'roof ponds' (105),
Baer collector/storage wall (106), Trombe/Michel solar
wall, heat pumps in solar systems, work of Sporn and
Ambrose (107), night sky radiation sooling, refrigeration
with solar energy, experiments of Chung, Löf, Duffie (108),
Brisbane solar refrigeration work (109), photovoltaic conversion (110), efficiencies of solar cells, integrated solar
thermal/electric systems (111), costs of solar cells, costs of
solar space heating (112), Löf and Tybout study (113),
urban 'sun rights', prospects for solar heating (115)

Acknowledgements

The range of subjects which this report attempts to cover is wide, and the treatment is accordingly superficial in places. I make no claims to any great originality in what is contained here; and I have relied very heavily for the most part on a number of other sources, in which each of the individual subjects has been treated by others much more completely and expertly than I am able to do. If there is any original contribution, it is perhaps in bringing together, digesting and in some degree coordinating a mass of information about what is now a very fast growing subject of interest both inside and outside the architectural profession; and where articles, documents and reports, many of them difficult to find and collect, are multiplying daily.

I have had the good fortune to be able, on behalf of the Academy, to collect together at least some of these publications; and also to visit many of the individuals, research groups and companies working in these areas around the country, and see a number of relevant buildings and experimental projects. My indebtedness to different published sources will be clear from the references in the text. I am very grateful to a large number of people for their help, for their courtesy, hospitality and kindness, and for valuable discussions both of their own work, and in many cases also of the whole subject of energy conservation and ecological approaches in building. Among those I would like to give particular thanks to are:

Harold Lorsch; University of Pennsylvania
Jerome Goldstein; Rodale Press, Emmaus, Pennsylvania
Robert Socolow, Dick Grot and Harrison Fraker; Princeton University
Daria Fisk; University of Texas
James Thring, Gerry Smith, Brenda and Robert Vale, Alex Pike, Ken Yeang; University of Cambridge, England
John Trela; University of Delaware
Richard Merrill; New Alchemy West, Santa Barbara
L. John Fry; Santa Barbara
Harold Hay; Sky Therm Processes and Engineering, Los Angeles
Paul and Cathy Relis; Community Environmental Council, Santa Barbara
Valentine Lehr; Lehr Associates, New York
Fred Dubin and Bruce Anderson; Dubin-Mindell-Bloome, New York
John Yellott; Phoenix
W. Beauchamp; University of Arizona
Steve and Holly Baer; Zomeworks, Albuquerque
Bob Reines, Jay Baldwin; ILS Laboratories, Tijeras N.M.
Richard Rittelmann; Burt, Hill and Associates, Butler Pa.
Malcolm Wells; Cherry Hill N.J.
Andrew MacKillop; Low Impact Technology, Cornwall, England
Everett Barber; Yale University
Ralph von Schneider; FAFCO, Redwood City Ca.

2

Also the many others who have kindly sent published and printed material in answer to my requests.

My special thanks are due to Peter Rickaby, who made the drawings with such care and skill.

Finally, I am especially appreciative of the great kindness and enthusiasm of Bill Marvel, with whom the idea for this report was originally conceived, and without whose support and friendship it would not have been carried through to completion.

Copyright permissions

I am grateful to the following individuals and publishers for kind permission to reproduce copyright materials:

Stanford Research Institute, Menlo Park, California, table on p.19
Fred S. Dubin, diagrams on p.24, diagram on p.43, diagrams on pp.56 and 57, and 'Conservation checklist' pp.59-62
Malcolm B. Wells, drawings on p.29
Atlantis Verlag AG, Zurich, drawing on p.33
Princeton University Press, diagram on p.37
Harvard University Press, maps on p.87
Dr Maria Telkes, map on p.89
Yale University Press, diagram on p.92, table on p.104
Frederick H. Morse and the NSF/NASA Solar Energy Panel, diagram on p.109
Arthur D. Little, Inc., diagram on p.110
Dr K.W. Böer, diagram on p.111, and drawings on p.152
Professor G.O.G. Löf, table on p.114, diagram on p.127
Dr H.G. Lorsch, list of solar heated buildings on pp.121-162
Dr H.E. Thomason, diagrams on p.141, drawing on p.143
Professor Dennis Holloway, drawings on p.146
Lama Foundation and Steve Baer, drawing on p.148
Professor Reyner Banham, diagram on p.161
P. Richard Rittelmann and Burt, Hill and Associates, drawing on p.166
Hackett Publishing Co., Indianapolis, drawing on p.190
Volunteers in Technical Assistance, drawing on p.196, diagrams on p.214, diagrams on p.216, table on p.219, drawing on p.260
Henry Clews and Solar Wind Co., table on p.197, table on p.201
Dr G.E. Smith, list of windmill manufacturers on pp.205-208, table on p.257
The James Leffel and Co., drawing on p.218
Richard Merrill and New Alchemy Institute West, diagram on p.224
John Wiley and Sons, New York, diagrams on pp.226 and 227
Dr R.B. Singh, diagram on p.235
R. Lindström and AB Clivus, diagram on p.247
Witold Rybczynski and Minimum Cost Housing Group, McGill University School of Architecture, drawing on p.262 and drawing on p.270
Richard Blazej, Grassy Brook Village, drawings on p.272
Nicholas Pole and Eco-Publications, Cambridge, diagram on p.287

Full details of the original sources of these materials are given on the pages indicated. While every effort has been made to contact copyright holders, this has proved impossible in one or two cases; but the publishers and author will be glad to make any corrections of which they are informed.

Bibliographies

The bibliographies which follow the chapters are catholic and uncritical. It will be obvious that I have not been able to see, let alone read, many of the works listed; but nevertheless I have thought it worthwhile to collate and present all the bibliographical material which I have been able to find – and so the listings are all-inclusive and not selective. This accounts for the lack of uniformity and incompleteness in some of the bibliographical details.

Although references have been collected from many sources, the bibliographies are in great part conflations of a number of existing bibliographies compiled by other authors, specifically the following:

Andrew MacKillop, Energy Bibliography and Equipment Sources, University College, London, mimeog., n.d.

Ken Yeang, Bibliography: Guide to Designed Ecosystems and Autonomous Housing Research, Cambridge University Department of Architecture, mimeog. April 1972

Bibliographical details listed in R. Church, G. Crouch and B. Vale, The Autonomous Servicing of Dwellings, diploma thesis, Cambridge University 1972

Bibliographical details listed in F. Daniels, Direct Use of the Sun's Energy, Yale 1964

Bibliographical details listed in B. Anderson, Solar Energy and Shelter Design, Master's thesis, Department of Architecture, MIT, 1973

And lastly the indispensable

'Bibliography Issue' of Alternative Sources of Energy, No.9, Feb.1973

Introduction

In April 1973, I was asked by the Academy of Natural Sciences
of Philadelphia to carry out some work in connection with the
new natural history Museum which the Academy some day hopes
to build to replace its old building on the Parkway at Logan
Circle. In several conversations which I had had with Academy
officials the previous year, we had talked about how particularly
appropriate it would be for the Academy – being an institution
devoted to the study of natural history and ecology – to try to put
'ecological principles' into practice in the design of a new Museum
building. Such a building would seek, through its architecture and
its engineering, to conserve materials and energy (insofar as any
new building may); to cause minimal disturbance to the landscape,
perhaps in some measure to restore and enhance the natural environment of its site; and to reduce to a minimum its contribution to
atmospheric and water pollution. These things seemed to be the
duty of the Academy at the very least. But much more than this,
there was the possibility that the Museum's design, in its physical
structure and its functioning, could teach lessons about the relation
of man to his environment, and about the natural world; so that the
the building could itself become an exhibit quite as much as the
displays which it would house.

At the time when Academy staff and I first talked about these subjects in 1972, there would have been no difficulty in convincing
most people of the reality of the 'environmental crisis' in America.
It is rather difficult now, since the winter of 1973/4, to believe that,
only that short time ago, the reality of an 'energy crisis' was by no
means as widely accepted. In the context of the design of buildings,
while research in solar heating for instance had been going on for
forty years or more, it was still the rather obscure and unpublicised
preoccupation of a visionary few, regarded probably – if thought
about at all – by the greater part of the architectural and engineering
professions as impractical and of marginal significance; while the
idea of drawing power for new buildings from the wind or from
methane gas would have been thought of as eccentric or even laugh-
able, subjects confined to the pages of such esoteric underground
publications as Undercurrents or the Alternative Sources of Energy
Newsletter. Today NSF and NASA are pouring millions of dollars
into solar heating, and one can hardly open the pages of the New
York or the London Times without finding feature articles or letters
from eminent scientists about methane generators or windmills.

In 1972 research and experiment into energy conservation and new
sources of energy for building, though going on in many places, was
scattered, fragmentary and not very widely written about, at least
not in the popular press. I myself, as one of the previously ignorant
and admittedly somewhat unconvinced members of the architectural
profession, had been introduced to some of the thinking in these
areas by my colleagues in the Technical Research Division of the

Cambridge University Department of Architecture. In April 1973 I was asked by the Academy to try to collect together information about research work and experiment going on in the United States and elsewhere, in universities, in commercial companies, in professional practices and in consulting firms, as well as work by private individuals; and this book reports my findings between May and October of that year, with some updating and correction of factual and typing errors.

There are many quite simple ways in which, without recourse to new technologies or systems, buildings can be designed to be much less wasteful than the overlit, overheated, overcooled, under-insulated glass-clad prisms that are today's commercial norm. By a greater sensitivity to local climatic conditions, a more tactful respect for the surroundings and topography, for trees and the environmental values of planting, by careful design and by in many cases a return to traditional materials and methods of building, there are long-term economic benefits in fuel savings to be had - quite apart from the benefits in terms of conservation, and the intrinsic good sense of such an approach.

But beyond this basic thriftiness and good housekeeping in building design and management, some architects and engineers are looking to new sources of energy for building which will avoid the present dependence on fossil fuels, and will lessen the environmental damage resulting from their use. Most estimates put the amount of energy which is consumed in residential and commercial buildings, for all purposes, at around 33% of total U.S. energy consumption; and so savings or changes effected in this sector can, in time, have an appreciable impact on patterns of overall energy use.

First among these 'new' possibilities is the use of power from the sun. When Gulliver visited that other Academy, the Grand Academy of Lagado, he viewed the activities of the projectors to whom he was introduced, with some scepticism. The first man he saw '... had been eight years upon a project for extracting sun-beams out of cucumbers, which were to be put into vials hermetically sealed, and let out to warm the air in raw inclement summers.' The projector told Gulliver that 'he did not doubt in eight years more he should be able to supply the Governor's gardens with sunshine at a reasonable rate.' The second of the Academicians that Gulliver met, was employed in a rather less savoury enterprise: 'an operation to reduce human excrement to its original food', the details of which work we can well pass over here.

Like several other details from Gulliver's Travels there is something uncannily prophetic (Swift's scorn notwithstanding) in this episode. Three hundred years afterwards our latterday projectors are having some success in getting the sun-beams into the vials; though one might argue that in one sense we have, for a very long time even before Swift, been using cucumbers (in their pickled form perhaps), as well as every other form of food, for the purpose of storing solar energy. Solar radiation is converted to chemical energy via the mechanism of photosynthesis in plants, and constitutes the fundamental energy source for all life. Not only is this the source of man's muscular energy and body warmth; but the same photosynthetic processes create the stored chemical energy which we release when we burn such biological fuels as wood, peat, dried dung, or those in fossilised form such as coal, gas and oil. In a completely literal sense all these constitute stored solar energy, 'let out to warm the air' and for a thousand other purposes, winter and summer. The realisation that the deposits of fossil fuels are limited in extent and – in the case of oil – in imminent danger of complete exhaustion in the fairly near future, has led many people to a reappraisal of our sources of 'income' solar energy (by contrast with our stored fossil fuel 'capital'); and it is with these sources and their application in building that the present report is largely concerned.

So far as 'income' solar energy goes, this is not just a matter of the direct use of solar heat and light, and of its indirect use through the biological system. There is the fact that the movements and temperature gradients of the atmosphere, of the rivers and of the oceans are caused (in part) by the intermittent heating effects of the sun's radiation, and are exploited by man as wind power and hydro-electric power.

For practical application at the scale of a single building the possibilities for direct or indirect use of the sun's energy (without recourse to fossil fuels) would include the following: direct use of solar radiation for space heating, domestic water heating and for cooling – using the solar heat to drive absorption refrigeration equipment: the use of photoelectric 'solar cells' to generate electrical power – though this is presently rather expensive: the use of wind power to generate electricity: and the use perhaps of small-scale water power. All of these power sources are quite nonpolluting. While the initial investment in capital equipment may be high, higher than for conventional heating, air conditioning and electric power systems, the fuel 'cost' thereafter, both in the sense of economic cost, and more importantly in this context, 'environmental cost', is very small. (Though there may be some questions of resource availability to consider, as for example the use of lead in electrical batteries, and the use of such metals as cadmium and copper in solar electric cells.)

The activities of Swift's second Academician might serve as an unattractive metaphor for the whole natural cycle by which dead or consumed organic material is decomposed and its constituent chemical materials returned to the soil and to the atmosphere, where they may once again be assimilated into plant growth, and so go on round the cycle. There is a (rather minor) source of fuel to be found in the decomposition of sewage and organic wastes, and that is methane gas which is produced when these materials decay in the absence of air (anaerobically). This methane can be burned to provide power and heat in exactly the same way as that which is more usually referred to as 'natural' gas. More importantly, there are ways in which the whole cyclic system of organic growth and decay has been abused and distorted in industrialised agriculture, and by improper or inappropriate treatment of sewage and other wastes in centralised urban societies. On a small scale the waste treatment systems of buildings may be redesigned so as to help contribute to righting this situation.

The new Academy Museum would, according to present plans, be a building of some 130,000 ft^2, comprising exhibition areas, an auditorium and classrooms, a schoolchildren's lunch room and a separate restaurant, administrative offices and workshops. It has been suggested that the central and unifying theme for the exhibit plan of the Museum, be 'energy' - the dependence of life on solar energy, the utilisation of energy from the sun in the process of photosynthesis going on in plants, the dependence in turn of animal life on plants for food and the energy stored in those plants in chemical form. The fact of the building housing the Museum being itself dependent on the sun for heat and power could provide a telling illustration of, and counterpoint to the exhibits on this same theme, solar energy, and its role in plant and animal life. But the possibilities for parallels between the various 'systems' which the building might comprise, and the subjects of exhibits picturing the natural world, do not stop here. The use of wind power in the building to produce electricity might be linked with discussion of the role of the atmosphere and the weather in transporting the gaseous compounds, oxygen, carbon dioxide, water vapour, essential to the support of life. The use of water power could be related to water systems and the cycle of evaporation, transport of water in the atmosphere, precipitation and flow of water through streams and rivers. The enclosure of the building itself and its function as a shelter against the weather and outside disturbances might be contrasted with shelters and protective defences evolved by animals and insects.

More directly than all of these - somewhat loose - analogies of process, there are ways in which man's relationship to nature could be made evident in microcosm in the building and its immediate surroundings, by showing all the transport of materials and energy around and through the building, and passing to and fro across the boundaries of the site. In this conception the Museum becomes like an island, or a relatively isolated ecosystem, and the extent of its independence from or dependence on the world around, is made clear.

There is the flow of energy from the sun and wind into the building, and its use and dissipation. There is the possibility if the site is to be used in part for gardening and horticultural exhibits, of growing food crops in a small way. Since the building is to include a restaurant, then this fresh produce from the gardens could form part of the menu. Following the fate of this material inexorably onwards;

there is the possibility of local processing of sewage from the building either by anaerobic digestion to yield methane gas – which can in turn be used for fuel – or else by aerobic composting, in either case producing effluent or humus which can be returned to the soil for its nutrient value. In addition to sewage there are other potential sources of organic waste material – kitchen wastes, garden wastes and manure from the Academy's menagerie of live animals – which might be subjected to the same composting process. Rainwater falling on the building and site could be collected and used, 'grey' waste water locally treated and recycled in the building or else used for irrigation of the garden crops. All this could teach lessons – in the most vivid way – about natural cycles of growth and decomposition, the food chain, problems of agricultural practice, urban waste disposal and its environmental effects, and many other topics.

How practical are these possibilities, first for the new Museum, and second in buildings more generally? The answers to that question in detail and in particular cases, are of course dependent on a great many variables: on technological and materials developments, on the particular nature and location of individual buildings, on what happens over the next few years to the cost of fossil fuels, on what tradeoff any particular building owner or user is prepared to make, of capital investment against running costs or against other scales of value. Some of these points are discussed in greater depth in the chapters that follow.

As regards the Museum building itself, this is clearly something of a special case. It may be possible here to experiment with previously untried arrangements, and to justify the inclusion of demonstration systems as part of the Museum's exhibits, which in the cold commercial world of speculative building might not stand up as economically competitive, or might not meet with general public acceptance.

Insofar as it is possible to make broad generalisations however, the fact is that the technology of most of what is discussed here is simple, well-tried and indeed in some instances very ancient. The so-called 'new sources of energy' turn out to be very old ones. The use of wind power is of course centuries old; and for generating electricity on a small scale, well tested in practice in all parts of the world over the last fifty or sixty years. Recent advances in energy storage methods, in battery design and fuel cell technology, increase the present-day attractiveness of wind power.

There are intrinsic theoretical reasons why the exploitation of wind power makes more sense on a large scale rather than on a small scale though. The power produced varies, other things being equal, with the square of the diameter of the windmill rotor, and with the cube of the windspeed. It follows that a rotor of twice the diameter will yield four times the power. And that in a wind of twice the velocity, the power produced increases eight-fold. Over level ground the speed of the wind is in general greater with increasing height. Therefore broadly speaking, the bigger the rotor and the taller the tower, the better.

Some very large windmills have been built in the past for generating electricity, and several proposals for giant new wind electric machines are presently in the air, so to say. It would seem that the smaller windmills suitable for supplying the power needs for a single building, would find more justification in remote and isolated sites; and particularly of course in those hilly and coastal regions where average wind speeds are highest. Small scale hydro-electric equipment has been and still is sold for use on ranches and remote farmsteads; but here again there would seem to be economies of scale operating, and the number of suitable sites is also limited.

Composting is one of the most ancient arts known to man; its scientific study and development dates from the early 1900s; many industrial scale composting plants have been built; and the use of methane as a fuel in sewage treatment plants is also quite usual. On a smaller scale many village and rural treatment plants for sewage and organic wastes of a very simple design have been built, especially in India. Aerobic composting toilets are on the market, and small gas production plants have been in use on farms in Europe and elsewhere for many years.

There are two chief drawbacks to the local digestion of human sewage for the production of methane as a domestic fuel. One is the possible danger of disease, which the centralised water-borne sewage system was originally designed of course to combat. The other is the simple question of the amounts of material available. British statistics show that the average quantity of sewage processed in municipal works yields $1 \cdot 2$ ft^3 of gas per person per day. The average use of (natural) gas in cooking alone in a three-person household is 32 ft^3 per day. The gas output may be augmented by the digestion of kitchen and garden wastes, and in smallholdings, with animal manure. But here again it seems that methane as a fuel has more promise at the larger scale, in particular as it is presently exploited in European sewage works, to power the works themselves, and on farms where there is intensive rearing of live-stock. None of this negates the general value of composting organic wastes, whether by aerobic or anaerobic means, and the return of nutrients to the soil.

As for direct solar energy, there was a flourishing market for solar water heaters in California and Florida before the Second World War; and today in Israel, North Africa, Japan and Australia, many designs are widely available. In Japan there are over $2\frac{1}{2}$ million solar water heaters installed, serving more than a quarter of all baths. At least two American companies now manufacture solar heaters for swimming pools, the principles of which are not dissimilar to heaters for domestic water supplies.

The use of solar energy for space heating in buildings has been the

subject of experiment since the 1930s. Some forty-five buildings -
described in the list in this report - using solar energy to a greater
or lesser degree have been erected in America, and a further nine
or ten elsewhere; mostly houses but including one office building,
four schools and a number of small laboratories. Several of these
buildings are in successful operation today, and interest and
research in the subject is growing very rapidly.

There are two reasons why solar energy is especially appropriate
for these uses in building, as distinct for example from industrial
scale power production in 'solar farms'. The first is that solar
radiation is diffuse, and reaches large areas of the earth's surface
in a more or less evenly distributed spread. It is thus immediately
available, so far as use in buildings is concerned, however dispersed or remote these might be; but must be concentrated
together by some means for industrial use. What is more it is
relatively simple to achieve the low temperatures - in the 100°
to 200°F range - which are required for space and water heating
and for refrigeration even. But it is more difficult to generate
the higher temperatures, from 300° to 600°F, suitable for steam
power and electricity production. This demands the use of
steerable, focussing collectors or specially treated collector
surfaces, and the plants are ideally sited in desert and arid
regions, at a distance from the potential users of the power so
produced.

Several large firms including Texas Instruments and the Lockheed
Missile and Space Co are involved in research and development
work on the design of low temperature flat plate solar collectors
(whose principal application is in building). And it seems probable
that the near future will see the emergence of new firms set up
exclusively for the manufacture of solar heating equipment. The
level of National Science Foundation funding for research work
in the universities on solar energy applications for buildings, has
risen to $5·6 million in 1974; and NASA also has a substantial
involvement in this area. The projections of the joint NSF/NASA
Solar Energy Panel study made in 1972 suggest that 10% of all
new buildings might be solar heated and cooled by 1985, and 10%
of all buildings, new and old, by 2000.

There is no doubt that solar heating is quite feasible technically,
and debate now centres around the comparative economics of
solar energy, and on the most suitable approaches for different
climates, sites and sizes of building, and so on. Solar cooling is
still at a prototype stage, and few buildings with solar-driven
refrigeration equipment, as distinct from simple evaporative cooling,
have been built until recently; although four or five have been
constructed during 1974, including houses at Colorado State and
Ohio State Universities, and trailer houses designed by NASA and
Honeywell. Solar cooling has a certain conceptual attraction,
since the periods of maximum demand coincide of course with the
periods of maximum energy supply.

The use of photovoltaic cells for producing electricity has been well proved in the space program, and 90% of earth satellites use this source of power. One house has been erected, at the University of Delaware, which makes use of solar cells. The main disadvantage is that they are at present a hand-made, 'cottage industry' product, and the cost is many times too great to be competitive, although there are hopes to bring the cost down drastically by mass production.

Several projects which are taking an integrated ecological approach in building design along the lines suggested here for the Academy's Museum, are already at an advanced stage. A private house built by Robert Reines in New Mexico is 100% solar heated and wind electric powered. Two houses designed by groups of architectural students and incorporating many ingenious energy-conserving and 'low impact technology' features have been completed: the 'Ecol Operation' in Montreal, Canada and 'Project Ouroboros' in Minneapolis. A house designed for Mrs A.N. Wilson by Burt, Hill and Associates, to be built in West Virginia, will incorporate solar heating and cooling, wind electric power and solar cells, and an aerobic waste treatment system. A condominium project in New Hampshire, Grassy Brook Village, will also employ solar power, wind power and local waste treatment systems.

In Britain an 'Eco-house' has been built by the architect Graham Caine and the 'Street Farm' group; and several more projects of a comparable kind are planned, including houses by Low Impact Design, in Cornwall, and by the Cambridge University Department of Architecture's Technical Research Division.

There has been some discussion, in particular in connection with these house projects, of the concept of total 'autonomy' in building design. Such buildings would be entirely (or almost entirely) independent of piped services and centralised mains supply; and would instead depend wholly on ambient sources of energy (the sun, the wind etc.) and on local processing and recycling of wastes. At the extreme this independence would extend to the growing of food and the raising of animals, so that the 'autonomous house' would amount in effect to a self-supporting smallholding. Questions arise among the purists as to the ethics of being connected to the telephone system, or say of using any form of petrol-driven transport. There is the further problem that a house which might immediately on completion be autonomous, could nevertheless be dependent subsequently on large scale centralised service industries for its maintenance (e.g. the replacement of electrical batteries), and for a continuing supply of spare parts to keep it running.

There is certainly something intellectually very attractive in taking such an extreme stand; it has a brave polemical value, and there is a considerable engineering challenge in demonstrating the feasibility of such an aim (as with the Reines house in

New Mexico). There is, no doubt, an even greater emotional
attraction, especially for the American spirit of pioneering
independence – some sort of combination Thoreau, frontiersman
and Robinson Crusoe syndrome perhaps. The autonomous house
represents a return to a state of harmonious balance with nature;
a readmission into Eden after our wanderings in the World of
advanced technology. It has an obvious appeal for those with a
yearning to get back to the land, to get back into close touch with
the simple rural life and with the basic labour of working the
earth.

At the same time one might detect here another rather different
thread of American tradition – that of the lone inventor, the
backyard tinkerer, the do-it-yourselfer. Much of the technology
involved in harnessing the 'alternative sources of energy' is
as already mentioned simple in principle, requires no exotic
materials, and is suitable for construction in the home handyman's
workshop; though still offering plenty of scope for ingenuity and
resourcefulness. There is more than a touch of Edison, not to say
Rube Goldberg about some of the characters involved in solar
heating of buildings or the various ingenious designs of water and
wind power device; and the fascination to the average mech-
anically-minded person of a system that can be built at home and
does not need some remote and incomprehensible technology for
its manufacture, is very great.

For yet another group the autonomous house forms part of a whole
'alternative technology' or 'radical technology' movement, with
a strong Anarchist flavour, and characterised by a serious distrust
of the concentration of political and economic power which is
represented by centralised industrial capitalism.

But despite these emotional, intellectual and political attractions
of the idea of complete autonomy or self-sufficiency in building,
there are clearly many degrees of relative independence possible,
many middle ways between the poles of the autonomous homestead,
and the fully centralised type of services distribution system
typical of our cities today. The University of Delaware solar
house for instance is intended as a prototype for a whole series
of such houses which would be connected to the utility company's
electrical network and would act as a source of supplementary
generating capacity. Then there is the concept of the Total Energy
system, whereby a complex of buildings or say a housing estate is
served by its own small combined electricity generating and
heating plant. And there are designs for water and waste treatment plants at this same scale too. It is unlikely that any large
proportion of buildings could ever be completely autonomous.
But it is certainly quite possible that a large proportion of
buildings could become much less dependent than today on
centralised mains services; and that this could happen soon. This
would have a very appreciable impact in energy conservation and
in environmental improvement.

To return to the Academy's own type of building: there are two institutions with similar interests to those of the Academy, the Massachusetts Audubon Society and the Cary Arboretum of the New York Botanical Gardens, which are both presently in the process of planning new office and administration buildings which will be solar powered and comprise other energy-conserving systems in their design. And a third such institution, the College of the Atlantic in Maine, largely devoted to the study of ecology, is to make substantial use of wind power for its new classroom and dormitory buildings.

At the present however it seems as though there are few if any projects of the size, significance and public prominence as that envisaged by the Academy, in which it is proposed to make use of all these energy-conserving and environmentally conscious poss- ibilities in design in a coordinated coherent whole. Nor is it likely that in many other buildings will there be a comparable opportunity for expressing such an approach, and of displaying it so well to public view. Philadelphia has been associated in the past with some of the early developments in solar and wind power. One of the first solar engines was built by Shuman in Tacony in 1908; and the biggest windmill ever built, the Grandpa's Knob machine, was made very largely by Philadelphia and Penn- sylvania firms. Recently some of the more significant theoretical and experimental work in solar heating, thermal energy storage and biological sources of fuel has been carried on at the National Center for Energy Management and Power at the University of Pennsylvania. The Academy's proposed new Museum building would provide a unique opportunity for carrying on this tradition, and for putting many of the ideas which are now talked about into real practical application.

Philip Steadman, Cambridge, England

October 1974

Notes on energy, environment and the architecture of the modern movement

The use of energy in buildings has not in the recent past been a great concern of architects. This in America has been as much a consequence of the (up-to-now) plentiful abundance of cheap energy, as anything else. But there are perhaps other traits or tendencies, in the philosophy of the modern movement in architecture, which have also contributed to this neglect. The functionalism of the '20s and '30s urged that the form of a building, and particularly its plan, should clearly reflect, express or make plain the nature of the activities carried on inside that building. Le Corbusier's 'The plan is the generator' catches this idea in a slogan. The building was designed from the inside out, so that the internal forms, spaces and functions would be made evident to the observer on the outside, by the pattern of openings, the external shapes, and the constructional details – almost, to use the biological metaphor then popular, as though the internal organs of a creature were to be seen bulging or protruding from its skin, 'ex-pressed' so to say onto the outside.

This same clarity of expression was to be carried into the material construction of the building, whose structural logic was to be exposed and not concealed beneath a cosmetic or decorative surface. The nature of the materials themselves was to be apparent, and materials were to be used only in circumstances and for purposes appropriate to their special properties. The result of all these exhortations about 'truth to materials' and to building function, was that the external containing envelopes of buildings became very largely just consequences, almost accidental resultants of their internal organisation and material structure. This emphasis was clearly in opposition to the alternative and in many ways more traditional approach in architecture, where the design of the external 'shell' of a building arose, certainly out of physical structure and materials of construction, but first and foremost as a protection from the elements, a shelter, both to keep out wind, rain, excessive sun, great heat and cold, and to keep the inside warm or cool according to the season. The activities and internal spaces were then fitted as best they might be into this containing shell.

It is true that the performance of much primitive architecture was and is very poor in terms of the control of climate. Rapoport, among others, has pointed to the many examples of 'anticlimatic' building designs to be found in primitive cultures – forms of dwelling and types of construction which seem to be fundamentally unsuited to the local conditions of weather and site (A. Rapoport, House Form and Culture, Prentice-Hall 1969). And the existence of extremely varied solutions to the problems of 'design with climate' in different primitive societies which coexist in identical climatic surroundings, gives the lie to any suggestion that building forms in those cultures arise directly out of environmental conditions through some sort of deterministic relationship; of form to climate.

The fact remains though that in much traditional building, both primitive and vernacular, some very ingenious solutions can be seen, to the architectural problems of resisting the weather and of maintaining comfortable conditions indoors when the climate is harsh outside. By necessity these solutions have worked with simple materials and through the manipulation of the geometry of building form, through the relationship of one building to another (so as to provide shading, windbreaks, control of cooling breezes, and so on), as well as through the relationship of buildings to topography, and by the use of trees and plants (again to provide shade, or to maintain humidity in courtyards in dry regions, for example). The result is an infinitely more subtle, economical, humane mode of design, one that is often formally and aesthetically very rich as a consequence; by contrast with the brute-force technological solutions of today which work in spite of climate, rather than working with the elements, and which rely on 'imported' energy and mechanical services, rather than using local natural forces, deflected or diverted to achieve the effects desired.

Some specific examples from primitive architecture will be given in the next chapter, including illustrations of the use of materials with high thermal mass, such as mud or adobe, to control diurnal temperature swings in desert regions; methods for natural ventilation in humid climates; the control of solar radiation, and its absorption or reflection through the colouring of building surfaces; and the use of shutters and other shading devices. Some beautiful photographs of vernacular building throughout the world in which these features are well demonstrated, are reproduced in Rudofsky's Architecture Without Architects (Museum of Modern Art, New York 1964). The principles involved are discussed by Victor Olgyay in his fine book Design with Climate (Princeton 1963), by the historian James Marston Fitch, with Daniel P. Branch, in an article 'Primitive Architecture and Climate' in Scientific American (CCVII, No.6, Dec.1960, pp.134-44), as well as by Rapoport - to mention only a few names from a whole wealth of books on this subject. The bibliography given by Rapoport is particularly useful.

In the modern movement in architecture, certainly in Europe, it is fair to say that this possible responsiveness of building form to physical environment, to the climate, was not something very generally considered. (In America one notable exception to this rule being Frank Lloyd Wright, at least in his earlier 'Prairie' houses and desert buildings. Reyner Banham has written of the ingenuity of Wright's systems of environmental control and servicing, as for instance the Baker, Gale and Robie houses - as well as the work of Gill, Maybeck and the Greene brothers in California (in The Architecture of the Well-Tempered Environment, Architectural Press, London 1969). But Wright and the Californians were the last heirs to a 19th century tradition, and many of their contemporaries or successors in this century looked not to their example but to those of the European groups and figures of the '20s.)

Another and largely unrelated tendency of the modern movement, acting also to divert attention from concerns with climate and site, was the formal aesthetic interest in rectangularity, or with simple geometric forms; partly in reaction to the over-ornamentation and historicism of the 19th century, partly in sympathy with the contemporary pictorial and sculptural concerns of the Cubists and of De Stijl. Thus the simple flat-roofed rectangular block became the norm for buildings of the so-called 'International Style' of the '30s - a name which in itself gives evidence of the lack of concern in design for the variations of climate between different parts of the world.

Where there was concern for the orientation and siting of buildings, and scientific consideration of their physical environment, this was largely in relation to natural lighting - this being associated with ideas of health, with a bright new uncluttered vision of the modern industrial way of life, and of course with the aesthetics of the play of light upon simple sculptural forms. Great efforts were made to open up the claustrophobic gloomy box-like architecture of the Victorians, to admit light and air, to exploit the new possibilities of plate glass in large areas of window. All this, however admirable, had the unfortunate and perhaps largely unconsidered side-effect of greatly increasing the rate of loss of heat from buildings in cold weather, and of introducing excessive solar radiation and thus over-heating the interior, in the summer.

Though a concern with economy of means - aesthetic economy, structural economy, economy in space - is a hallmark of the functionalism of the modern movement, this is not an economy which, curiously, extended to the use of power or energy. Indeed there are elements in for example most characteristically the program of Futurism, of a quite opposite philosophy, believing in the unlimited capacity of modern technology to produce cheap electricity amongst other wonders in boundless supply, so freeing man (and woman, viz. housewife) finally and completely from the burdens of physical work. Modern architects have many of them been infatuated with technology, there are many secret and not-so-secret Futurists among their number; and so an ethic of energy conservation and of environmental restraint has been foreign to much of the theory and polemic of architecture until the last few years.

The subjects of landscape or 'townscape' design, and gardening, have not been so much a part of modern architectural practice and education as they would have been say in the 18th or 19th centuries. This is partly a result of the decline of private patronage, no doubt; but more importantly can I think be linked with some of the other central ideas in the philosophy of the modern movement already mentioned. Because great stress is laid on the internal organisation of the building, and its particular individual function, attention is correspondingly drawn away from the external spaces surrounding buildings.

In civic architecture up to the 19th century, buildings were conceived more often than not as component parts in the overall urban fabric, to be subordinated to the larger composition of streets, squares or terraces. Their external form was dictated as much by considerations of siting and neighbourliness, and the need to fit into some greater organizational or aesthetic whole, as by considerations of the activities which they housed. But the method of working from the inside outwards, of using the (individual building) plan as the 'generator', can be seen as encouraging an opposing view: of the building as an isolated object, a monument, to be seen three-dimensionally, sculpturally in the round - rather than as a flat facade flanked by other facades - and designed almost independently of the features of the site for which it is destined.

One result is that the means for environmental control within and around buildings which was formerly achieved through effects of mutual shading, enclosure and wind protection, are lost or must be replaced by mechanical substitutes, each building independent of every other. The present disintegration and collapse of civic form, and the visual incoherence of outdoor urban space - arguably as much a consequence of this aesthetic trend as it is of real estate speculation and the ravages of highway engineering - is paralleled by a collapse of the coherence of the street, square or other larger configuration of buildings as a means for the control of climate; witness the sun-baked shadeless plaza, the gale which blows around the foot of any freestanding high-rise structure, the windswept hinterland of so many a public housing development.

One of the great architectural visions of the 1920s in Europe was Mies van der Rohe's dream of soaring crystalline towers, transparent and glittering, monuments to the new technology of steel and glass. The vision has come to be realised many times over, by Mies, and in often debased forms by many others, in the office blocks of all modern cities. Both the financial logic and the aesthetic conception which dictate their form are in direct contradiction to a logic of energy conservation, which they acknowledge neither in their shape, their orientation - which seldom takes much account of the direction of sun or of prevailing wind - nor in their structure and materials - which are often light-weight and so poorly insulating, and in the large areas of glass typical of 'curtain wall' construction allow the passage, in different directions, of excessive amounts of solar radiation or of lost heat, so that in certain situations the same building may require simultaneously heating and cooling on its opposite sides. Brave efforts have been made to counter these problems with the use of specially treated glass, with blinds and shades; but the problems are ones which should perhaps not have been allowed to arise in the first place. Mies' gnomic dictum 'Less is more', though it might convey the formal asceticism of his works, is little better than a bad joke in the context of the energy performance of his buildings, for which 'Less with more' might be apter.

One feature of the organisation of modern architectural practice

which has led to wastefulness in energy use – unrelated to any
aesthetic or formal preoccupation – arises from the increasing
complexity of the technology of building and of the engineering
design of the mechanical services in large modern buildings in
particular. With this increasing complexity has come specialisation,
and the division of responsibilities in design between several professions; so that the individual architect no longer has grasp of the
entire design process, but instead seeks the advice of consultants.
Unless the collaboration is very close, as in some multi-professional
joint practices, the situation can and does arise, frequently, where
the building is designed in outline without reference to problems of
mechanical servicing; and this more or less finished scheme is then
handed to consultants whose job is to provide heating, ventilating,
air conditioning and other systems of a sufficient capacity to carry
the given load. The fact that the fees paid to these consultants
are calculated as a percentage of the cost of the equipment and
installation of the service systems which they specify, means that
there is no direct incentive to economy on their part – rather the
opposite. To counter this problem, the architect must consider,
from the beginning, how the overall form, the details and the construction of the building may be adapted so as to reduce the total
requirements for servicing, and thus cut energy use. Either the
engineering consultants must be involved in design from an early
stage, or else the relationship of building form and materials to
energy consumption must be better understood by the architect
himself.

One final factor. The great demand for housing built quickly and
cheaply, especially since World War II, has encouraged the development of industrialised and prefabricated systems of building.
While these systems have merits as an answer to these pressing
problems, the requirements for cheapness and for ease of transportation of units have led to the adoption in many cases of rather
lightweight construction. This often compares badly, from an
insulation and energy conservation point of view, with the more
massive masonry or brick structure typical of much traditional building.
Again the use of prefabricated systems means that buildings are
designed less specifically to accommodate to, or exploit the unique
conditions and local climates of individual sites. The logical
extreme point of this tendency is represented by mobile homes, now
accounting for more than a quarter of all new dwellings in the
United States, in which lightness of structure – to the point of
flimsiness – is at an absolute premium, where the identical design
is sold from coast to coast, and which are in Jay Baldwin's words,
' an energy disaster'.

Energy conservation measures in building

Before turning to alternative sources of energy other than those provided by the fossil fuels, consideration should be given first to the many ways in which the total consumption of energy – from whatever source – in buildings, at present wildly wasteful, can be reduced. Energy is used in buildings for space heating and cooling, for water heating, for lighting, for cooking and for refrigeration, and for running a variety of appliances and machines. The table below, taken from the Stanford Research Institute's Patterns of Energy Consumption in the United States (Nov. 1971), gives a detailed breakdown of consumption by use in the residential and commercial sectors, with comparative figures given for 1960 and 1968 and the annual rate of growth computed over this period.

Energy consumption in the United States by end use, 1960–1968
(Trillions of Btu and Percent per year)

Sector and end use	Consumption 1960	1968	Annual rate of growth	% of national total 1960	1968
Residential					
Space heating	4,848	6,675	4.1%	11.3%	11.0%
Water heating	1,159	1,736	5.2	2.7	2.9
Cooking	556	637	1.7	1.3	1.1
Clothes drying	93	208	10.6	0.2	0.3
Refrigeration	369	692	8.2	0.9	1.1
Air conditioning	134	427	15.6	0.3	0.7
Other	809	1,241	5.5	1.9	2.1
Total	7,968	11,616	4.8	18.6	19.2
Commercial					
Space heating	3,111	4,182	3.8	7.2	6.9
Water heating	544	653	2.3	1.3	1.1
Cooking	98	139	4.5	0.2	0.2
Refrigeration	534	670	2.9	1.2	1.1
Air conditioning	576	1,113	8.6	1.3	1.8
Feedstock	734	984	3.7	1.7	1.6
Other	145	1,025	28.0	0.3	1.7
Total	5,742	8,766	5.4	13.2	14.4

It will be seen that the total for the two sectors taken together accounted in 1968 for almost exactly one third (33.6%) of overall national energy consumption. Four uses, space heating and cooling, water heating, refrigeration and cooking, accounted for 88% of residential energy requirement, and 77% of commercial requirement. One particular figure to note is the very rapid annual rate of increase for residential air conditioning of 15.6%, representing a net tripling of consumption over the eight year period. In the commercial sector the growth of use for air conditioning is also fast, at 8.6% p.a.

The chart below, based on projections made by the U.S. Bureau of Mines, shows the anticipated increase in total energy consumption divided into major uses, up to 1990. Though residential and commercial consumption drops as a percentage of the total, there is still a substantial absolute increase.

U.S. energy consumption : consuming sectors
Figures from Bureau of Mines, Department of the Interior

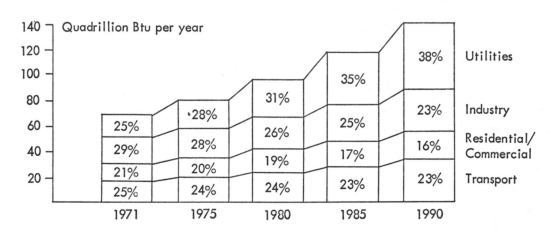

(The percentages for residential and commercial consumption in this chart and in the foregoing table are calculated in different ways. This is to do with the fact that when electricity is generated in central power plants and then distributed, substantial energy losses occur both in conversion (of fuel to electricity) and in transmission. In the figure these losses appear as consumption in the utilities sector: in the table they have been assigned to the relevant end uses in the commercial and residential sectors).

It should be mentioned that these projections from the Bureau of Mines are not as high as those made by some other analysts, and are themselves based on the assumption of certain energy conserving measures, including better insulation in new dwellings.

In their report to the President on The Potential for Energy Conservation (Oct. 1972), the Office of Emergency Preparedness make a broad and useful distinction within energy conservation measures of all kinds, into the categories of what they call "belt tightening" and "leak plugging". "Belt tightening" in their words 'is defined as those measures which would reduce energy output at fixed efficiency

"Belt tightening"

"Leak plugging"

levels. "Belt tightening" can take the form of long-term efforts to reduce consumption or emergency measures to prevent or mitigate brownouts or blackouts... "Leak plugging" is defined as those measures which would retain performance while increasing efficiency. Thus, "leak plugging" would rely on applications of extant technology, such as improved insulation in buildings, and other measures which would improve the efficiency of energy use in the short and mid-term.' To give an example from transport: leaving your car at home and going to work on foot, by bus, or sharing in a car pool, would be "belt tightening", whereas having the engine of your car tuned to improve the mileage per gallon would be "leak plugging".

Space heating is the most substantial component of energy use in buildings, and is the most likely candidate for saving in the residential and commercial sectors. There are any number of ways in which these economies can be effected. These may be "leak plugging" measures again, such as improved insulation as mentioned, or for example increasing the efficiency of furnaces and boilers. Or they may be "belt tightening" expedients such as for example maintaining thermostat settings at some few degrees lower than is presently normal.

Space heating and cooling

A good overall analytic understanding of the problem of heating buildings can be gained with the help of a useful formal statement of the economic space heating equation, given by Hottel and Howard. This equation relates the annual cost of heating to fuel costs, capital equipment costs, and maintenance costs.

Seasonal heating cost ($/year) =

fuel cost + capital cost + maintenance cost

This assumes the maintenance of some given level of temperature for comfort within the building, and of course depending what this chosen level of temperature is, so the total cost will vary. Assuming a fixed temperature for the moment; the components of the equation may be broken down further into their constituent factors. Not all these factors can be exactly quantified, and so it is not possible to optimise mathematically for minimum cost; neverthless a formal expression of the problem does show up clearly the various different ways in which energy consumption can be reduced.

The fuel cost may be expressed thus :

$$\text{Fuel cost} = \frac{0.0024F}{E} \ (D \ (\lesssim AU + cn) - g)$$

Where E is the thermal efficiency of the fuel used, as a percentage
F is the fuel cost in $/$10^5$ Btu
D is the 'degree days' /year. This is a means of expressing the temperature conditions, during the heating season, of some particular location and climate. It is assumed for these purposes that no heating is needed on days when the

average outside temperature exceeds 65ºF. For all days when the temperature falls lower then this, the difference is taken between the average temperature and 65. The sum of all these differences gives the degree days/year. Typical figures would be for example, 1,161 for Jacksonville, Florida, as compared with 7,989 for Minneapolis, Minnesota.

ΣAU is the sum of all the areas A of heat transfer coefficient values U ('U-values') making up the external skin of the building, in Btu/ºF/hour

c   is the heat capacity of the air contained in the building, in Btu/ºF (0.018 x volume in ft^3)

n   is the number of air changes in the building per hour

g   is the heat gain from sources other than the heating system: from appliances, from the occupants, from the lights, from insolation on the building surface or through windows, or from ventilation, in Btu/year

(The unit of heat energy used here, Btu is the British thermal unit. 10^5 Btu = 1 therm.)

The capital cost component is the equation may be expressed as $\dfrac{Ci}{100}$

Where C is capital expenditure in dollars on all parts of the heating system, including insulation, double glazing and any other feature of the building designed to save heat, some of these very difficult to attribute precise costs to.

i   is the interest, plus depreciation, on the capital investment, as a %/year

Finally the maintenance cost is expressed as an annual figure in dollars.

Substantially the same range of factors enter into calculations of the cost of cooling in summer, where this applies, with the obvious main differences that the heating effects of artificial lighting, solar gain etc. then represent an additional load, rather than a bonus as they do with the heating equation; and also calculation must be made on the basis of the number of days on which the outside temperature rises above some given figure (and how high above).

Fuel efficiency and fuel cost

To go back to the first part, the expression for fuel cost. The first term in this expression E, the thermal efficiency of the fuel, relates to the particular choice of fuel to be used, while the second term F, the fuel cost, follows as a consequence of this choice. Some typical efficiencies for different fuels are :

Anthracite, hand-fired	60% – 75%
Bituminous coal, hand-fired	40% – 65%
Bituminous coal, stoker fired	50% – 75%
Oil and gas fired	65% – 80%
Electricity	100%

The figures for combustible fuels are dependent on the adjustment of furnaces, and efficiency may be reduced by 5% or 10% as a result of poor maintenance.

The 100% figure for electricity is deceptive, since this refers to efficiency 'at the socket' and conceals the fact that where electricity is generated in central power plants a considerable part (about 65%) of the energy in theory available from the combustion of the fuel used to fire the plant is lost as waste heat, and other losses (perhaps another 5%) occur in electricity transmission; so that the net efficiency is little better than 30%. The waste heat in the mean time is thrown away, either in the cooling water drained into streams and rivers, or else to the atmosphere – all this contributing to thermal pollution.

Electric heating

Electric resistance heating is popular, particularly in private houses put up by speculative builders, because of the low first costs. But this is extravagant and inefficient generally in energy consumption by comparison with other forms of heating. It has been the practice in the past to provide higher standards of thermal insulation in many electric-heated buildings, in order that the heating costs be competitive with oil and gas. But of course there is no reason why these same high standards of insulation should not be provided in gas and oil heated buildings, equally. Electricity is only really appropriate for 'spot' heating to bring parts of a building quickly up to the required temperature; or in rooms or buildings which are only used and heated for short periods at intervals. The use of electricity is appropriate too, to drive heat pumps (described below); but this is not properly a form of electric heating in itself.

Total Energy systems

A means of cutting the losses inherent in the central generation of electrical power, is represented by the introduction of so-called 'Total Energy' systems. The theory here is to bring onto the site of a large building complex or, say, a housing estate, for example, a miniature electricity generating plant which supplies the needs of that development alone. Not only are the losses in power transmission so avoided, but the heat produced by the plant, which would otherwise go to waste, can be used to supply the space and domestic water heating needs of the adjacent buildings. Alternatively, in summer, the heat can be used in absorption chillers for air-conditioning systems. The electricity generator may be driven either by a gas-fueled turbine, or with a gas or oil-fired engine. Under the best conditions, the energy efficiency of the whole process may be increased from the 30% for central generating stations, to 70%; though for various reasons these best conditions cannot always be created. It goes without saying that the greater efficiency of fossil fuel use in Total Energy systems results in a considerably lowered contribution to air pollution.

Matching of loads in Total Energy systems

One of the difficulties which tends to reduce the efficiency of Total Energy installations, is the fact that the demand for heat does not

Efficiency comparison:
Total Energy with
central station

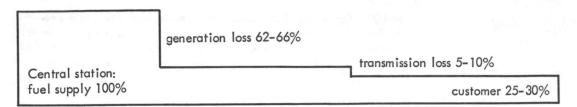

generation loss 62–66%

transmission loss 5–10%

Central station:
fuel supply 100%

customer 25–30%

conversion loss at point of use 15–35%

Total Energy:
fuel supply 100%

customer 65–85%

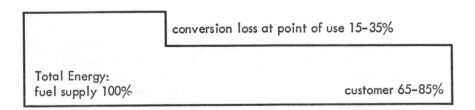

Adapted from Fred S.
Dubin, 'Total Energy for
Mass Housing – Why it
Makes Sense', Actual
Specifying Engineer,
Feb. 1973 p.79 fig.7

Below: typical load profiles in winter for 1,000 houses, each of
1,200 ft^2. Total heating demand is shown by the heavy solid line
at the top of the figure. The thin solid line shows the pattern of
base electric demand. In a Total Energy system, the heat produced in generating this electricity (indicated by the lower of
the heavy solid lines) can be recovered and used. The difference
between this recovered heat, and the total heating demand is thus
represented by the area within the heavy solid lines.

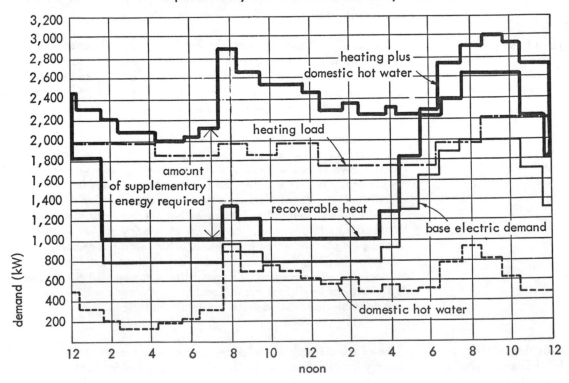

always coincide precisely in time with the demand for electricity, either on a seasonal or on a daily basis. During the daytime in winter, the requirements for heat in housing developments will in general greatly exceed what is available as a by-product of generating the required electricity, although during the evenings the loads are better matched. The summer matching is dependent in large degree on what proportion of dwellings are air-conditioned. There is good scope for using Total Energy systems in mixed developments, say schools with apartments, or offices with apartments, where the heating and electricity demands can be spread more evenly over the whole twenty-four hour period. (Opportunities for multiple uses of space in such developments offer, incidentally, another area for potential energy conservation). Total Energy systems are presently in operation at Rochdale Village, the Wabasse housing complex in Brooklyn, and the Kings Plaza Shopping Centre, all in New York, at the HUD Jersey City 'Operation Breakthrough' site, and at Wingate Village in Indianapolis, among other places. Battersea power station in London uses its 'waste' heat for space heating in local housing around the station. One of the largest and oldest Total Energy systems in the world is Consolidated Edison's combined electricity and piped steam system in Manhattan.

In a broader context, the term 'total energy' has been used rather loosely and perhaps improperly to describe the integration of a wider range of building and urban power systems. For example the heat produced in the incineration of garbage can be exploited for useful purposes. Again the 'waste' heat from electricity generation might find uses besides those in buildings - in agriculture, aquaculture or in the digestion of sewage sludge. Some of these possibilities are discussed in later chapters.

Fuel costs

The comparative costs of gas, oil or electricity for heating can vary in different parts of the country. For the reasons already indicated electricity is universally the most costly form of energy of the three for space heating and cooling. Oil is generally cheaper than gas, but this can vary with location. In making cost and energy consumption evaluations of proposed systems for buildings, consideration should be given to the fact that prices of oil and natural gas are likely to rise sharply over the next few years. Nuclear power is still some way off supplying any great proportion of electricity demand, and even such contribution as it presently makes is at a much higher cost than promised in the days of nuclear power optimism in the '50s and '60s. Reserves of coal are more extensive and expected to last much longer than those of oil and gas - for several centuries possibly. But both coal-fired and nuclear powered electricity generating stations are presently 'under a cloud' so to say, literal and metaphorical, because of the pollution threats they pose. The net results of all this is that although cheap and plentiful electricity from nuclear power and coal gasification may be a possibility in the long run, in the short term electricity prices are bound to continue to rise steeply, in step with the price increases in gas and oil.

Rising fuel costs and
'life-cycle' costing

Buildings that are designed today, in the middle 1970s, may be expected to have a useful life at least up to 2010 and after; and it is arguable that in energy and conservation terms we should be designing buildings for much longer life-spans than the forty year norm which this represents, perhaps for 60, 100, even 200 year lives. In any case it is worth observing the implication of this: that most buildings erected from now will have lives beyond the date at which, according to most expert opinion, world oil and gas production will peak and go into decline. Buildings are not like other products, such as cars, in this respect, where the technology can, at least in principle, be rapidly changed. The whole stock of cars might be replaced with some new kind, smaller, electric-driven perhaps, within a few years. With buildings this is not possible, and we are stuck, for better or worse, with existing stock for up to half a century or more. When considering the comparative economics of solar energy for space heating and cooling for example, covered in detail in later chapters, although it is true that direct solar energy cannot compete economically with the use of oil and gas at today's prices, on the basis of 'life-cycle costing' (see p.44) and with the perspective of what is likely to happen to gas and oil over the life-cycle of all new buildings, this picture of the economic attractiveness of solar energy may prove very different - setting aside its other benefits in terms of resource conservation and reduction of pollution.

Degree days

Going back to our earlier heating cost equation, the next term in the fuel cost expression is D, the number of 'degree days' per year, this being an expression of the average outside temperature conditions during the heating season and at some particular location. For any specific project this is a given, of course; but depending on the local climate conditions in each particular place, so the relative appropriateness of various heat-conserving or heat-rejecting measures - insulation, control of building orientation, control of building shape, areas, angles and orientation of glazing, and many other factors - will vary. A proper consideration of and response to these factors can perhaps bring a new regionalism back into architecture, so that an office building say in Phoenix would be clearly recognisable from one in Washington, or one in Montreal - not always the case today.

Insulation

Of all the very many factors in building design the one with the most immediate and substantial potential benefits to offer for energy conservation is the factor of insulation. The insulating properties of the building shell are expressed in our heating cost equation as $\leq AU$, that is the sum of all the areas A of the outside surface of the building, multiplied in each case by an appropriate factor, the 'U-value', expressing the ease with which heat passes through the construction of that particular surface. Thus the U-value is the combined thermal value not only of the different materials making up a wall for example (brick plus insulation material plus plaster say), but also of the air spaces or air films - which can have considerable insulation value - trapped within the structure. The lower the U-value, the better the insulation. Typical values are 1.13 for a single sheet of glass, 0.85

for 4 inches of solid concrete, and 0.06 for a good exterior stud wall with $3\frac{1}{2}$ inches of fibreglass insulation. The insulating properties of the building shell may be improved either by reducing A, the surface areas or by reducing the coefficients U.

Minimum surface area

For minimum surface area a building would be of compact shape and at the extreme theoretical case round in plan or spherical in shape. Such buildings are represented in practice by Fuller's geodesic domes, or by for example Robert Reines' dome house in New Mexico (see p.149) whose shape is chosen for just this minimal surface for given volume property (amongst other reasons). Buckminster Fuller has always urged this as a virtue of his domes, and has pointed to the fact that as the absolute size of the dome increases so the ratio of volume to surface goes down, thus giving even better heat savings – since while the volume increases by the cube, the surface area increases only by the square. A similar consideration accounts for the fact that ice cubes melt at a much faster rate than icebergs; and all this is related to the biological 'principle of similitude', one of whose consequences is that animals of very large size such as elephants or hippopotami must generally have means of losing heat continuously (in elephants the ears act to some extent as cooling 'fins'); while small warm-blooded creatures such as mice and birds, with high relative surface areas, must be well-insulated and be continuously eating to keep up their body temperature.

Back in the architectural context, Fuller again has pointed out how the overall three-dimensional form of Manhattan island, with its thousands of separate building 'spikes' could hardly have been better devised as a means of increasing surface area and so of losing heat – much like the cooling fins on a motorcycle engine or a car radiator. For summer cooling in Manhattan this is of course a good thing. Fuller's proposal to cover the island with a single giant dome is partly based on a notion of reducing heat loss by an effective reduction of this enormous surface area.

The hemispherical dome form assumes from a theoretical point of view a building surface of uniform U-value, and also that the insulating properties of the ground surface are good. In general round and dome forms are inconvenient on a number of counts other than their thermal properties, and factors such as lighting and the internal layout of rooms work in favour of less compact, more elongated and generally rectangular geometries. For simple rectangular blocks with surfaces (not counting the ground) of equal U-value, the best form for low heat loss is the half-cube; but where the U-value of the roof is not equal to that of the walls, as typically is the case, the optimum form will be different, and in general this theoretical 'model' is highly artificial and simplistic, because of all the complicating effects in real terms of windows, orientation, the wind and other factors.

Thermal mass

Traditional heavy construction – in brick, masonry or concrete – had good insulating properties, and the great weight of heat-retaining material acted to increase the 'thermal mass' of the structure, so saving the heat from the daytime to be released during the night, and thus damping out the considerable diurnal swings in temperature which can occur in light-weight structures. Much indigenous and primitive building made ingenious use of insulating materials and features, often by half-burying houses in the ground, or with the use of earth berms and sod or earth-covered roofs. Rudofsky shows pictures of entire cities in China where the houses are all below the earth's surface, dug into the ground, and lit by courtyards or light-wells.

Earth roofs

In modern buildings the incorporation of heavy roof structures, carrying layers of earth and vegetation, could combine the advantages of better insulation with the delights of roof-gardens and planted terraces. A number of designs along these lines have been developed by the architect Malcolm Wells. Wells' own office in Cherry Hill, New Jersey, is an underground structure with three foot of earth and planting carried over the roof area, Wells' philosophy being concerned as much with causing minimal disturbance to the landscape and to the natural ecosystem, as with the insulating benefits of below-ground architecture. Adobe is a traditional material with good insulating properties, as is the snow used by Eskimos for building. In traditional Alpine houses the roofs are designed not with steep slopes to throw the snow off, but instead with shallow slopes so that a layer of snow builds up and acts as additional winter insulation, which in summer of course disappears.

Reduction of glazed areas

The poor insulating performance of modern building has been brought about not just by lightweight construction, but by the introduction of large areas of glazing, particularly in office and commercial buildings. Some increase in performance is certainly possible with the use of double and even triple glazing, but in most cases the total area of glass can be reduced radically from present day norms without significant loss in terms of natural lighting or views from the inside out. There can be savings in capital cost as well as heating (and cooling) cost by cutting glazing areas. In domestic architecture (as distinct from commercial buildings, e.g. supermarkets or theatres, where windowless structures are common) probably the most extreme example of reducing glass area so as to cut heat loss is provided by the Reines dome house, where the windows are little more than peepholes.

But much can be done, without going to these limits, to retain a reasonable view of the outside world from windows, by the design of eye-level horizontal 'vision slots' for example rather than floor-to-ceiling picture windows (with their dizzying vertigo-inducing effects on the upper floors of some multistorey buildings). From an overall energy conservation point of view there may be some tradeoff between the savings in heating made by decreasing glazed areas, and the savings in lighting costs possible where natural illumination can be used in preference to artificial. In general the heating costs are the larger. The situation is further complicated by the effects of glazing on solar heat gain through the windows, which may be a benefit or a disadvantage depending on on the climate and the time of year. The question of solar heat gain is discussed in more detail in a later section. Some of the properties of different types and combinations of glass, both in insulating and in the transmission of solar radiation, are illustrated also in that section.

Malcolm Wells' under-
ground office in Cherry
Hill, N.J., completed
1973: plan and perspec-
tive. Adapted from M.B.
Wells, 'Confessions of a
Gentle Architect',
Environmental Quality
July 1973 pp.51 and 52

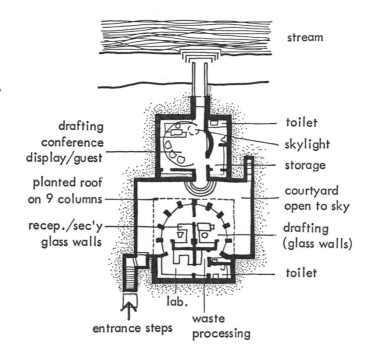

stream

drafting
conference
display/guest

toilet

skylight

storage

planted roof
on 9 columns

courtyard
open to sky

recep./sec'y
glass walls

drafting
(glass walls)

toilet

lab.

entrance steps

waste
processing

Window shutters	One or two methods have been suggested whereby heat losses through windows could be reduced in certain seasons and particularly at night – when the window is not needed generally for light or view of course, but also when the outside air temperature is lower. Storm windows can be fitted for the winter season. Traditionally the use of heavy curtains, together with the air space trapped behind them, provided an insulating effect. A proposal made by Fred Dubin for the General Services Administration's demonstration building in New Hampshire (see p.55) amounts to a more effective version of the curtain, and would consist of well-insulated and tight-fitting shutters closing automatically over the windows at night-time. (Dubin doubts whether the occupants could be relied on to be sufficiently energy conservation minded to close them by hand.)
'Beadwall'	A more elaborate mechanical system invented by Dave Harrison and patented by the Zomeworks Corporation is intended for a similar purpose. This is the 'Beadwall', consisting of two sheets of glass with a space between, containing styrofoam pellets. These pellets can be withdrawn to a storage chamber, by means of the suction provided by an ordinary vacuum cleaner fan. The insulation properties of the empty 'window' condition and the filled 'wall' condition differ by a factor of ten.
External insulation	Where special insulating materials are used to decrease the U-values of surfaces with composite construction, it is general practice to place these materials in the centre or on the inner face of the 'sandwich', often because their weather-resisting properties are poor. But in certain circumstances, depending on factors such as the mass of the structure and the exposure of surfaces to the sun, it may be advantageous to place insulation on the outside instead, so that heat is retained better in the structural materials themselves. This could apply particularly for instance to basement walls and floors, which being of concrete usually, can have high thermal mass, and through which, despite the insulating properties of earth, some considerable heat losses can still occur.
Exposure to wind	The basic calculation of U-values for different forms of construction is made on the assumption of still air on both sides, in and out, of the building surface. Where the outside is exposed to windy conditions, this increases the effective U-value (i.e. lowers the insulating properties) by an amount (the 'chill factor') dependent on the wind speed. According to Victor Olgyay, a 20 mph wind can double the heat load of a house normally exposed to 5 mph winds. Good protection from the prevailing winter winds, provided either by the shielding effects of other buildings, walls, or by specially planted windbreaks of evergreen trees, can therefore be effective in cutting heating requirements.
Increasing insulation	Some Federal action has recently been taken towards encouraging higher insulation standards in buildings. Interim Revision 51a introduced in 1971 into the Federal Housing Authority's Minimum Property Standards, made mandatory requirements for better insulation in single family dwellings, and in 1972 a revised specification was issued applicable to multi-family dwellings. A study made by

the Intertechnology Corporation (The U.S. Energy Problem, Vol.II, Appendix A, November 1971) suggests that for an extra investment of $280, thermal losses for a 1,500 square foot house in Washington D.C. could be halved from the level required as a minimum by the F.H.A.s Revision 51a, and for $890 these losses could be cut to one third. Dubin is of the opinion that U-values for the external walls and roofs of buildings could and should be universally brought down to a figure of around 0.06.

Ventilation, and heat losses through infiltration

Going back again to our algebraic expression for costs of fuel, the next component entering into this calculation relates to the flow of air through the building and is given by cn, where c is the heat capacity of the air contained within the building, and n the number of times this entire volume of air is replaced on average with outside air, per hour. These factors enter in, since heating the inside of the building must clearly involve first of all heating the air contained within the structure (as well as the material of the structure itself); and if this air leaks to the outside, or is changed to provide ventilation as it must be, heat is lost this way to the surroundings. Leakage of heated air to the outside takes place particularly through cracks around ill-fitting doors and windows, and these losses can be substantially cut by effective weatherstripping or sealing. In large and especially in tall buildings considerable infiltration of cold air occurs at ground level entrances, because of the creation of vertical convection currents in the warmed air inside (the 'stack effect'), thus sucking outside air in at the base of the building. This effect can be lessened by shielding the entrances from prevailing winds and by the use of vestibules, or better, revolving doors, which are very effective air locks.

Stack effect

Experimental studies in housing

The extent to which doors and windows are left open in winter can have great effects on fuel consumption. In a study of developer-built row-houses in the new community of Twin Rivers in New Jersey, Grot and Socolow have found that the consumption of gas for heating identical houses, with the same orientation, set side by side in the middle of a terrace, and occupied by families of similar composition and income, can vary by as much as 50%. One tentative explanation for this surprising finding, among several possibilities, is to do with the habits of the occupants, in particular how much they leave the windows open. In general this observation emphasises the importance in energy conservation of human factors, and in influencing people's habits, as much as of mechanical and material improvements.

An earlier study made of two specially instrumented one storey houses in St. Paul, Minnesota by the Wood Conversion Co. in 1961, gives an indication of the relative magnitudes of the heat losses via different routes from such buildings. The test houses were well insulated, with double windows and doors, and the rate of ventilation was one air change per hour. They were not occupied, but the opening and shutting of doors and the production of body heat as well as heat from electric lights and the use of appliances, were all simulated. The resulting winter heat losses were 15% through the walls, 13% through the roof, 5% through the floor, 27% through doors and windows, and 40% through air exchanges.

Artificial ventilation

With artificial systems of ventilation, or with air-conditioning, energy is consumed not only in heating or cooling the incoming air, but also in moving it about the building. Fred Dubin has questioned whether current standards for ventilation are not rather high; whether

Current standards

5, 10 or 15 ft^3/minute per person are really necessary, and whether these figures might not be reduced to 3 or 4 ft^3/min. (less in buildings with high ceilings) without significant loss of comfort or amenity. Dubin points out that in many circumstances the outside air ('we used to call it "fresh air", he says) is of dubious quality anyway. Instead of bringing air in from the outside to dispel cigarette smoke and odours by dilution, charcoal-activated filters or even ultra-

Odour control devices

violet lamps could be used instead to filter and clean the inside air. Where requirements for ventilation are particularly high, as in kitchens and toilets, local odour-control devices can be employed. Also these areas may be grouped together possibly, and served by a separate ventilation system, so that standards for the whole building do not need to be determined by the ventilation requirements of special individual spaces. In buildings such as offices there can be some savings by the adoption of the open type of plan, so that air does not need to be supplied to many small rooms but can be introduced through a central service 'core', from which it filters naturally to the periphery. There are efficiencies from the heating point of view here too, in the way in which warmth also migrates naturally from where it is produced, by people, light fittings and machines, at the buildings's centre, out to the edges.

Fume hoods

One way in which great volume of heated or cooled air can be lost to the outside, is via fume ducts and extraction hoods over equipment in laboratories, kitchens or laundries. The number of such hoods should be minimised and their use controlled only to when equipment is actually in use. What is more they can be supplied directly with outside air rather than with air which has been previously expensively conditioned, simply to be rejected again to the outdoors.

Where ventilation standards are reduced, it follows that not only are fuel costs cut, but there are possible economies in capital investment because the size of heating and cooling equipment, fans and ductwork is correspondingly reduced. Of course if the ventilation of the building can be effected naturally, in mild climates, by the use of openable windows, and by appropriate siting and orientation of the building to take advantage of natural air currents, then the extra financial and energy costs associated with artificial ventilating equipment can be totally avoided.

In his book Architecture without Architects, Rudofsky illustrates a design of natural air conditioning device in use for over five hundred years in the lower Sind district of Pakistan. A feature of the local climate is that during the hottest summer months, a cooling breeze blows from one prevailing direction; and the houses carry flat sail-

The natural air-
conditioners of
Hyderabad Sind,
Pakistan: adapted
from Dr M. Hürlimann,
India, the Landscape,
the Mountains and the
People, Atlantis Verlag,
Zurich, by kind per-
mission of the
publishers.

like windscoops or 'bad-gir' set up on the roofs, which act to deflect the air down into each room.

Heat exchangers

Devices are available which can recapture the heat (or 'cool') from conditioned air before it is exhausted from the building, and transfer this heat to the incoming air supply. According to Dubin the use of such devices should be contemplated in all buildings where the requirement is for greater than 2,000 ft^3 of incoming air per minute.

Thermal wheels

One such device is the rotary heat exchanger, or thermal wheel, which sits half in one duct and half in the other, and revolves slowly. It is packed with aluminium or stainless steel wool, somewhat like a giant rotating Brillo pad. Alternatively an asbestos medium can be used. Heat is picked up by the wheel on the warm side and rejected to the cooler side. Such wheels are capable of exchanging not only sensible heat, but also the latent heat of evaporation of water. Moisture is absorbed from the humid airstream by a dessicant, lithium chloride, and is released again to the dry airstream. One such design of wheel, the Enthalex, is manufactured by the Wing Company, a division of Aero-Flow Dynamics Inc.

Other types of heat exchanger

An alternative type of heat exchanger is the water-cooled coil type, which consists of a closed loop with finned coils in both incoming and outgoing air ducts, and which transfers the heat from one to the other via the water medium. Although this system is not capable of transferring latent heat, it can, unlike the thermal wheel, be used to transfer sensible heat between widely separated locations. Finally, other types of air-to-air exchanger and, as a more exotic and advanced method, the use of 'heat pipes' - an invention coming out of the space program - can also be employed to transfer heat between outgoing and incoming air. Overall, the use of heat exchangers can reduce winter energy consumption by around 30% to 35%, and summer air-conditioning energy consumption by 15% or 20%.

Heat recovery wheel

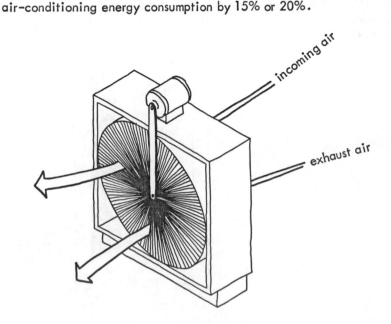

Extra heat inputs from solar gain, heat of lights, etc.

The very last term in our original expression for fuel costs, g, takes account of the gratuitous heating bonus provided by other sources than the heating system itself. Even when outside temperatures are sufficiently low to warrant heating a building, there will still be some substantial heating effect coming from winter sunshine falling on the surfaces of the building, and more so from solar radiation entering through the windows, since this is then trapped inside the building by the 'greenhouse effect'. The radiation, once through the glass, acts to heat up both the air inside, and the internal surfaces. These surfaces re-radiate the energy, but at a longer wavelength, to which the glass is opaque. Much energy is still lost back to the outside by conduction through the glass. But the net effect can be, as with greenhouses, for the internal temperature to rise above the outside temperature with no other source of heat than the sun.

The greenhouse effect

Body heat

Other sources of additional heat which can be quite appreciable, are the heat given off by light fittings (up to 80% of the electrical energy input to lights ends up as heat); and the body heat given off by the building's occupants, which is correspondingly greater as the building becomes more densely occupied, as for example in schools and auditoria, and as these people's activities become more strenuous, as in dance halls or gymnasia. In schools, because of the great heat production of their small but numerous and vigorous occupants, as well as the heat from lights, there can even be a need for cooling the building when outside temperatures are as low as 20°F. A very remarkable design of school classroom building which exploits all these effects to the full, was built by the English architect Emslie Morgan at Wallasey near Liverpool in 1961. The principal feature of the design is an enormous 40 foot high 'solar wall' on the south side. This wall consists of two glass skins, separated by a gap of 24 inches, the outer face being clear glass and the inner face largely obscure glass, so that the wall admits diffuse light right through to the interior. The remainder of the inner skin is made up of opaque panels, aluminum painted white on one side and black-painted on the other, which are reversible so as either to reflect or absorb heat according to the season. Apart from this special design of the solar walls, the building is massively insulated, both in the thickness of the wall, and in the polystyrene foam covered concrete roof slab. (The large air space within the two skins of the solar wall also acts as insulation).

St. George's School, Wallasey

The classroom lights are turned on early in the morning to preheat the building, and it is estimated that the pupils themselves provide perhaps one sixth of the heat input to the school per average winter day. The building is not strictly solar heated in the sense of using special collecting surfaces and heat storage methods (as described in later chapters). Nevertheless it does rely on trapping radiation from the winter sun (even in the murky North of England climate) for a substantial part of its heat; and it is reported that although a secondary boiler system was installed because of official doubts whether the solar wall arrangement would work, this has never had to be put into use. The workings of the building, not entirely understood in the architectural and engineering professions, since the designer Morgan died without recording his methods and calculations, have been the subsequent subject of study by a team from the Thermal Research Group of the Department of Building Science at Liverpool University.

Depending on the particular climate or location, solar heat gain can be either an embarrassment or a blessing. In Morgan's building in Wallasey, the main requirement is for winter heating rather than summer cooling, and it is probable that the building is unoccupied in any case during the hottest summer months. In such northerly climates it may well be appropriate to face the largest area of glazing south, and even perhaps to turn the windows on the east and west faces of the building towards the south also by means of a setback or saw-tooth arrangement in plan.

'Solar houses' of 1940s

Some of the 'solar houses' for which there was a fashion in the 1940s, were simply 'solar' in this sense, that they had large picture windows facing south. One experimental version was built by G.F. Keck near Chicago under the sponsorship of the Illinois Institute of Technology. Another such house was constructed in 1945 by F.W. Hutchinson at Purdue University, as part of a series of experiments supported by the Libbey-Owens-Ford Glass Company. The results of these experiments seem to be equivocal. The savings in heat with Keck's house were reported as 18%, and fuel savings of up to 30% have been claimed for other 'solar houses'. On the other hand Hutchinson's experimental house used more energy for heating than did an exactly similar house constructed alongside for comparative purposes, and differing only by having a smaller area of south-facing glass.

These houses seem to have been successful, almost too successful, in trapping winter sunshine. In Hutchinson's solar house the temperature could reach 80°F on clear days in mid-January, when the outside temperature was below freezing, without any other source of heating than the sun. Keck's house could also become overheated on sunny winter days. On the other hand large quantities of heat were lost through the large glazed areas on cloudy days or at night. It is these losses which were presumably responsible for the increased energy consumption (16%) of Hutchinson's solar house. In general the problem was one of very considerable and essentially uncontrollable swings in temperature between day and night, and between one day and another, because of the insufficient thermal mass in the interior to retain the incoming heat and release it slowly. The logical development, in order to overcome these problems, would be to systematise the collection of solar energy; not to allow it to penetrate directly and uncontrolled into the interior space, but instead to store the heat in some form to be released at a steady rate, more or less independently of the particular conditions of weather or of the time of day. This amounts in fact to proper solar heating for buildings, as generally understood, and such methods will be discussed in detail in the next chapter. In the meanwhile, it seems that the simple use of south-facing glass to allow the penetration of winter sunshine is most appropriate for mild climates where the

37

'Basic forms and building
shapes in different
regions', from Victor G.
Olgyay, Design with
Climate: Bioclimatic
Approach to Archi-
tectural Regionalism
(copyright (c) 1963 by
Princeton University
Press), fig.174. By kind
permission of Princeton
University Press.

Btu's and shapes

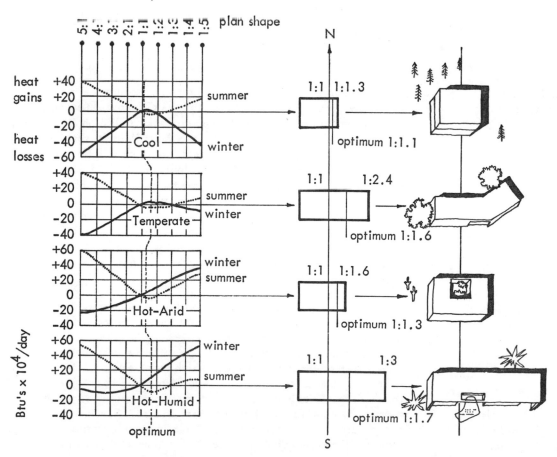

conduction losses through the glass are not too great.

Solar radiation through south facing windows

It is a curious and unappreciated fact that the amount of solar energy received through a south-facing window (in American latitudes) on an average sunny day in winter is greater than that coming through the same window on an average sunny day in summer. There are a number of reasons for this, but chief among these are the facts that although in summer the sun takes a longer path around from its point of rising north of east to its point of setting north of west, it is nevertheless on the south face for just the same amount of time as it is in the winter, despite the days being longer overall. And that in the winter the angle of the sun is much lower, so that not only is the effective intercepted area of the window greater, but the amount of radiation reflected at this more nearly normal angle of incidence is less. Calculations by Socolow and Grot in their studies of Twin Rivers (latitude 40°) confirm this point, and indicate that south-facing windows have an advantage both in admitting heat gain from low sun during the winter heating season, and in allowing less heat gain than west or east-facing glazing during the cooling months of summer.

It is this cooling load resulting from summer solar heat gain which is the overriding consideration in building design for most parts of America. In this context the best position to put large areas of glass would be by contrast on the north face of the building, this having the additional advantage of providing glare-free natural light (as in artists' studios).

Shading and orientation

Various means are possible for shading and orienting the building to cut down the amount of sun reaching its surfaces. In summer the wall receiving the greatest amount of solar radiation is the west, and so for example planting trees along the building's west face can be useful. If these trees are deciduous, they will have a shading effect in the summer when in leaf, and then in winter when they drop their leaves, they will allow the penetration of low angle sunshine which in this season may be advantageous. A building in Philadelphia designed according to these principles is Mitchell and Giurgola's office headquarters for the Philadelphia United Fund. The north wall is entirely glass; while the west wall has recessed strip windows with deep concrete sunbreaks to shield the glass from the afternoon summer sun.

Olgyay studies of building shape

Some calculations made by Olgyay of the optimum shape for buildings taking into account both heat loss in winter and heat gain in summer, show that for simple rectangular plans the most effective shapes would be those elongated in the east-west direction, since it is the east and west faces which receive the greatest summer radiation, and therefore which should be reduced in area; while the south face receives radiation in the winter but not so much in the summer, and can thus best be increased in size. Similar considerations led Henry Niccols Wright in a study of the orientation and planning of houses in the New York area in

Henry Niccols Wright study of orientation

Comparison of effects of solar radiation on a house in the New York area, in two perpendicular orientations; from Henry Niccols Wright, 'Solar Radiation as Related to Summer Cooling and Winter Radiation in Residences', New York 1936

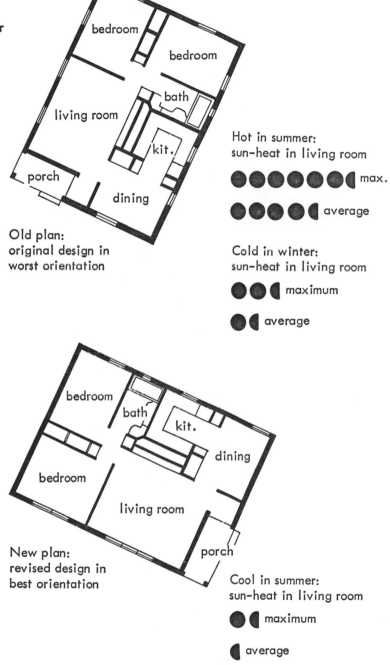

bedroom

bedroom

bath

living room

kit.

porch

dining

Old plan: original design in worst orientation

Hot in summer: sun-heat in living room

max.

average

Cold in winter: sun-heat in living room

maximum

average

north

bedroom

bath

kit.

bedroom

dining

living room

porch

New plan: revised design in best orientation

Cool in summer: sun-heat in living room

maximum

average

Warm in winter: sun-heat in living room

maximum

average

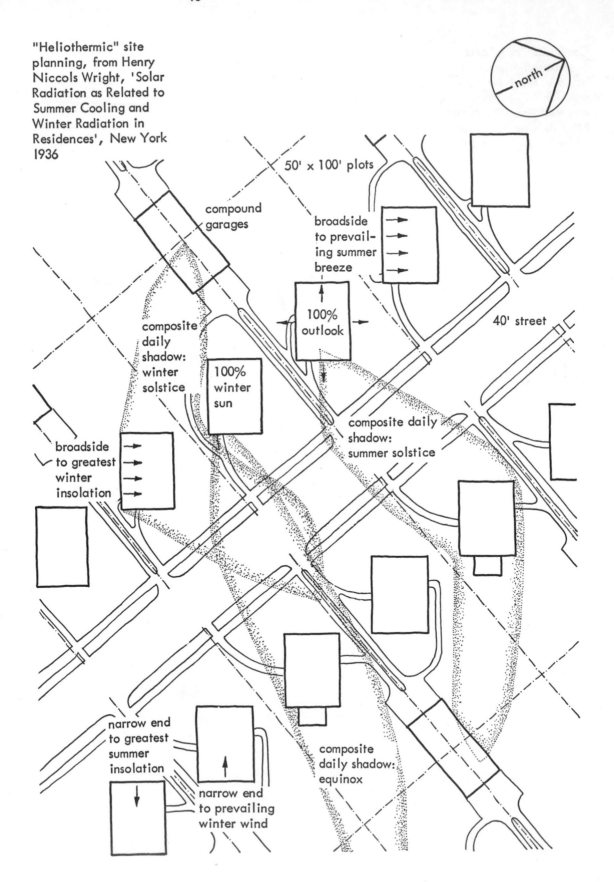

"Heliothermic" site planning, from Henry Niccols Wright, 'Solar Radiation as Related to Summer Cooling and Winter Radiation in Residences', New York 1936

north

50' x 100' plots

compound garages

broadside to prevailing summer breeze

composite daily shadow: winter solstice

100% outlook

40' street

100% winter sun

broadside to greatest winter insolation

composite daily shadow: summer solstice

narrow end to greatest summer insolation

narrow end to prevailing winter wind

composite daily shadow: equinox

relation to solar radiation during the 1930s, to recommend
that most of the important rooms and large windows be placed
on the south and south-west, to take advantage of winter sun,
and that a minimum of windows be introduced on the west-
northwest end, because of the excessive solar radiation in
summer. A diagram from Wright's report illustrates the vices
and virtues of two 'before and after' situations where the same
plan is turned through 180° to give the optimum orientation
which Wright recommends. Wright extended his thinking on
orientation of buildings for solar radiation into the larger-scale
problems of what he called 'heliothermic' site planning; and
the second diagram reproduced here shows a housing layout
which he devised to take account not only of summer heat gain
and winter heat loss but also shadowing effects, outlook and best
orientation for prevailing winds.

There are some further possibilities for shading buildings so as to
prevent solar radiation reaching its surfaces, particularly the
windows. Where a building is surrounded by masonry or hardtop
surfaces these may act to re-radiate the heat which they receive
onto the building itself. This effect is avoided by the use of
planting and of grass. The absorption or reflection of heat is
affected by the colour of the building surfaces, and the use of
light colours, particularly for roofs, is effective in reducing
heat gain. In Israel and other parts of the Mediterranean, houses
were traditionally whitewashed in spring to reflect the summer sun;
and then in autumn the rain would wash off the whitewash again,
exposing a darker coloured surface to absorb the winter sun.

Colours of
surfaces

Shading of
windows

The penetration of solar radiation through windows can be controlled
through the judicious use of awnings, special blinds which can be
drawn between the two panes of double-glazed sashes, by deep
reveals, and by a variety of types of externally projecting shades
which may take the form either of vertical fins or else horizontal
'eyebrows' which cut off high angle summer sun but allow low level
winter sun to enter.

Steve Baer at Zomeworks has invented an automatic shutter to be used
in skylights, of great elegance and conceptual beauty. It is called
the 'Skylid'. It consists of a series of delicately balanced pivoting
slats, linked together. On the outside and the inside are two metal
bottles, joined by a tube, and partially filled with Freon, a
low boiling point liquid. When the outside temperature is
greater than that inside, the Freon is boiled from the outer into
the inner bottle, and the resulting transfer of weight tips the
shutter open. As the internal temperature rises through solar
heat gain, or if the external temperature drops, so the Freon
may be boiled back to the outer bottle, and the Skylid closes
again. There is a manual override by which the shutter can be
kept fixed open or shut.

Self-shading of
inward sloping walls

A self-shading effect may be achieved by having the wall of the
building undercut, or sloping diagonally inwards from top to

bottom. Michael and Kemper Goodwin are the architects of a
municipal building in Tempe, Arizona, whose all-glass walls
slope inwards in this fashion at an angle of 45°, thus giving
shading to the glass. Where the sun's rays do strike the walls,
it is at much more oblique engle of incidence than with vertical
walls, so that more radiation is reflected and less transmitted.
Similar intentions lie behind the design of an office building for
Blue Cross and Blue Shield in North Carolina, by Odell Associates
Inc., whose form is that of a rhomboid leaning to the south and
west.

Special glass

Finally, the glass itself can be given special properties, either
heat-absorbing or reflective. Such special glasses are largely
the product of research stimulated by the awesome solar heat
gain problems experienced in all glass walled commercial buildings.
Some diagrams prepared by Dubin to illustrate the comparative
performances of different combinations of clear, heat-absorbing
and reflective glass in transmitting, reflecting, re-radiating and
convecting, and conducting solar energy, are reproduced here.

Heat of lights

A second source of 'free' heat, after solar heat gain, is that generated
by electric lighting. Again, as with solar gain, this is more often
in the American climate an additional load on the air-conditioning
system, than it is a bonus in the space heating equation. In recent
years the standard levels of lighting installed in public buildings,
offices and schools, have crept steadily upwards, largely at the
instigation of companies and trade organisations in the light fitting
business, to a point of almost absurd excess. The possible lowering
of these lighting standards back to more reasonable levels is discussed
separately. But while these high levels have prevailed, they have
brought as a consequence the generation of considerable amounts of
heat in the light fittings, which must be disposed of somehow in the
cooling season, and is often wasted. Two possibilities are available
for drawing this heat away from the fittings and putting it to
useful purposes. One is by exhausting air from the rooms through
slots around the fittings – thus drawing up to 80% of heat away
from the lights – and out through the ceiling plenum duct. The
heat in this exhausted air can be recovered and used to preheat
incoming air, with the use of heat exchangers as already described;
or the hot exhaust air may be blended directly with incoming cold
air to yield a mixture of appropriate temperature for reintroduction
back to the rooms again. An inherently more efficient process than
air-cooling of light fittings, is to cool the lights with water, using
a so-called 'wet troffer' system. Water circulates through jackets
around the lighting troffers and takes up the heat. This heat might
be transferred to a water storage tank, whence it could be extracted
as needed (for space heating, water heating) with the use of heat
pumps. Wet and dry systems can be used together in conjunction.
The use of heat-of-light systems is appropriate when illumination
levels exceed 75 footcandles (this is high). Whether the extracted
heat is reused or not, the fact of the lighting fittings being cooled
means that the air-conditioning load is correspondingly cut, and

Wet troffer
system

Reactions of different glazing configurations on typical summer and winter days in the NE United States; from Fred Dubin, 'Energy for Architects', Architecture Plus July 1973

'Note how the positions of the double glazed panes change in winter and summer – this is not usually possible to do in a building, but a building should be designed according to the prevailing weather conditions it will encounter. The calculations are hypothetical and should be taken for their relative values only. Also, note how even reflective glass can be installed to allow solar heat into the building during the winter through proper double glazing.'

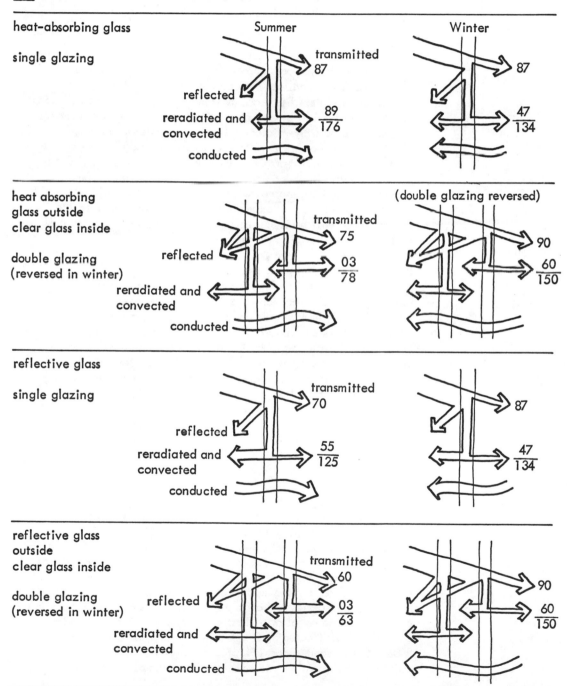

heat-absorbing glass

single glazing

Summer

Winter

heat absorbing glass outside clear glass inside

double glazing (reversed in winter)

(double glazing reversed)

reflective glass

single glazing

reflective glass outside clear glass inside

double glazing (reversed in winter)

savings both in energy and in capital cost of the system follow.
The light bulbs themselves are more efficient in light production
(more lumens per watt) when run at lower temperature, also.

**Heat recovery from
refrigeration units**

Refrigeration units offer a further source of recoverable heat. The
firm of Dubin-Mindell-Bloome designed a heat recovery system for
the Star supermarket chain, in which the use of otherwise waste heat
rejected from the commercial refrigeration units filled the entire
requirement for space heating. A 33% saving on the total energy
consumption of the stores was achieved by this means.

**Lifecycle
costing**

To return yet again to the seasonal heating cost equation : we have
now covered the various factors affecting the annual fuel costs,
and it remains to consider the costs of capital equipment, and
maintenance costs. There are certain measures which can be adopted
for reducing the initial cost of heating (and cooling) installations –
without jeopardising efficiency – by not oversizing the equipment
or using excessive safety factors for example; and these represent
no doubt minor savings from an energy and materials conservation
point of view. In general though we are faced with a complex
process of weighing increased capital expenditure and increased
use of materials – as for example more insulation – against the
savings these will bring in energy conservation and reduced fuel
costs while the building is operating.

In many cases in the past, and in the face of overwhelming
pressure from clients or from the purchasing public, the
tendency has been for architects and engineers to design
systems for buildings which would minimise first costs. This
tendency has been reinforced recently by the enormous rate
of inflation in the cost of building. There is an understandable
psychological predisposition, which we all are prey to, when
we are buying any kind of appliance or item, let alone buildings,
to be attracted by a low price tag, without giving too much
thought to the additional real costs which may well be involved
in owning and using that item over the longer term. There is
also the real difficulty of raising immediate extra capital to pay
for investments even when these are known to promise overall
savings in the long run. But the necessity for energy conservation
and the rising cost of energy, is now provoking designers and
clients to look again at these various tradeoffs. The concept of
'lifecycle costing' has been introduced, whereby the total costs
of constructing, owning and operating a building over its entire
estimated lifetime, are looked at together. In a recent publication
devoted to energy conservation in schools, Educational Facilities
Laboratories estimate that for school buildings with an anticipated
life of 40 years, the breakdown of lifecycle costs, taking into
account staff salaries and all the teaching costs as well as building
costs, would be as follows: first cost, 8%, maintenance and
operation costs (including fuel) 12%, teacher/administration costs
80%. In this same report EFL present details of methods for
calculating lifecycle costs, with worked examples, taking into

account interest charges, inflation, anticipated rises in energy costs and maintenance costs, in order to compare the relative advantages of various proposed systems and investments.

Efficiency of heating and cooling installations

A number of features of the design of heating and cooling installations, and their efficiency, can have bearing on the balance of capital with running costs. The use of more sensitive thermostats, and the automatic control of air-conditioning, shutting down refrigeration equipment when the outside temperature is below 55°F, can both bring energy savings. Large central air-conditioning and heating plants can be more efficient, and use up to 10 or 15% less energy than decentralised package units; though this is very dependent on the layout and pattern of use of buildings, since decentralised units are controlled locally and can be switched on and off as needed. In order to be competitive in energy use, central systems must be given the same control and flexibility of operation; though they are inherently more efficient because of economies of scale, and the use of water to condense the refrigerant rather than air. Many of the designs of small air-conditioning units for installation in walls or windows are very inefficient, and units giving equivalent performance can vary as greatly as 80% in energy consumption. This variation is greater in 115 volt than in 230 volt air-conditioners. Federal specifications establish lower limits for the efficiency of window air-conditioning units bought by the Federal Government, and it seems possible that these standards could be enforced generally by legislation. Michael Corr of the American Association for the Advancement of Science Committee on Environmental Alterations calculates that if all air-conditioners were designed to the present maximum efficiency, this could yield a 36% overall saving in power consumption.

Terminal reheat systems

A widely popular technique of air-conditioning which is wasteful of energy is the 'terminal reheat' type of system. The principle here is to cool all incoming air to the lowest temperature required anywhere in the building, and then progressively to reheat the great proportion of this same air back up to the various higher temperatures required in other spaces. The method provides very flexible control of temperature and humidity, but it is clearly wasteful, not only in the fact that energy is consumed first to cool and then immediately to reheat the same air, but in that additional heat produced from the extra cooling is often wasted also. Much more economical of energy is the 'variable volume' type of system which cools only a proportion of the air appropriate to the particular cooling needs. The control of humidity in summer is not so effective as with the 'terminal reheat' method, but this seems a small penalty for the increased efficiency of energy use.

Pilot lights

One practice which could theoretically save a lot of energy nationwide, is to install electric ignition on gas-fired boilers (and other appliances) in preference to gas pilot lights, which are calculated to consume 223 billion ft^3 of gas per year in American gas-heated homes alone.

Heat storage

Many of the methods for energy conservation so far described consist in collecting the heat produced incidentally or as a by-product of other processes, storing it by some means, and then putting it back to work for other purposes. The subject of heat storage is treated in some detail in the chapter on solar heating since storage is a key feature of such systems. Broadly speaking heat may be stored in buildings in two ways, first by heating up some large body of material with high thermal mass, i.e. storing sensible heat. Appropriate materials are concrete, rock, metals or most especially water in large tanks. Water has the advantage as a storage medium that heat penetrates the body of the water through the stirring action of convection currents; it is also cheap and may be pumped easily from place to place. The thick walls of desert (and other) houses act as a kind of thermal storage system, soaking up heat during the daytime, and releasing it at night. The designs of solar heated houses by Harold Hay and Steve Baer (see pp. 137, 147) use a similar principle in their different ways, in these cases with bodies of water, either in the roof or on the walls, which again pick up heat from the sun and store it for use at night-time or on cloudy days.

Water tanks and rock bins

Storage radiators

In Britain and West Germany the principle of heat storage is used to even out the loads on the electrical power network, by means of 'storage radiators'. These are box-like cabinets, containing ceramic bricks, magnesia blocks, or water, which stand in the room, and are heated by electric resistance heating during off-peak periods, generally at night. The stored heat is released continuously throughout the twenty-four hours. Water tanks are used for heat storage on a much larger scale in the headquarters of the New Hampshire Insurance Company, in Manchester, N.H. The three tanks in this building hold 16,000 gallons each, and are heated with electrical resistance heaters, between the hours of 8pm and 7am. Heat is extracted from the tanks via heat exchangers for space heating and domestic hot water. By this means the working day power consumption is reduced to 20% of total consumption.

Heat of fusion materials, and latent heat storage

The second means of heat storage which can be used involves special chemical materials, generally salts or possibly waxes, which have a melting point, or which undergo chemical change, within the range of temperature over which heat is to be stored. By this means these materials effectively store latent as well as sensible heat; and can retain a much greater quantity of heat for given volume than can for example water tanks or rock beds. Equivalent systems may be used to store 'cold' for air-conditioning purposes.

Heat pumps

As has already been mentioned, the use of electricity for resistance heating is inefficient, and a much more effective use of electric power in heating can be the use of heat pumps, which in large sizes can be very efficient both for heating and cooling. They may be driven by gas engines better still than by electric motors. The most familiar form of heat pump is that contained in the domestic refrigerator, and all refrigeration uses the principle of the heat pump in which, in the usual arrangement, some volatile liquid used as the

refrigerant is circulated in a closed cycle through two sets of coils.
A motor, generally an electric motor, drives a compressor, which
raises the pressure of the refrigerant vapour and causes it to
condense to the liquid form, in the coils of the condenser half
of the cycle. The liquid is then passed through an expansion valve
to the coils of the evaporator half, where a lower pressure causes
it to evaporate again. The vapour passes back then to the compressor,
and so on round the cycle. In the process the refrigerant takes up
its latent heat of vapourisation from the external surfaces surrounding
the evaporator, and rejects this again to the external surroundings
of the condenser. In its most general use in the domestic refrigerator
the heat pump withdraws heat from inside the refrigerating cabinet,
and releases it to the surrounding air. The refrigerating components
of air-conditioning systems work in a very similar way. To put it
figuratively one might say it was as though the building were the
cabinet of a giant refrigerator, the heat extracted from the building
being released to the atmosphere in a similar fashion on a larger
scale.

Instead of being used for the purposes of cooling air, heat pumps
may be used in an exactly equivalent manner to extract heat from
bodies of water, for example the water in heat storage tanks, and put
it to use for say space heating purposes.

Heat pumps may be run alternatively either way around, so to speak,
for use in either heating or cooling modes. For the purposes of air
cooling for air-conditioning, the condenser is outside the building,
and the evaporator inside, as already described. For space heating
the positions are reversed, the evaporator being outside and the
condenser inside. In both cases heat is rejected at the condenser.
In the arrangement for heating, the heat pump thus acts to extract
heat (very largely solar heat) from the outside air, or else from the
surrounding earth, or from local bodies of water (wells, ponds or
streams), and use this for heating the building. Alternatively a
special purpose solar radiation collector may be used as a heat
source; this type of application of heat pumps is discussed further
in the following chapter. This function of the heat pump has been
described by Putnam as analogous to a kind of mechanical coal
miner, which for a small energy input is able to 'mine' and bring to the
surface much larger quantities of energy stored in the ground or in
the water. The energy 'mined' is, in the average performance of
heat pumps of this kind presently in operation, about three or four
times that required to run the compressor. Electrically driven heat
pumps can provide a means of heating which can be $2\frac{1}{2}$ to 6 times
more efficient than other electrical heating methods. In 1955
according to Daniels about 6,000 heat pumps for building heating
were installed and working in the United States, the majority in
California, Florida and the Southern states. G.E. Smith has
reported on the economics of some British experiments with the
use of heat pumps for space heating - notably the installation at the
Festival Hall in London which used the river Thames as a heat source,
as well as buildings in Norwich, and at Nuffield College, Oxford.
Generally, the most promising heat pump applications seem to be

in larger buildings, for both heating and cooling, and used in conjunction with waste heat recovery systems.

Maintenance

Lastly in the economics of energy conservation in heating and cooling for buildings, we come to the question of maintenance. According to Fred Dubin, improved maintenance practices in existing and new buildings in the U.S. could reduce energy consumption by better than 15%, without any resulting increase in maintenance labour costs. This can be done with the use of proper automated data control centrers, by instrumentation, by the regular cleaning or replacement of filters, by regular checking of weather seals on doors and windows, and checks for leaking taps and radiators. Preventive maintenance programs of inspection and adjustment of machinery should be instituted, and the systems in new buildings should be accompanied by operation manuals outlining the proper procedure for their use. Great waste of energy is caused presently by mistakes or lethargy in maintenance, because thermostat settings are changed, blowers switched off, or the automatic controls are altered on furnaces which are intended to operate on a seven-day clock and to be set to lower temperatures during times when the building is unoccupied, in ignorance of their function.

Furnace inefficiencies

Another source of inefficiency is in furnaces, where, with poor combustion, soot can built up on the heat transfer surfaces, so requiring more fuel for the same heat output. Bad furnace maintenance also results in more smoke and air pollutants being emitted to the atmosphere. According to architect P. Richard Rittelmann, the occupants of buildings often reduce the speeds of air-conditioning fans (to cut down fan noise; so clearly a quiet design of fan and ducting system is in order), which can cause icing over of the surface of cooling coils, and so drastically reduce performance.

Evidence of the importance of good maintenance for energy conservation is given by a comparative study made by Dubin of two identical Connecticut schools with all-electric heating, ventilating and air-conditioning systems. One school had nearly double the energy consumption of the other. The causes of this were traced to unnecessarily high thermostat settings, the unnecessary lighting of spaces during periods in which they were not occupied, to dirty filters, and to continuous inactivation of the outside damper control.

Standards of heating (and cooling) for comfort

All of the calculations of the costs of heating and cooling of a building start initially from the decision as to what temperature or range of temperatures should be maintained within the building for comfort. ASHRAE, the American Society of Heating, Refrigerating and Air-Conditioning Engineers, define the range of 73°F to 77°F as 'thermal comfort conditions', and designs are usually calculated to achieve 75°F, the mid-point of this range. The heating and cooling systems are sized so as to maintain the target temperature range for $97\frac{1}{2}\%$ of the time, given the average weather conditions of the region. It can be questioned whether the prevailing standards for summer and winter temperatures could not be raised and lowered respectively. By raising the summer design temperature from $75°F$ to $78°F$ savings of 10% in energy consumption in the air-conditioning systems could be achieved on average.

Overheating and overcooling

The European coming to America (and it is something which Charles Dickens remarked on, in the 19th century) is continuously surprised at the necessity to keep taking off and putting on clothing, as he enters and leaves buildings in winter, even when it is quite mild out of doors. This overheating can actually cause discomfort, and it is not unusual for the occupants of apartment buildings to keep their windows open in winter time to get rid of the heat which their building superintendent is so zealously producing down in the basement below. Meanwhile in the summer many air-conditioned buildings are positively cold, and we have the phenomenon of people actually putting on warm clothes to go indoors for instance into restaurants. European standards of temperature for winter heating are lower than American; too low, no doubt, in the view of many a suffering American tourist. But it should certainly be possible to make reductions in American standards without any real sacrifice of comfort; and is it too heretical to suggest that people might wear sweaters rather than turn the thermostat up? As for the $9/\frac{1}{2}\%$ condition standard, Dubin has proposed that with the exception of certain special cases such as hospitals, housing for the elderly, or special temperature sensitive industrial processes, this standard might be reduced to 95%, which would mean that temperatures would be higher or lower than the 'comfort' range for only 50 hours per year more on average.

Relative humidity and comfort

Our sensation of being comfortable is related not just to absolute temperature, but to the relative humidity of the air as well, and it is possible to endure high temperatures without discomfort so long as the atmosphere is very dry (as in the South Western states). Conversely, in winter, if the temperature is somewhat lower but at the same time the humidity is somewhat higher, we experience the same subjective feeling of comfort, because we lose less body heat through respiration. The problem of maintaining relatively high humidities in buildings during the winter, is that moisture then condenses on the cold inside surfaces of windows. But with double or triple glazing this difficulty can be avoided, and insulation values are simultaneously improved of course too.

Domestic water heating

After space heating and air conditioning, the next largest user of energy in buildings is domestic water heating. Much energy is lost when hot water from baths, showers, sinks, washing machines etc., is drained to the sewers while it is still warm. With the use of heat exchangers this energy can be recovered and stored for different purposes, most appropriately to preheat incoming cold water from the mains supply, so that less energy is used overall for water heating. Other savings are possible with better insulation of hot water tanks and pipes, and also obviously by prompt repairs to leaking hot taps. In the water heater itself, if it is a gas or oil-fired type, the heat transfer surfaces should be kept free of soot, and the heat from the combustion gases might be recovered for use in space heating, rather than being lost to the outside. Electric ignition is to be preferred to the use of gas pilot lights.

Lighting

The use of energy for lighting is relatively minor compared to other energy uses in building, but it nevertheless constitutes a substantial component of electrical energy use generally (24% of national electricity consumption; 40% for Con Edison in New York City). In modern office buildings up to 50% of electricity used can go to lighting. This is another area where standards can quite well be cut, indeed they can be cut drastically, not only without loss of amenity but actually with great improvements in the quality and visual interest of interior illumination.

Lighting standards

The recent history of lighting standards is very curious. Some indication of what has been happening is given by the fact that the total output of electric light in the United States increased $5\frac{1}{2}$ times between the years 1948 and 1966. An analysis made by William M.C. Lam of Massachusetts and described in a paper given to the American Association of School Administrators in February 1964, charts the steady rise in recommended lighting levels for schools over the last sixty years or more. Before 1910 the standard was 3 foot candles, between 1910 and 1930 this was raised to 18 foot candles, and after 1930 raised again to 30 foot candles. Since 1950 the recommended standards have shot up to quite extraordinary levels, between 70 and 150 foot candles. As Lam points out, the properties of the human visual apparatus set a limit to what may be seen and distinguished ('visual acuity') at any illumination, and 30 foot candles will provide sufficient light to come within 7% of this theoretical limit. The increase in recommended school lighting levels after 1950, from 30 to 150 foot candles, gives an increase of only a further 3% or 4% in this performance.

Lighting criteria are established in terms of the light required to carry out given visual tasks. As the architect Richard Stein (reported in EFL's The Economy of Energy Conservation in Educational Facilities) points out, 'The basic standard for school lighting is reading hard pencil on cheap, grey foolscap. Why, asks Stein, choose such an arbitrarily difficult task? Why can't the student use a softer, more legible pencil, or even better paper?' After a visit to the Illuminating Engineering Research Institute, and with their expert advice, the Chairman of New York State Public Service Commission Joseph C Swidler was inspired by an urge to conserve energy and removed nine out of the 21 fluorescent lighting fixtures which were installed in his office in Albany, N.Y. The lighting level is still 80 foot candles over the work area. According to Swidler, 'The corridor outside contained a practically continuous series of fluorescent tubes, more than enough for fine needlework, miniature painting, or engraving counterfeit money, although it was used only for walking from office to office.'

The waste of energy in lighting is thus twofold. The level of illumination is excessively high over work areas where it is needed, and this same high level is provided generally even in many areas where the requirement for lighting is much less. To lower illumination levels from 150 to 50 foot candles results in a 90% reduction in energy consumption. A level of 50 foot candles or lower is quite satisfactory for most work with the exception of very fine and delicate tasks. Corridors, staircases and the peripheries of rooms may be lit to lower levels still. It may not only be more economical of electricity to use local desk lights, or for example swivel and adjustable lamps for drafting tables; but this lighting can also provide better individual control of glare and shadows, and can be turned on and off as needed. In modular layouts it is possible to provide flexibility in the control of the ceiling fixtures with the use of 'high-low' ballasts, so that for say particular working arrangements, the fittings over desks may be set at 'high', while all others are set at 'low'. Some of the most pleasant and visually interesting lighting effects are achieved in restaurants, private houses or in museums by the selective lighting of particular areas or objects of attention, and by the resulting counterpoint of light and shade, with a very modest use of electrical power.

Selective lighting

High-low ballasts

Switching lights off

One obvious means of conserving energy for lighting, is by turning the lights off when the space is not in use. Curiously in some office buildings this is not even possible. When New York State Public Service Commissioner Mrs. Carmel Marr moved into her new office in the World Trade Center (surely one of the world's most energy-prodigal buildings) she, being a conscientious energy conservation enthusiast, looked around for a light switch so that she could turn the lights out on leaving, or when the natural light from the windows was sufficient without artificial supplement. There was no switch. Only after considerable agitation did she manage to have a switch installed, at a cost of $200, no doubt enough to pay for burning lights in the room for a few years into the future.

Even where separate switching is installed to control the lighting in different rooms of the building or different parts of the same room, there may be difficulties in persuading the building occupants to remember to use these switches. EFL cite a cautionary tale about an energy consumption study carried out in a high school in Las Vegas. This revealed that 30% of all the energy used in the school building was consumed between the hours of 4pm and midnight, when all the 1,100 staff and pupils had gone home leaving only the three maintenance staff on duty working at cleaning and clearing up. The study calculated that if these staff had switched off lights, heating, ventilation and air-conditioning as they worked, as much as 15% or 20% savings in energy could have resulted. Another similar example is given by Richard Stein who designed Public School 55 on Staten Island with the light fittings closest to the window walls on separate switches, so that they might be turned

Automatic
switching

off when natural lighting was sufficient. On several visits to the
school he discovered these lights on in broad daylight however.
Stein, who was hoping for 8% savings in the total daytime lighting
cost, is now resigned to the view that photo-electric switching will
be necessary in similar future schemes. This should not be necessary
with proper public awareness of the energy conservation issue, but in
EFL's words 'It may be the only way to combat the wasteful habits
programmed into the American psyche.' Who knows, one might even
see a revival of those fiendish time-switch devices which control
the staircase lights in the more decrepit of French hotels and boarding
houses, which give you so many seconds to dash up the stairs before
blackness descends and you are stranded in mid-landing.

Efficiency of
fittings

Quite apart from lowered standards, and provisions for switching,
whether manual or automatic, there are means by which the actual
efficiency of the bulbs and fittings themselves may be improved.
Frequent replacement of bulbs, and cleaning of lamps, fixtures,
reflectors and shades is one measure. Fluorescent lights are three
times as efficient as incandescent; and longer fluorescent tubes are
more efficient than short ones. Four 4-foot tubes will give 40%
more light than eight 2-foot tubes of the same total wattage. U-
shaped tubes are more efficient than straight ones. In their report
on energy conservation, the Office of Emergency Preparedness wonder
whether it might not be possible to develop a compact design of
fluorescent lamp which could fit in a screw socket and give off a
soft pleasant light comparable to incandescent bulbs, but with the
power consumption typical of fluorescent. Lights run more efficiently
at lower temperatures (as for example when cooled in heat-of-light
systems). Another way of cutting operating costs and improving
lamp life and performance, is by the use of high frequency lighting,
running at 3000 cycles/sec. instead of the standard alternating
current frequency of 60 cycles/sec.

Overall, the estimates of a joint National Bureau of Standards
and General Services Administration panel are that energy
consumption for lighting could be reduced by at least 25% in
new buildings and by 15% in existing buildings. Other estimates
go higher, aiming for as much as a 50% reduction. Outside
buildings there is a great deal of electrical energy expended on
advertising, display lighting, floodlighting and wall washers,
some of which could no doubt be dispensed with. In New York
City about $7\frac{1}{2}$ million kWh/year are used for these purposes.

Appliances

Refrigerators

Cookers

Some energy savings are possible through the design of household appliances - cookers, refrigerators, dryers - which account for most of the remainder of energy consumption in dwellings after the uses already considered. Self-defrosting freezers and refrigerators use much more energy than normal types, and their use might be discouraged. All refrigerators might be better insulated. Since hot air rises and cold air falls, refrigerators which have the door on the top lose less 'cold' when they are opened than those with doors at the front. In cookers much heat is lost from the burners on ranges, and is often exhausted directly through hoods and fans to the exterior. This waste could be controlled by having the bottoms of pans fit tightly over the burners, and by insulating the sides and lids of the pots. Cooking inside the oven is generally a more efficient use of energy, since the heating is intermittent, much heat is retained within the material of the oven walls, and there are smaller convection losses.

'Save a Watt'

Two pamphlets issued by Con Edison, '101 Ways to Conserve Electricity at Home' and '10 Ways to Save a Watt', are very largely devoted to ways in which the householder can save electricity both in the purchase of more efficient appliances, and in the times and ways in which these appliances are used. The second pamphlet is reproduced here as an appendix. One of the main purposes of Con Edison's 'Save a Watt' campaign is to distribute demand for electricity more evenly over the day and week and particularly to cut summer loads which because of air-conditioning give rise to the highest annual peaks. If these peaks can be smoothed, then less generating capacity is required, equipment can be run more continuously and so at greater efficiency, and inefficient stand-by generators need not be brought into operation.

Electricity supply

Load-shedding

Ways are available for cutting the peak loads in larger buildings automatically, so as to help in smoothing the pattern of electricity demand. There is generally an economic incentive for the consumer to do this of his own initiative, since utility billing rates or surcharges are often based on the maximum demand made by the particular consumer over the year, and if the extreme annual peaks can be cut, then the rate at which electricity is charged for, over the whole twelve months, is reduced. 'Load-shedding' or 'permissive load control' devices act to disconnect less essential circuits such as those supplying the heating of corridors and stairwells, or domestic water heating, when the load goes over a certain predetermined level.

Transmission

There are energy losses in the transmission of electricity at low voltages, and the General Services Administration for example has found it worthwhile for new buildings to purchase power at 13,800 volts, and distribute this to local sub-stations within the building or complex, where it is transformed to 277/480 volts for lighting, heavy equipment and power, and then down again in a second series of transformers to 120/208 volts for small equipment.

The energy costs
of building materials

If the building is to be conceived as a complete energy and materials system over its whole lifecycle, then analysis should properly begin with the extraction of the raw materials used in the building's construction, the transport and assembly of these materials; and then at the end of the building's life, when it is demolished, account would be taken of how the materials were dispersed and perhaps reused. In practice this is something of a counsel of perfection, and little precise data is presently available on the consumption of energy in the manufacture and transport of building products. Energy conservation considerations would certainly seem to weigh in favour of the use of locally found materials - wood, earth and clay products; all of which can usually find some new use or are at least bio-degradable after the building's demolition. There are certain classes of material which are known to use great amounts of energy in their production, in particular plastics and synthetics with a petro-chemical base. The example which is always quoted in

Aluminum

this connection is aluminum, and the analysis made by Richard Stein of the construction of a high-rise building, which showed that it would take 0.77 million kWh of electric energy to produce the 5.75 million pounds of stainless steel required for the skin of the building, as compared with a consumption of 2.1 million kWh to cover the same surface with 4 million pounds of aluminum. One publication which does present some figures on the comparative energy expenditures associated with different forms and materials of building construction is Archiecoframe, a report by Beckman and Weidt of the University of Minnesota Department of Architecture.

MacKillop has published some figures ('Low Energy Housing', The Ecologist Vol.2 No.12, Dec.1972 pp.4-11) giving the total consumption of materials and energy in construction, in Britain; and also estimates of the typical input of materials and energy into a three-person semi-detached house, including consideration of energy consumption in transport of materials. Data on energy costs associated with manufacture and materials processing across the whole of American industry are given in A.B. Makhijani and A.J. Lichtenberg, An Assessment of Energy and Materials Utilization in the U.S.A., College of Engineering, Univ. of California, Berkeley 1971.

Potential savings
from energy conservation
measures

Because of the complexity and systematic interrelation of the many factors determining the use of energy in buildings, any estimate of what the total savings might be resulting from the implementation of some or all of the measures described above, must necessarily be very approximate. Most of the estimates that have been made are more by way of exhortations or target figures, rather than the product of detailed scientific analysis. The Ad Hoc Committee on Energy Efficiency in Large Buildings of the Interdepartmental Fuel and Energy Committee of the State of New York are of the opinion that with the implementation of all the measures which they put forward in their report, more than 50% energy savings could be achieved in large buildings, over typical present practice, for an estimated average building life span of 50 years. The President's Office of Emergency Preparedness gives a breakdown by different uses of estimated savings in the residential and commercial sectors in 1980 with the introduction of a variety of measures, among the most significant of which are better insulation in buildings, the use of more efficient domestic applicances and air-conditioning equipment and the general public adoption of a number of energy conservation habits. A table showing this analysis is presented below.

Annual energy savings possible in the Residential/Commercial sector in 1980.

	Savings: Trillion of Btu/year	Percentage of total residential/ commercial sector[1]	Percentage of total national consumption[2]
Residential			
Space heating and cooling:			
(a) existing homes	1,100	3.1	1.1
(b) new homes	1,100	3.1	1.1
Water heating	250	.7	.3
Cooking	50	.1	.05
Refrigeration	100	.3	.1
Air conditioning equipment	500	1.4	.5
Other, including lighting, clothes drying etc.	500	1.4	.5
Residential total	3,600	10.1	3.7
Commercial			
All commercial uses	1,500	4.2	1.6
Total	5,100	14.3	5.3

This energy saving is equivalent to 2.4 million barrels per day of crude oil.

1. Percentages calculated on basis of a denominator of 35.6 quadrillion Btu. This is the energy consumption of the residential/ commercial sector including electrical energy, expected in 1980.
2. Percentages calculated on basis of a denominator of 96 quadrillion Btu which is the total national consumption for all sectors expected for 1980.

GSA demonstration office building, Manchester, N.H.

One instance in which a detailed systematic analysis has been made of the possibilities for energy conservation in large commercial buildings is the recent study carried out by Dubin-Mindell-Bloome Associates for the General Services Administration (Fred S. Dubin, 'GSA's Energy Conservation Test Building - A Report', Actual Specifying Engineer, Aug.1973 pp.84-92).
The GSA proposes to build a demonstration energy conservation test building in Manchester, New Hampshire. The accommodation will comprise 126,000 ft^2 of offices, planned on six stories.

Results of computer studies on the design of the GSA's proposed demonstration energy conservation office building to be erected in Manchester, N.H. (engineering consultants Dubin-Mindell-Bloome). Adapted from F.S. Dubin, 'Energy for Architects', <u>Architecture Plus</u>, July 1973.

The first diagram (Run 1) represents the original breakdown of the total amount of energy used in the building (which is of 126,000 ft^2, planned on 6 stories), assuming normal construction and current standards. Expected energy consumption is 13,150 x 10^6 Btu per year. The givens include walls, floor and roof with U values between 0·3 and 0·2, single glazing, 50% wall/window ratio, a year-round shading coefficient of 0·5, a 2:1 length to width ratio with the long axis running north/south. The following pie charts show how changing one factor of this building program affects total energy requirements in the building. Percentage energy savings are indicated by heavy outline.

Run 1: Typical office building

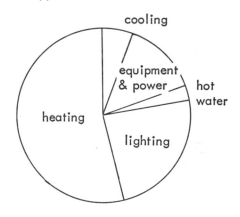

Runs 2-7: Increasing thermal resistance of walls, floor, roof (decreasing the U-value)

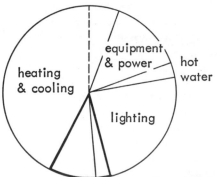

21½% saved in heating and cooling by reducing U-value to 0·1

6½% saved in heating and cooling by reducing U-value to 0·06

Runs 8 and 9: Using double and triple glazing

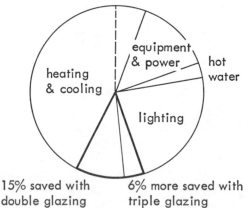

15% saved with double glazing

6% more saved with triple glazing

Runs 10 and 11: Reducing the amount
of shading

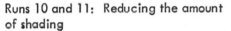

2½% saved by increas-
ing shading coefficient
from 0·05 to 0·75

2% more saved by in-
creasing shading co-
efficient to 1·0 (max)

Runs 12 and 13: Decreasing glazing

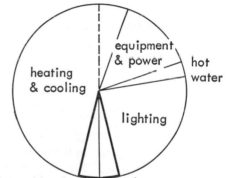

8% saved by decreas-
ing window-wall ratio
from 50% to 30%

8% more saved by
decreasing window-
wall ratio to 10%

Run 16: Changing aspect ratio
(length/width)

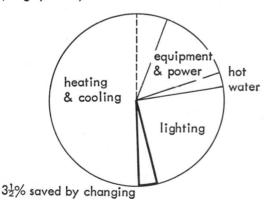

3½% saved by changing
from 2:1 (north/south
longitudinal axis) to 1:1

Run 18: Changing orientation

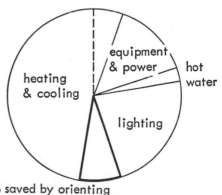

9½% saved by orienting
the longitudinal axis
east-west

Calculations were made first, using a computer program developed by the National Bureau of Standards, of the total energy consumption in the building assuming conventional standards of construction, typical current design practice and using electrical, gas or oil power. Some of the details of the calculated pattern of energy use are illustrated in the accompanying 'pie chart' diagrams.

The form of the building is a simple rectangular block. The U-values of wall, floor and roof construction were assumed to average 0·3, 0·25 and 0·2 respectively. Single glazing was assumed, and a window: wall area ratio of 50%. The year-round shading coefficient was taken as 0·5, and the aspect ratio (length: width) taken as 2:1, with the long axis aligned north-south.

Dubin-Mindell-Bloome's calculations show that on this basis, in the New Hampshire location, the building would require an input of 116,000 Btus/ft^2 per year, equivalent to about 216,000 Btus/ft^2 per year of primary source energy. (Many similar sized existing office buildings, they say, consume as much as 600,000 Btus/ft^2 per year.) Using the NBS computer program, they then went on to examine the effects of various changes in these initial design parameters, on the annual total consumption of energy. They looked at the implications of altering the number of stories, the story height, the shape and orientation of the building, the insulating properties of walls, roofs and floors, the proportion of window area to wall area, and the shading coefficient, as well as other factors. Results of the different computer runs in which these factors were varied one at a time, are illustrated in the pie charts.

The overall conclusion of the study was that even with no change in the mechanical systems of heating, ventilating and air conditioning, and no change in lighting installations or levels of artificial illumination, the annual energy consumption could be cut by 48,000 Btus/ft^2 at the building (with a corresponding reduction in requirement for primary source energy). With improvements to the efficiency of the mechanical systems, recovery of waste heat and rationalisation of the artificial lighting systems, this figure could be further reduced to about 56,000 Btus/ft^2 per year at the building; or an overall saving of 48%. (38% reduction in primary source energy requirement.)

Dubin-Mindell-Bloome have also studied the possibility of supplying part of the heating and cooling load in this building from a roof-mounted solar collector; some details of these proposals are reported at the end of the next chapter.

Energy conservation: Appendix 1

Conservation checklist
from Fred Dubin, 'Energy for Architects', Architecture Plus
July 1973

I. To make an existing building more efficient

1. Analyze the fuel and electrical bills in terms of
    consumption patterns and equipment needs.

2. Analyze the potential ways to conserve energy, given
    existing lifestyles and working patterns.

3. Use a computer program (similar to one offered by the
    U.S. National Bureau of Standards) to establish an energy
    profile of the building - hour by hour, day by day, month
    by month, etc., separating the energy requirements of
    each building system.

4. Analyze where energy is going in the building and the
    relative effects of exposure, infiltration, ventilation, etc.

II. To make a new building more efficient

1. Reduce environmental requirements:

Maintain lower temperature in winter, except in such special
facilities as those for health care of the elderly.

Design for 95%, not 97.5% minimum standards.

Do not heat, cool or illuminate unoccupied spaces to the same
degree as occupied spaces. Passages, lobbies and other non-work
areas are included.

Provide lower level, but better quality illumination (with less
glare and contrast) than current standards. Maintain lower levels
in non-seeing task zones.

Limit the flow of cold and hot water at each tap in lavatories,
showers and sinks.

Prepare energy/benefit, as well as cost/benefit analyses for
all mechanical and electrical systems and for all building
materials, such as insulation, windows etc.

2.   Make energy conservation integral to design and
       construction

Reduce glazing to vision strips where extensive exterior views are
not required.

Use double and triple glazing, heat-absorbing glass and reflecting
glass on east and west exposures.

Insulate walls and ceilings to a U factor of .06 or less in cold
climates.

Employ external solar control devices, such as fins, eyebrows,
awnings, special blinds in double sash, movable louvers, trees,
and site to take advantage of surrounding buildings for shade.

Use an operable sash where outdoor air quality permits and
infiltration does not excessively raise heat loads.

Specify thicker walls and roofs so that mass can provide insulation
and noise reduction qualities.

Build all or partially below grade and employ berms to reduce solar
loads and transmission losses.

Consider multi-use panels that integrate thermal, acoustical, power
and structural functions to reduce energy requirements and capital
costs.

Use light-reflecting wall finishes.

Construct models and make wind-tunnel tests on all new buildings
with objectionable emissions.

3.   Refine calculations to prevent oversizing mechanical equipment :

Use computer programs for load calculations and for energy load
profiles to prevent overdesign.

Make realistic heating and cooling calculations, taking advantage
of lights, people and storage effects.

Do not use excessive safety factors.

4.   Practice heat conservation in specifying heating, cooling
       and illumination systems:

Employ heat-recovery devices, i.e. thermal wheels, heat pipes
and coil-to-coil transfer devices, to transfer energy from exhaust
air to outdoor air, and within sections of the building, interior
to perimeter.

Employ heat-of-light systems when light requirements are necessarily high anyway.

Use rejected heat of compression from refrigeration units for terminal reheat and for space heating or process.

Recover heat from solid and liquid waste disposal plants.

Use large heat pump systems.

Use electrical demand limiters with load-shedding devices.

Make wide use of Total Energy and energy storage systems.

5.   Select efficient mechanical and electrical systems:

Use low-resistance filters, ducts (material and size), registers, grilles and coil to reduce air horsepower.

Avoid large supply fans with high static electric pressure power requirements – use separate air handlers and wet-media energy transmitters in central systems.

Avoid large terminal reheating systems and make more extensive use of variable volume. Avoid absorption refrigeration, except when using waste heat – use gas engine drive, centrifugal and reciprocating compressors.

Employ modular design on boilers, cooling towers, pumps etc.

Provide sufficient zones of temperature control so areas are not overheated or overcooled.

Use more central HVAC systems to increase diversity and use more efficient large-scale equipment. Use district heating and cooling systems where available.

Use higher voltage distribution outside and inside buildings.

Install capacitors where necessary to correct power factor.

Use more sensitive and heat-anticipating temperature controls and computerized systems to avoid wide temperature swings.

Limit the kWh per Btu output for window units and all incremental units. In general, do not use window air conditioners.

6.   Recycle water, sewage and solid wastes:

Pipe hot water discharge from kitchens, laundries and lavatories through heat exchangers to preheat service hot water.

Use effluent from the sewage system for irrigation and flushing purposes, reducing water requirements and sewage and water treatment plant requirements.

Recycle water within buildings, using "grey" water for flushing.

7. Locate buildings with high energy requirements near power plants and heat-generating waste-disposal systems to increase Total Energy efficiency.

8. Use building materials that require less energy to produce. For example, it takes six times more energy to produce a ton of aluminum than it does a ton of steel. However, it takes only 5% as much energy to produce recycled aluminum as it does virgin aluminum.

9. Avoid non-bio-degradable products.

10. Choose materials and components with long useful lives; obsolescence can no longer be tolerated.

11. Practice preventive maintenance:

Install a preventive maintenance program, using a detailed maintenance and operations manual prepared by the design engineers.

Use a data control center for maintenance and operation to indicate operating hours and conditions of filters, pumps and other equipment.

Instrument each mechanical, electrical and hydraulic system for both the maintenance program and to gather data on operating and energy costs. This can be valuable for future building designs, as well as for maintenance.

12. Operate and integrate building facilities and systems for maximum efficiency.

Precool buildings – start the system later and turn off cooling earlier.

III. To improve outlook

1. Provide incentives to the owners and designers of energy-conserving buildings and systems.

2. Create educational programs, and disseminate environmental data to the public, engineers, architects and maintenance personnel.

Energy conservation: Appendix 2

10 Ways to Save a Watt
Pamphlet published by Con Edison, New York

1.   During the day, when no one is at home, turn the air conditioning off.

2.   When using air conditioners, select moderate or medium settings rather than turning your unit on high. During the day keep windows closed and adjust blinds and shades to keep out the sun so that air conditioners won't have to work so hard.

3.   Whenever possible, plan to run major appliances – and smaller appliances as well – before 8am and after 6pm.

4.   If possible, use dishwashers just once a day – after the evening meal.

5.   If possible, plan washer and dryer loads for evenings and weekends. Do one full load instead of many small loads.

6.   Keep lights off when it's daylight except for safety, health and comfort reasons (the heat from lighting requires more air conditioning).

7.   Never leave a kitchen range or oven on when not actually in use.

8.   Turn off television and radio sets when you are not looking or listening.

9.   If you can, save once-in-a-while jobs like vacuum cleaning or working with power tools until the weekend.

10.   When buying an air conditioner, look for the right size unit for your needs. Select one that gives you the maximum amount of BTU's of cooling for every watt used.

Energy conservation bibliography

Air Conditioning and Refrigeration Business Magazine, 'How Employees and
Employers can Conserve Energy', in issue of March 1972

Ad Hoc Committee on Energy Efficiency in Large Buildings, Report to the
Interdepartmental Fuel and Energy Committee of the
State of New York, March 7, 1973

Architectural Record, 'A Round Table on Energy Conservation Through Higher
Quality Building' in issue of January 1972

Jeffrey E. Aronin, Climate and Architecture, Reinhold, New York 1953

Maurice Barrangon, 'Conservation of Resources, How Total Energy Saves Fuel',
GATE Information Digest, March 1971

Beckman and Weidt, Archiecoframe, University of Minnesota, Minneapolis
1973 (figures on energy costs of different building materials
and methods)

David Bird, 'Energy in the Home Being Tested at Twin Rivers', New York Times
May 27th 1973, News of New Jersey section pp.49, 65

Building to Save Energy, report of a seminar sponsored jointly by New York State
Council of Environmental Advisers, New York Chapter
of American Institute of Architects, Consolidated Edison
Company of New York Inc., New York April 13, 1973.

Walter Bunning, Homes in the Sun, W.J. Nesbit, Sydney, Australia 1945

Frank L. Codella, 'Effect of Energy Conservation on Architecture', paper presented
at Workshop on Total Energy Conservation in Public
Buildings, Albany, New York, January 12 1972

Barry Commoner, 'Alternative Approaches to the Environmental Crisis', paper
presented to the Royal Institute of British Architects'
annual conference 1972, published in RIBA Journal,
October 1972 pp.423-9. Also shortened version in Design
No. 285 pp.62-5, 87

Congressional Record, introduction of proposed National Fuels and Energy
Conservation Act by Senator Jackson, with text of Act,
reported July 13 1973 pp.S13358-S13362

Consolidated Edison, 101 Ways to Conserve Electricity at Home, pamphlet,
New York 1973

C.H. Coogan, 'The Residential Heat Pump', Connecticut Light and Power Company,
Waterbury, Conn. 1948

M. Corr and D. MacLeod, 'Getting it Together', Environment, November 1972
(energy conservation through communal living)

G.M. Davies, 'Model Studies of St. George's School Wallasey', Journal
of the Institute of Heating and Ventilating Engineers,
July 1971, Vol. 39 pp.77-80

G.M. Davies, N.S. Sturrock and A.C. Benson, 'Some Results of Measurements
in St. George's School Wallasey', Journal of the
Institute of Heating and Ventilating Engineers, July
1971, Vol. 39 pp.80-4

'Designing for Survival', reports of Royal Institute of British Architects' Conference
University of Lancaster, England, 19-22 July 1972;
published in RIBA Journal, September 1972
pp.366-386 and October 1972 pp.421-432

R.M.E. Diamant, Total Energy, Pergamon 1970

R.M.E. Diamant and J. McGarry, Space and District Heating, Iliffe Books,
London 1968

Fred S. Dubin, ed., 'Life Support Systems for a Dying Planet', special issue of
Progressive Architecture, October 1971, including,
'Available Now: Systems that Save Energy' and 'Can
Building Codes Help Protect the Environment ?'

Fred S. Dubin, 'The New Architecture and Engineering', paper presented at
Workshop on Total Energy Conservation in Public
Buildings, State University of New York, Albany,
January 12 1972

Fred S. Dubin, 'Energy Conservation Needs New Architecture and Engineering',
Public Power, March/April 1972, pp.20-3, 56

Fred S. Dubin, 'Total Energy Systems and the Environment', paper presented at
Connecticut Clean Power Symposium, St. Joseph's
College, Connecticut, May 13 1972

Fred S. Dubin, 'Energy Conservation through Building Design and a Wiser Use
of Electricity' , paper presented at Annual Conference
of American Public Power Association, San Francisco,
June 26 1972

Fred S. Dubin, 'Total Energy Systems and the Environment', Actual Specifying
Engineer, October 1972, pp.58-63

Fred. S. Dubin, 'If You Want to Save Energy ...', American Institute of Architects
Journal, December 1972 pp.18-21

Fred S. Dubin, 'Total Energy Systems for Mass Housing – Why it Makes Sense',
Actual Specifying Engineer, February 1973, pp.69-82

Fred S. Dubin, 'Energy Conservation through Building Design in Perspective', paper
presented to Energy Conservation Conference, University
of Minnesota, Minneapolis, May 23 1973

Fred S. Dubin, statement on energy conservation before Subcommittee on Energy
of the House Science and Astronautics Committee,
June 12 1973

Fred S. Dubin, 'GSA's Energy Conservation Test Building – A Report', Actual
Specifying Engineer, August 1973 pp.84-92

Fred S. Dubin, 'Energy for Architects', Architecture Plus, July 1973

Dubin-Mindell-Bloome Associates, Total Energy – A Technical Report from
Educational Facilities Laboratories, New York May 1970

E-Cube, computerised method for evaluating energy requirements; service available
through South West Research Institute, 8500 Culebra
Road, San Antonio, Texas 78284. Also from Control Data
Cybernet Centers (contact James Ousley, E-Cube
national marketing manager, Omaha, Nebraska)

Edison Electric Institute, Alternate Choice Comparisons for Energy System
Selection (ACCESS), New York

Educational Facilities Laboratories, The Economy of Energy Conservation in
Educational Facilities, EFL, New York 1973

Electric Energy Association, Design Concepts for Optimum Energy Use in HVAC
Systems, New York

Energy International, 'Total Energy Evaluated' in issue of February 1972

Rudolf Geiger, The Climate Near the Ground, Harvard University Press 1950

R.A. Grot and R.H. Socolow, Energy Utilization in a Residential Community,
Working Paper W-7, Princeton University Center for
Environmental Studies, School of Engineering, Feb. 1973

Group to Advance Total Energy (GATE), Total Energy – A Decade of Progress, 1971

GATE Information Digest, monthly from South West Research Institute, 8500 Culebra Road, San Antonio, Texas 78284

M.V. Griffith, 'Some Aspects of Heat Pump Operation in Great Britain – with particular reference to the Shinfield Installation', Proc. of IEE , Dec. 1956 pp.262-78

J.P. Harmsworth, An Introduction to Total Energy Systems

Eric Hirst and Robert Herendeen, 'A Diet Guide for Chronic Energy Consumers', Saturday Science Review, October 28 1972

Eric Hirst and John Meyers, Improving Efficiency of Energy Use: Transportation and Space Heating and Cooling, Oak Ridge National Laboratory, Tennessee 1972

H.C. Hottel and J.B. Howard, New Energy Technology – Some Facts and Assessments, Massachusetts Institute of Technology Press 1971

Illuminating Engineering Society, Optimizing the Use of Energy for Lighting, draft January 24 1973

Interdepartmental Fuel and Energy Committee of the State of New York, Action Plan for Energy Conservation and Efficiency in Large Buildings, Appliances and Transportation August 9 1972

George F. Keck, 'Solar House', Architect's Journal, December 6 1945

B.Y. Kinzey Jr. and H.M. Sharp, Environmental Technologies in Architecture, Prentice-Hall, Englewood Cliffs N.J. 1963

John L. Kmetzo, 'When Computers Assume Building Operations', American Institute of Architects' Journal, December 1972

Helmut E. Landsberg, 'Use of Climatological Data in Heating and Cooling Design', Heating, Piping and Air Conditioning, Vol. 19 No. 9 September 1947, pp.121-5

Metin Lokmanhakian, ed., Procedure for Determining Heating and Cooling Loads for Computerized Energy Calculations. Algorithms for Building Heat Transfer Subroutines, ASHRAE, New York 1971

A.B. Makhijani and A.J. Lichtenberg, An Assessment of Energy and Materials Utilization in the U.S.A., Memorandum ERL-M310, Electronics Research Lab., College of Engineering, University of California, Berkeley, September 22 1971

G. Manley, 'Microclimatology – Local Variations of Climate Likely to Affect the Design and Siting of Buildings', Royal Institute of British Architects Journal, 3rd series, Vol.56 No. 7 pp.317-323

John C. Moyers, The Value of Thermal Insulation in Residential Construction: Economics and the Conservation of Energy, Oak Ridge National Laboratory, Tennessee, December 1971

National Mineral Wool Insulation Association Inc., Impact of Improved Thermal Performance in Conserving Energy, April 1972

Office of Emergency Preparedness, The Potential for Energy Conservation, A Staff Study, Executive Office of the President, Office of Emergency Preparedness, October 1972

Victor G. Olgyay, 'The Temperate House', Architectural Forum Vol. 94 No. 3, March 1951 pp.179-194

Victor G. Olgyay, Design with Climate, Princeton University Press 1963

Joe B. Olivieri, 'A Consultant Looks at Heat Recovery Systems', Air Conditioning, Heating and Refrigeration News

Robert Rodale, 'Avoid the Energy Crunch - Organically', Organic Gardening and Farming, February 1973 pp.42-7

Bernard Rudofsky, Architecture without Architects, An Introduction to Non-Pedigreed Architecture, Museum of Modern Art, New York 1964

Maron J. Simon, Your Solar House, Simon and Schuster, New York 1947

Stanford Research Institute, Patterns of Energy Consumption in the United States, 1972

Richard G. Stein, 'Architecture and Energy', paper presented to AAAS meeting, Philadelphia, December 28-29 1971

Richard G. Stein, 'Spotlight on the Energy Crisis: How Architects Can Help', American Institute of Architects Journal, June 1972

Richard G. Stein, 'A Matter of Design', Environment October 1972 p.17

W.F. Stoecker, ed., Proposed Procedures for Simulating the Performance of Components and Systems for Energy Calculations, ASHRAE

Total Energy, monthly from Total Energy Publishing Co., 522 Briar Oaks Lane, San Antonio, Texas 78216

J.A. Sumner, 'Norwich Heat Pump', Proc. Inst. Mech. Eng. Vol. 158 No. 1 1948, pp.22-9, 39-51

United States Department of Commerce, The First Symposium on the Use of Computers for Environmental Engineering Related to Buildings, 1970

United States Department of Commerce, Office of Consumer Affairs, 7 Ways to Reduce Fuel Consumption in Household Heating... through Energy Conservation, 1971

United States Department of Commerce, Office of Consumer Affairs, 11 Ways to Reduce Energy Consumption and Increase Comfort in Household Cooling, 1971

United States Department of Commerce, The Application of Total Energy Systems to Housing Developments, March 1972

United States Department of Commerce, Use of Modern Computer Programs to Evaluate Dynamic Heat Transfer and Energy Use Processes in Buildings, March 1972

United States House of Representatives, Committee on Interior and Insular Affairs, 92nd Congress, Energy "Demand" Studies: An Analysis and Appraisal, Washington, September 1972

United States National Bureau of Standards/General Services Administration, Action Plan for Power Conservation in State and Local Facilities, Summer 1972

United States National Bureau of Standards/General Services Administration, $e=mc^2$, report of Roundtable on Energy Conservation in Public Buildings, Public Buildings Service, July 1972

United States, National Research Council Conference, Weather and the Building Industry, Washington 1950; includes paper by J.M. Fitch, 'Buildings Designed for Climate Control'

R.G. Werden, 'Weather Data vs. Operating Costs', ASHRAE Journal, October 1964

Henry Niccols Wright, 'Solar Radiation as Related to Summer Cooling and Winter Radiation in Residences', preliminary study for John B. Pierce Foundation, New York, January 20 1936

Wood Conversion Co., The Invisible Family Test House, St. Paul, Minnesota, 1961

Solar energy

In contrast to the prehistoric periods, lasting many millions of years, over which the earth's deposits of fossil fuels - coal, oil, natural gas - were formed, the time taken for their extraction and combustion by man is a mere instant, even on the scale of human history. The energy expert King Hubbert makes this dramatically clear in a discussion which puts the 'epoch of exploitation of fossil fuels' into historical perspective. The best estimates seem to be that the time required to exhaust 80% of the world's petroleum fuels will be about a century - and we are now nearing the mid-point of that hundred years. And the time required to exhaust the same proportion of all coal deposits, perhaps 300 to 400 years. As Hubbert says, on a time scale measured only in millennia, 'it is seen that the epoch of fossil fuels can only be a transitory and ephemeral event - an event, nonetheless, which has exercised the most drastic influence experienced by the human species during its entire biological history.'

The sun is man's primary source of energy - and the fossil fuels may be thought of as a kind of concentrated store of solar energy, fixed in chemical form through the processes of biological photo-synthesis over the enormous eons of pre-history. During the brief era of exploitation of fossil fuels, then, we can be said to be living off 'capital'; and before these fuels are gone, we will have to reorganise our energy economy, so that we are able to live off our solar 'income', or else we will have to look elsewhere than to the sun for our sources of energy.

Solar heat and light create on earth the basic conditions, of temperature etc., which make life possible at all. It is solar radiation, through the mechanism of photosynthesis, that provides the energy for the whole biological system. Through the complex food chain of plant and animal life, we in turn derive from this source the warmth and muscular power of our own bodies. Man has systematised his dependence on this process, of course, in the activity of agriculture; and he has augmented the power of his own muscles with the employment of draft animals. He has also traditionally made use of a variety of renewable biological sources of fuel such as wood, peat and animal dung, burnt mostly for the purposes of house heating or to fire small chemical processes. In historical times there has been little use made by man of direct solar energy as such - with a few minor exceptions like the drying of agricultural produce. On the other hand there are several indirect forms besides in agriculture in which the sun's energy has been exploited.

It is the sun's energy which provides the motive power, through its unequally distributed heating effects, for the circulation of the atmosphere, the oceanic currents and the transport of water

through the cycle of evaporation, precipitation as rain or snow,
and flow through streams and rivers. The capture of this energy
on a small scale through the development of windmills and water
wheels is described in later chapters. Historically more recent
and larger scale harnessings of these sources are represented by
hydro-electric projects, and the proposals presently advanced
for giant wind-electric generators, or for power plants to exploit
the gradient in temperature between the upper and lower levels
of the oceans.

Total quantities of solar energy available

The amount of energy which reaches the earth's surface from the
sun is colossal; quite enough in principle to supply all our
foreseeable energy needs for the almost indefinite future.
According to Farrington Daniels in his admirable book Direct Use
of the Sun's Energy, the thermal solar power available at the
mean distance of the earth from the sun, outside the earth's
atmosphere, amounts to 0.139 watts/cm^2; and the quantity of
solar power intercepted by the cross-sectional area presented by
the earth's disc is 17.7×10^{16} watts. This, says Hubbert, is
roughly $100,000$ times as much as the entire world's presently
installed electric power capacity. The amount is reduced
substantially and in varying degree by the effects of the earth's
atmosphere, cloud cover and so on. Nevertheless, again quoting
Daniels, a mean figure for the available solar power at the earth's
surface would be about 0.024 watts/cm^2, averaged over the whole
day. This is just over one sixth of the value outside the atmosphere.

Efficiency of photosynthetic conversion

The average efficiency with which plants convert solar energy,
through photosynthesis, to the form of chemical energy, is very
low. Most plants store only something like 0.1 to 0.2% of available
radiation annually. Under intense cultivation some agricultural
crops have been reported to yield as much as 40 tons of dry material
per acre per year; which, assuming an average heat of combustion
of these dried materials of 16×10^6 Btu/ton, gives a conversion
efficiency of up to 3%. There are some water plants which have
in relative terms a very high conversion efficiency, such as the
water hyacinth. And under favourable controlled laboratory
conditions some types of algae may be capable of converting up
to 30% of radiant energy from the sun. A small scale pilot algal
culture plant has been in operation at the University of California
at Berkeley since 1959; and many other promising experiments have
been made in Germany, Israel and in Asia, mostly in connection
with the cultivation of algae as a high-protein food.

Cultivation of algae

Biological fuels

It is not conceivable that ideal laboratory conditions could be
matched in the large scale cultivation of plants intended as fuel
for power generation. Proposals have been made recently nonetheless (e.g. by the NSF/NASA Solar Energy Panel) that the
potential be investigated for growing specialised crops, either
fast growing trees, grass crops, water plants or algae, and
processing the harvested material on an industrial scale to fuel
electric power stations. It is estimated that a 1,000MW power

plant could be continuously supplied with timber grown over an area of 400–500 square miles. Other possibilities for biological sources of fuel are agricultural and urban wastes. These may be either burned direct as fuel, or, in the case of organic wastes, may be digested to produce methane gas. The potential of these latter sources is discussed in more detail in a later chapter. In general, though biological fuels offer a useful energy source with no great technological difficulties to their exploitation, their role in the energy economy as a whole must be regarded as restricted, because of the inherent limitations of the efficiency of photosynthetic conversion; and, in the case of organic wastes, the simple matter of the total quantities of material available.

Hydro-electric power

Limited also, though still useful too, are the resources of water and wind power. As secondary effects of the sun's radiation, they must of their nature represent substantially smaller potential sources than does the exploitation of solar energy direct. There is an ultimate capacity for hydro-electric power fixed in theory by the total flow of stream and rivers. For the United States this is calculated – by the Federal Power Commission – to be about 161,000 megawatts. Although this theoretical potential is very large, there are serious limitations on the number of appropriate sites; there are limits on the extent to which it would be possible or desirable to flood large areas of beautiful mountain scenery to provide the necessary reservoirs; and what is more, these reservoirs are bound in a matter of a few hundred years to become entirely filled up with sediment, at which time a whole series of new sites must again be found.

Wind power

As for wind energy, it has been calculated that the power potential in the winds over the continental United States is about 10^8 megawatts; but this is a figure of theoretical significance only, and the practical possibilities are restricted again by the availability of suitable sites. More seriously, the effective power potential is a factor of the total cross-sectional area of air flow which may practically be intercepted with rotors or other devices; and the engineering problems of a large scale wind power program, though well understood and presenting no theoretical obstacles, would be prodigious. (No more so than those of the nuclear power program, all the same).

Non-solar energy sources

Nuclear power

Geothermal power

As for possible sources of energy besides the sun, these are several; the one which presents the greatest promise in quantitative terms, as well as the greatest threat in terms of danger to environment and health, being of course nuclear power, both atomic fission and in time perhaps atomic fusion. In addition there is geothermal energy, that is essentially heat from the earth's interior and manifested at the surface in volcanic activity and hot springs. Geothermal power was first exploited for generating electricity in Tuscany in Italy at the beginning of this century, and other plants are working in New Zealand, California, Iceland, Japan and elsewhere. And there is tidal

Tidal power

energy, which may be harnessed by constructing barriers across the mouths of tidal estuaries, and by using the water-flow - in either direction - to drive electric turbines. The first such scheme was put into operation in northern France in 1966, and others have been since built in Russia. The significance of geothermal and tidal energy on a global scale is minor however, the maximum potential amounting in either case to only 2% and 1% respectively of the world's potential water power from conventional inland hydro-electric plants.

It is the purpose of this report to examine sources of energy as they are likely to affect building design: and in this context most of the above-mentioned alternatives to the fossil fuels represent new means for the centralised large scale generation of electrical power, and their resulting impact on architecture and on the engineering services in buildings as such would be minimal. The fossil fuel alternatives which do seem to have important implications for building are first and foremost the direct use of solar energy, which is the subject of the present chapter; as well as the possibilities, of perhaps rather lesser significance, for small scale wind-electric, hydro-electric and methane power applications which are the subjects of later chapters.

Application of solar energy in buildings

There are special reasons why solar energy finds particular application in buildings, of all possible uses. As we have seen from the Stanford Research Institute's figures given at the beginning of the last chapter, the major uses of energy in buildings are for space heating, water heating and air conditioning. These are all relatively low temperature applications, of the order of 100° to 200°F, by contrast with the temperatures of 300° to 600°F required for mechanical or electrical power production. It is rather wasteful to use the kinds of fuel which can readily yield these higher temperatures, to meet the relatively low grade energy requirements of building heating and cooling. (Especially is this so, as we have already seen, where fossil fuels are used to generate electricity centrally, this electrical supply distributed, and then converted back to thermal energy via electrical resistance heating). A second important factor is that solar radiation arrives already distributed so to speak in a more or less even spread over the earth's surface. For the very dispersed pattern of use which is represented by buildings, this is quite convenient; the energy supply is every-where locally available and no distribution network with its consequent transmission losses (and possible unreliability !) is required.

It is precisely the converse of these considerations which present the main difficulties in the way of large scale industrial or commercial applications of solar power. In this case it is necessary to collect solar energy from very large areas of collector surface, perhaps spread over many acres or square miles even; and to do so probably in desert or in arid sites remote from the industrial users of the power produced. It will also be virtually obligatory to use some form of focussing device or specially treated absorbing surface to achieve the high temperatures required; something which so far as space and water heating applications go, is, as we shall see, quite unneeded. Despite these problems, the outlook for solar power stations on a large scale has promise, and we shall look briefly at the history and potentiality of solar power developments before turning to the subject of water and building heating in greater detail.

History of solar power applications

Farrington Daniels gives a short history in his book of the experiments made over the last hundred years with direct applications of the sun's energy. Some historical information is also given by Hans Rau in Solar Energy (Macmillan 1964). The first achievement of practical significance seems to have been the building, almost exactly a century ago, of a solar distillation plant in the desert of northern Chile. The sloping glass plates of the distilling apparatus covered an area of 51,000 ft^2, and provided a supply of 6,000 gals. of fresh water daily to the saltpetre mines of Las Salinas. This part of Chile remains today one of the most favourable sites geographically and meteorologically for solar power applications, with its cloudless skies, its endless sunshine, and the particular hard saline composition of the desert floor, which reduces blowing dust. (This is a problem with other desert sites, since dust and sand can settle on, obscure, or have a pitting effect on the collector surfaces.)

Chilean solar distillation plant

Principles of solar stills

The process of solar distillation consists generally in setting out a series of shallow black trays into which the salt water is run. The trays are covered with transparent sloping roofs constructed from glass or plastic sheet. As the temperature rises inside the stills, as a result of the 'greenhouse effect', so the water is evaporated from the trays and condenses again onto the under side of the transparent roofs, whence it runs down to be caught in separate channels which lie at the edges of the stills. From these the distilled water is drawn off to a reservoir. The transparent cover to the still has the additional function of protecting the water from any cooling effect of the wind. Other designs have been built using tilted wicks of black cloth. The wick is soaked continuously in salt water, and the distilled water condenses onto a transparent cover sheet, and is collected as before. Solar distillation of water is an application which has continued to attract interest, since it is cheap and simple by comparison with other methods, and meets an obvious and widespread need in arid and in underdeveloped regions.

Burning glasses

The principle of using lenses and mirrors for producing high temperatures by focussing solar radiation, in order to melt metals, or more mundanely to cook food, has been the subject of experiment since the seventeenth century. Indeed it is is possible that the idea was known to the Greeks; Archimedes is reputed to have set fire to the Roman fleet at Syracuse with the use of mirrors. And the possibilities of solar burning glasses or furnaces have from time to time occupied the interest of several scientists well known in other fields, including amongst them the naturalists Buffon and de Saussure, the astronomers Cassini and Herschel, the chemist Lavoisier (who had a lens made of four foot diameter, and with it generated temperatures of 3,000°F and more), and Sir Henry Bessemer of steelmaking fame.

Mouchot solar engine, Paris

One of the first public demonstrations of the use of solar energy to generate steam and hence mechanical power, was by Mouchot and Pifre in Paris in 1882. Their solar steam engine was used to drive a small printing press, on which was printed a newspaper called Le Soleil. To produce the temperatures required for making steam it is usual to focus the sun's rays - as with burning glasses - directly onto a boiler. It is somewhat impractical and expensive to use glass lenses of the size required however, and curved mirrors are generally used for the purpose. (A mirrored dish was used in the Paris demonstration.) These are ideally of parabolic section, with the reflecting surface made of mirrored glass, of polished metal, or today of aluminized plastic sheet material.

Focussing collectors

Either the mirror can take the form of the paraboloid of rotation, or else it can be extended into an elongated trough shape with parabolic section. In very large collectors such as those built for furnaces, and in which temperatures of several thousands of degrees may be achieved, the parabolic form is often made up from a series of flat mirrored pieces appropriately tilted and assembled into a parabolic frame. The same principle may be applied on a small scale; and a design of parabolic reflector made from a mosaic of mirrored tiles has been produced commercially. It is not in fact strictly necessary to have a parabolic form of reflector to achieve high temperatures, and it is sufficient for many purposes, as well as being more convenient in the manufacture, to use a hemispherical shape or else a cylindrical trough form. One further possibility for focussing devices is the Fresnel lens, which refracts the radiation through a series of circular concentric grooves cut in a sheet of plastic, or through a series of concentric rings of aluminized plastic or polished metal.

Tracking the sun

In order to keep the focussing collector pointed continuously at the sun it must be capable of being steered. This is done by mounting both collector and target - be it boiler, furnace or whatever - together on a cradle or gimbals. The sun is then tracked either by moving the assembly manually, by clockwork or by other mechanisms triggered by moving shadows falling across photocells, for instance. Some forms of cylindrical collector can be oriented and tilted so as not to need moving for the greater part of the day; and require only slight adjustments of their overall alignment on a daily or weekly basis.

Ericsson solar engine

The Swedish-American John Ericsson, inventor of the ironclad ship Monitor, built a solar powered steam engine of $2\frac{1}{2}$ hp

Shuman solar
engine, Pasadena

Work of
A.G. Eneas

Shuman solar
engine, Philadelphia

capacity using an 18 foot diameter concave mirror, which he put on show in New York State in the 1870s. A model of this engine is exhibited at the Franklin Institute in Philadelphia. In 1901 Frank Shuman built a solar motor in South Pasadena, with a huge reflector 36 feet across made from small plane mirrors, and steered by clockwork. The output was said to have been 10 hp. Some few years later, in 1907, the Californian inventor A.G. Eneas built a solar steam engine, also in Pasadena, at the Cawston ostrich farm; and later another in Arizona.

In 1908 Shuman built a second solar engine in the Philadelphia suburb of Tacony. This time he made use of so-called 'flat-plate' collectors, of which we will hear more in connection with building heating applications. A flat-plate collector consists in its simplest form of a plane sheet of blackened metal, covered with one or more sheets of glass or transparent plastic, with an air space between metal and cover. This is set up facing south and at an angle appropriate to catch the sun. The blackened surface absorbs solar radiation, and the temperature of the metal plate, and of the air contained in the collector, rises, as a result of the familiar 'greenhouse effect'. The loss of heat from the back surface of the collector is controlled by means of a layer of insulating material, and the sides and cover are also carefully sealed. Heat is drawn off by withdrawing the heated air continuously from the air space; or else by circulating some liquid heat-transfer medium, usually water, through a series of pipes or coils embedded in, or sitting on or behind the metal collector plate.

Shuman's apparatus had two glass cover sheets, an air space of 1", a series of blackened pipes acting as the collector surface, and a 2" thick layer of cork insulation backing. The heat transfer medium was ether, chosen for its volatility and low freezing point, which carried heat from the pipes in the collector, via a heat-exchanger, to a low pressure steam engine with an average output on a daily basis of 14 hp. The collector was equipped with two large plane (not focussing) mirrors, set at an appropriate orientation and tilt to the sun, whose function was to reflect the radiation down onto the collector which was itself set horizontally, in a large wooden box. The steam engine which it powered was used for pumping water, for the purposes of irrigation.

In its essentials Shuman's design remains the model for most flat plate collectors used in water and space heating since, with the exception that the heat transfer medium is most usually water – or water mixed with ethylene glycol as antifreeze – and the collector itself is generally tilted, rather than having reflecting mirrors with a horizontal collector, as in Shuman's arrangement. This engine of Shuman's shows that it is possible to produce steam, and mechanical power, using a flat plate and not a focussing collector. But the maximum achievable temperature is low, and the thermodynamic efficiency of the engine correspondingly small.

Shuman and Boys
plant, Cairo

In 1913 Shuman, with the consulting engineer C.V. Boys, built a very large solar plant at Meadi near Cairo in Egypt. Here Shuman reverted to the use of steerable focussing mirrored collectors, this time in the form of parabolic troughs, 572 in all, which were used directly to heat the boilers of an equal number of steam generators. The steam was used to drive a 50 hp irrigation pump which pumped water from the Nile. Meanwhile in the years before the First World War, two other American solar pioneers, E.E. Willsie and J.F. Boyle, had been working

Work of Willsie
and Boyle

on the design of solar engines, in St. Louis and at Needles in the desert of south-eastern California. In 1918 they built a 15 hp engine which used as solar collector a glass-covered water tank; and they experimented with a variety of volatile heat-transfer liquids, including ammonia, ether and sulfur dioxide under pressure. One other experimenter of this period was

Harrington solar
engine

J.A. Harrington, working in New Mexico, who ran a steam engine with a focussing collector, and used the power to pump water into a high level tank (so storing potential energy). This head of water was used in turn to drive a water turbine. In this way Harrington was able to overcome the fundamental problem of the intermittent nature of the sun's radiation, and the consequent need for some form of energy storage during the nights and over cloudy periods.

Work of
C.G. Abbott

Between the years 1920 and 1950 there appears to have been little activity in the field of solar energy as a whole, with the exception of the work of C.G. Abbott of the Smithsonian Institution, whose own life has spanned just over the hundred years from the time the Chilean distillation plant was installed in 1872. Abbott exhibited a 2 hp solar steam engine at the International Power Conference in Washington in 1936, and a second engine of 1/5 hp in Florida in 1938.

The '30s saw the widespread introduction of commercially produced domestic solar water heaters, mostly in Florida, California and the southern states; as well as the setting up by the wealthy Boston businessman Godfrey L. Cabot of a $600,000 fund intended for solar energy research, and of which the main fruits have been a series of experimental solar heated houses, built at the Massachusetts Institute of Technology since 1939. More of these developments later.

Russian work

F. Molero

Meanwhile in the field of solar power applications, the main centre of activity in the immediate post-war years was the U.S.S.R. From 1941 to 1946 F. Molero worked on the development of solar steam engines; and a series of parabolic reflectors with diameters of up to 33 ft were subsequently built in Tashkent, for powering ice-making and refrigeration machinery. One of the leading Soviet solar scientists is V. Baum, who in 1958 revealed that for the previous three years planning had been going on, for a site on the plains of Ararat near the Turkish border, of the most ambitious solar power project up to that date. This scheme was to have involved the building of a large steam boiler set on a

Solar power
plant, Ararat

tower, 130 ft tall. Around this tower were to have run a series of twenty-three concentric circular tracks, with a total of 1,293 plane mirrors, each 160 ft^2 in area, mounted on cars, and the cars running on the tracks. The position and tilt of the mirrors were to have been controlled automatically to focus onto the central boiler tower. The whole plant was planned to produce steam for heating and industrial processes, as well as electricity generation, sufficient for a town of 20,000 people. It was not built.

Since the 1950s interest and activity in solar research has grown steadily, both through increasing levels of institutional and university support, and as a result of a series of important international meetings and conferences devoted to the subject. (The published proceedings of a number of these conferences are referenced at the beginning of the bibliography section which follows this chapter). In 1949 one session of the centennial meeting of the American Association for the Advancement of Science, held in Washington, was devoted to new energy sources, including solar energy. In the next year a symposium on solar house heating, the first of its kind, was held at MIT. In 1953 the National Science Foundation supported a symposium on applications of solar energy generally, at the University of Wisconsin; and from 1955 a program of solar energy research was supported at Wisconsin with grants from the Guggenheim Fund and the Rockefeller Foundation.

Association for Applied Solar Energy

In 1954 the Association for Applied Solar Energy was founded in Phoenix, Arizona. This organisation, since renamed the Solar Energy Society, has sponsored research, conferences, the holding of an architectural competition for the design of a solar heated house, and the publication of the Journal of Solar Science and Engineering (now Solar Energy). Also in 1954 an important international conference was organised jointly by UNESCO and the Indian government, on solar and wind energy, held in New Delhi. In 1955 the Association for Applied Solar Energy put on two very large and significant conferences in Arizona, the first of which, at Tucson, stressed basic research, and the second, in Phoenix, the applications of solar energy. Amongst other conferences held since, some of the more important have been a United Nations symposium on 'New Sources of Energy' in Rome in 1961, a seminar on solar and aeolian energy at Sounion in Greece also in 1961, and in 1973 a big international meeting in Paris, sponsored by UNESCO and the French government, and organised by the International Solar Energy Society together with French and European solar energy organisations.

Work of H. Tabor on solar 'power ponds'

The scope of work over the last twenty years has very much widened, and any attempt even at a brief survey must be selective. In the fields of power and larger scale applications one might point to the work of H. Tabor in Israel, who, among other interests, has made experiments with 'solar ponds'. These ponds consist of large shallow water tanks with black-painted bottoms, ideally covering several acres, and acting as collectors for low temperature, low pressure steam turbines. In order to inhibit heat losses from the surface of the ponds, a very concentrated salt solution is used for the lower layers of liquid, with plain water lying over the top. When the salt solution becomes heated, it remains at the bottom of the pond, due to its greater density: and so the 'thermal stirring' action which would otherwise occur is prevented. It is possible for water temperatures of up to 200°F to be achieved. Other similar 'power ponds' have been equipped with transparent plastic cover sheets, again to cut the surface heat losses. One further interesting development by Tabor is a relatively cheap design of large cylindrical focussing collector. This consists of a transparent thin plastic bag which is inflated to the cylindrical shape and held rigid by the internal air pressure. The lower part of the inside surface of the bag is aluminized and so acts as a reflector; and steam is generated in a central pipe at the focus.

F. Trombe and solar furnaces

In France much of the recent work in solar applications is associated with the name of Felix Trombe, who has devoted his energies especially to the building of solar furnaces. These furnaces employ large parabolic focussing reflectors; and their use is mainly in high temperature chemical research. The collector and target may be moved together to track the sun, as previously explained. Otherwise, with big installations, where moving the very large diameter parabolic reflectors is cumbersome, it is preferable to use 'heliostats'. This is the arrangement adopted by Trombe, where a focussing reflector is placed in a fixed position facing north, and an array of steerable plane mirrors is set out opposite, with which the sun's radiation is reflected back onto the parabolic mirror. Trombe has experimented with a series of progressively larger furnaces. One built at Fort Mont-Louis in the Pyrenees in 1952, has a focussing reflector of 35 ft diameter, and has produced 70 kW of power, and temperatures over 5,000°F. In 1970 a gigantic furnace was completed, the largest in the world, at Odeillo near Mont-Louis. This has a parabolic reflector of 130 ft diameter, and is capable of generating 1,000kW.

Current U.S. Solar research

In the last two or three years, largely as a result of growing awareness of the imminent shortage of petroleum fuels and the difficulties and dangers of nuclear power, the scale of solar energy work has expanded out of all recognition. A recent Staff Report of the Committee on Science and Astronautics of the House of Representatives reviews current research and development (at December 1972) in the United States. There are contributions in this report (Solar Energy Research : A Multidisciplinary Approach) from four bodies: the National Aeronautics and Space Administration, the National Science Foundation, the National Bureau of Standards and the Congressional Research Service. The testimony of the NBS is largely devoted to the heating and cooling of buildings by solar energy, and its economic and technical feasibility; and the report of the Congressional Research Service discusses for the most part the requirements for chemical and materials research created by solar energy applications.

National
Aeronautics and
Space Administration

As for NASA, the Administration have been interested since the late '50s in the specific application of photovoltaic cells, which convert sunlight to electrical energy (see p.110), in connection with the power systems of spacecraft and satellites. Much of the progress in photovoltaic technology over this period is due to their sponsorship. More recently NASA have turned their attention to terrestrial applications of solar power, including solar electric and solar thermal power generation, heating and cooling of buildings, and the intensive cultivation of biological fuels. A joint study was set up with the National Science Foundation in 1972, in which a panel of experts from many disciplines came together to assess ' the potential of solar energy as a national resource and the state of technology in the various solar application areas'. The Panel made recommendations for research and development priorities and for levels of governmental funding of solar work.

In the fiscal year 1973 NASA is spending $1 million on research into terrestrial applications, and about $1.5 million on the continuing support of solar cell technology for space missions. Over the next three years the total NASA solar energy budget is up to $30 millions a year. The most spectacular solar power proposal associated with the name of NASA, in fact originates from the consultancy company Arthur D. Little and Associates, and its president Dr. Peter Glaser.

Glaser satellite
solar power
station

Glaser's scheme is to build a giant satellite solar power station placed in synchronous orbit around the earth's equator. Such a satellite not only receives solar radiation at an intensity several times greater than that reaching the earth's surface, but it is also exposed to the sun for the full twenty-four hours of the day (with the exception of short periods around the equinoxes).

The scale of Glaser's proposal is staggering. Two square arrays of photovoltaic cells would be assembled, each with overall dimensions of 4km by 4km, and surrounded by a larger area of concentrating mirrors. The electrical power generated would be used to power a microwave beam, transmitted to earth by means of a transmitting antenna 1km in diameter on the satellite, and a receiving antenna 7km in diameter on the earth's surface. The net power output would be about 10,000 megawatts. The feasibility of the scheme depends on the use of the NASA Space Shuttle for building the station in orbit, and on a reduction of the present per square foot cost of solar cell arrays by a factor of 100 or so. W.R. Goddard of NASA's Goddard Space Flight Center believes that an earth-based solar electric power plant would offer more promise, despite the problems of intermittent operation, battery or other storage, and the reduced levels of solar radiation at ground level – one sixth or so of those in space.

Meinel
'solar farm'

A competing power scheme using a solar thermal conversion system has been put forward by Professors Aden and Marjorie Meinel, formerly of the Department of Optical Sciences at the University of Arizona and now running their own solar power consultancy firm, Helio Associates. The Meinel's proposal calls for the setting up of large 'solar farms' in the deserts of the American south-west. The solar farm idea is not dissimilar in principle to the Shuman and Boys Cairo plant of 1913. But a number of new materials and other developments now make possible much higher levels of efficiency.

A great number of focussing collectors are set out, and the heat so captured is transferred via receiver pipes placed at the foci, to central heat storage facilities and to steam turbines, which in turn generate electrical power. The Meinels have built an advanced prototype design of focussing collector, with a parabolic section trough-shaped mirror, and an evacuated glass tube at the focus. This tube is silvered on the inside, somewhat like a 'thermos' flask, with the exception of two narrow slit windows to admit the radiation. In this way heat losses by re-radiation, convection and conduction from a steel absorber pipe inside the glass tube, are prevented.

Selective coatings

The steel pipe is covered with a specially prepared absorbing surface, which increases the ratio of short wave radiation absorbed to infrared radiation re-emitted (the a/e ratio) to a very high value. This is done by vacuum deposition of alternating thin layers of aluminum oxide and molybdenum onto the steel substrate. Though the temperatures achieved with these selective coatings and the focussing collector (up to 1,000°F) are very encouraging, the Meinel's tests have revealed that even in the Arizona climate the proportion of time during which the output is affected by cloud or hazy conditions is greater than had been anticipated. A parabolic focussing type of collector, or a Fresnel lens (as the Meinels have else where proposed as an alternative possibility) collects radiation from the sun's disc itself; and when the sun is obscured the collection ceases. A great deal of radiation however also reaches the ground in a diffuse form from the remainder of the sky.

Meinel 'planar' collector

It is both diffuse and direct solar radiation which are collected with a flat plate receiver, which despite its lower efficiency and lower operating temperature, is able to work for a greater number of hours per day and days per year than a focussing collector. The Meinels are now proposing a method for getting the best of both worlds, with what they call a 'planar' collector. This is developed from a device used in the space program to reject heat from spacecraft, and called a 'space radiator'. The planar collector has a double cusp section, and collects radiation from the whole sky, which it reflects onto an absorbing pipe encased in a vacuum tube as before, set at the apex of the cusp. The Meinels have published schemes for solar farms covering many square miles, and are presently seeking funding for the construction of a 1 acre test bed. They estimate that all anticipated American electrical power needs in the year 2000 could be met by a plant area of 10,000 square miles.

National Science Foundation

To return briefly to the subject of National Science Foundation support of solar energy research, the evidence given to the House Science and Astronautics Committee shows that in the fiscal year

1971 the NSF/RANN (Research Applied to National Needs) program was supporting work at two universities, to the extent of $1·2 million, and in 1972, work at ten universities and to a total of $1·6 million. The projects supported range over photovoltaic applications, solar thermal power systems, biological methods for the production of hydrogen and methane as fuels, ocean temperature gradient power plants and computer modelling of solar heating and cooling systems for building. In 1973 NSF support for research has risen to $4 million, and the projected figure for 1974 is $12 million, of which nearly half is to be devoted to solar energy for buildings.

Work by commercial firms

Commercial firms active in the field of solar power applications include McDonnell Douglas Astronautics of Huntington Beach, Ca.; Gulf General Atomics Co. of San Diego; Honeywell Inc. in Minneapolis; The Aerospace Corporation of El Segundo, Ca.; and Sandia Laboratories of Albuquerque, New Mexico. Companies involved in building applications or in the design of low temperature flat-plate collectors include Texas Instruments, the Lockheed Missiles and Space Co. in Palo Alto, and Thermo Electron Corp. of Waltham, Mass. Several of these companies are working in collaboration with NSF-funded university research groups.

Applications of solar energy in buildings

As already indicated, there are three main functions to which solar energy can be usefully applied in buildings. These are, in ascending order of difficulty, the heating of domestic water supplies for bathing, washing etc.; space heating; and space cooling. The same methods which are used to heat domestic water can be applied to heating swimming pools. In addition there have been a variety of designs developed for solar-powered cookers, although these are intended for cooking outdoors and when the sun is shining only, and so their usefulness is rather limited. And it is possible to make use of solar distillation for the local purification of water supplies. Finally there is the prospect in the future of being able to exploit the photoelectric cell to generate electricity from solar radiation locally, for use in buildings; and one experiment along these lines is presently under way.

With solar thermal applications, the fundamental principles are similar throughout. In all cases it is necessary to have some form of solar collector, with which to trap the solar heat; and since the sun shines only intermittently, during the daytime and not always with any great strength even then, it is necessary to have some form of storage reservoir, in which to retain this heat, and from which it may be released slowly as needed. The solar collector is generally of the flat-plate type, as used by Shuman in his 1908 solar engine and already described in that connection, set up facing south (or, in the southern hemisphere, facing north), and at a tilt which might vary anywhere between the vertical and the horizontal. The subject of heat storage reservoirs has been discussed briefly in the last chapter. There are broadly two possibilities: to store sensible heat in some large body of material with high thermal mass, such as a tank of water or box of rocks; or else to store latent heat in a material which melts, or by a chemical reaction which takes place over the range of temperature in question. The most popular, simplest and cheapest form of heat storage is in large tanks of water; and in the case of solar water heaters, or solar swimming pool heaters, it is the water tank or pool itself which acts in effect as the heat storage reservoir.

Whether solar heating is technically feasible or not, whether it is economically competitive, and what the particular size and config-uration of the collection and storage system should be, are all clearly questions which are related to the particular climate and locality in which the building is situated; as well as to the size, nature, construction and use of the building itself. Let us look first at the problem of geography and climate in relation to solar heating.

Solar radiation reaching the earth's surface

Solar radiation at the earth's surface is measured in <u>langleys</u> per minute. One langley is equal to one calorie of radiation energy per square centimetre. (This figure refers to measurements made on a horizontal surface.) Putting this into the units of heat energy more conventionally used with reference to building design, 1 langley/min. = 221 Btu/ft^2/hour. The intensity of solar radiation reaching any given point on earth varies with geographical latitude, with the season, with the time of day, with the proportion of cloud cover and with the amount of dust or haze in the atmosphere. These factors can result in a variation of intensity between 0 and about 1.5 langleys/minute. A reasonably average figure for radiation received by a surface tilted to face the sun and under cloudless skies, is 1 langley/min. According to Daniels, a house roof of 100 m^2 (or 1,076 ft^2), receiving an average of 1 langley/min. for 500 minutes (or roughly 8 hours) per day in bright sunshine, is exposed to 5×10^8 calories of radiation energy; or the equivalent in heat energy of burning something like 14 gallons of gasoline.

Variation of solar radiation with the seasons

Ignoring for the moment the effects of the earth's atmosphere on solar radiation reaching the ground, we must first take account of the factors of latitude, season and time of day; which in turn are essentially dependent on the geometry of the earth's orbit around the sun, and of the earth's rotation on its own axis. Imagining the orbit of the earth round the sun in a path which, although strictly elliptical, is in fact very close to a true circle; then this circular path can be seen to establish a conceptual 'plane of rotation', passing through the sun. The polar axis on which the earth itself spins, is tilted in relation to this plane at an angle of $23\frac{1}{2}°$; and this angle remains unchanged throughout the whole of the orbit – that is to say, the polar axis is at all times parallel throughout the whole year. The consequence is that at one side of the orbital path, the northern hemisphere is tipped somewhat toward the sun, this period corresponding to the summer for that hemisphere; while at the opposite side of the orbit the converse situation obtains, and the southern hemisphere is tilted to the sun and in turn enjoys its summer.

During the summer season in either case, the effect of the tilt is that the hemisphere in question is exposed to the sun for a greater part of the 24 hour cycle of rotation of the earth on its own axis; that is to say the hours of daylight become lengthened. The effect reaches an extreme in the northern hemisphere on the solstice, June 22nd, at which date the days are at their longest, and from that time start to become shorter again. The effect is furthermore increasingly pronounced at higher latitudes, towards the poles; and during the whole summer season the polar area is exposed to continual daylight. (Living in northern latitudes, we are conventionally used to referring to this date of June 22nd as the 'summer solstice'; but it represents in fact the summer season of long days and more sun for the northern hemisphere only, while the southern hemisphere is undergoing the opposite, winter conditions.) Conversely, during the winter season, the days (in northern latitudes) shrink ever shorter, to reach a minimum on the winter solstice, December 22nd; and the higher latitudes are now in continual darkness.

Midway between the dates of the two solstices, are the equinoxes, March 21st and September 23rd, at which times the length of both day and night is exactly 12 hours everywhere on earth. On the equinoxes, the sun is directly overhead at noon on the equator; and between these two dates it is directly overhead at noon at a degree of latitude which moves between a northward extreme at the Tropic of Cancer ($23\frac{1}{2}°N$), reached on the summer solstice, and a southerly extreme at the Tropic of Capricorn ($23\frac{1}{2}°S$), reached on the winter solstice. At all other latitudes and times of day the sun's rays strike the surface of the earth obliquely. In general of course the sun's angle is lower at higher latitudes, and lower in the mornings and the evenings than at midday. As a consequence, taking an imaginary 'beam' of sunlight of given cross-sectional area, this beam is spread over a larger area of the earth's surface; and so its intensity per unit of ground area is less.

Passage of solar radiation through the atmosphere

There is a further result of the fact of the sun's rays striking the earth at an angle, and this is to do with the passage of the radiation through the atmosphere. Even when there is no cloud, the effect of the atmosphere and of water vapour and dust particles is to diffuse the sun's radiation quite appreciably - hence the fact that the clear sky appears blue and not black - and the proportion of diffuse radiation to direct even in cloudless conditions can be as high as 10%. As the depth of the atmosphere through which the solar radiation must pass increases, so the amount which is lost by absorption and scattering increases, and the proportion reaching the ground is reduced. When the sun is directly overhead at noon on the equator or at the lower latitudes, this depth of atmosphere is at its minimum, and the amount of radiation reaching the ground directly is at a maximum. The path which the radiation must take gets longer as the angle of incidence becomes shallower, towards the higher latitudes, and in the mornings and evenings; and the diffusing effect of atmospheric particles is correspondingly greater.

The meteorological records which are kept of solar radiation measure the energy received on a horizontal surface of given area. The two considerations mentioned, which follow from the fact of the solar radiation falling at an oblique angle, result in the observed values being generally reduced in higher latitudes and at the ends of the day, as explained. There is no way of avoiding the problem of the sun's longer path through the atmosphere in these situations. It is possible however in solar energy applications to take action in response to the other consideration - that the same 'beam' of sunlight arriving at an angle is spread over a larger area of ground surface, and its measured intensity on the horizontal plane is thus diminished. The answer is, naturally, to tip the surface of any solar collecting device to an angle, ideally perpendicular to the sun's rays - and this is what is generally done in collector design. The figures for radiation received on a horizontal surface, must be adjusted therefore to derive values for the radiation reaching an inclined collector.

Tilt and orientation of solar collectors

Ideally the flat surface of a solar collector would be continuously moved, on two axes, so as to be normal to the sun's radiation both at different times of the day and on different days of the year. This is not often done in fact, because of the complication and inconvenience, not to mention expense, of steering the collector with some automatic mechanism; and it is usually simpler to use a fixed collector of rather larger area to compensate for the consequent loss of efficiency, and at a compromise position for the average pattern of radiation. In higher latitudes a vertical surface receives more radiation in winter than does a horizontal one; and we shall see how for space heating applications, designs have varied from a horizontal type of collector, mounted on a flat roof perhaps, at the lower latitudes (say up to 35°), through progressively steeper pitches of collector, to a vertical 'collector wall' type which is most appropriate in latitudes around 45° or 50° and above.

Diffuse radiation

In cloudy weather diffuse radiation can form the greater part of the total received, and this is frequently the rule in the higher latitudes. 'In much of Europe', says Daniels, 'about half of the total radiation is diffuse, with a higher proportion in winter and less in summer. At a station in Massachusetts 40 per cent of the total annual solar radiation is diffuse, and in South Africa in relatively sunny climates the diffuse radiation is 30 per cent of the total.' According to Drummond, on a bright, cloudy day a north window in the northern hemisphere may receive ten times as much radiation as on a cloudless day. As explained earlier, the flat-plate type of solar collector is capable of collecting both direct and diffuse radiation, unlike the focussing type - and so the quantity of diffuse radiation available is an important consideration in solar heating design, especially in cloudier climates. A method has been put forward by Liu and Jordan ('The Interrelationship and Characteristic Distribution of Direct, Diffuse and Total Solar Radiation', Solar Energy Vol.4 No. 3, 1960 pp.1-19) by which, in the absence of separate measurements, estimates may be derived for the proportion of diffuse radiation, from figures for the total radiation. This method uses an index for average cloudiness during different months of the year.

Numbers of consecutive cloudy days

It is not only the average conditions of solar radiation which are significant, but the extremes; particularly, for solar heating, the extreme low conditions. The frequency with which numbers of consecutive cloudy days are likely to occur in any location has important implications for the requirements for thermal storage capacity in heating installations. In some of the southern parts of the United States, the maximum continuous period of cloudy weather likely to be encountered is about seven days; in the north this can rise as high as ten days. With the introduction of computers, many meteorological records, giving hour-by-hour observations, are now kept on magnetic tapes. These very detailed tape records have been used in some recent simulations of solar heating systems, and can be preferable to the use of average values, precisely because of this reason, that the particular pattern and sequence of sunny and cloudy weather has an important bearing on the resulting performance.

Albedo

Radiation to the night sky

Two other meteorological phenomena which can be significant in solar energy applications are the reflection of solar radiation back off the ground surface, particularly off snow and water, and known as the albedo; and also re-radiation of long-wave infrared radiation from the earth to the sky, when the former is at a higher temperature than the latter (e.g. at night). The ground absorbs solar radiation during the day, and becomes warmed. Then, during the night, when the sky's temperature drops, the heat energy is re-radiated to the sky again. The amount of this radiation is greatest when the night sky is cloudless, so acting as a 'black body' (an ideal absorber of radiation), and can rise as high as $0 \cdot 1$ cal/cm^2/min (20 Btu/ft^2/hr). When the sky is overcast, then little re-radiation takes place, since the temperature of the clouds is generally much the same as that of the ground. The re-radiation effect is so pronounced in some dry and desert regions of the world, that it is possible to freeze water (even though the air temperature remains above freezing) by setting it out in shallow pans under the night sky; and this method was employed for making ice in the Middle East in historical times. Some recent solar-heated houses have used the same principle to achieve a cooling effect on summer nights, by running the system 'the other way round', using the solar collector as a radiator, and the thermal storage reservoir to store 'cool' instead of heat.

Meteorological data

Sine the revival of interest in solar energy research in the 1950s, much work has been done on collecting relevant meteorological data, both for the United States and on a world-wide basis. A great deal of this coordinated information was presented in a report by Löf, Duffie and Smith, World Distribution of Solar Radiation (Report No. 21, Solar Energy Laboratory, College of Engineering, University of Wisconsin) published in 1966. Rather counter to expectations from the foregoing discussion perhaps, it is not the equatorial regions of the world which are most favourable for solar energy applications. Here the humidity is high, and there is persistent cloud cover. More suitable are the broad bands lying between latitudes 15° and 35°, both north and south, and it is in these regions that are found the great deserts of the world – the Mojave and the American south-west, the Sahara, Arabia and the Gobi in the northern hemisphere, the deserts of northern Chile and of central Australia, in the southern hemisphere. These are the most promising areas for industrial scale solar power applications. A map showing the annual number of hours of sunshine in different parts of the United States appears at the end of this section on pp.

It is not simply the total yearly available amount of sunshine which is important in relation to the use of solar energy in buildings however. In the case of solar water heating, there is a fairly constant year-round pattern of demand; and supplies of hot water are as much needed in hot climates as they are in cold. But with solar space heating or air conditioning, there is little need of the one in hot climates or of the other in cold climates, of course; and the pattern of demand in both cases varies greatly with the seasons.

There is a certain neatness and symmetry about the use of solar energy for refrigeration, since there is most need for cooling buildings at those times of day and on those days of the year when the supply of energy with which to achieve that cooling is greatest. For these reasons the requirements for thermal energy storage in solar cooling systems would be less than those for solar heating. The prospects for solar cooling in tropical countries are most particularly appealing.

Solar heating and climate

So far as solar heating goes however, the converse applies, and it is during the winter months, when the amount of sun is least, that the requirement for space heating is, naturally, at its greatest. Roughly speaking, one can say that the ideal kind of climate for solar heating is one with cold winter weather, but with plenty of winter sunshine. Such conditions do occur, particularly at high altitudes, for instance in New Mexico; but they are not the general rule.

Map by P.A. Siple

There is a map, drawn by the engineer P.A. Siple, which has been frequently reproduced in the literature, and which is intended to show the relative feasibility of solar heating systems for different parts of the United States. In this map the country is divided, like Gaul, into three parts: a 'region of maximum feasibility' covering Florida, the south-east, the Gulf of Mexico, Texas and the south-west including southern California; a 'region of minimum feasibility' comprising northern New England, New York, Pennsylvania, Virginia, Ohio, Michigan, Wisconsin, Minnesota, North Dakota, Montana, Idaho, Washington and Oregon; and a 'region of engineering feasibility' which covers all the central parts of the country in between. The map is in some ways misleading however. Florida and the south-west are certainly the areas where, from an engineering point of view, it is simplest to construct a collector and heat storage reservoir of sufficient size to carry the required heating load. It is in these regions that solar water heating has been a commercial proposition in the past, from the 1930s to the early 1950s. But the requirement for space heating in these same areas is small; and the capital investment in equipment, which would be used only for a short season in the year, might not be justifiable.

Solar radiation, in lang-
leys, in the United States
east of the Rocky
Mountains on June 21;
adapted from S.S.
Visher, Climatic Atlas
of the United States,
Harvard 1954 p.183

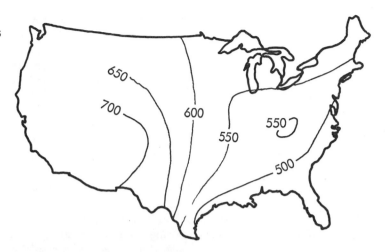

What is important in considering different geographical areas with
a view to solar space heating, is the relationship in each case
between the average winter solar radiation, and the average winter
temperature conditions as expressed typically in 'heating degree days'
(see p.21). The short table below, taken from Daniels (p.40), gives
some typical figures for average solar radiation in langleys per day
(on a horizontal surface) for different months of the year, in four
different parts of the United States.

	December	March	June
New York and Chicago	125	325	550
S. California and Arizona	250	400	700
Florida	250	400	500
Nevada	175	400	650

(September radiation is similar to March)

The accompanying maps, above and below, adapted from Visher's
Climatic Atlas of the United States (Harvard University Press 1954
p.183) illustrate the same information for two particular dates, June
21 and December 21, throughout the whole of the country east of
the Rocky Mountains.

Solar radiation, in lang-
leys, in the United States
east of the Rocky
Mountains on December
21; adapted from S.S.
Visher, Climatic Atlas
of the United States,
Harvard 1954 p.183

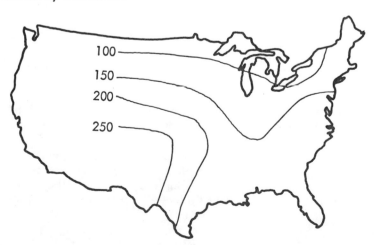

These figures for radiation in langleys do not, as already explained, give a precise indication of what would be available for collection with a tilted receiver – particularly at higher latitudes. They do however provide some basis for approximate comparison of solar heating potential between different locations. One comparative index has been devised by G.O.G. Löf, in a paper from 1961 in which he reviewed several of the solar heating projects up to that date ('The Use of Solar Energy for Space Heating, General Report' (UN: Rome) E 35 Gr-S14). This index he calls a 'weather factor', and it represents an approximated ratio of solar radiation to heating degree days per year. Löf takes the figure for January radiation in langleys/day for the particular location, and multiplies this by 3·69 to convert to Btus/ft^2. He then multiplies the resulting quantity again by 1·5, which is the approximate ratio of the average solar radiation during the entire heating season, to the January radiation. Finally he multiplies the whole resulting total by 200 for the number of days in the heating season. The figure obtained thus represents an estimate of the total quantity of solar radiation received over the whole period during which heating is required, expressed in Btus/ft^2. It is divided by the figure for heating degree days per year for the given location, in order to yield the 'weather factor'.

Index devised by Löf for favourableness of climate for solar heating

The actual numerical value has no physical meaning, but the relative values for different geographical sites do serve the purpose of making comparisons in terms of the favourableness or otherwise for solar heating applications. The particular figures computed by Löf in his paper vary between 30 for Massachusetts at the least favourable, through values in the 40s for Washington DC and Colorado, values of 59 for the island of Capri in Italy and 67 for Tokyo (all places where solar buildings had then actually been put up), to a maximum of 190 for Arizona as by far and away the 'mildest' site studied.

Telkes map of degree days per sunshine hour

A slightly different index, but serving essentially the same comparative purpose, has been proposed by Dr Maria Telkes. This is illustrated here in the form of a map, on which are plotted relative values for the whole of the country. The figures on the map represent the ratio in each case of the degree days to the total hours of sunshine, measured over the months of December and January. The higher the value, the more severe is the climate from the point of view of solar space heating, and the larger is the heating system required. Sample figures range between 7·2 for Boston, 6·6 for Washington DC, 5·4 for Denver to 1·8 for Phoenix.

Performance of flat-plate collectors

The principles of the simple 'flat-plate' collector of solar radiation have already been expounded; and the design of collector developed by Shuman for his experiments in Tacony has been specifically discussed. The theoretical aspects of the thermodynamic performance of flat-plate collectors were first set out in an important paper of 1942 by Hottel and Woertz ('The Performance of Flat-Plate Solar Heat Collectors', Trans. Am. Soc. Mech. Eng., Vol.64, 1942 pp.91-104).

A proportion of the solar radiation striking the transparent surface of the cover of the collector is reflected (depending on the angle of incidence); but the greater part passes through and is absorbed by the blackened collecting surface behind. The collecting surface rises in temperature as a result. Some energy is re-radiated back through the transparent cover sheets, but again the greater part is trapped because of the opacity of these materials to the longer wave-length infrared radiation (the greenhouse effect). Some heat is lost from the collector by convection and conduction to the surrounding air, and some by conduction to the adjacent parts of the collecting system or supporting structure. The remainder is drawn off to the heat storage reservoir via the heat transfer medium of air, water or other fluid.

At a steady state of constant temperature, these various flows of energy are balanced against each other, and the quantity of useful heat energy obtained is given by subtracting the various heat losses from the quantity of incoming energy from the solar radiation. Losses by convection are substantially increased as the speed of the wind increases. Radiation losses are proportional to the fourth power of the temperature, and therefore rise steeply at higher temperatures.

Some of the most important variables in the design of flat-plate collectors are, first of all, the area, and the angle of tilt; then the optical properties of the glass or other transparent material of the cover sheets; the absorbing properties of the blackened surface; and the insulating properties of the construction of the box which contains and supports the collector.

The required area of collector is obviously dependent on the particular climatic conditions, and on the total heating demand, as well as many factors of performance efficiency. Some of these will be discussed in more detail later, but to give a <u>very</u> rough indication

Map by Dr M. Telkes showing degree days per sunshine hour, based on December and January data. From 'A Review of Solar House Heating', <u>Heating and Ventilating</u> reference section, Sept. 1949, fig.1 p.71

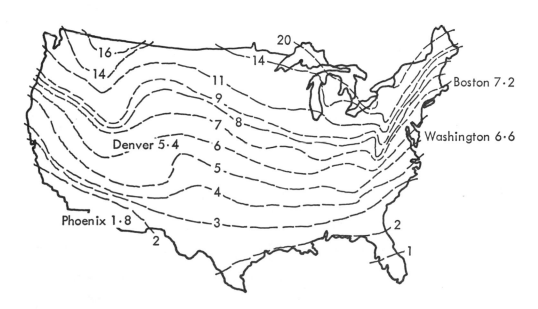

here of the orders of magnitude involved: a collector for a domestic water heater might be perhaps 30 ft^2 to 60 ft^2 in area; while for latitudes around 30° to 45°, for space heating applications, a figure for the collector area equal to about half the floor area of the building, might indicate the sort of size required. It is immediately clear that the collector is a very large piece of apparatus indeed, and poses serious problems for its incorporation into the architectural form of any building.

Tilt of collector

As for the tilt, a rough rule of thumb is, for the collection of winter radiation, to set the collector at an angle with the horizontal equal to the latitude plus 15° (i.e. at latitude 30°, the collector is tilted at 45°). This would be most appropriate for space heating applications. If the angle is to be optimal for summer radiation, then a value equal to the latitude minus 15° is recommended. In practice the performance of collectors is not too sensitive to the angle of tilt, and a variation of up to 30° from these recommended angles appears to be acceptable.

Architectural incorporation of the collector

From the point of view of architectural convenience, and for space heating installations, it may be possible in the appropriate latitudes to set the collector on the surface of a pitched roof, and so achieve the required tilt quite neatly. In other circumstances, and in lower latitudes, the flat roof surface of the building may be used for mounting a horizontal collector; and this is probably the arrangement which is least obtrusive and easiest to accommodate visually. Another possibility is to mount a series of smaller elongated tilted collectors on a flat roof surface in sawtooth arrangement, or like a large scale Venetian blind. These principles were used in a house designed by Löf at Denver, Colorado, and in a house in Phoenix which was the winning entry in a competition for solar house designs organised by the Association for Applied Solar Energy.

Collector walls

In higher latitudes where the optimal winter angle of tilt approaches the vertical, then it will probably prove best to incorporate the collector into the construction of the south wall – though this has the obvious disadvantage of conflicting with any requirement for south-facing windows in the building. Collectors which are more nearly vertical have the virtue of not collecting dust and dirt so badly, and of being cleaned automatically by the rain; although it is reported that collector efficiency is not too seriously affected by dirty glass. It is not absolutely essential that the collector be mounted on the building itself, and it might possibly be a free-standing structure. This has the disadvantage that heat losses from the back of the collector are involved; where with a wall or roof-mounted collector, heat given off from the back passes into the interior spaces. One problem to be borne in mind is the vulnerability of the collector glass – especially if it is at ground level – to accidental damage or vandalism.

Variation in collector orientation

As for any possibility of variation from the optimal orientation of the collecting surface towards the south (or towards the north in the southern hemisphere), a recent study at the University of Pennsylvania has shown that a 23° deviation either side of the exact southerly orientation, during the critical heating months of December and January and for central U.S. latitudes, involves a reduction in insolation of only 5%; and a 33° deviation either way involves a 10% reduction. These figures refer to vertical collecting surfaces. Any deviation greater than 45° results however in the collector walls being exposed to more radiation in the summer than in the winter, which is something very much to be avoided.

Cover sheets to collectors

A range of possibilities have been tested for the transparent cover sheets to solar collectors. Because these transparent materials are poor conductors of heat, and are separated from the absorbing surface by layers of static air, they have an important role in reducing heat losses. The most usual cover material is glass. The greater the number of sheets, the more effective is the reduction of convection and radiation losses; but at the same time the reflection of incoming radiation from the multiple glass surfaces is increased. The optimum spacing of sheets is about 1" apart, and it has been found that, for central U.S. latitudes, two sheets gives the optimal balance of reduction of heat losses against increased reflection losses - although for the extreme south of the country, e.g. in Florida and the south-west, one sheet may be sufficient. There do exist special methods of treatment whereby the reflectivity of the glass can be reduced, but this raises the cost.

Number of glass sheets

Comparative merits of glass and plastics for collector covers

For best transmission of solar radiation, the glass should be as thin as structural considerations allow; and the use of greenish glass with high iron content should be avoided, since this has lower transmissivity. Two problems with glass, in comparison with the alternative transparent plastic materials, are its cost and fragility. Some difficulties have been experienced in flat-plate collectors where the considerable fluctuations of temperature have given rise to substantial thermal movement of the supporting structure, and this has resulted in high rates of glass breakage. On the other hand, plastic film materials, despite their being cheap and tough, have other disadvantages which render them less suitable for collector covers. Under the influence of the ultraviolet radiation in sunlight, many plastics deteriorate rapidly, becoming yellowed and brittle (though treatments are available to inhibit this action). Other plastics are softened by the high temperatures reached. Several workers who have experimented with plastics have returned to using glass covers in the end; and at present glass appears to remain the most suitable material, all factors considered.

Design of absorbing surface

The absorbing surface itself must be black, and is usually of metal, with a matt paint applied. The detailed design is affected particularly by the heat transfer medium chosen. Water or any other liquid must be channelled through pipes or tubes in the collector. Either these pipes, coiled back and forth, or linked in parallel arrays, are themselves formed into the collecting surface; or they may lie on top of, or beneath a sheet metal surface. Another possibility is for channels to be formed within the thickness of some sheet material. Or channels may be constructed quite simply by welding a corrugated metal sheet

Types of flat–plate
collector suitable for
water heating, from
F. Daniels, Direct Use
of the Sun's Energy,
(copyright (c) 1964 by
Yale University), p.113.

Water heater with
corrugated iron
soldered to sheet
metal plate

Tube–in–sheet water
heater formed with
hydraulic pressure

Corrugated iron
soldered to metal
sheet enclosing tight-
fitting plastic tube

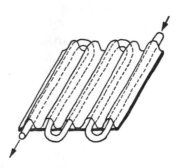

Solar water heater
with storage tank

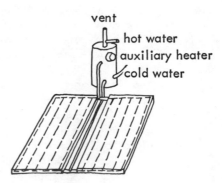

vent
hot water
auxiliary heater
cold water

to a second, flat sheet. The water may be passed through plastic piping, which is threaded along a series of metal tubes; in which case the fit must be a tight one, in order to ensure effective heat conduction. Some experimenters have simply used a single sloping black sheet of corrugated metal, with the water trickled over its surface from a perforated pipe at the top edge, and collected by a gutter at the bottom edge.

Air as a heat transfer medium

In those collectors where the chosen heat transfer medium is air, the problem is to bring the air into contact with the greatest possible area of absorbing surface, while still allowing relatively unimpeded air flow through the collector. G.O.G. Löf has devised a design consisting of a series of small overlapping glass plates, very much on the principle of roof tiles. One third of each plate is blackened, and the plates are staggered such that each black area is beneath two clear sheets. The whole array is contained within a box under a single glass cover sheet; and air is forced through the box and over and between the lapped plates. The design is illustrated on p. Other workers have used sheets of black gauze or fabric mesh through which air is forced; or else multiple layers of black-painted expanded metal mesh.

Insulation of back surface of collector

It is important that the back surface of the collector be well insulated to reduce conduction losses from this under side; and that the junction of the glass cover with the collector frame be well sealed so as to create an airtight joint and thus cut convection losses. The frame itself is usually of wood, plastic or thin metal and is again designed to minimise conduction losses.

Selective black surfaces.

With an ordinary matt black paint coating it is possible for over 95% of radiation reaching the collector surface to be absorbed, and only fractional amounts reflected. With special chemical treatment it is possible to increase the ratio of radiation absorbed to radiation re-emitted (the so-called 'a/e ratio'); and surfaces so treated are referred to as 'selective radiation surfaces'. Interest and research in selective surfaces is mainly directed towards their application in solar power schemes, where high temperatures and so high efficiency collecting surfaces are required. But a cheap form of selective coating would have great value in increasing the performance of flat-plate collectors for building applications, as for instance may be required in solar cooling systems.

Work of B. Seraphin at University of Arizona

Most selective surfaces which have been produced to date, make use of interference effects occurring in microscopically thin layers of alternating metal and black metallic oxide films. An alternative approach presently being pursued by B. Seraphin at the University of Arizona, is to use silicon as the absorbing material, covered with very thin non-reflective layers of material to dull its surface. This increases its absorptivity. The heat which builds up is conducted to a steel substrate, and this steel sheet is coated with a thin layer of highly reflective metal such as gold or aluminum, which substantially cuts down the re-radiation from the plate in the infrared.

The development of special treatments for materials to give particular optical properties in terms of absorption and emission has acquired some importance in the construction industry in connection with special glasses for curtain-walled buildings (perhaps an unnecessary solution to an unnecessary problem?). Here the aim is the opposite, of decreasing rather than increasing solar heat gain. Daniels mentions the possibilities of developing 'selective white' paints which besides reflecting short wave radiation would also maintain a high level of emission in the infrared, and could be used on buildings in sunny climates to help keep them cool.

Materials for absorbing surfaces

The metal used in conventional untreated flat-plate absorption surfaces is either iron or aluminum. Copper has been employed in the past, but its scarcity and price now put it out of the question. It is possible that asphalt or tar might be used; and H.E. Thomason has designed one house in which the collector surface is formed from black asphalt shingles. These are not covered with any glass sheet though; and clearly, if they were covered, problems with melting would be experienced even at fairly low temperatures. Daniels has suggested that cheap simple collectors might be made from transparent plastic containers filled with charcoal. One design of commercially manufactured collector intended for swimming pool heating is made from black ABS plastic with an ultraviolet inhibitor; but here again the operating temperature is low, and under glass covers and at higher temperatures the same material would soon begin to deform and melt.

Efficiency of flat-plate collectors

Various figures for the net efficiency of flat-plate collectors are quoted, and a value of 40% to 45% - for the ratio of usable heat energy collected to radiation energy falling on the collector - seems average. About 55% of radiation may be collected on clear days, and 35% on partly cloudy days. The low efficiency results from reflection off, and absorption by the cover glass; as well as re-radiation and conduction losses from the absorber surface. Efficiency is increased when the difference in temperature between the collector and the heat storage reservoir is greater; and is lowered when the difference in temperature between the collector and the outside air is greater. Efficiency increases as the speed of circulation of the heat transfer medium through the collector increases, up to certain optimal flow rates; and in ideal circumstances the transfer medium should pass evenly at a constant rate over the whole absorbing surface.

Collector costs

As for collector costs the figures usually mentioned lie between $2.00 and $4.00 per ft^2; but the bottom end of this range seems to be unjustifiably optimistic for one-off, tailor-made installations, and would at best cover the cost of materials only, without account taken of labour, overheads and profits. According to the fullest and most rigorous analysis of the economics of solar heating, by Löf and Tybout ('Cost of House Heating with Solar Energy', Solar Energy Vol.14, 1973 pp.258-78), it is reasonable to assume that the large size of collectors required for house heating could be mass-produced and marketed for around $4.00/ft^2, and that in time the costs might, in volume production, be brought down towards the $2.00 mark. Löf and Tybout quote figures for commercially produced solar water heaters currently on the market of from $5.95 to $7.90 per ft^2 of collector for sample Israeli designs, and $6.40 to $8.90 for U.S. manufactured units. These are costs for the whole heater including tank and plumbing, divided by the collector area, however; and it would be fair to expect that with the larger area collectors needed for space heating, the incremental cost per additional square foot would go down considerably. This is because of the lower 'surface to edge' ratio by comparison with the smaller water heater collectors.

Solar water heaters

One of the simplest and so far the only commercially succesful application of solar energy in buildings is the solar water heater. Daniels estimates that in 1964 there were about half a million solar water heaters in use throughout the world, and today this figure must be at least five or six times greater. There was a flourishing solar heater business in the United States during the '30s and continuing on into the '50s until cheap natural gas forced it out of the market; both in California, and in Florida where several firms operated including G. & L. Roofing Co., the Solar Water Heater Co. and the Bolinger Company. By 1951 there were about 50,000 solar water heaters in use in the city of Miami alone. A very full review of the history of the subject was published by B.V. Petukhov (Solar Water Heating Installations, U.S.S.R. Academy of Sciences, Moscow) in 1953. Another account, of then current work, was made by T. Hisada and I. Oshida in 1961 ('Use of Solar Energy for Water Heating' (UN: Rome) E35 Gr-S13).

The heater comprises in most cases a flat-plate collector panel or panels, a well-insulated storage tank, and the associated simple plumbing and controls. It is generally agreed that a temperature of about 135°F is required for domestic hot water uses - for bathing and for washing clothes and dishes. Standards of hot water consumption vary widely from country to country, and between households; and no doubt there is much scope for conservation by appropriate design of appliances and by changes in people's habits of hot water use. Israeli figures suggest a daily consumption for a 4-person family of 120 litres (32 gals). An average U.S. figure might be 20 gals per day per person; and so on this basis a family of four might be supplied from a tank of something over 80 gals capacity. In sunny climates a rough guide to the required area of collector would be 0·75 ft^2 per gal of hot water. A heater for a four-person 80-gal family would therefore need a collector of about 60 ft^2 in area.

Standards of hot
water consumption

For water heating purposes, where the demand continues year-round, then the optimal tilt of the collector is equal to the latitude plus 10°. It is possible to effect the circulation of the water from the tank to the solar collector, and through the collector itself, by means of natural thermal action, without the use of pumps. The tank must be placed above the collector, and cold water from the bottom of the tank is piped to the bottom of the collector. As it is warmed, this water rises, because of its lower density, through the collector and

Circulation of water
through collector

back to the tank again through a return pipe. The bottom of the tank should be at least two feet above the top of the collector, to prevent a reverse cycle taking place at night, when water in the collector may be cooler than water in the storage tank. If the arrangement of tank above collector is inconvenient architecturally, then a pump can be used to circulate the water.

Freezing of water in collector

One problem which can occur in winter, is freezing of water lying in the metal pipes of the collector, at night. This can happen even when air temperatures do not fall below freezing, because of the effects of radiation from the collector surface to the clear night sky. One answer, though this complicates the heater design, is to use a special closed heat transfer loop from collector to storage tank, in which a water/ethylene glycol (antifreeze) mixture is circulated; and to transfer the solar heat to the domestic water reservoir via a series of immersed coils. With most simple designs of solar water heater it is neither practicable nor economic to try to meet the whole demand for hot water right through the winter with solar heat. It is usual to incorporate some means of auxiliary heating back-up, which can be switched to take over automatically, using a thermo-stat, when the water temperature falls below say 135°F. This might be an electric immersion heater, of perhaps 2kW capacity for an average domestic installation; or else a heater fired by oil or natural gas could be employed.

Need for auxiliary heat supply

Solar water heating in Japan

The country in which the solar water heater has gained widest acceptance is Japan. Daniels reports that in 1964, heaters made from plastic were selling at a rate of 60,000 a year; and a more recent Japanese account calculates that there were, in 1970, 2·6 million solar water heaters installed in that country, serving 26 to 27% of all baths. One of the most rudimentary types in use in Japan consists just of a shallow horizontal wooden box, lined with black polyvinyl plastic, and furnished with a hinged glass window cover on the top. Designs along these lines were first introduced some 25 years ago. Another very simple type, probably the simplest

Typical design of solar water heater

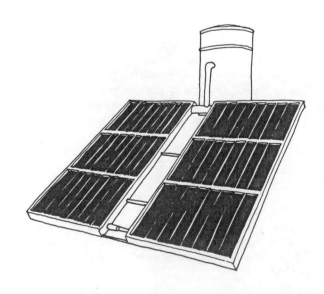

Pillow type of water heater	of all, is a black polyvinyl plastic water-filled pillow, set out in the sun and allowed to heat up. These pillow type heaters were being sold in Japan for a price in 1964 of $10.00, and are good for two years' use. In winter the pillow may be placed under a rigid transparent plastic cover to achieve a higher water temperature. The drawback to these very simple heaters is their low efficiency, due to their horizontal position, their poor insulation and their high resulting heat losses. Furthermore, they are not capable of being connected directly to the mains, because of the hydraulic pressure of that supply, and must be filled and emptied as needed. For greater efficiency and convenience the tilted type of 'closed' design with separate storage tank is preferable, although more expensive.
Costs of solar water heaters	As for costs, some figures quoted by manufacturers for particular designs are given below; and average costs per ft^2 of collector as computed by Löf and Tybout have been mentioned above. The capital cost of the installation would in general be higher than that for electric resistance, gas or oil heaters; since, although the cost of water tank and plumbing is comparable, the solar collector represents a sizable extra expense. It appears that in many parts of the world, and particularly latitudes below 35°, the fuel costs saved by solar water heating are sufficient to balance these additional collector costs, in 18 months to three years of operation. In Japan designs are sold with capacities of 180 to 210 litres for prices around $80 to $100.

Manufacturers of solar water heaters

The following is a list of some manufacturers of solar water heaters, with details of designs and costs where known:

Radiasol Corporation	Casablanca and Paris (selling heaters in North Africa and France)

22 ft^2 collector with 53 gal. water tank; delivers daily average of 40 gals. hot water during nine months of the year at 104°-122°F. This unit was priced in 1961 at the equivalent of about $340. Also 40 gal. model yielding daily average supply of 29 gals. Units may be connected together in parallel to give larger installations with daily capacity of up to 1,600 gals. for hospitals, schools, industrial buildings. |

Miromit	Miromit Ashkelon Metal Products Ltd, 44 Montefiore Street, Tel-Aviv, Israel

This company has sold tens of thousands of heaters, to various designs, since 1955. 30-35 gal. tank with two collectors and stands costs $420 including freight to U.S. (1973 price). Collectors use Miromit Selective |

Black coating. Water circulation by thermosiphon action. Combination solar/electric designs available, and the use of banks of collectors in parallel is possible for larger buildings.

Silves Ltd   7 West 14th St., New York, N.Y.10011

Marketing the 'Amcor' combination solar/electric unit. Galvanised sheet metal collector treated by 'Pyrene' process, double panel collector 4" x 31½" x 75", polyurethane insulated 35 gal. tank.

Low-Impact Technology   73 Molesworth St., Wadebridge, Cornwall, England

Agents for the 'Suntrap' solar water heater Mark IIB. This has a 6'7" x 4'3" x 3" collector formed from copper tubes, painted with 'Solarblak' formula paint. The frame is wooden, and insulated with glass wool. Two collector panels will supply 200 litres of water per day at temperatures of 105°F and above during the months of April to September in Britain and for more of the year further south.

Plans for home-made solar water heaters are available from:

VITA   Volunteers for International Technical Assistance, 3706 Rhode Island Ave., Mt. Rainier, Maryland 20822

Village Technology Plan No.5513.2, 'Glass Plate Solar Water Heater'. The original of this unit was built in Afghanistan in 1961. It consists of a galvanised iron panel made from two 3' x 6' sheets joined at the edges to form a 'pillow'. It is set on a sloping support of mud bricks. Circulation of water to and from a raised 18 gal. tank is by thermosiphon action. The water is heated to 140°F in a full sunny day. Cost (in 1961): $15.00

Brace Research Institute   McGill University, Ste Anne de Bellevue 800, Quebec, Canada

How to Build a Solar Water Heater, Do-it-Yourself Leaflet No.L-4, Feb.1973. Collector made from one corrugated and one flat galvanised steel sheet, with glass cover and fibrous insulation. Water tank is standard 45 gal. oil drum. The unit produces 30 to 40 gals. of hot water per day, at temperatures between 130° and 140°F, in tropical countries. Cost, at 1965 prices: materials $45.00, labour $40.00. The leaflet gives lists of required parts and detailed step-by-step instructions for assembly.

A simple home-built design of heater is described by Daniels in Direct Use of the Sun's Energy pp.116-119.

Solar swimming pool heaters

FAFCO

A design of solar heater for swimming pools is manufactured by FAFCO, 2860 Spring St., Redwood City, California 94063. This is made from thin black ABS extruded plastic sheet panels with a cross-sectional structure rather similar to corrugated cardboard. Water is passed through the channels via perforated pipes welded to the head and the foot of each sheet. The panels come in two sizes, 10' x 4'4" or 8' x 4'4", and are clamped together in parallel and set out on the house roof, or on a flat or sloping surface by the pool. Water is circulated using the normal pool pump, and the flow to the collector is controlled by an automatic sunlight sensing device. A water temperature of 80°F can be maintained throughout the summer season and into the spring and fall. Costs are $61.00 and $76.00 respectively for the two sizes of panel, and $96.50 for the controls. A typical complete installation for a 450 ft^2 pool in California, with 245 ft^2 of collector panels, cost $673, installed by the owner.

Fun and Frolic

A second commercial design of solar pool heater, the Solarator, is manufactured by Fun and Frolic, Madison Heights, Michigan 48071. The 40" x 75" collector is made from two sheets of black PVC, heat welded to create internal passages through which the water flows. The cost is $18.75

Solar Heat Ltd

One British design is manufactured by Solar Heat Ltd., 99 Middleton Hall Road, Kings Norton, Birmingham 30, England. This is a more conventional flat-plate collector design of 2·7 m^2 area, costing £58.50 without glazing, plumbing, controls or installation.

Solar space heating

The first truly solar heated building was erected at the Massachusetts Institute of Technology in 1939, as part of the long-running program of solar energy research established there by the Boston businessman Godfrey L. Cabot. Since that time something between forty-five and fifty solar heated buildings of various kinds have been constructed in America; and eight or so in other parts of the world.

Virtually all buildings receive some heat from the sun and trap this in their structure. This universal 'solar heat gain' effect can be desirable or not in different circumstances, and can be ingeniously exploited in design in various ways as described in the last chapter. The criteria which we shall use here (and which are used generally) to distinguish solar heated buildings described as such - though it is perhaps only a distinction of degree - are that they should employ some special purpose collectors of solar heat, and should employ some special purpose storage reservoirs, other than the mass of their structure, for storing that heat and controlling its transfer to the occupied spaces or rooms.

There is set out in the second half of this present chapter an extensive list of past and present solar heated buildings, with detailed data and some remarks on the particular features of each design. The format of the presentation and much of the data has been adapted from a table prepared by H. G. Lorsch and published in a paper Solar Heating Systems Analysis, Report No. NSF/RANN/SE/GI 27976/TR72/19, National Center for Energy Management and Power, University of Pennsylvania (pp.1-2 to 1-5, table 1). That list covered twenty-one solar heated buildings as defined here. The description has been amplified in most cases, and comparable data for a further twelve buildings has been added, as well as a number of illustrations. Nine of these buildings were laboratories or experimental structures intended to simulate houses, one is an office building and one a school classroom block. The remainder are houses occupied and used as such. A map showing the location of solar buildings in the U.S. appears at the beginning of the list, on pp.118-9. (See p.117 for note on solar buildings erected in 1974.)

The purpose in this introductory preamble will therefore be to concentrate on general and theoretical issues in solar space heating; and the reader is referred forward to the list of buildings for the analysis of specific designs. The data presented in standard format for each building covers some or all of the following: date and place of construction, designer, use of building, and floor area; details of the solar collector; details of the thermal energy storage system; details of the heat transfer system from collector to storage and from storage to space ('loops'); the latitude of the site and the heating degree days at that location; details of performance and costs; any other remarks; and bibliographical references to published descriptions and other documents relating to the building.

Heat storage

Storing summer heat for use in winter

Proposal of E. Schönholzer

The subject of flat-plate collectors has been treated at length already; and almost all that has been said applies equally to collectors for space heating applications. In solar heating installations, as well as collection, the question of heat storage becomes crucial. The first ever solar building, MIT Solar House No.1, was designed to trap solar heat in the summer and to store it for winter use - the only building so far to attempt this. The building used a basement water tank as the heat storage reservoir; and the capacity of this tank, 17,400 gals., was quite colossal in relation to the very small volume heated - two rooms, with total floor area of 500 ft^2. The idea has been more recently raised again by E. Schönholzer, who in 1969 proposed a scheme for the long-term storage of summer solar heat in very large volume, heavily insulated underground water tanks, holding many thousands or even millions of gallons of water, and serving groups of perhaps a hundred dwellings.

It has been recognised however since the MIT experiment that, at least for single buildings, to try to carry heat from one season to the other involves a storage capacity which is quite uneconomic; and storage over ten days is about the maximum attempted in subsequent buildings. According to Löf and Tybout's study, the heat storage capacity for minimum solar heating cost, for nearly all U.S. locations where solar heating is feasible, is 10 to 15 lbs of water (or its thermal equivalent in other materials) per ft^2 of solar collector. This is sufficient for one or two days winter heating requirement in cloudy weather. (One cubic foot of water weighs $62\frac{1}{2}$ lbs, and contains about $7\frac{1}{2}$ gals.)

Required heat storage capacity

100% solar heated buildings

Only four buildings have attempted and succeeded in drawing 100% of their space heating requirement from the sun with no auxiliary back-up source of heat. The first was the Telkes-Raymond-Peabody House built in Dover, Massachusetts in 1944, which had heat storage to cover up to one week of cloud - though for special reasons this storage capacity was effectively reduced after the first year's operation, and the 100% solar heated performance was maintained only for that one year. The second was a bungalow belonging to the U.S. Forest Service in Amado, Arizona and modified for solar heating by R.W. Bliss Jr. in 1955. Here the climate is very favourable, the building was small (672 ft^2), and an extremely large heat storage reservoir, in the form of a tank filled with gravel, was installed, sufficient for ten days' storage, and much bigger than could be justified on economic grounds. A solar heated laboratory in Princeton N.J., built in 1959, had no auxiliary source of heat; but the heating demand was in all probability reduced by the building's only being occupied during working hours. Most recently Robert Reines has built a hemispherical steel dome house in Tijeras N.M. which is 100% solar heated. Although the cost is low, it is fair to say that the performance has been achieved at the expense of some reduction in standards - of floor area, window size and on occasion of internal air temperature - as well as by accepting the rather restrictive geometry of the dome form.

Solar collector area for given heating demand

It is the combined consideration of these three main factors, the climate, the size of the building, and what proportion of the resulting heating demand is to be supplied by the solar system, which largely determine the required area of solar collector and the required thermal capacity of the heat storage reservoir. In the already cited economic study, Löf and Tybout calculate the optimal collector size for minimal solar heating cost for a (large, upper middle income) house with a heating demand of 25,000 Btu/degree day, in eight climatically characteristic locations in different parts of the United States. This assumes the use of solar heat for both water and space heating; but assumes that auxiliary back-up heating is also provided for both uses, and that the balance of solar to auxiliary heating is calculated for minimum costs over a twenty year life. The resulting optimal collector areas were found to vary from 208 ft^2 in Charleston South Carolina (carrying 55% of the annual heating load) to 521 ft^2 for Omaha, Nebraska (carrying 47% of the load). In Santa Maria, California, a 261 ft^2 collector was found to be able to supply 75%

of the annual heating requirement. The size of collector required increases substantially as greater fractions of the load are carried by solar heating.

Löf 'heating design index'

In his comparative study of eight existing solar buildings made for the Rome U.N. Conference of 1961, Löf develops a 'heating design index' with which to evaluate the various designs, and which is defined as the ratio in each case of the area of solar collector in ft^2 to the heating demand in Btu/degree day. The bigger this ratio, the more generously is the system designed, broadly speaking, for the size of building and for the location and climate. The computed values for the different buildings range between 0·008 and 0·12, with several values clustering around the 0·05 to 0·08 level in between. The highest value of 0·12 relates to a house built in Washington DC by H.E. Thomason, and the lowest to a laboratory building in Nagoya, Japan (which was intended only for daytime use however).

Löf 'design adequacy index'

The product of this index multiplied by the 'weather factor' defined by Löf and described earlier, serves to give an overall indication of design adequacy of the solar system for climate and heating demand in each case. The highest value for this product, of the buildings studied, was 17, achieved by a laboratory building at the University of Arizona designed by Bliss. The lowest value, 0·76, is for a house built by Löf himself in Denver, Colorado. These are extremes, and values in the middle range vary around 1·6 to 5·6. One would expect, generally speaking, that the higher this number, the larger should be the fraction of the heating load provided by solar heat. In the case of the University of Arizona laboratory, this fraction worked out in practical operation as 86%; for the Löf house at Denver it was 26%. Two buildings in the middle range with equal values for the overall 'design adequacy index' of 1·6, a house/laboratory in Capri, and the fourth solar house in the series built at MIT, both drew around 50% of their heat from the sun.

Materials for heat storage

Water

The two other practical possibilities for heat storage materials besides water, are first rock in the form of gravel or small stones, and second some kind of material which undergoes reversible physical or chemical change when its temperature is raised by the solar heat, and when the temperature falls again as heat is withdrawn. Water is cheap, although the large size of tank needed to hold the quantities involved may be expensive. With heat storage in a water tank and water used as the heat transfer medium from the collector, and to the spaces, then the need for heat exchangers from one medium to another is avoided. In a large tank there may be set up stirring currents resulting from the difference in temperature between water at different levels, and this can increase the rate of heat loss. The losses can be controlled though by dividing the tank into a series of compartments.

Rocks

At least four buildings have used rock beds as the sole heat storage medium: two houses designed by G.O.G. Löf in Colorado, the U.S. Forest Service Desert Grassland Station at Amado, Arizona, and the Earl Palmberg residence in Topeka, Kansas. The average size of rock pieces used varied from 2" to 4". According to Daniels, if the pieces are roughly spherical and of a uniform size, then whatever this size might be, the geometry of their packing together results in about one third of the volume being taken up by air spaces. The rock bed is used in conjunction with an air heat transfer system. The contact between the air and the very large surface area of stone in the bed results in a most effective transfer of heat – although it requires a blower to drive the air through the stones and this in itself consumes some energy. The heat capacity of the stone is much less than that of water, but its density is greater. The result is that about one third as much heat can be stored in a given volume of rock, as can be stored in the same volume of water (20 Btu per °F in a ft^3 of solid rock, 62·5 Btu per °F in a ft^3 of water). (The figure for rock beds with air spaces is correspondingly lower.)

Position of heat storage reservoir

Although some designers have placed the heat storage reservoir outside the building, this is not ideal from the point of view of heat loss. The reservoir must always be well-insulated, but nevertheless some heat will still escape; and if the reservoir is placed inside or beneath the building, say in the basement, then this escaping heat passes to the interior spaces. A further advantage of placing the storage tank in the basement is that the conductivity through the surrounding earth is low, and even if heat does escape to raise the temperature of this earth, it may be retrieved again in part when the temperature of the tank drops. In effect the earth acts as additional storage capacity. (In a water heat storage system, placing the tank below the collector means that the water can be drained out of the collector by gravity at the approach of freezing weather, and on winter nights.) In Löf's Denver house, the rock storage is placed in two cylindrical bins which extend right through the house from basement to roof. H.E. Thomason uses a combination of water storage with gravel surrounding the tank. The heat transfer is by circulation of water. Here the gravel acts partly as additional storage, partly as insulation to the water tank.

Latent heat storage

The significance of latent heat storage, by contrast with the storage of sensible heat as in water or rocks, is in reducing the volume required for given thermal capacity. When a substance melts, it needs heat to do so, which it must withdraw from its surroundings. Supposing a material melts at 90°F. The heat required to raise its temperature from 89° to 91°F, and to effect the transition from solid to liquid phase, is very much greater than that needed to raise it say from 87° to 89°F or from 91° to 93°F. When the temperature of the liquid material drops again, back below 90°F in this case, as heat is withdrawn, so it re-releases this 'latent heat of fusion', and solidifies once more. It follows that by storing this latent heat, rather than sensible heat only, a reservoir of very much smaller volume is required; and this reservoir may also operate at lower temperatures and need less insulation.

Besides physical changes of state, like melting, latent heat may also be stored by certain chemical reactions. For instance one of the most

Glauber's salt:
$Na_2SO_4.10H_2O$

widely used chemicals for latent heat storage has been Glauber's salt or sodium sulfate decahydrate, whose chemical formula is $Na_2SO_4.10H_2O$. It is a relatively inexpensive substance, and much smaller quantities are required in any case than with rocks or water. When Glauber's salt is raised above 90°F it dissociates into the anhydrous form Na_2SO_4, and water; and the result is a concentrated solution of the salt in water. The reaction is:

$$Na_2SO_4.10H_2O \rightleftharpoons Na_2SO_4 + 10H_2O$$

Below:
Table showing heat storage capacity of various materials, from F. Daniels, Direct Use of the Sun's Energy (copyright (c) 1964 by Yale University), p.141 Reproduced by kind permission of Yale University Press.

Much heat is absorbed as the reaction progresses in the one direction, and much heat is given off again in the other. For particular applications what is needed is a chemical reaction or a physical change which takes place over the range of temperature at which heat is being collected and stored; and for space heating the reaction of Glauber's salt at 90°F is in this respect very appropriate. The table below, reproduced from Daniels (p.141) gives comparative figures for the heat capacity of water tanks, rock beds·and $Na_2SO_4.10H_2O$ - where the water and rocks are both assumed to be raised through 20 degrees C (or 36 degrees F) in operation at around room temperature.

temperature	$cal\ g^{-1}$ $degree^{-1}$	$Kcal$ $litre^{-1}$	Btu lb^{-1}	Btu ft^{-3}
Water	20°C (36°F)			
	range	1	20	36	2,240
Pebble bed (rocks with $\frac{1}{3}$ voids)	20°C (36°F)			
	range		8.0		864
$Na_2SO_4.10H_2O$	32·3°C (90°F)		84.5	104	9,568

Work of Telkes on latent heat storage

Dover house

The scientist who has given the deepest study to the problems of storing latent heat for solar energy applications is Dr Maria Telkes. It was she who designed the solar heating system for the first house to use latent heat storage, built in Dover, Massachusetts in 1944. $Na_2SO_4.10H_2O$ was the material chosen there, and the salt was contained in 5 gal. drums in three closets in the space of the house. Unfortunately, some difficult problems were encountered with this system. After a number of cycles there was a tendency for the reverse reaction not to occur with the fall in temperature. Instead of crystallisation of the salt, a 'supersaturated solution' was formed. There was a further tendency that, where crystals of the salt were formed, these settled to the bottom of the containers; and this stratification also interfered with the reversibility of the cycle. As a consequence the heat storage performance of the salt reservoir deteriorated after the first year of the life of the house.

Buildings using latent heat storage

Three more buildings have used latent heat storage since the Dover house: a laboratory built at Princeton by the Curtiss Wright Corporation, and a solar house at New Mexico State College, both of which also used $Na_2SO_4.10H_2O$; and most recently the University of Delaware's 'Solar One' house. Dr Telkes is in charge of the design of the heat storage system for the Delaware house. Three types of salt are used, one in a base heat reservoir and melting at 75°F; and two salts in a secondary reservoir, in alternating containers, melting at 50°F and 120°F respectively. Special stacked trays containing the salts have been designed, so that the surface area of container brought in contact with the air which transfers the heat can be maximised.

Research into latent heat storage at the University of Pennsylvania

A program of experiments has been carried on recently at the National Center for Energy Management and Power at the University of Pennsylvania, into methods and materials for latent heat storage. A series of salts have been examined, as well as several paraffin waxes which seem to have promise. Efforts have been made to prevent the stratification which occurs with $Na_2SO_4.10H_2O$ (and other materials), by suspending the salt in an inert gel or thickening medium such as clay, plaster of Paris, starch or rubber foam - but without great success so far. This University of Pennsylvania group has been interested in latent heat storage for other purposes besides use in solar heating systems; for example, in air conditioning applications, where 'cool' rather than heat is stored, and a reaction occurring at appropriately lower temperatures (perhaps around 55°F) is required. Using heat storage reservoirs, an air conditioning plant may be run at night or throughout the twenty-four hours instead of just during the daytime peak. The power loads are thus evened out, a much reduced (perhaps 40% smaller) tonnage of refrigeration equipment can be used, and there is an added bonus achieved by storing 'coolness' during the night-time when outside air temperatures are lower.

Storage of 'cool' for air conditioning purposes

Latent heat 'storage radiators'

Two experiments were tried during the early '60s, both in Pennsylvania, with latent heat storage in conjunction with off-peak electrical resistance heating, along the lines of the (sensible heat) 'storage radiators' in use in Europe. The first experiment, the Cryotherm system installed in a demonstration house in Allentown, Pa. in 1962-3, used an inorganic salt melting at 154°F, and a water heat transfer system. The second experiment, made by the Edison Electric Institute, in Philadelphia, involved sodium hydroxide units with a forced air heat transfer system to the rooms, installed in ten houses of employees of the Philadelphia Electric Co. Although the performance was satisfactory, the use of the toxic and potentially dangerous caustic soda was a drawback, and the units were removed after two years.

Combination of solar collector with heat storage

Hay 'roof ponds'

In several solar houses there has been no separation made between solar collector and heat storage reservoir, and instead the storage medium has been heated directly by exposure to the sun. This is the method adopted by the designer Harold Hay, whose system involves the use of 'ponds' of water lying on the roofs of buildings. The first structure of this kind, built in Phoenix in 1967-8 by Hay and John Yellott, was a small experimental test building, with a series of plastic bags containing water, on the roof. The bags were retained within troughs lined with black plastic sheet, formed between the roof beams. Over the top of the water bags was a large movable insulated panel sliding horizontally on metal trackways.

The principle of operation of Hay's system is that, on sunny winter days, the insulation is moved back to expose the collector pond, which becomes heated. At night and on cloudy days the insulation is replaced to cover the pond, which now acts as heat storage reservoir. Heat is conducted and radiated downwards through the steel decking of the roof of the building, into the rooms below. In the Phoenix structure Hay and Yellott also achieved a radiative cooling effect during summer nights by exposing the water bags to the clear night sky. If the surface of the bags was to be flooded with a thin layer of water exposed to the open air in this arrangement, then additional cooling might be produced through evaporation.

In 1973 Hay, with a group from the California Polytechnic Institute at San Luis Obispo, completed a house working on the same prin- ciple as the Phoenix building, with a 1 ft deep water pond over the whole roof of the one-story structure, and movable insulation panels stacking, when drawn back, over the adjacent garage and patio area. The method is simple and effective for low latitudes – according to Hay, up to 35° – and could possibly find wide accept- ance in underdeveloped countries. The horizontal roof collector is well integrated with the architectural form of the house and presents no obstruction for daylighting or views. It has the dis- advantage of retaining fallen leaves and, in less clement climates, snow, however; and the use of roof ponds is impractical where freezing temperatures may be expected.

Since heat storage is combined with collector, and heat is transferred from storage to space directly by conduction and radiation, Hay's house has no need of mechanical systems of pumps and blowers – although motors and some automatic control devices are needed for moving the insulation panels back and forth. One problem with the heat storage reservoir being so directly adjacent to the rooms of the building, is that the flow of heat from one to the other is controlled only with difficulty. On an unexpectedly fine day in the heating season, the rooms might well become overheated; though this effect could be countered of course by opening windows etc.

Baer collector/ storage wall

Essentially the same approach as Hay's has been adopted by the designer Steve Baer, but with vertical collector/storage walls as opposed to roof ponds. Baer's own house in Albuquerque has a series of glazed south-facing areas of wall behind which are piled a number of metal drums filled with water. The exposed ends of the drums are painted black, so that their surface, behind the glass, acts like a conventional flat-plate collector, and the heat so trapped is transferred directly to the water in the drums. During winter nights, and in summer, the collector walls are covered with large insulating doors, faced with aluminum, and hinged at their bottom edges. When the doors are let down on winter days, their inside faces act as reflectors and thus increase the radiation falling on the collecting surface.

Trombe/Michel
solar wall

The vertical collector wall has more application in the higher latitudes, because of its angle in relation to the low winter sun, as
explained. The French solar scientist Félix Trombe, together with
the architect Jacques Michel, has developed a design of combined
collector and heat storage wall unit which they have tried out in
houses in the Pyrenees and in central France. Again the principle
is very close to Baer's approach, but instead of water as the heat
storage medium, Trombe and Michel use a thick concrete wall
painted black on its outside face. A sheet, or sheets of glass are
placed in front of the concrete, and air circulates in the space
between glass and wall. Air from the rooms of the building is allowed
to pass through openings at the foot of the wall, into this space
within the collector. It rises naturally through the collector as it
is heated, and passes back into the building again through a second
set of openings at the top. The effect is of a type of large storage
radiator acting as a flat-plate collector (with air as the heat transfer medium) on its outer exposed face. Since the air circulation
is by natural convection, there are no moving parts whatever. In
order to stop the air flow, in summer, the openings in the wall are
blocked with shutters.

Heat pumps as part
of solar heating
systems

Seven of the buildings in the list which follows this section made
use of heat pumps as part of their solar heating systems. The
purpose of the heat pump here is to allow usable solar heat to be
collected at lower temperatures than otherwise, and also to be able
to withdraw heat from a storage reservoir when its temperature is
too low for use in space heating direct. The heat pump boosts the
solar heating system's performance and extends the range of climatic
conditions over which it may be operated.

The principles of heat pumps have been covered briefly in the last
chapter, on pp.46-7. Their application to solar heating and cooling
systems for building has been discussed in papers by Sporn and
Ambrose ('The Heat Pump and Solar Energy' (Phoenix) pp.159-70)
and Morgen ('The Heat Pump' (Solar Energy Research) pp.69-70).

Experiments by
Sporn and Ambrose

In the experiments made by Sporn and Ambrose for the American
Electric Power Corporation of New York, in 1950, the refrigerant
used was Freon, circulated between solar collector panels and a
water tank heat storage reservoir. In the winter heating cycle, the
Freon was evaporated in the solar collector and condensed with a
5 hp electric-driven compressor to release its heat to the water
storage tank. In the reversed cooling cycle in summer, the refrigerant was vapourised by the house heat. The solar collector
surface, cooled by convection and radiation, was used to remove
the heat from the condensed vapour when it was compressed again.

Solar collector/
heat pump in New
Haven, W. Virginia

A heat pump installation in a house in New Haven, West Virginia,
in use from 1950 to 1955, transferred heat from air in the solar
collector to air in the rooms directly, without any thermal storage
reservoir. In several other buildings heat pumps have been
installed to operate between two water storage tanks held at different temperatures. One tank is heated from the solar collector,

and this is used as a heat source by the heat pump (on its 'cold' side), from which it transfers heat to the second tank and thus raises it to a higher temperature. Heat from the second tank is used to heat the building.

The problem with heat pump installations, especially in conjunction with solar collectors, is their high capital cost. And when driven by electricity, they do not represent so much of a net saving in energy, as they would say when powered directly by gas or oil burning engines. Dubin has demonstrated how the annual load profiles in large commercial buildings with a requirement both for space cooling and heating as well as water heating, may be less peaked and hence more advantageous for solar heat utilisation than are those for single dwellings. In such buildings too there is the opportunity for the efficient recovery of quantities of waste heat which can be dumped into heat storage tanks together with the solar heat; and the prospects for using heat pumps, in both cooling and heating modes, in this context are very promising.

Cooling by radiation to the night sky

Apart from cooling with heat pumps, which makes no use of solar energy, those solar heated buildings which have incorporated any kind of cooling have mostly achieved this by systems for radiation to the night sky from the solar collector surface on summer nights. These include the U.S. Forest Service building at Amado, Arizona, the University of Arizona Solar Energy Laboratory at Tucson, the Hay/Yellott test building in Phoenix, Hay's recent house in California, and the houses built in Washington DC by H.E. Thomason. Thomason has also employed a method of evaporative cooling whereby water is pumped to the ridge of the roof using the same pipes and pump as for the heating system; but instead of being run through the collector on the south-facing slope, it is trickled down open channels in the north-facing slope of the roof.

Refrigeration with solar energy

Absorption refrigeration

Only a few attempts have so far been made to power refrigeration equipment proper with solar energy. The main difficulty is to produce temperatures high enough for the purpose, with flat-plate collectors. Most of the absorption types of refrigeration unit now on the market need water under pressure at 270°F or steam with which to operate; but some large units may be run at lower capacity with water at only 210°F or lower, and other small units are capable of being modified to do the same. According to Daniels a lithium bromide/water system can be run with temperatures of 170°F at a minimum, and this can certainly be achieved with efficient flat-plate collectors. Although such systems are not capable of making ice or of reaching low temperatures, they do serve very well the purposes of air conditioning.

Experiments of Chung, Löf and Duffie

Chung, Löf and Duffie have reported experiments in cooling a number of rooms, 1,200 ft^2 in total area, with a 102 ft^2 solar collector and a commercially produced 3 ton lithium bromide/water absorption cooling unit, the Arkla DUC 5-2 ('Solar Space Cooling', Chem. Eng. Progr., Vol.55 No.4, April 1959 p.74). The

Solar refrigeration
experiments in
Brisbane, Australia

Below:
Residential heating and
cooling with solar
energy: schematic
diagram of one alter-
native. From NSF/
NASA Solar Energy
Panel, Solar Energy as
a National Energy
Resource, University of
Maryland 1972 p.14

collector supplied only a part of the heat used by the unit, the remainder being made up from a piped steam supply. The results of the experiments indicated that on a bright calm day a solar collector of 200 ft^2 would be able to power 1 ton of refrigeration. Similar experiments were made by Sheridan and others in Brisbane, Australia. Here again a 3 ton lithium bromide/water absorption air conditioner was used, supplied with heat in part by 64 ft^2 of solar collector and the balance made up to simulate a larger collector area, with water preheated by electricity. 'Cool' storage was provided both in a water tank and in a gravel bed. The University of Florida Solar Energy Laboratory has been the scene of other experiments in solar powered refrigeration under the direction of E.A. Farber.

Two diagrams are reproduced here which illustrate possibilities for combined solar heating and cooling systems in buildings. The first is from the report of the NSF/NASA Solar Energy Panel, and shows a solar collector with water used as the heat transfer medium to a

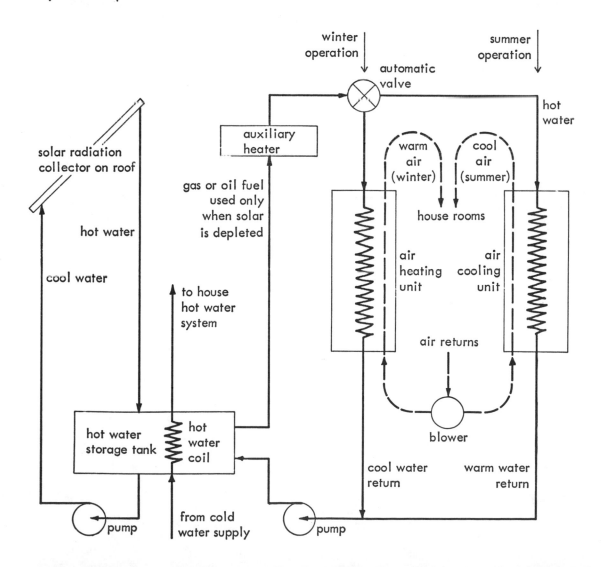

water tank heat storage reservoir.   The domestic water supply is heated via a heat exchange coil immersed in this tank.   The hot storage water is pumped either, in winter, to a unit where heat is exchanged with the air used to warm the building; or else, in summer, to an absorption air conditioning unit.   The second diagram shows a system devised by Arthur D. Little Inc., with an alternative arrangement for heat pump operation added by Dubin.   The layout is similar in many respects, with domestic water supply, heat storage tank and the generator of an absorption cooling machine all heated from the solar collector.

Photovoltaic conversion

Below:
Combined solar heating and cooling system, from a sketch by Arthur D. Little Inc.

All the discussion so far has been concerned with solar thermal applications in buildings – means for trapping and using the sun's heat.   The exploitation of photovoltaic effects, that is the production of electrical currents in certain materials or combinations of materials under the action of light, offers the further opportunity for using sunlight, for generating electricity in buildings.   Photovoltaic cells have already been widely used for this purpose on earth satellites and space vehicles, and it is the space program

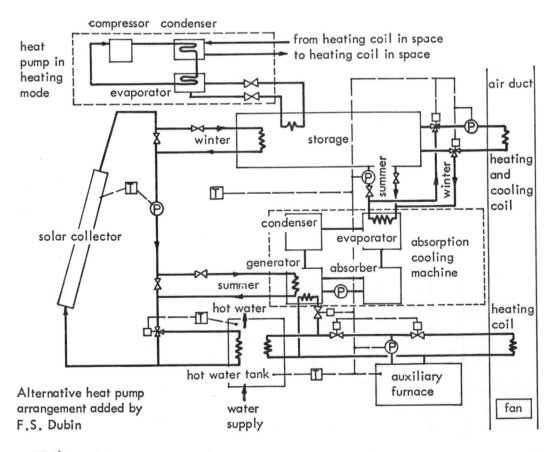

Alternative heat pump arrangement added by F.S. Dubin

🆃 thermostat
🅟 pump

which has given great impetus since the '50s to the development of solar cell technology. The two most efficient and best studied types are the silicon cell and the cadmium sulfide (CdS/Cu_2S) cell. The first and only building in which electricity is generated from the sun is the University of Delaware's Solar One house, in which the cadmium sulfide type of cell is used.

Efficiencies of solar cells

The theoretical limit of efficiency of conversion of solar radiation in a solar cell is 22% (since only the short-wave radiation is converted), and cells with efficiencies of up to 15% have already been produced. In the Delaware house, the director of the project Dr K.W. Böer anticipates a conversion efficiency for the cadmium sulfide cells of 7%. It is thought that this value might be pushed up to 10% in time. The particular attraction of solar cells in buildings is that they may be integrated into a combined thermal collector and electrical energy generator, so that the space heating, air conditioning and water heating may be achieved, and the electricity for lights, appliances and motors provided by one and the same unit. Buildings so equipped could be independent for much of the year from all centralised power and fuel supplies. Since the efficiency of thermal energy collection may be around 50%, the combined efficiency of conversion of solar energy can be as high as 60% overall.

Integrated solar electric and thermal installations

A diagram of the cross-section of the collector panel used in the Delaware house is shown below. The arrays of solar cells are sealed behind transparent sheets and lie beneath a plexiglas cover with an air space between. Since the cells present a black upper surface they act simultaneously to produce electric current and to absorb solar heat. The heat is removed from the back surface of the cells with air, driven through insulated ducts. The integration of thermal collector with photovoltaic array brings intrinsic savings in the cost of materials and components. The whole Solar One electric system is more fully described under the entry in the list of solar buildings which follows.

Cross-section through a solar electric/thermal flat-plate collector as proposed for the University of Delaware's Solar One house. From K.W. Böer, 'The Solar House and its Portent', Chemtech July 1973 p.396 fig.2

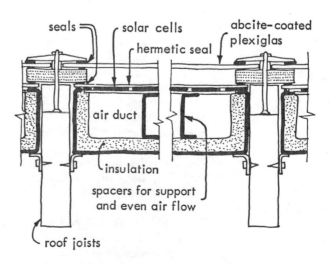

According to the NSF/NASA Solar Energy Panel report, 'about three times the present average household consumption of electric power can be collected from average-size family residences, even in the northeastern U.S.' If the problem of local electricity storage could be effectively and economically solved (using electrolysis of water with hydrogen-burning fuel cells, flywheels, or, as in Solar One, conventional electrical batteries) this surplus electricity might be used they suggest to power electric cars.

Costs of solar cells

So far the manufacture of solar cells has been on a very small 'cottage industry' scale – though to exacting standards of quality and by skilled craftsmen. The present cost is of the order of $70 per ft^2 for silicon cell arrays for terrestrial applications ($1,000 to $8,000 per ft^2 in spacecraft). For generating electricity economically on earth, it would be necessary to bring these costs down to $3.50 per ft^2 for silicon cells, 50c to $1.00 per ft^2 for cadmium sulfide. It will also be necessary to extend the working life of the cells to twenty years or more, where the present life is ten years for silicon cells, two only for cadmium sulfide.

Costs of solar heating of buildings

The subject of costs for solar thermal applications in buildings is a deep and complex one, and many variables enter in. Two systematic studies have been published of the cost of solar heating of houses in the United States, one by Buchberg and Roulet ('Simulation and Optimization of Solar Collection and Storage for House Heating', Solar Energy Vol.12, 1968 pp.31-50), and the other already referred to by Löf and Tybout who in 1973 produced a revised version of a study previously published in 1970 (Tybout and Löf, 'Solar House Heating', Natural Resources Journal Vol.10 No.2, April 1970 pp. 268-326).

The cost figures assumed by Löf and Tybout for solar collectors have been quoted previously. Capital costs for other parts of the solar heating system were derived on the basis of figures for existing solar buildings, and expressed as functions of the collector area, as follows:

Storage = $0.05 per pound of water stored
= $0.05K (collector area, ft^2), where K is a parameter
equal to pounds of water storage per square foot of collector
Controls = $150.00 regardless of system size
Pipes, fittings = $100.00 + $0.10(collector area, ft^2)
Motors, pumps = $50.00 + $0.20(collector area, ft^2)
Heat exchangers = $75.00 + $0.15(collector area, ft^2)

The costs of equipment for heat distribution to the spaces were not included, since these would be comparable whatever type of energy source were employed.

For their studies, Löf and Tybout took eight cities in the United States which are representative of the various climates encountered through the country: Miami, Albuquerque, Phoenix, Santa Maria,

Ca., Charleston, S.C., Seattle-Tacoma, Omaha and Boston. They studied two typical sizes of house, expressed in terms of heating demand per degree day: a 15,000 Btu/degree day figure, corresponding to an average middle income house, and a 25,000 Btu/degree day figure for an average upper middle income house. For each location, actual detailed weather records were obtained for a sample year including data on radiation, temperature, wind, solar altitude, cloud cover and humidity. Equations were developed for the theoretical performance of solar collectors and heat storage systems, assuming sensible heat storage in water or rocks. A series of design parameters were introduced including, besides the heating demand, the area, tilt and thermal capacity of the collector, the number of transparent cover sheets to the collector, the storage capacity and the insulation of the heat storage reservoir, and the demand for domestic hot water. Two of these parameters, the thermal capacity of the collector and the insulation of the storage reservoir, proved in the analysis not to have, over the range of values in common practice, any significant effects on system performance. A computer simulation of performance was used to relate these system design parameters to capital costs and running costs; and that design was identified which gave lowest annual heating costs calculated over a twenty year period at a discount rate of 6%.

The table reproduced below provides a summary of the results in terms of system costs. Comparison is made with the prevailing costs of alternative forms of heating, by electricity, oil or gas, in the eight different locations. No account is taken of the capital cost of furnace or electrical resistance heating equipment, since the design of the solar system is optimised always to take the fraction of the heating load which gives least cost. This fraction varies between 40% for Boston and 75% for Santa Maria, Ca. In all cases an auxiliary heating installation must be provided in addition to the solar heating system, with almost equal capacity to that needed if the whole year-round heating load were carried. The savings offered by solar heating are thus wholly in the area of fuel costs. Two cost figures are given, an upper and a lower, corresponding respectively to the cost of components available from manufacturers at the time of the study, and to estimates of lower component costs achievable in the special purpose manufacture of collectors, to a similar design.

In six instances the cost of solar heat is less than that of electrical heating, the two exceptions being Seattle and Miami. In Seattle electric power is unusually cheap; and in Miami there is only a small heating demand and so the capital cost of the installation weighs heavier in proportion. In only two cities, Santa Maria and Albuquerque, was the cost of solar heat found to be competitive with oil or gas-fired heating.

There are two considerations however which will make this picture rather different today and in the future. The first is the spectacular rise in oil and gas prices, which may be expected to continue at accelerating rates. The second concerns the assumptions made by Löf and Tybout for the sake of their analyses about the average

Costs of space heat (United States)
From G.O.G. Löf and R.A. Tybout, 'Cost of House Heating with
Solar Energy', <u>Solar Energy</u> Vol.14, 1973 p.274, table 2

	Least cost solar heat, ($/10⁶Btu, 1961)				Electric heat, electricity cost only, ($/10⁶Btu, 1967)			Conventional heat fuel cost only, ($/10⁶Btu, 1962)	
	15,000 Btu/DD house		25,000 Btu/DD house		20,000 kWh/yr	30,000 kWh/yr			
	Low	High	Low	High				Gas	Oil
Santa Maria	1·35	1·84	1·10	1·59	4·51*	4·36*	California	1·42	1·62
Albuquerque	1·70	2·31	1·60	2·32	4·89	4·62	New Mexico	0·89	2·07
Phoenix	2·55	3·55	2·05	3·09	4·56	4·25	Arizona	0·79	1·60
Omaha	2·65	3·16	2·45	2·98	3·30	3·24	Nebraska	1·05	1·32
Boston	2·70	3·15	2·50	3·02	5·49	5·25	Massachusetts	1·73	1·76
Charleston	3·15	4·16	2·55	3·56	4·50	4·22	S. Carolina	0·96	1·55
Seattle–Tacoma	2·85	4·05	2·60	3·82	2·26**	2·31**	Washington	1·83	2·00
Miami	5·85	6·48	4·05	4·64	5·16	4·90	Florida	2·81	1·73

*Electric power costs are for Santa Barbara. Electric power data
for Santa Maria were not available
**Electric power costs are for Seattle

Source: Solar heat costs are from optimal design systems by inter-
polation from graphs given earlier in the same paper. Electric
power heat costs are from U.S. Federal Power Commission, <u>All
Electric Homes</u> (1967), Table 1. Conventional heat fuel costs are
derived from prices per million Btu reported in P. Balestra, <u>The
Demand for Natural Gas in the United States</u> (North Holland Publishing Co., 1967), Tables 1.2 and 1.3. Fuel prices were converted
to fuel costs by dividing by the following national average heat
(combustion) efficiencies: gas, 75 per cent; oil, 75 per cent.
Heat efficiencies are from American Society of Heating, Refrigerating and Air Conditioning Engineers, <u>Guide and Data Book</u> 692–
694 (1963 edition).

---

heating demand in houses. The smaller of the two sizes of house
studied, with a requirement of 15,000 Btu per degree day, is taken
to represent a middle income house of about 1,000 ft^2 in area.
Means of reducing the heating requirements of buildings quite
drastically from present typical performance have been discussed at
length in the last chapter; and simply the application of the F.H.A.'s
new Minimum Property Standards relating to insulation would, in
the particular case of this size of house picked for the Löf and
Tybout study, cut the heating requirements to about 8,000 Btu per
degree day, that is to say almost by half. The significance of this
lies in the fact that the capital cost of a solar heating system is
rather sensitive to the size of heating demand; more so than are,
in domestic installations, the costs of conventional systems. And
since the high capital costs of solar heating installations may be

one of the chief deterrents to prospective purchasers, any reduction in these costs is psychologically and from the point of view of mortgage financing all to the good.

Figures given by the NSF/NASA Solar Energy Panel suggest a capital cost for a solar house heating system at present prices, of between $1,500 and $2,500 (including collector, heat storage and controls); and for a combined solar heating and cooling installation, between $3,000 and $4,000.

Integration of solar heating into pre-fabricated building systems for housing

It is possible that if a sizable solar heating industry were to develop, then complete package units might be produced, including for example designs which could be integrated with prefabricated building systems. The University of Pennsylvania group have made detailed studies of how a modular design of collector and heat storage unit might be incorporated into town houses and row houses in existing planned residential developments. One company in France is about to go into business this year with an industrialised steel building system for houses which will incorporate 'solar walls' of the Trombe-Michel type.

Urban 'sun rights'

There are many problems in the organization of the building industry and in the financing of buildings which have important consequences for the prospects of widespread introduction of solar heating and cooling systems. Not the least of the legal problems involved will be how the owners of solar powered buildings may be protected from being overshadowed by subsequent building or by newly planted trees on adjacent sites – the problem of preserving urban 'sun rights' like the rights to light which have been traditionally protected by the building codes of the past.

Prospects for solar energy use in buildings

To conclude this general examination of solar energy and its use in buildings, mention should perhaps be made of some predictions of the rate and extent of the introduction of solar heating (and cooling) systems which might be expected, into the stock of buildings in the country as a whole. A report to President Truman in 1952, The Promise of Technology, made the prediction that by 1975 there would be a market for 13 million solar-heated houses in the United States. The time is now very short for that particular prophesy to come true; and this in itself might make us wary of predictions generally. The NSF/NASA Solar Energy Panel have been bold enough nevertheless to make some very recent projections. They estimate that 10% of all new buildings could have combined solar heating and cooling systems by 1985; and that 10% of all buildings old and new could have solar heating by 1990 and combined systems by 2000. Ultimately, between 30 and 80% of fuels and electricity used in space heating and cooling could be saved, they predict.

Directory of existing and past
solar heated buildings

The following is a list of solar heated (and cooled) buildings
constructed to date. If it is not complete, then it must be
very nearly so.* It is based very largely on the list compiled
by H.G. Lorsch, Solar Heating Systems Analysis, Report
No. NSF/RANN/SE/G127976/TR72/19, National Center
for Energy Management and Power, University of Pennsylvania,
Nov. 1972 pp.1-2 to 1-5 Table 1; and the presentation here
follows Lorsch's format with some additional information
included. Information on twelve more buildings not covered
in Lorsch's list is also added.

Other useful general reviews of the field are:

H.C. Hottel, H. Heywood, A. Whillier, G.O.G. Löf, M. Telkes and R.W. Bliss Jr.,
'Panel on Solar House Heating', Proceedings of the World
Sympsium on Applied Solar Energy, Phoenix, Arizona 1955,
Stanford Research Institute, Menlo Park California 1956 pp.103-58.
Progressive Architecture, 'Roundup: Recent Solar Heating Installations' in issue of March 1959
G.O.G. Löf, 'The Use of Solar Energy for Space Heating, General Report', United Nations
Department of Economic and Social Affairs, New Sources of Energy
and Energy Development (Proceedings of U.N. Conference on
New Sources of Energy, Rome 1961), United Nations, New York,
E 35 Gr-S14
Bruce Anderson, Solar Energy and Shelter Design, M. Arch thesis, Massachusetts Institute of
Technology Department of Architecture 1973

An appendix is added here giving descriptions of a number of
published unbuilt schemes for solar heated buildings, and of some
current proposals in the planning stages or of a fairly 'firm'
character.

---

* Note added October 1974. This it turns out was a rash claim to
make. Since writing the above, several additional existing solar
heated buildings have come to my attention. What is more, a
substantial number of others have been erected during 1974; and
it seems that very soon any attempt at a comprehensive list will
become unmanageable.

A continuously updated list, already through several editions, is:
W.A. Shurcliff, Solar Heated Buildings: A Brief Survey, distributed by Solar Energy Digest,
PO Box 17776, San Diego, California 92117, price $4.00. The
4th edition (July 1974) lists a total of 58 past buildings, existing
buildings and firm projects.

Older houses which I had missed include, in the United States:
the Saunders House in Weston, Massachusetts (1960), the Henry

Mathew House in Coos Bay, Oregon (1967), a house by R. Crowther
in Denver, Colorado (1972) and two houses by P. van Dresser in
New Mexico, the first built around 1949/50, the second a conversion in 1956 of an existing adobe house in Santa Fe. An architect working in London, D. Michaelis, was occupied during 1973
on the design of a solar house being manufactured in England and
to be assembled at a site in Jucas, France. This will incorporate
a windmill and solar electric cells, as well as solar space and
water heating. E.J.W. Curtis built an experimental 'solar house'
at Rickmansworth, England in 1956, incorporating a heat pump
for heating and cooling; but the design had no special purpose
solar collectors or solar heat storage.

A survey of solar heating work in Britain, mainly devoted to
solar water heating and swimming pool heating, or with experimental rigs only, is given in:

M. Shain, C. Stousland, D. Ross, S. Chippa (Polytechnic of Central London Department of
Architecture), 'Survey of Solar Heating Installations in the U K',
paper 5, International Solar Energy Society, U K Section,
Conference on Low Temperature Thermal Collection of Solar
Energy in the U K, Polytechnic of Central London, April 1974.
This and other papers from the same conference report on the work
of Curtis, J.C. McVeigh, S.V. Szokolay, the late Dr Harold
Heywood and others.

Solar heated buildings erected, or existing buildings converted to
solar heating, during 1974, include:

Solar heated and cooled test house at Marshall Space Flight Center
(NASA), Huntsville, Alabama
Meinel House, Tucson, Arizona (cf. p.167)
Crowther House No.2, Denver, Colorado
Colorado State University House, Fort Collins, Colorado (engineer
G.O.G. Löf)
Pinchot Garage House, Guilford, Connecticut
House on Connecticut shoreline designed by E.M. Barber (engineer)
and D.I. Watson (architect)
National Bureau of Standards Solar House, Gaithersburg, Maryland
Timonium Elementary School, Timonium, Baltimore, Maryland
Grover Cleveland Middle School, Dorchester, Boston, Massachusetts
Honeywell Mobile Solar Laboratories Nos.1 and 2, Minneapolis,
Minnesota
North View Junior High School, Osseo, Minnesota
Ouroboros East, conversion of existing house in St. Paul, Minnesota
Eccli House, New Paltz, New York
Ohio State University Solar House, Columbus, Ohio
Pennsylvania Power and Light Co. House, Schnecksville, Allentown,
Pennsylvania
Fauquier County Public High School, Warrenton, Virginia (install-
ation by Intertechnology Corporation)

As this list indicates there has been growing activity in the field
during this year with two new areas of development emerging:
(continued on p.120)

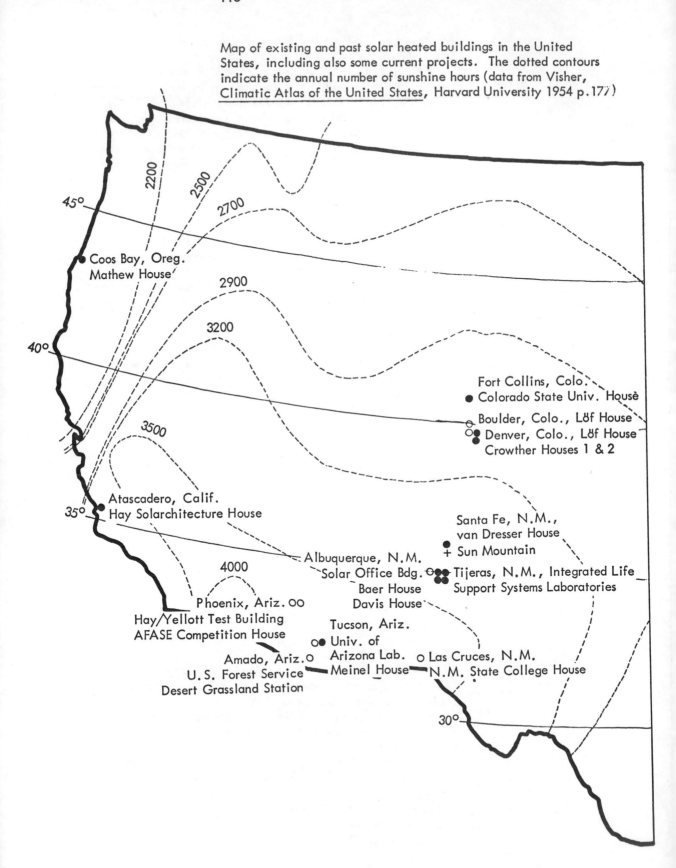

Map of existing and past solar heated buildings in the United States, including also some current projects. The dotted contours indicate the annual number of sunshine hours (data from Visher, Climatic Atlas of the United States, Harvard University 1954 p.177)

Past solar buildings ○
Solar buildings known to be currently operating ●
Projects for solar buildings +

Manchester, N.H., GSA Test Building
Lincoln, Mass., Audubon Society
Weston, Mass., Saunders House
Boston, Mass., MIT Houses I to IV
Grover Cleveland Middle School
Dover, Mass., Telkes-
Raymond-Peabody House

2200

East Warren, Vt., Dimetrodon Condominium
Newfane, Vt., Grassy Brook Village

Osseo, Minn., North View
Junior High School
Minneapolis, Minn., Honeywell
Mobile Solar Labs 1 & 2
Rosemount, Minn.,
Project Ouroboros
St Paul, Minn.,
Ouroboros East

Guilford, Conn., Pinchot
Garage House, Barber House,
Barber/Watson House

New Paltz, N.Y., Eccli House
Millbrook, N.Y., Cary Arboretum
Saginaw, Mich.
GSA Post Office

Schnecksville, Pa.,
P.P.&L. House

Bethpage L.I.
Grumman Corp.

45°

Princeton N.J. Lab.

Newark, Del.
Solar One

Martinsburg,
W.Va.,
Wilson House

Columbus, Ohio
Ohio State Univ. House

40°

Topeka, Ka.
Earl Palmberg Residence

Warrenton, Va.,
Fauquier County Public High School

Baltimore, Timonium
Elementary School
Gaithersburg, Md.,
NBS Solar House
Washington D.C.,
Thomason Houses 1-4

Hampton, Va.,
NASA Langley Center

2500

2700

35°

Huntsville, Ala., MSFC Test House

+ Dallas/Fort Worth
Blum Apartments

Gainsville, Fla.
Univ. of Florida Solar House

30°

Tampa, Fla., Lake Padgett Solar 1

(continued from p.117) the application of solar heating to buildings larger than houses or experimental laboratories, specifically
in the four schools mentioned; and several new experiments with
solar driven refrigeration systems, including G.O.G. Löf's house
at Colorado State University in Fort Collins, the Ohio State
University house on the Ohio State Fairgrounds in Columbus,
NASA's test house at the Marshall Space Flight Center in Huntsville, Alabama and Honeywell's mobile solar laboratories in
Minneapolis. Of these, the first three use lithium bromide/water
absorption refrigeration systems (cf. p.108); and the NASA and
Honeywell buildings are both trailers.

The Meinel house in Tucson (one-storey, 2000 ft^2) has a 300 ft^2
vertical collector wall, forced air heat transfer loops, and a heat
storage reservoir containing 1000 water-filled plastic bottles of 1
gal. capacity each, stacked up and spaced apart to allow the
passage of air between the bottles. An evaporative cooling system
is incorporated.

Löf's house at Fort Collins (architects Crowther, Kruse and Williams)
is one-storey, 3,000 ft^2 in area, including a heated basement. A
two car garage is also heated. The roof collector is of 760 ft^2 at a
tilt of 45°, and heat storage is in a 1,100 gal. basement water
tank. Collector to storage loop, water; storage to space loop, air.

The house on the Connecticut shore built by Everett Barber and
Don Watson (one and a half storey, 1,900 ft^2) has 450 ft^2 of solar
collector in three rows of panels set at 45° on a flat roof. Heat
storage is in a 1,500 gal. basement water tank. Collector to
storage loop, water; storage to space loop, air.

The Ouroboros group at the University of Minnesota School of
Architecture, under Dennis Holloway, have converted an existing
house (Ouroboros East) in St. Paul. The house is on two storeys,
floor area 2,000 ft^2. Extra insulation has been introduced, and
a solar heating system with 600 ft^2 of collector at 45° tilt on the
roof, 500 ft^2 collector on the south wall. Heat storage is in a
2,000 gal. water tank in the basement. Collector to storage loop,
water; storage to space loop, air.

The house built by Eugene Eccli in New Paltz, N.Y. has a 270
ft^2 collector, of which half is Thomason-type with trickled water,
and the remainder a 'greenhouse' with floor of high thermal mass.
Insulating shutters are used at night.

The Ohio State University house is a one-storey building with
2,200 ft^2 of heated living area. Heat losses are cut by very substantial insulation and small windows. 800 ft^2 of collector is in
three sections of roof, tilted at 45°, and is made up of a total of
forty 3' x 6' panels. Heat storage is in two 2,000 gal. water tanks.
Collector to storage loop is water. Solar driven refrigeration uses
a LiBr/water absorption system. A heat pump is used to back up
both heating and cooling systems.

MIT Solar House No.I

1939-40	Cambridge, Massachusetts Two room laboratory, usable area 500 ft^2 Constructed as part of Cabot Solar Energy Research program, under the direction of H.C. Hottel
Solar collector	Size 408 ft^2, tilt 30° Collector was of blackened copper sheet, covered by three glass panes
Thermal energy storage	Sensible heat, in 17,400 gal. water tank
Loops	Collector to storage : water Storage to space: air
Latitude	42°N Heating degree days 5,800

Schematic section of
MIT Solar House No.1,
from H.C. Hottel,
'Residential Uses of
Solar Energy' (Phoenix)

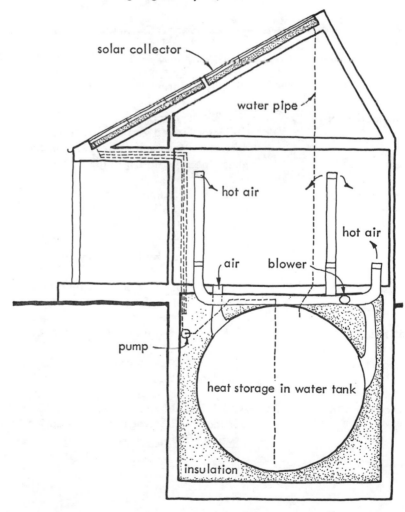

solar collector

water pipe

hot air

hot air

air   blower

pump

heat storage in water tank

insulation

Heating performance	Stored summer heat for winter use, but inefficient, storage too large. Heat loss 10,500 Btu/hr at $0°F$
Remarks	Collector tilt not favourable to winter sun
	Analysis of performance of solar collectors in H.C. Hottel and B.B. Woertz, 'The Performance of Flat-Plate Solar Heat Collectors', Trans. Am. Soc. Mech. Eng., Vol. 64, 1942 pp.91–104
Description in	H.C. Hottel, 'Residential Uses of Solar Energy', Proceedings of the World Symposium on Applied Solar Energy, Phoenix, Arizona 1955, Stanford Research Institute, Menlo Park, California 1956

MIT Solar House No.II

1947-8	Cambridge, Massachusetts Seven-section laboratory, 14' x 44' x 8' high, divided into seven 4' wide cubicles, plus instrument room, usable area 600 ft^2, experimental area 400 ft^2
Solar collector	Size 224 ft^2, vertical Collector formed vertical south wall, made up of seven different types each of 32 ft^2. Six sections had double glass, the seventh triple glass
Thermal energy storage	Various, including no storage. Storage was immediately behind glass collector surface; either water or else heat of fusion materials. Storage could be insulated from glass at night by shades; heat output from back of storage to rooms also controlled by internal shades
Loops	Storage to space: transfer either by direct radiation, or convection using forced air.
Latitude	$42°N$ Heating degree days 5,800
Remarks	Louver and shade operations unreliable. Converted to M.I.T. Solar House No.III
Description in	A.G.H. Dietz and E.L. Czapek, 'Solar Heating of Houses by Vertical Wall Storage Panels', reprint ASHVE Journal Section, Heating, Piping and Air Conditioning

MIT Solar House No. III

1949–53	Cambridge, Massachusetts M.I.T. Solar House No. II modified as dwelling, usable area 600 ft^2
Solar collector	Size 400 ft^2, tilt 57° Collector was built on roof of building, constructed of 3/8" copper tubes at 6" centres, backed with aluminum foil and 4" mineral wool insulation
Thermal energy storage	Sensible heat, in 1,200 gal. water tank under insulated roof. Electric resistance booster heater
Loops	Collector to storage : water Storage to space: air
Latitude	42°N Heating degree days 5,800
Heating performance	75% of space heat from sun. The collector wall area of House No. III was converted to 180 ft^2 of window, 26 ft^2 with double pane, 154 ft^2 with triple pane. Heat loss 20,000 Btu/hr ul 0°F.
Remarks	Collector was framed in wood which cracked from overheating. Collector was kept dry until its temperature was 5° above storage temperature, then pump was started. Water was drained back to storage when collector temperature dropped again, thus avoiding freezing problems. House was destroyed by fire in auxiliary oil heater
Description in	A.L. Hesselschwerdt, 'Heating by Sunpower: A Progress Report', Heating and Air Conditioning Contractor, Oct. 1956 p.44 – H.C. Hottel, 'Residential Uses of Solar Energy', Proceedings of the World Symposium on Applied Solar Energy, Phoenix, Arizona 1955, Stanford Research Institute, Menlo Park, California 1956

MIT Solar House No. IV

1959-61	Lexington, Massachusetts Two-storey house, usable area 1,450 ft^2
Solar collector	Size 640 ft^2, tilt 60° Collector consisted of 60 panels of 0.025 black aluminum, with $\frac{3}{4}$" copper tubes at 5" spacing, covered with two glass panes, backed with fibreglass insulation. 43% efficiency
Thermal energy storage	Sensible heat, in 1,500 gal. water tank. (Also 275 gal. back-up tank, oil-heated to 135°-150°F) Heat storage adequate for three cloudy days
Loops	Collector to storage : water Storage to space: air
Latitude	42°N Heating degree days 5,800
Heating performance	48% of space heat from sun. Attempted to collect 77% of insolation. Heat loss 30,000 Btu/hr. at 0°F
Cooling performance	$\frac{3}{4}$ ton refrigeration cooled water tank, to provide cooling for living room.
Remarks	Domestic hot water also supplied from thermal storage. In summer all solar energy used for water heating
Description in	C.D. Engebretson and N.G. Ashar, 'Progress in Space Heating with Solar Energy', Paper No. 60-WA-88, Winter ASME Meeting, December 1960 C.D. Engebretson, 'Use of Solar Energy for Space Heating, M.I.T. House IV', United Nations Department of Economic and Social Affairs, <u>New Sources of Energy and Energy Development</u> (Proceedings of U.N. Conference on New Sources of Energy, Rome 1961), United Nations, New York E35-S67 (Engebretson was the M.I.T. program's chief engineer, and himself lived in House No. IV)

Telkes-Raymond-Peabody House

1944-53	Dover, Massachusetts Private house, single storey, usable area 1,456 ft^2 Owner, Amelia Peabody; solar system designer, Dr. Maria Telkes; architect, Eleanor Raymond
Solar collector	Size 720 ft^2, vertical Collector formed upper part of south wall, consisted of black galvanised plate with two glass covers and a 5/8" air duct. Efficiency of 40%
Thermal energy storage	Latent heat, in $Na_2SO_4.10H_2O$ (Glauber's salt), 470 ft^3 (21 tons) in 5 gal. drums in three closet bins. Heat exchange surface 2,400 ft^2. Stored 4.7×10^6 Btu, sufficient for 5-7 cloudy days
Loops	Collector to storage : air, three fans at 1,100 cfm Storage to space: air, five fans at 60 cfm, 1/15 watts Loops could be combined
Latitude	42°N Heating degree days 6,000 +
Heating performance	First season 100% of space heat from sun, later seasons less. Collector yielded 3.5×10^6 Btu/day. Heat loss 8,400 Btu/ degree day
Cost of installation	Materials only; collector $940, storage $635, ducts, fans and controls $290, total $1,865. Estimated cost of a mass- produced unit, $3,750. Cost of equivalent conventional unit for comparison, $800.
Cost in operation	Cost saving was estimated at $300/year. At this rate cost of solar installation would be amortized (at 6%) in 16 years. Would require 22 years to amortize cost with $250/year savings, 40 years with $200/year savings
Remarks	Performance dropped after the first year because of segregation of the Glauber's salt and the resulting imperfect reversibility of the storage cycle. 170 ft^2 of windows added 10^6 Btu/day in winter. House was enlarged in 1953, and the heating system replaced.
Description in	M. Telkes, 'Space Heating with Solar Energy'. The Scientific Monthly, Vol. LX1X No. 6, Dec. 1949

Löf House, Boulder

1945 -7	Boulder, Colorado Existing five room bungalow, usable area 1,000 ft^2 Heating system designed and added to house by G.O.G.Löf for himself
Solar collector	Size 463 ft^2, tilt 27° Collector consisted of sheet metal troughs, 3" x 2' x 4', containing a stepped arrangement of glass plates, with part of each sheet blackened, such that each black surface was beneath two clear surfaces. Whole trough was also glass covered
Thermal energy storage	Sensible heat, in 7 cubic yards of gravel (8-9 tons) in bin
Loops	Collector to storage : air Storage to space : air Loops could be combined
Latitude	40°N Heating degree days 5,500
Heating performance	20-25% of space heat from sun. Used auxiliary gas furnace with hot air heating system
Remarks	Insufficient insulation, leaky dampers, initially high rate of collector glass breakage
Description in	H.C.Hottel, H. Heywood, A. Whillier, G.O.G. Löf, M. Telkes and R.W. Bliss Jr., 'Panel on Solar House Heating', Proceedings of the World Symposium on Applied Solar Energy, Phoenix, Arizona 1955, Stanford Research Institute, Menlo Park, California 1956

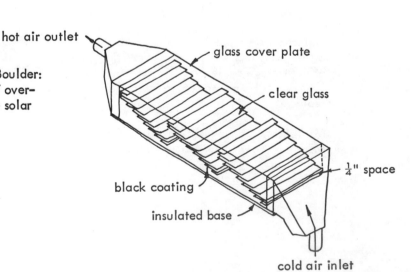

Löf House, Boulder:
schematic of over-
lapped plate solar
air heater

hot air outlet

glass cover plate

clear glass

$\frac{1}{4}$" space

black coating

insulated base

cold air inlet

Löf House, Denver

1958	Denver, Colorado Private house, single storey with partial basement, usable area 2,050 ft^2 Owner and solar system designer, G.O.G. Löf; architect, James Hunter
Solar collector	Size 600 ft^2, tilt 45° Collector is in two staggered sections 12' x 25' on the roof. The design consists of overlapping glass plates, on the same principle as the Boulder house. Efficiency of collector 35%
Thermal energy storage	Sensible heat, in 230 ft^3 (12 tons) of rock pieces 2" in diameter stored in two fiberboard drums 3' in diameter, 16' high from basement to roof. Normal maximum air temperature 140°F
Loops	Collector to storage : air Storage to space: air Loops can be combined

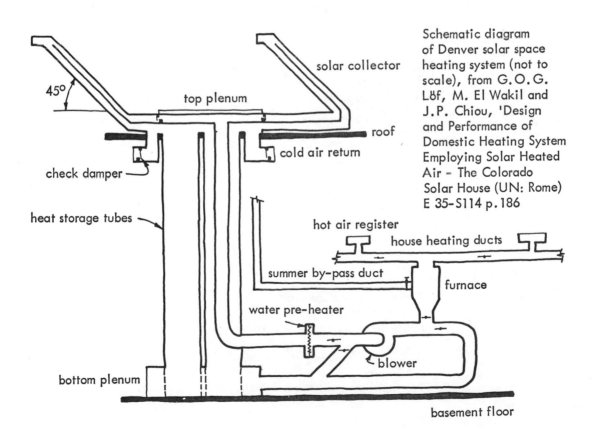

Schematic diagram of Denver solar space heating system (not to scale), from G.O.G. Löf, M. El Wakil and J.P. Chiou, 'Design and Performance of Domestic Heating System Employing Solar Heated Air – The Colorado Solar House (UN: Rome) E 35-S114 p.186

Latitude	40°N Heating degree days 5,700

Heating performance

26% of space and water heating from sun, remainder supplied by natural gas. Attempted collection of 72% of insolation (average January radiation 220 langleys/day)

Cost in operation

Saved $80 in cost of natural gas/year; this saving could be increased to $100–$130 by redesign. Needed $60 more power to drive fan.

Remarks

Auxiliary gas heater. Collector air passes through 80 gal. domestic hot water tank before reaching storage or rooms. Had reflective-lined draperies

Description in

H.C. Hottel, H. Heywood, A. Whillier, G.O.G. Löf, M. Telkes and R.W. Bliss Jr., 'Panel on Solar House Heating', Proceedings of the World Symposium on Applied Solar Energy Phoenix, Arizona 1955, Stanford Research Institute, Menlo Park California 1956

US Forest Service Desert Grassland Station

1955

Amado, Arizona (30m south of Tucson)
Existing bungalow, usable area 672 ft^2
Modified by Raymond and Mary Bliss

Solar collector

Size 315 ft^2, tilt 53°
Collector was separate from house, on a structure 34' x 10', and consisted of four layers of black cotton screens under a single glass pane. Collected 315,000 Btu on clear day

Thermal energy storage

Sensible heat, in 1,300 ft^3 (65 tons) of 4" diameter rocks, in a bin next to the house. Bin was insulated with 4" concrete floor, 7" concrete walls, 8" rockwool roof. Stored 1.35×10^6 Btu between 140°F and 90°F for ten average days

Loops

Collector to storage : air
Storage to space: air
Loops could be combined. Ducts above ground

Latitude

32°N   Heating degree days 525 for January

Heating performance

No auxiliary heat needed; system was overdesigned

Cooling performance	Cooling provided by means of a single porous cloth over collector, air cooled by cold night air, plus 2°F sky radiation. Comfort equivalent to evaporative cooling, but not up to air conditioning standards
Cost of installation	$4,000. Should cost $2,000 - $3,000 for subsequent models. Conventional heating unit would have cost $700 installed $12/year (equivalent bottled gas cost, $80/year). Cannot amortize solar unit through operating savings. Might become economical if hot water and cooling systems incorporated
Remarks	Storage should have been under house, not next to it; 25% of heat collected is lost this way
Description in	H.C. Hottel, H. Heywood, A Whillier, G.O.G. Löf, M. Telkes and R.W. Bliss Jr., 'Panel on Solar House Heating', Proceedings of the World Symposium on Applied Solar Energy, Phoenix, Arizona 1955, Stanford Research Institute, Menlo Park, California 1956

Schematic view of air-heating collector and heat storage rockpile; and below, air cooling 'night radiator', in US Forest Service Desert Grassland Station. From H.C. Hottel, A. Whillier, G.O.G. Löf, M. Telkes and R.W. Bliss Jr., 'Panel on Solar House Heating' (Phoenix)

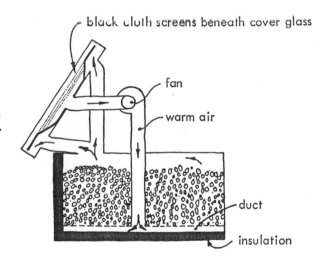

black cloth screens beneath cover glass

fan

warm air

duct

insulation

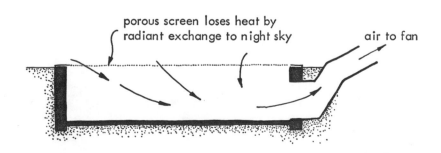

porous screen loses heat by radiant exchange to night sky

air to fan

Solar Office Building

1956–65	Albuquerque, New Mexico Single-storey office, usable area 4,300 ft^2 System design by F.H. Bridgers and D.D. Paxton
Solar collector	Size 790 ft^2, tilt 60° Collector covers south wall, consists of black aluminum plate with copper tubes, behind single glass pane
Thermal energy storage	Sensible heat, in 6,000 gal. water in insulated underground tank
Loops	Collector to storage : water Storage to space : water, at 90–110°F in floor and ceiling panels
Latitude	35°N Heating degree days 4,400
Heating performance	Used heat pump booster. Storage for three days, then needed city water on cold side of pump
Cooling performance	7.5 ton heat pump evaporative cooling to air. For low loads evaporator chills water without heat pump
Cost of installation	$17,400 ($4/ft^2), $58,500 for building ($13.60/ft^2)
Cost in	First season's heating $78 (would cost $318 to heat with heat pump, $163 with natural gas)
Remarks	The heat pump is part of the solar heating system, not an auxiliary; it extracts heat from the water storage. The tank may be used to store 'coolness' by running the heat pump at night. Building is no longer solar heated, uses natural gas
Description in	F.H. Bridgers, D.D. Paxton and R.W. Haines, 'Performance of a Solar Heated Building', Heating, Piping and Air Conditioning Vol. 27, Nov. 1957 p.165

AFASE Competition House

1958	Phoenix, Arizona Single storey house with central court and swimming pool Winning design in competition held by Association for Applied Solar Energy (now Solar Energy Society) and Phoenix Association of Home Builders, by Peter R. Lee, then a student at the University of Minnesota. Lee associated himself with Robert L. Bliss, architect, for the construction of the house, which was built with funds made available by G. Robert Herberger
Solar collector	Size 700 ft^2, variable tilt Collector consisted of 68 tiltable louvers in 17 rows, covering the court and two patio roofs
Thermal energy storage	Sensible heat, in 2,000 gal. (8.5 ton) water tank undergound
Loops	Collector to storage : water Storage to space : air (heat pump when water not hot enough)
Latitude	33°N Heating degree days 1,500
Remarks	Heat pump used as a booster for heating, also for cooling use with water from aerated swimming pool. Heat pump is part of solar heating systems, not an auxiliary means of heating; it extracts heat from water storage. Collector louvers acted to shade south-facing windows
Description in	Phoenix Association of Home Builders, 'The Solar House', <u>Sun at Work</u>

University of Arizona
Solar Energy Laboratory

1959	Tucson, Arizona Single storey simulated home, usable area 1,440 ft^2
Solar collector	Size 1,623 ft^2, tilt 15°+ Collector is integral with roof, made of green copper sheet and tubes, with no glass, efficiency 29%
Thermal energy storage	Sensible heat, in 4,500 gal. water tank, divided into two sections which may have temperature differences of 10°F. Tank is above ground, insulated
Loops	Collector to storage : water Storage to space: water at 110°F in ceiling panels covering all rooms
Latitude	32°N Heating degree days, 1,800
Heating	86% of space heat from the sun. 1.5 hp heat pump booster. 435 ft^2 of double pane windows. Heat loss 12,000 Btu/hr at 30°F
Cooling performance	Roof radiates up to 0.5×10^6 Btu per night from 70°F water
Cost in operation	For heating and cooling, 8,500 kWh/year: $215. Gas heat and electric air conditioning would cost $400
Remarks	Heat pump is part of solar heating and cooling system, not auxiliary heating. Heat pump operates between two tank sections with temperatures of 115-105°F in winter, 70-60°F in summer $\pm$ 5°F.
Description in	R.W. Bliss Jr., 'Performance of an Experimental System Using Solar Energy for Heating and Night Radiation for Cooling a Building', United Nations Department of Economic and Social Affairs, New Sources of Energy and Energy Development (Proceedings of U.N. Conference on New Sources of Energy, Rome 1961), United Nations, New York 1964 E 35-S30

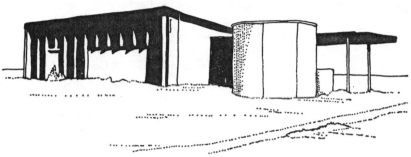

General view of
University of Arizona
Solar Energy Laboratory
looking south-east.
Note vertical fins for
shading of north-facing
windows. And below:
flow scheme of
experimental heating-
cooling system in Univ-
ersity of Arizona Solar
Energy Laboratory.
From R.W. Bliss Jr.,
'Performance of an
Experimental System
Using Solar Energy for
Heating and Night
Radiation for Cooling
a Building (UN: Rome)
E 35-S30 pp. 149, 151

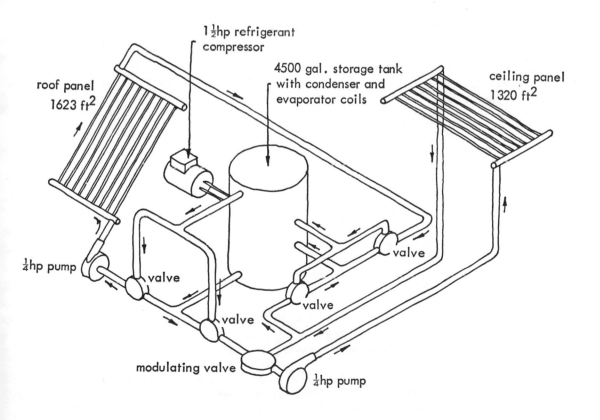

Solar heat pump, New Haven

1950–55	New Haven, West Virginia
Solar collector	Size 112 ft^2 Collector consisted of glass covered evaporator plate (for heat pump), 1" away from 3" insulation No thermal energy storage
Loops	Collector to space: heat pump
Latitude	39°N
Heating performance	Collected 60% of all insolation. From January 10th to 20th, 400 Btu/ft^2 collected (20% of all insolation)
Remarks	On warm days (March, April) ambient air temperature also heats refrigerant, so that heat collected may exceed total insolation

Earl Palmberg Residence

1962–3	Topeka, Kansas
Solar collector	Size 600 ft^2, vertical Collector was south-facing, constructed of black corrugated metal plates covered with plastic fabric material
Thermal energy storage	Sensible heat, in 1,350 ft^3 of limestone rocks, maximum size 2½"
Loops	Collector to storage : air Storage to space: air
Latitude	39°N
Remarks	System used two 2½ hp heat pumps of which one used heated air from the solar collector. Supplementary electrical resistance heating was also provided
Reported in	G.R. Mowry, 'Solar Energy Supplemented Rural-Home Heat Pump', Solar Energy Vol. 8 No. 1 1964

New Mexico State College Solar House

1953	State College, Las Cruces, New Mexico One and a half storey house, usable area 1,100 ft^2
Solar collector	Size 457 ft^2, tilt 45° Collector faced south and southwest, was made of black steel plate with glass cover
Thermal energy storage	Latent heat, in 2 tons of $Na_2SO_4.10H_2O$ (Glauber's salt) in 5 gal. cans. Stored 0.5×10^6 Btu
Loops	Collector to storage: air Storage to space: air
Latitude	32°N
Heating	Approximately 50% of space heat from the sun; although estimated average December collection was 0.5×10^6 Btu/day, which is 25% larger than required
Remarks	Segregation of Glauber's salt progressively decreased storage capacity. This can be avoided by proper design.

University of Florida Solar House

1968	Gainsville, Florida One storey house, originally test house of Mechanical Engineering Department, University of Florida
Solar collector	Size 350 ft^2, made up of ten panels each 5' x 8'
Thermal energy storage	Sensible heat, in 3,000 gal. water tank in basement
Loops	Collector to storage: water Storage to space: water
Latitude	$29\frac{1}{2}$°N
Remarks	House was converted to partial solar heating in 1968, and to full solar heating in 1973
Reported in	E.A. Farber, 'Solar Energy, Its Conversion and Utilization', Solar Energy 1973 Vol.14 pp.243-52 E.A. Farber et al., 'The University of Florida Solar House' (Paris) C11

Princeton Laboratory

1959-60	Princeton, New Jersey Single storey laboratory, usable area 1,200 ft^2
Solar collector	Size 600 ft^2, vertical Collector was of black sheet metal with two sheets of glass, efficiency 46%
Thermal energy storage	Latent heat, in 275 ft^3 (12 tons) of $Na_2SO_4.10H_2O$ (Glauber's salt), storage capacity 2.5 x 10^6 Btu
Loops	Collector to storage : air Storage to space: air
Latitude	40°N Heating degree days 5,100
Heating performance	No auxiliary heat needed. Typical January heat load 12,000 Btu/hr
Description in	A. Olgyay, 'Design Criteria of Solar Heated House', United Nations Department of Economic and Social Affairs, New Sources of Energy and Energy Development (Proceedings of U.N. Conference on New Sources of Energy, Rome 1961), United Nations, New York 1964 E35-S93

Hay/Yellott Test Building

1967-8

Phoenix, Arizona
Single room experimental structure, area 120 ft^2
Designers, Harold Hay and John Yellott

This building, since demolished, was a well-insulated,
white painted structure with a 12 ft^2 south-facing window
beneath an overhanging carport roof.

**Solar collector
and thermal
energy storage**

Solar collector and thermal storage were combined in the form
of a pond of water on the roof contained within a series of
transparent plastic bags. The bags were retained in troughs
formed by the roof beams and metal ceiling, and lined with
10 mil. black polyethylene sheet. Over this pond was a 1.5"
thick panel of polyurethane insulation, sliding on aluminum
trackways. The principle of the system's operation was to draw
back the roof insulation over the carport and expose the pond
to collect heat during winter days; and to re-cover the pond with
the insulating panel during the nights, to stop heat losses.
The heat stored in the body of water in the pond was radiated
downwards through the ceiling into the space below. In summer
the mode of operation was reversed, and the pond was covered
during the day, and uncovered during the night, when some
cooling effect could be achieved by radiation to the night sky,
providing the weather was clear, or there was little cloud cover.

Latitude

33°N   Heating degree days 1,500

**Diagrammatic cross-
sections of Hay
ceiling ponds**

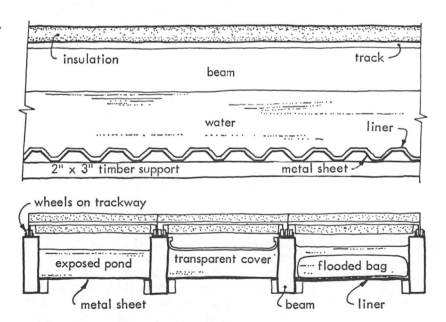

Heating performance	Pond water could reach a temperature of 85°F by the end of the day. Room was kept in the 66°–73°F range when outside temperatures were at freezing point
Cooling performance	Using night sky radiation to cool the pond, temperatures were kept between 74 and 77°F when outside maximum temperature was 100°F and when 24-hour outdoor temperature average was 84°F. With outdoor maxima of 108°F and 24-hour averages of 87°F, internal temperatures were maintained between 77° and 82°F by flooding the plastic-enclosed ponds with a thin layer of water at night, and allowing this to evaporate thus cooling the pond water itself. At higher temperatures still, fan-driven forced air circulation was needed between the ponds and the room.
Remarks	The system is clearly inappropriate for climates where temperatures much below freezing occur. The principles are not complex however, and simplified versions could be built cheaply in the lower latitudes in underdeveloped countries. According to Hay, the use of roof ponds is possible between latitudes 35°S and 35°N. The size of the pond must be large, since in its very nature it must be horizontal, and thus as a collector is not optimally oriented. The transfer of heat from storage to building is essentially uncontrollable, although if temperatures rise too high in winter, the roof insulation may be drawn back and windows opened etc.
Description in	H.R. Hay and J.I. Yellott, 'Construction and Operation of a Naturally Air-Conditioned Building', Winter Annual Meeting of the Am.Soc.Mech.Engrs., New York.Dec.1968 H.R. Hay and J.I. Yellott, 'Natural Air Conditioning with Roof Ponds and Movable Insulation', Semi-Annual Meeting of ASHRAE, Chicago, Jan. 1969 J.I. Yellott and H.R. Hay, 'Thermal Analysis of a Building with Natural Air Conditioning', Semi-Annual Meeting of ASHRAE, Chicago, Jan. 1969 H.R. Hay and J.I. Yellott, 'A Naturally Air-Conditioned Building', Mech. Engng. 92 (1), 1970 pp.19-25

Hay Solarchitecture House

1973	Atascadero, north of San Luis Obispo, California Single storey family house, usable area 1,100 ft² approx., excluding garage, patio System design by Harold Hay, architectural design by Ken Haggard, house constructed and to be evaluated by Solar and Night Sky Radiation Research Group,

School of Architecture, California Polytechnic Institute,
San Luis Obispo

This recently completed house has been financed with a
grant from the department of Housing and Urban
Development, who are also sponsoring a program of
evaluation of the house, including instrumentation of the
system and structure to measure thermal performance, as
well as economic and sociological evaluations. The house
represents a full scale application of the principles of the
Hay/Yellott Phoenix test building (see above), with a
roof pond of equal area to the house itself and movable
insulation.

Solar collector

The roof structure is of steel decking, and carries 10"of
water contained within a three-layer polyethylene sheet
liner, the first two layers being cross-laminated to eliminate
leaks, and the third a 'sacrificial' layer which will be
replaced at intervals, since the polyethylene deteriorates
under the action of the ultraviolet radiation in sunlight.
The movable insulation over the pond consists of three
sets of 12 ft span polyurethane panels running on aluminum
channel tracks at 8 ft spacing. The panels are moved by
motors, controlled automatically; and when the pond is
uncovered, they stack three deep above the patio and
garage areas at the end of the house.

Solar wall

Incorporated into the design of the house is an experimental
solar wall, on the south side, 12" thick, and which is to be
filled with water in plastic containers in a central cavity.
It will be painted in a dark colour on the outside face, and
will act as a combined collector and means of heat storage,
somewhat like the roof (or like Steve Baer's water-filled
drum wall, q.v.); at one stage it was intended that it be
covered, in a similar way, with (vertical) movable insulation.
One effect of this wall is to further increase the thermal
mass of the building; and in other parts of the house the
cavities in the block construction are filled with sand, for
the same reason. Hay is interested in making experiments
with solar walls, either of concrete blocks, as at Atascadero,
or of metal, for application in designs for sites north of
latitude 35°.

**Cost of
installation**

The cost of the house with land is $40,000, of which
Hay calculates $7,000 can be attributed to extra costs due
to its being a prototype. The overall cost of the roof
structure is $5.20/ft^2, which again Hay estimates could
be brought down to between $3.40 and $2.70 with mass
production.

Description in

H.R. Hay, 'Natural Air Conditioning in the California
Solarchitecture House', paper presented at 'The Sun in the
Service of Mankind', International Congress, Paris July 1973

Thomason Houses 1 to 7

Harry E. Thomason is the inventor of the 'Solaris' system of solar heating, and the founder of Thomason Solar Homes Inc., 6802 Walker Mill Rd. S.E., Washington D.C. 20027. Since 1959 Thomason has built four solar houses (Nos. 1 to 4) in Washington. House No. 5 planned for a South Carolina firm, was never built. House No. 6, built in Mexico City, though following Thomason principles, was not constructed strictly according to his recommendations. House No. 7, the Solaris 'Sunny South Model', exists so far in the form of plans only.

House No. 1

1959	Washington D.C. Single storey house with basement, storage space beneath pitched roof/collector, usable area 1,500 ft^2
Solar collector	Size 840 ft^2, tilt 60° on lower (wall) section, 45° on upper (roof) section Collector is on south-facing wall and roof, made of corrugated metal sheet under one layer of clear plastic, one sheet glass cover
Thermal energy storage	Sensible heat in 1,600 gal. water tank surrounded by 50 tons of gravel, acting both as storage and insulation. 275 gal. domestic water pre-heater tank
Loops	Collector to storage: water, 135°F maximum Storage to space: air, circulated through rocks and around water tank
Latitude	39°N Heating degree days 4,300
Heating performance	95% of space heat from sun. Auxiliary oil heater used 50 gal. one season. Heat storage sufficient for five cloudy days
Cooling performance	For cooling, same system is used as for heating, but with water run during night over bare metal north-facing roof to produce cooling by evaporation, convection and radiation. On hot humid nights with clouds and no wind, little cooling effect
Cost of installation	Cost of collector $1 per ft^2 approx. Cost of whole system $2,500
Cost in operation	Annual fuel saving $180-$200
Remarks	House has been in continuous operation for thirteen years. After five years the collector was rebuilt in more long-lived

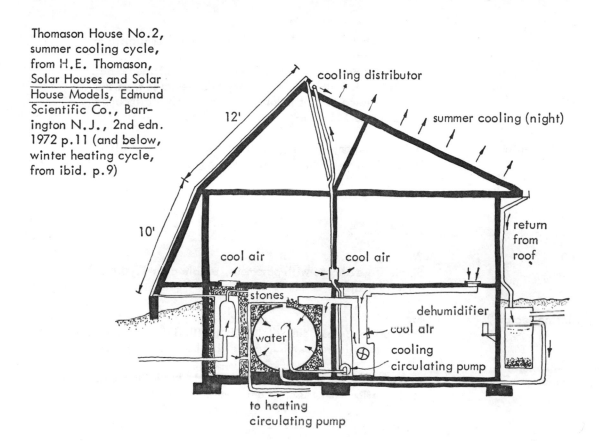

Thomason House No.2, summer cooling cycle, from H.E. Thomason, <u>Solar Houses and Solar House Models</u>, Edmund Scientific Co., Barrington N.J., 2nd edn. 1972 p.11 (and <u>below</u>, winter heating cycle, from ibid. p.9)

12'

10'

cooling distributor

summer cooling (night)

return from roof

cool air

cool air

stones

water

dehumidifier

cool air

cooling circulating pump

to heating circulating pump

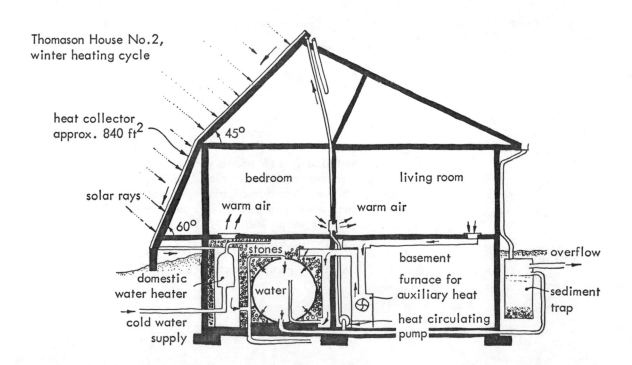

Thomason House No.2, winter heating cycle

heat collector approx. 840 ft^2

45°

60°

solar rays

bedroom

living room

warm air

warm air

stones

water

domestic water heater

cold water supply

basement

furnace for auxiliary heat

heat circulating pump

overflow

sediment trap

materials but with lower efficiency. The mylar plastic on the collector is subject to deterioration. The fact that the collector covers the whole of the south side of the house results in good insulation, and any heat leakage from the back of the collectors is into the house itself – although this can result in over-heating on occasion.

Description in	H.E. Thomason, 'Solar Space Heating and Air Conditioning in the Thomason Home', Solar Energy Vol. 4 No. 4 Oct. 1960 pp.11-19

House No. 2

1960	Washington D.C. Single storey house with basement, usable area 1,000 ft^2 (675 ft^2 heated)
Solar collector	Size 560 ft^2 Same principle as House No. 1, but with 336 ft^2 horizontal aluminum reflector extending out from bottom of collector
Remarks	In other respects similar to House No. 1, but with a $\frac{3}{4}$ hp refrigeration compressor to chill water and rock storage at night (using off-peak electrical power). Problems were experienced with excessive humidity
Description in	H.E. Thomason, 'Solar-Heated House Uses $\frac{3}{4}$ HP for Air Conditioning', ASHRAE Journal Nov. 1962 pp.58-62 also in Sun at Work, First Quarter 1961 pp.16-17

House No. 3

1963	Washington D.C. Single storey house with basement, usable area 3,400 ft^2 (1,500 ft^2 heated)
Remarks	Water tank constructed of concrete blocks. Better dehumidification than House No. 2. Collector on roof only, constructed of 4' x 16' panels with glass covers in aluminum frames; adjacent flat roof of indoor swimming pool and sun porch covered in aluminum, to act as 300 ft^2 reflector. Solar heating of pool (7,000 gal.) by pumping water through collector periodically
Description in	H.E. Thomason, 'A Solar House Completed – Another Begun', Sun at Work, Fourth Quarter 1963 pp.13-16

House No. 4

A-frame house with 60° tilt collector consisting of black asphalt shingles, with water trickled over surface. Heat storage is in the form of a shallow pond of water beneath the floor. Described by Thomason as a 'pancake' storage system, this is constructed on a 2" bed of sand, with polyurethane and foamed glass insulation on top, and a polyethylene sheet liner, to give a water tank 12"-15" deep. Problems were encountered with leaks in the polyethylene tank liner, and with leakages and low efficiency in the asphalt shingle collector.

House Nos 5-7

House No. 5 was planned for a South Carolina firm in 1965 but never built.

Below: Thomason House No.3, Washington DC, from H.E. Thomason, Solar Houses and Solar House Models, Edmund Scientific Co., Barrington N.J., 2nd edn. 1972 (front cover). Flat roof of pool and porch at extreme left is aluminum covered, and acts as a reflector onto the inclined collector roof surface

House No. 6 was built in Mexico City, and is a large luxurious home but with no insulation in the walls, an inadequately sized heat storage bin, a collector of only 300 ft^2 with no insulation, and with a blue collector surface! Thomason's designs were not followed, and the performance as a result is very poor.

A new design by Thomason for a flat roof system is being tested in India. Thomason has also recently put forward plans for a house design No. 7, the Solaris 'Sunny South Model'. This incorporates 'pancake' under-floor heat storage in shallow water tanks, of the type used in House No. 4, together with a roof-pond solar collector similar to the Hay/Yellott system (q.v.). This pond is edged with vertical aluminum reflectors along its north side. On sunny mornings in winter water is pumped from the under-floor storage tank to the roof pond, and at night the warmed water is drained back to the storage again. (Thus no movable insulation is required over the collector pond, as with the Hay/Yellott design). In summer the cycle is reversed to provide cooling by means of night sky radiation and/or evaporation.

Descriptions of Thomason's work as a whole are to be found in :

H.E. Thomason, 'Three Solar Homes', American Society of Mechanical Engineers Paper No. 65-WA/-SOL-3, 1965
H.E. Thomason, .'Experience with Solar Houses', Solar Energy Vol. 10 No. 1 1966 pp 17-22
H.E. Thomason, Solar Houses and Solar House Models, Edmund Scientific Co., Publication No. 9069, Barrington N.J., 2nd edn. 1972
H.E. Thomason and H.J.L. Thomason Jr., 'Solar Houses/ Heating and Cooling Progress Report', Solar Energy Vol. 15 No. 1, May 1973 pp.27-39

Project Ouroboros

1973	Minneapolis, Minnesota Two-storey dwelling, usable area 1,500 ft^2 Live project by 160 students of the University of Minnesota School of Architecture and Landscape Architecture, under the direction of Professors Dennis Holloway and Tom Bender
Solar collector	Size 576 ft^2 in 12 panels, 4' x 12' Collectors are of Thomason-type design, corrugated galvanised sheet metal with two sheets of glass cover
Thermal energy storage	Sensible heat, in 1,250 gal. insulated water tank with 1½ hp circulation pump, and 55 gal. domestic hot water tank
Loops	Collector to storage : water Storage to space: water
Latitude	45°N Heating degree days 8,000
Remarks	Plan form is trapezoidal, with largest (collector) wall facing south, and northern wall smallest to minimise wind exposure. Earth berms and sod roof are also used for wind protection, insulation and summer cooling. Auxiliary heating provided by electric immersion heater, wood fired stove. The use of heat pumps is contemplated for some later stage of the project.
Description in	Lyle Frost, 'Ouroboros', Dimensions (Northern States Power Magazine), Summer 1973 Andrew P. Corty, 'Solar Homes : The "Clan" is Growing', Environmental Action Bulletin, Sept. 22 1973 pp.4-6

Project Ouroboros,
University of Minn-
esota, Minneapolis:
plan, and <u>below</u>,
diagrammatic section.
Drawings by courtesy
of Professor Dennis
Holloway.

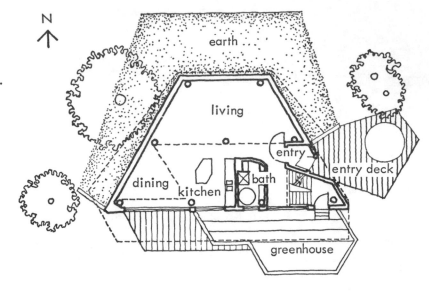

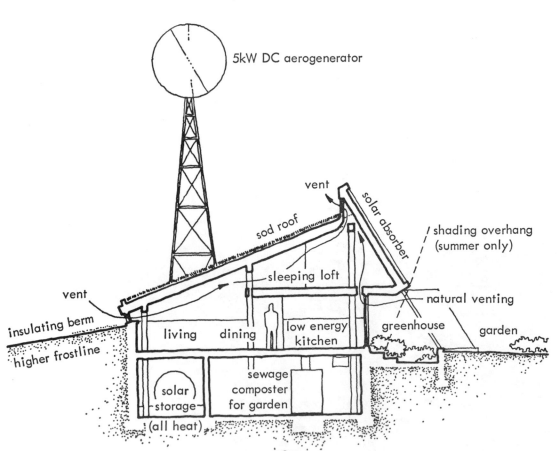

Baer House

1972

Corrales, Albuquerque, New Mexico
House of zonohedron ('zome') geometry designed for
himself and family by Steve Baer (Zomeworks), usable
area 2,000 ft^2

Solar collector

Size 400 ft^2 overall, 260 ft^2 net exposed surface of
drums. Thermal energy storage and collector are combined,
and consist of 91 metal drums 22$\frac{3}{4}$" diameter and 34$\frac{3}{4}$" deep,
stacked on their sides up to five deep, and filled with water.
The total capacity of the drum is 4,800 gals. The ends
exposed to the outside (south) wall are painted black, and
covered with a single sheet of glass. The ends on the
interior are painted white. The collector surfaces are
covered during the night or in cloudy periods by four
insulating doors, approx. 9'6" square each, made of 3"
styrofoam with aluminum skins on both sides. These doors
are folded down when the sun shines, and the interior

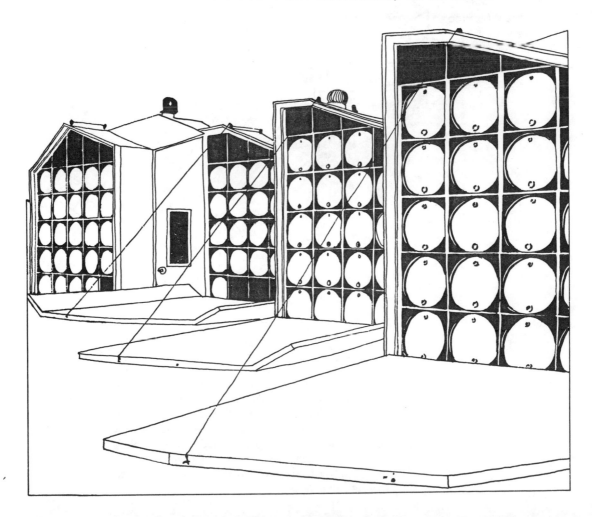

aluminum surfaces then act as reflectors. The collector picks up 1,200 Btu/ft^2/hr. Radiant heat output from the inside face is controlled with the use of curtains. Auxiliary heating is provided by a wood-burning stove.

Latitude   35°N   Heating degree days 4,400

Description in   Steve Baer, 'Solar House', Alternative Sources of Energy No. 10, March 1973 p.8
'The Plowboy Interview with Steve and Holly Baer', The Mother Earth News No.22 July 1973 pp.6-15

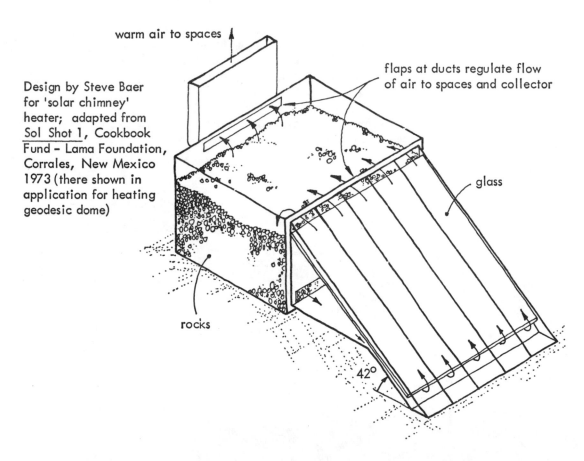

warm air to spaces

flaps at ducts regulate flow of air to spaces and collector

Design by Steve Baer for 'solar chimney' heater; adapted from Sol Shot 1, Cookbook Fund – Lama Foundation, Corrales, New Mexico 1973 (there shown in application for heating geodesic dome)

glass

rocks

42°

'Solar chimney'   Baer has also designed or collaborated in the design of other solar heated houses in Albuquerque and elsewhere in New Mexico. For the Davis house (one storey, 1,000 ft^2) next to his own, in Corrales, New Mexico, he has built a 'solar chimney' heater. This consists of a 36' x 12' sloping collector set into the hill below the house, with five layers of black painted metal mesh spaced apart and set beneath glass. Air is introduced at the bottom of the collector and circulates naturally upwards by convection. Heat storage is provided in a rock bin situated at the top of the collector and beneath the floor of the house. Hot air is admitted into the house from the storage bin by means of registers in the floor.

Integrated Life-Support Systems Laboratories

1972	Tijeras, Albuquerque, New Mexico Hemispherical dome house 31'6" diameter, usable area 655 ft^2 at ground level, 200 ft^2 in loft space. The dome is built from pressed steel segmental sections, with 3" internal flame-resistant polyurethane foam insulation. An airlock is formed by the 7' long entrance hallway. The dome has 19 portholes of $8\frac{1}{2}$" diameter, and a 6' skylight at the top, with 11 circular fixed lights of varying sizes, and one rectangular opening light to act as a vent. Second similar-sized dome (built 1973) used as workshop. Designer Robert Reines
Solar collector	Conventional flat-plate, separate from house, two sheets glass cover. Workshop dome has collectors integral with the structure.
Thermal energy	Sensible heat, in 3,000 gal. water tank separate from house, heavily insulated with polyurethane foam. Contains small tank for domestic hot water.
Loops	Collector to storage : water-glycol medium Storage to space : water, run through a ring of radiators at the base of the dome, thus giving a torus pattern of hot air circulation throughout the space by convection.
Latitude	35°N Heating degree days 4,400

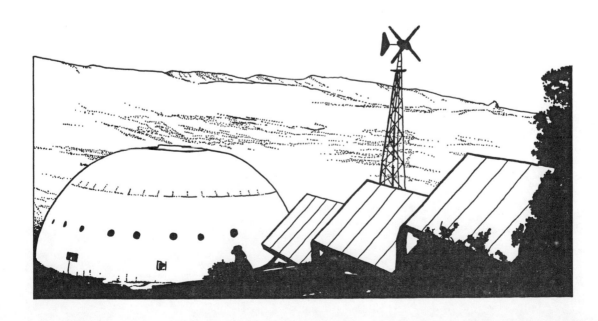

Heating performance	100% of space heat and water heating from sun. Indoor temperatures have been maintained in the range 65°-85°F with outdoor temperatures ranging from -5°F to 100°F+. Storage capacity sufficient for seven sunless days.
Cost of installation	Total cost of dome house (including wind electric power system) $12,000
Remarks	It is intended that experiments be made with running the solar system at night in summer for cooling purposes. The house is 100% solar and wind powered (with the exception of a butane stove); the electrical power for running lights (150 watts total), stereo, radio, tv, power tools, Thetford electric toilet and solar system pumps, being supplied from reconditioned wind machines, of which there are presently three in operation, generating a total of 4 kW. Electricity storage is in 16 lead-acid batteries, with a capacity sufficient for seven windless days; the house circuit is at 110v AC. The parts for two further domes have been fabricated and await erection. Experiments have been begun with hydroponic horticulture, using plastic foam insulated, solar heated beds.
Description in	J. Dreyfuss, 'Unique Dome Home Harnesses Sun and Wind: New Mexico House is First Totally Heated, Powered by Elements', Los Angeles Times Jan 1 1973

University of Delaware Solar One

1973	Newark, Delaware Two-storey family house with basement, usable area 1,500 ft^2. House has been built by the University of Delaware Institute of Energy Conversion, Director Karl W. Böer. Heat storage system design by M. Telkes, architectural design by Harry Weese Associates. House construction and associated research program financed with funds from University, Institute, National Science Foundation RANN program, Office of Naval Research and Delmarva Power and Light Co.
Solar collector	Size 800 ft^2, tilt 45° Combined solar electric and thermal collector, consisting of 25 4' x 8' panels installed on roof. It is intended in time that all 25 panels will incorporate solar electric cells, but so far only one panel is so equipped, and the remainder are conventional flat-plate thermal collectors with double sheet plexiglas covers. The single combined electric and thermal panel incorporates CdS/Cu_2S thin-film solar cells acting simultaneously to generate electricity and to absorb heat from solar radiation. Heat is picked up from the back of the cells, using air as the transfer medium. The cells are covered by two plexiglas sheets with a separating air space. Total conversion efficiency of the collector is 50% (5% conversion to electricity, 45% to thermal energy). Six additional flat-plate thermal collectors are to be installed on the south wall at a later date.
Thermal energy storage	Latent heat, in eutectic salt storage reservoirs. A base reservoir (200,000 Btu capacity) contains salts with melting point near 75°F. A secondary reservoir of approx. 200 ft^3 (1,000,000 Btu capacity) contains two eutectics with melting points near 50°F and 120°F, in alternating containers, for use in cooling and heating modes respectively. A heat pump operates between the two reservoirs.
Loops	Collector to storage : air Storage to space: air
Electrical power storage	Lead-acid batteries with capacity of about 20 kWh. Most circuits in the house use DC, and there is an inverter to provide AC for selected loads.
Latitude	40°N Heating degree days 4,750
Cost of installation	The total cost of the project is around $130,000, of which roughly $40,000 is attributable to the house itself. The present cost of CdS/Cu_2S cells produced individually

University of Delaware
Solar One: view of
south side of house with
collector surfaces on
roof. The spaces
between the windows
will allow room for the
future installation of
additional vertical
thermal collectors.

Schematic section of
Solar One, adapted from
K.W. Böer, 'The Solar
House and its Portent',
Chemtech July 1973
p.397 fig.3

1. Base heat reservoir
   at 75°F
2. Heat pump
3. Secondary heat
   reservoir at 120°F
   or 50°F, with heat
   exchanger
4. Auxiliary heater
5. Battery
6. DC to AC inverter
7. Socket outlets
8. Fan
9. Range
10. Light
11. Heater

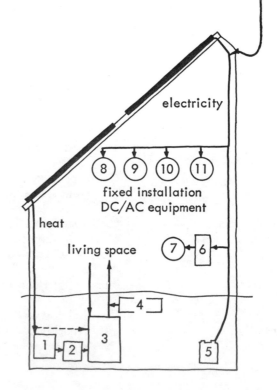

in the laboratory is very high. Böer quotes figures however to suggest that future mass production costs might be of the order of $1/ft^2. Total costs for combined solar electric/ thermal collector panels would on this assumption work out at $2.25/ft^2; that is $1,800 for the 800 ft^2 array on Solar One. Thermal storage (in mass production) would cost $900. Allowance must also be made for the cost of battery storage, auxiliary heater and other equipment. On this basis Böer calculates that the total cost of the solar electric/ thermal system exceeds that of a conventional system by about $3,000.

Cost in operation

Böer obtains an estimated figure of $360/year for the resulting cost of energy, allowing for interest rates, amortization, maintenance and insurance. Assuming the system to produce 80 million Btus and 24 kWh of electric energy, the unit prices would be $1.50/million Btus and 2.7c/kWh. If the power utilities were to be servicing the system, the annual cost would rise to $480/ year, and the unit costs of energy to $2/million Btus and 3.7c/ kWh - energy costs at a level which it is conceivable may be reached generally in the late '70s.

Remarks

The house is the first to combine solar electric and thermal systems, and the first building to use solar electric cells. It is designed to derive 80% of total power requirements from the sun. When the solar electric system is fully installed, it will not provide for the complete electrical power needs of the house. But it will allow the shifting of the use of auxiliary electric power from the mains supply, to off-peak periods, thus - if numbers of similar houses are built - helping to flatten the curves of overall demand on the utility companies. The incorporation of thermal storage capacity in the house designed for storage of 'coolness' in summer operation, also allows air-conditioning equipment to be run at night, so contributing further to the evening out of electrical power demand. (Some cooling effect is obtained by radiation to the night sky from the collectors.) On occasions when electrical power is produced at such a house in excess of requirements and in excess of storage capacity, it may be transmitted to the utility company and the house-holder credited appropriately; thus a network of such houses would provide effective extra generating capacity for the power company. The batteries in the house will only be discharged to a certain minimum level, which not only gives longer battery life, but also provides an emergency power supply at all times in the event of mains failure.
A program of testing and evaluation of the house is under way. In the first year of experimentation the occupation of the house will be simulated. In later years the house will be occupied by university guests, and the second storey, presently given over to measuring equipment, will be converted to additional bedrooms.

Description in   K.W. Böer, 'The Solar House and its Portent', Chemtech
                        July 1973 pp.394-9.
                        K.W. Böer, A Description of the Energy Conversion System
                        of the University of Delaware Solar House, Institute of
                        Energy Conversion University of Delaware, July 20 1973
                        K.W. Böer, A Solar House System Providing Supplemental
                        Energy for Consumers and Peak-Shaving with Power-on-
                        Demand Capability for Utilities, Publication No. 166,
                        Institute of Energy Conversion, University of Delaware,
                        n.d.

Yanagimachi Solar Houses I and II

I.   Tokyo, Japan
II.   Funabashi City, Japan
Both houses incorporated solar heating and cooling, with water as heat transfer and storage medium, and the use of heat pumps. The second house is described below:

House No. II
Two storeys, usable area 2,460 ft^2

Solar collector	Size 1,410 ft^2, tilt 15° Collector is on roof, consists of blackened corrugated aluminum sheet, unglazed, and includes an area for domestic water heating.
Thermal energy storage	Sensible heat, in 9,600 gal. and 2,700 gal. water tanks, made of concrete, in basement
Loops	Collector to storage : water at 55°-80°F Storage to space : water (in ceiling panels)
Latitude	36°N Heating degree days 3,800
Heating performance	70 - 75% of space heating from sun. Collects better than 22% of insolation. A 3 hp motor operates a heat pump for auxiliary heating (and cooling)
Cooling performance	Uses same system as for heating. Water runs in the roof corrugations, which radiate heat at night
Remarks	The heat pump operates between the two water tanks, the cold side being preheated by the sun
Description	(of House No. I) in M. Yanagimachi, 'How to Combine Solar Energy, Nocturnal Radiation Cooling, Radiant Panel Systems of Heating and Cooling, and Heat Pump to Make a Complete Year Round Air-Conditioning System', Transactions of the Conference on the Use of Solar Energy: The Scientific Basis, University of Arizona Press, Tucson 1958 Vol. 3 pp. 21-31 (of House No. II) in Yanagimachi, 'Report on Two and One-half Years Experimental Living in Yanagimachi Solar House II', United Nations Department of Economic and Social Affairs, New Sources of Energy and Energy Development (Proceedings of U.N. Conference on New Sources of Energy, Rome 1961), United Nations, New York 1964 E35-S94

Solar Heated Laboratory, Japan

Nagoya, Japan
Usable area 880 ft^2

Solar collector	Size 300 ft^2, tilt 35° Collector consisted of expanded tubes in corrugated sheet aluminum, with no glass cover
Thermal energy storage	Sensible heat, in two tanks holding 1,480 gal. of water each
Loops	Collector to storage : water at 55° – 80°F Storage to space : air
Heating performance	70–75% of space heat from the sun. Collected better than 22% of insolation
Cooling performance	Used same system as for heating, with water running in roof corrugations which radiate heat at night
Remarks	3 hp heat pump operated between the two water tanks, the cold side being preheated by the sun. Building is now abandoned
Description in	N. Fukuo et al., 'Installations for Solar Space Heating in Gerin', United Nations Department of Economic and Social Affairs, New Sources of Energy and Energy Development (Proceedings of U.N. Conference on New Sources of Energy, Rome 1961), United Nations, New York 1964 E 35 S112

Swedish Solar House, Capri

Isle of Capri, Italy
Swedish laboratory (Stazione Astrofisica Svedese) and house, two storeys, usable area 1,940 ft^2

Solar collector	Size 320 ft^2, vertical Collectors were in the walls, made to look like black windows. They were constructed of metal, one with a plastic cover, the other glass
Thermal energy storage	Sensible heat, in 800 gal. water tank

Loops	Collector to storage : water Storage to space : water (radiators)
Latitude	40°N Heating degree days 2,640
Heating performance	Designed for 50% of space heat from sun. Used auxiliary gas or electric resistance heating
Description in	G.V. Pleijel and B.I. Lindström, 'Stazione Astrofisica Svedese – A Swedish Solar-Heated House at Capri', United Nations Department of Economic and Social Affairs, New Sources of Energy and Energy Development (Proceedings of U.N. Conference on New Sources of Energy, Rome 1961), United Nations, New York 1964 E 35–S49

Brisbane Solar House

Brisbane, Australia
Experimental house operated by Research Committee on Solar Energy and Tropical Housing, University of Queensland, Australia, air-conditioned area 1,318 ft^2

Solar collector	Design allowed for 1,024 ft^2, on roof, made up of 16 sections 16' x 4'. Only one of these sections (64 ft^2) was made and installed. The hot water output of this section of collector was mixed with other water preheated by electricity, to simulate the larger collector area
Thermal energy storage	Sensible heat, first of 70 gal. water tank, later in 30 tons of $\frac{3}{4}$" gravel
Loops	Collector to storage : water Storage to space : air, up to 1,500 cfm
Cooling performance	House air-conditioned with lithium bromide/water absorption 3 ton air conditioner receiving heat supply from collectors
Reported in	N.R. Sheridan and W.H. Carr, A Solar Air Conditioned House in Brisbane, Solar Research Notes No. 2, University of Queensland 1967
	N.R. Sheridan, 'Performance of the Brisbane Solar House', Solar Energy 1972 Vol. 13 pp.395–401

Trombe/Michel Solar Wall, and Michel Solar Houses

The French solar scientist Prof. F. Trombe has developed a design of 'solar wall' for space heating, the principles of which have been applied in three houses built by the architect Jacques Michel. Of these the first two prototypes were built neat Montlouis in the Pyrenees (latitude 43°N). One, at Odeillo, is described in detail below. The third was completed in 1971 at Chauvency-le-Chateau in the Meuse district (latitude 49°N).

Solar collector and thermal storage

The system consists essentially of a combined solar collector and heat storage unit in the form of a massive concrete south wall, painted black on the outer face and covered with one or more glass sheets. Air from the house is admitted into the space between wall and glass cover via low level openings, and circulates up through the collector and back to the space via a second set of openings at the top, by natural convection. The lower duct openings are somewhat above the bottom of the collector, so that early in the morning and on cloudy days a reverse cycle cannot take place, and instead cool air sinks and is trapped. In summer the hot air in the collector is vented to the outside at the top of the wall, which thus acts as a thermal chimney, sucking air from the house through the lower openings and providing a cooling effect by forced ventilation.

Heating performance

According to Michel, at the Montlouis latitude and for a well-insulated structure, one square metre of solar wall is sufficient to heat ten cubic metres of internal space. At the winter solstice, the wall receives 7 kWh/m^2/day; and 1.7 kWh/m^2/day at the summer solstice. The two prototype houses in the Pyrenees had walls of 35 cm thickness, and drew half to three quarters of their winter heating requirement from the sun, with outdoor temperatures going below freezing. The remainder was supplied by electric heating.

Remarks

The house at Chauvency-le-Chateau has a usable area of 106 m^2 and the area of the solar wall is 45 m^2. Michel has also published plans for a circular solar house. In 1973 he exhibited designs for a steel prefabrication system for housing, based on a 3.6 m square grid, and incorporating solar walls on the south and on parts of the east and west faces of the component square units. This system is scheduled to go into production shortly.

Michel Solar House

1970	Odeillo, France Single storey, usable area 75 m^2
Solar collector	Size 48 m^2, vertical Collector comprises 12m x 4.9m south wall, with exception of 4m x 2.7m door opening. Two glass panes and air space in front of black painted concrete storage block
Thermal energy storage	Sensible heat in 35 cm thick concrete wall behind entire collector, insulated on internal face. Capacity 40,000 Btu/$^\circ$F
Loops	Collector to storage : none Storage to space: air
Latitude	43°N

Descriptions in	Jacques Michel, 'Chauffage par Rayonnement Solaire', Architecture d'Aujourdhui No. 167 pp.88-93 'Le Soleil - Source Permanente de Confort', L'Usine Nouvelle No. 26, June 29 1972 (Solar wall principle) F. Trombe, A Le Phat Vinh and Mme Le Phat Vinh, 'Etude sur le Chauffage des Habitations par Utilisations du Rayonnement Solaire', Revue Generale de Thermique Vol IV, No. 48, December 1965

Diagrammatic section to show principles of Trombe-Michel solar wall

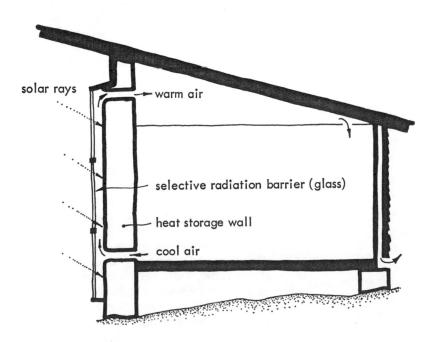

solar rays

warm air

selective radiation barrier (glass)

heat storage wall

cool air

St George's County Secondary School

1961

Wallasey, Cheshire, England
Classroom, science laboratory and gymnasium blocks
Architect and heating system designer Emslie Morgan

This building has already been described in the chapter
on energy conservation (pp. 35-6). According to a
legalistic definition it might not perhaps qualify as a
truly solar heated structure, since it has no special-
purpose heat storage reservoir, but instead stores heat
in the substantial thermal mass of its heavy brick and
concrete construction (covered, on the roof and north
wall, with 5" of external expanded polystyrene insulation).
It has frequently been referred to in the context of solar
heating systems however, and for that reason if no other
deserves inclusion here.

Sources of
heat

The building's heat comes in fact from three sources;
heat of lights, heat produced by the occupants and from
the large south-facing solar wall. Of these solar heat,
in the majority of conditions, appears to be the most
significant contributor. Some doubting critics have in
the past questioned whether the contribution of solar
energy was at all important; and because of the contribution
of heat of lights, have persisted in regarding it as an electrically
heated building. According to a study group from the
Liverpool Department of Building Science under Dr. G.M.
Davies, however, 'the mean solar gain over one day might
reach $120W/m^2$ (compared to a mean occupancy gain of
$21.5W/m^2$ and mean winter lighting gain of $38W/m^2$).
This is of course an extreme value. In cloudless conditions
in winter it is reduced to nearly half and cloud cover of
sufficient density could reduce the solar gain to virtually
zero.' There is no auxiliary back-up heating. (Though
a hot water radiator system was originally installed, it has
since been removed.)

Solar wall

The vertical solar wall measures 230' x 27' and consists of
two glass skins, the outer clear, the inner largely obscured
glass, separated by a 2' air space. For the most part the
wall acts to admit solar radiation direct, and thus functions
somewhat like the 'solar houses' of Hutchinson, Keck and
others. In parts the inner skin is clear glass however, and
is backed with black-painted opaque panels, the whole
acting therefore as a series of flat-plate collectors. In
summer the backing panels may be covered with hinged
shutters, originally with a polished aluminum surface and
now painted white, so as to reflect rather than absorb
radiation. In other sections the inner glass skin of the
wall is replaced by black-painted masonry. These areas

St. George's School,
Wallasey: general
view of the solar wall

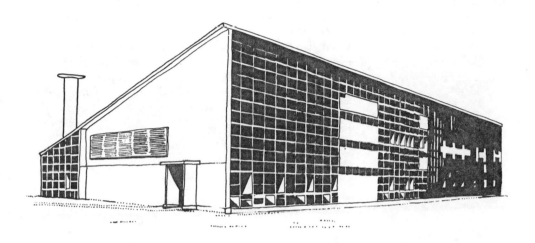

St. George's School,
diagrammatic section.
From R. Banham, The
Architecture of the
Well-tempered Environ-
ment, Architectural
Press, London 1969
p.283

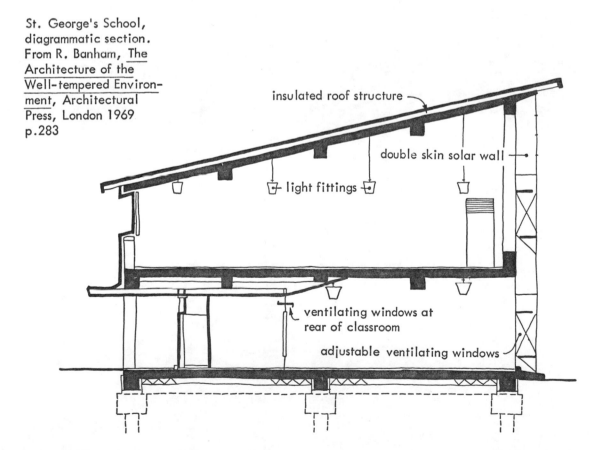

insulated roof structure

double skin solar wall

light fittings

ventilating windows at
rear of classroom

adjustable ventilating windows

act similarly as collector surfaces. The absorption of
heat in summer is controlled in the same way with the use
of white-painted shutters. One disadvantageous feature
of the very large glazed area of the solar wall is the
resulting heat loss by conduction in winter and at night.

Latitude   53°N

Description in   G.M. Davies, 'Model Studies of St. George's School
                  Wallasey', Journal of the IHVE July 1971, Vol. 39
                  pp. 77-80
                  G.M. Davies, N.S. Sturrock and A.C. Benson, 'Some
                  Results of Measurements in St. George's School Wallasey',
                  Journal of the IHVE July 1971, Vol. 39 pp. 80-4
                  see also Reyner Banham, The Architecture of the Well-
                  Tempered Environment, Architectural Press, London 1969
                  pp. 280-3

Projects and published schemes for solar buildings

The following is an annotated list of unbuilt schemes for
solar powered buildings, including some details of current
proposals. It is difficult to define what should qualify
precisely as a 'proposal', since clearly almost anyone anywhere
might decide idly to put up a solar building, with a very
variable probability of the project ever actually coming to
fruition. I have tried to include here only projects of a fairly
firm character which seem to have a good chance of getting
off the drawing board, or else which have some intrinsic interest
to their design. In the nature of such a list it must be very
fragmentary, and is biased presumably towards the inclusion of
those schemes which have received the greatest advance publicity.

America

GSA Test
Building,
Manchester N.H.

Engineering consultants Dubin-Mindell-Bloome Associates of
New York, together with Professor E. M. Barber of Yale
University, have carried out a feasibility study for a solar heating
and cooling system for the General Services Administration's
planned energy conservation test building to be built in Manchester,
New Hampshire. The overall building area is to be 126,000 ft^2,
assumed for the purposes of the study to be disposed on seven floors,
with a 15,000 ft^2 solar collector on the roof supplying the heating
and cooling requirements of three floors. The collector design is
of saw-tooth configuration to reduce wind-loads and construction
costs. The shape also constitutes a wind barrier, cutting down heat
losses from the collector surfaces. The light-coloured roof areas
on the north-facing slopes of the saw teeth act as reflectors.

Calculations of performance were made for various angles of collector
tilt from 57° to 35°. The collector design comprises a rolled bond
collector sheet with selective surface, two sheets of glass cover and
4" of polyurethane insulation backing. Heat storage is as sensible
heat in water tanks, sized for $1\frac{1}{2}$ winter days' supply. Fred Dubin
writes: 'Two modes of heating have been considered. In the first,
water from storage tanks is circulated through coils in air handling
units serving the building interior and each individual perimeter
area. In the second, hot water from the storage tank supplies a
closed water loop which serves as a heat source for heat pumps located
to serve perimeter zones in the building. The heat pumps chill the
water in the loop and utilize their heat of compression to warm the
air which is supplied to the occupied space. The second heating
mode employs much lower water temperatures (50° to 70° instead of
120° to 180°). The collector efficiency is increased, or can be
reduced in size when used to service heat pumps. For space
cooling, a heat-activated refrigeration system was selected. The

water heated by the solar collector to 210° to 220°F is circulated to absorption refrigeration units which generate chilled water for air conditioning.' The GSA building system would require for three floors approximately 65 tons of refrigeration operating at 210°F. The exhaust and jacket water heat is recovered from an engine-driven generator powering a central heat pump, and used for absorption units, space heating and domestic hot water. Any auxiliary heating needed beyond that supplied by the solar system and recovered waste heat, is provided by a small gas-fired boiler.

Dubin estimates that about 65% of the annual energy required for heating the three floors, and about 90% of the energy required for cooling from May to September, could be supplied from the sun, at a life-cycle cost 20% higher at current prices than gas heating and electric compression cooling, and 25% lower than all-electric heating and cooling. This assumes an equipment life of 30 years, a 7% interest rate, and a cost for the solar collector of $4.00/ft^2, with an additional $1.25 per ft^2 of collector for the cost of storage, pumps and other equipment. (Reported in F.S. Dubin, 'GSA's Energy Conservation Test Building - A Report', Actual Specifying Engineer August 1973 pp. 84-92).

New York
Botanical
Gardens

A 30,000 ft^2 solar powered office and laboratory building is to be erected at the Cary Arboretum of the New York Botanical Gardens in Millbrook, New York. Solar energy will be used for space heating, cooling and water heating. The architect is Malcolm Wells and the engineers are Dubin-Mindell-Bloome.

GSA Post Office,
Saginaw, Mich.

The General Services Administration plan a post office of 53,000 ft^2 in Saginaw, Michigan with solar collectors as heat sources for heat pumps.

NASA Langley
Center,
Hampton, Va.

The National Aeronautics and Space Administration plan to equip a system office building at their Langley Center with a solar energy system for heating and cooling.

Grumman Corp.,
Bethpage, L.I.

At Bethpage, Long Island, the Grumman Aerospace Corporation is considering the installation of a solar collector on the roof of one of their existing 200,000 ft^2 buildings. Dubin-Mindell-Bloome Associates are the engineering consultants on an energy conservation program for Grumman.

Massachusetts
Audubon
Society

The Massachusetts Audubon Society is to build an addition to their present headquarters in Lincoln, Mass. which will use solar energy for space heating and cooling. The building will comprise 8,000 ft^2 of office, lecture hall and library accommodation, and will cost $75,000. The system designer is Dr. P.E. Glaser of Arthur D. Little Inc., otherwise known for his orbiting satellite solar power station proposal. The building will have a 45° collector on the roof, using water as the heat transfer medium. Heat storage will take the form of a water tank with capacity sufficient to carry over three cloudy days at a maximum. It is planned that from 60 to 85% of the energy required for heating and air-conditioning should be supplied by the sun. (Reported by John C. Devlin, 'Energy from Sun will Heat and Cool an Office Building', New York Times August 12 1973)

Condominium, East Warren, Vt.

Harry Thomason reports (in Solar Houses and Solar House Models, Edmund Scientific Co., Barrington N.J. 1972) that architectural students from the University of Pennsylvania are building a solar heated condominium for five families in Warren, Vermont, using the Thomason 'Solaris' system.

Grassy Brook Village

A ten-unit condominium project in Brookline, Vermont will use solar energy for space heating and domestic water heating. The developer is Richard Blazej, the architects People/Space Co. of Boston, and the engineers Dubin-Mindell-Bloome.

Fort Worth/Dallas Apartments

Professor H.A. Blum of the Department of Aerospace and Mechanical Engineering at Southern Methodist University in Dallas, has put forward proposals for a solar-powered 100-apartment complex to be built in the Fort Worth /Dallas area.

Sun Mountain Design

Hermann G. Barkmann of Sun Mountain Design is reported as planning a solar-heated housing project in Santa Fe, New Mexico.

Mrs. A.N. Wilson House, Shanghai, West Virginia

The architectural firm of Burt, Hill and Associates, of Butler, Pennsylvania, is responsible for the design of a house to be built for Mrs. A.N. Wilson at Shanghai, West Virginia, six miles southwest of Martinsburg. The plan form of the house itself is roughly square, with a deep 45° double-pitched roof; it is connected to a separate garage structure through a linking greenhouse. There is 1,400 ft^2 of living area in the house, and 350 ft^2 of space for mechanical equipment. The solar collector is 588 ft^2 in area, and made up of a series of modular 32" x 96" aluminum pan units. The bottom of the pans are lined with 2" of fibreglass insulation, over which is laid aluminum sheet and aluminum tubing, all black-painted, a double layer of Mylar film and a top cover of glass. The heat transfer medium from collector to storage is a 50% ethylene glycol solution.

Heat storage is in two water tanks beneath the house, with capacities of 2,400 gal. and 400 gal. The operating temperature range of the larger tank is 90°F to 130°F, and the heat storage capacity 768,000 Btus. The smaller 400 gal. tank can be heated either by the collector, or else during the winter with an auxiliary 84,000 BtuH oil-fired heater; it is used for heating the domestic water supply and for standby space heating capacity when the temperature of the large tank falls below 90°F. Its working temperature range is 130°F to 150°F and its heat capacity 192,000 Btus. A forced air distribution system is used to heat the house. It is anticipated that in early May and late September the large storage tank may reach capacity, in which case heat from the solar collector is dumped to the smaller tank. In summer the collector will be used to maintain the temperature of the small tank only, for domestic water heating and occasional space heating use.

Provisions have been made in the design for an absorption air conditioner, using the 400 gal. water tank as a heat source. The tank temperature would be boosted to 180°F, using the auxiliary heater if necessary. In this arrangement the 2,400 gal. tank would be used as an evaporator and for 'coolness' storage. A photovoltaic conversion system for generating electricity from the sun has also been mentioned as a possibility.

Heat losses from the windows of the house will be controlled by means of a technique of triple glazing, whereby a standard double pane is used on the exterior, separated by a three foot air gap from a single openable pane on the interior. The space within the glazing is to be used for house plants. The greenhouse linking the house proper to the garage acts as an airlock to the main outside door. A large central wood burning fireplace and chimney provide an additional source of supplementary heat. (Description in Burt, Hill and Associates, The Technological and Economic Feasibility of Solar Assisted Heating and Cooling Systems, Butler, Pennsylvania, August 1973)

Schematic of solar system for Mrs A.N. Wilson House, from Burt Hill and Associates, The Technological and Economic Feasibility of Solar Assisted Heating and Cooling Systems, Butler, Pa. 1973

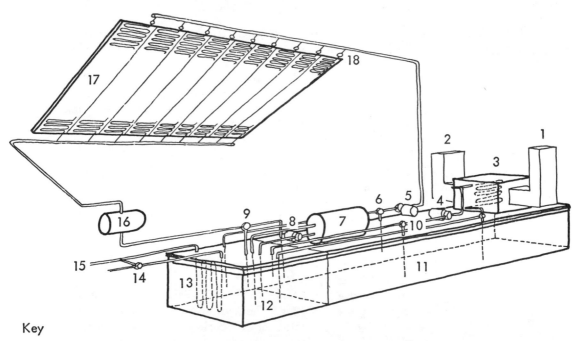

Key

1. Return air (70°)
2. Supply air, 85° min – 125° max
3. Fan-coil unit, 660 – 1600 cfm
4. Fan-coil circ. pump, 4 gpm
5. Solar collector circ. pump, 12 gpm
6. Season changeover 3 way valve, manual
7. Auxiliary heater, 84,000 Btu output
8. Auxiliary heater circ. pump
9. Season changeover 3 way valve, manual
10. Suction selection valve – 90° min
11. 2400 gal storage tank, 90° – 130°
12. 400 gal storage tank, 135° – 150°
13. Domestic hot water immersion coil
14. Domestic hot water tempering valve
15. Cold water inlet
16. Expansion tank and collector receiver
17. Solar collector modules
18. Balancing valves

Meinel house, Tucson	Aden and Marjorie Meinel, founders of Helio Associates Inc., and authors of a 'solar farm' proposal for generating power from the sun on a commercial scale with focussing collectors and steam turbines, have installed an 8' x 32' solar collector at their own home in Tucson, Arizona, which is presently used for heating their swimming pool, and is planned to be used later for space heating purposes. The collector is of a type referred to by the Meinels as 'planar' (not flat-plate). It is of double-cusp section, lined with reflective material, and reflects radiation both direct and diffuse, from the sun and from a large part of the sky, onto a black plastic absorber pipe at the apex of the cusps.
Chahroudi 'Biosphere'	Day Chahroudi has published details of a 'Biosphere' house (broadsheet published by Biotechnic Press, Albuquerque, April 1973), with a 40° tilt collector (for central U.S. latitudes) and movable external insulation. This insulation might consist of hinged foam plastic shutters faced with aluminum sheet, along similar lines to the Baer house; or else would employ the Zomeworks 'Beadwall' principle (see p. 30). Several forms of heat storage are mentioned, both sensible and latent.

Yale University engineering professor Everett Barber is building a solar house for himself in Connecticut (architect, Charles Moore).

Notes on developments during 1974 appear on p. 170

Europe and elsewhere

Safwat/Souka house, Giza, Egypt	H.H. Safwat and A.F. Souka have presented plans for a 2,500 ft^2 house at latitude 30°N in Giza, Egypt ('Design of a New Solar-Heated House Using Double-Exposure Flat-Plate Collectors', Technical Note, Solar Energy Vol. 13 1970 pp. 105-119). One novel feature of this house is the design of double-sided collectors with reflectors, a series of which are to be arranged in parallel rows on the flat roof. Heat storage is in a water tank, with auxiliary electric immersion heating; and hot water is pumped through under-floor panels to heat the space of the house itself.
Gupta/Chopra solar heater	A simple solar powered storage heater intended for use in high altitude conditions (where winter skies are clear but temperatures are low) has been developed by J.P. Gupta and R.K. Chopra at the Defence Laboratory, Jodhpur, India. It consists of a flat-plate collector at the side of the building, connected to a tall thin water tank inside the space, which acts as a storage radiator. Thermo-siphon action circulates the water (with added anti-freeze) from the bottom of the radiator tank to the bottom of the collector, and back from the top of the collector to the top of the radiator again.
Ganneskov house Copenhagen	The engineer Svend Ganneskov is working on a solar heated house in Copenhagen. The house area is 163 m^2. Heat storage is in two

large concrete tanks of water, of capacity 100 m^3, one of which will be used in addition as an indoor swimming pool. Heat is extracted from the storage both by circulated hot water, and by means of a water to air heat pump system. Further heat storage is provided in two bins of stones with heating pipes embedded. Ganneskov expects to cover two thirds of the heating demand with the solar system, and to provide the remainder with supplementary electrical heating. By late 1973 construction of the house had got to the point of completion of foundations, basement and heat storage tanks.

Developments in France of the Trombe-Michel solar wall

Proposed future developments of the Trombe-Michel solar wall system in France have already been referred to. A group of architects in Marseilles (Architectes DPLG, Group ABC Marseille-Luminy) have published plans for housing developments incorporating Trombe type south-facing solar walls in concrete, covered by movable shutters (J.L. Izard and J.P. Long, 'Habitation Economique Utilisant Le Flux de Chaleur Resultant de l'Absorption du Rayonnement Solaire', (Paris) Eh 30). Plans have also been published by D. Chanson and P. Claux ('Recherches sur un Habitat Collectif et en Terrasses Climatisé Grace a l'Utilisation Rationnelle de l'Energie Solaire', (Paris) Eh 74), for multi-story terraced apartment buildings at a ski resort in the Alps, which will again make use of the Trombe solar wall principle.

BRAD Community, Wales

It was at one time proposed that a solar wall of the Trombe-Michel type be built into the south-west side of a house being converted and extended at Janine and Robin Clarke's Biotechnic Research and Development (BRAD) Community near Church Stoke, Montgomeryshire, Wales (following similar earlier experiments in Brittany). The collector was to have been in two panels, each of 18 m^2, with a storage wall thickness of 60 cm and a double pane glass cover at a distance of 15 cm from the wall. (Reported in R.J.D. Vale, Services for an Autonomous Research Community in Wales, Working Paper 5, University of Cambridge Department of Architecture, Technical Research Division, June 1973). Vale estimates that a 36 m^2 wall at the site in question would receive approximately 6,000 kWh over the heating season. With an assumed efficiency of 40% this would yield 2,400 kWh of usable energy.

Low Impact Design, Cornwall, England

The architectural collective Low Impact Design of Wadebridge, Cornwall, England is producing plans for a solar heated boys' school to be built in the Andorran Pyrenees.

Vale Autonomous House

Brenda Vale has published plans for a house designed to be independent of all mains services, and suitable to be built in the area of Cambridge, England. The house is on two storeys with an elongated rectangular plan aligned east and west, a monopitch roof facing south with solar collector incorporated, and a conservatory along the whole length of the south wall. The tilt of the roof/collector surface is 30°, and its area 115·5 m^2. The collector is constructed from black-painted corrugated aluminum sheets on a timber sub-structure, covered by two sheets of corrugated PVC, held apart by spacer bars. There is 15 cm of expanded polystyrene insulation backing. Water is trickled down the corrugations in the metal sheeting from a perforated gutter at ridge level, and collected at the lower edge in a second gutter, whence it is pumped to a 3,000 litre storage tank. The heated water is used largely for the domestic supply, and the temperature is held to a maximum of 50°C, while any excess heat is transferred via a hot air fan-driven heat exchanger to a bed of wet sand (volume 18 m^3) used as additional heat storage capacity, beneath the floor of the house. The sand is also heated with embedded electrical resistance heating coils, using electricity generated by a windmill. There is a small electric booster heater for the domestic hot water supply, again using wind-generated electrical power. Some space heating is achieved by virtue of air being warmed in the conservatory, and by solar heat gain as a result of radiation passing right through to the glazed back wall of the conservatory and into the body of the house itself. Heat losses from the house are reduced by covering the windows with polystyrene shutters at night. (Description in B. Vale, The Autonomous House, part of dissertation submitted for 5th Year Diploma in Architecture, University of Cambridge 1972)

A group of students at Brunel University in London are planning to build a somewhat enlarged version of the Vale House, and have been allocated a site in the University for the purpose.

Crouch Autonomous House

G. Crouch has designed a comparable autonomously serviced house, also for a Cambridge, England site, whose general arrangement has affinities with the Thomason House No.4. It is and A-frame structure containing two floors, total area 94 m^2. The solar collector covers the entire south wall, and has an area of 90 m^2 with a tilt of 60°. The collector is constructed from a series of black chlorinated PVC water trays, covered by sealed double glazing units and backed with 16 cm of glass fibre insulation. Water is pumped to a perforated pipe at the ridge of the roof, and trickled down the collector surface to a collection pipe at the bottom edge, in a manner similar to the Vale (and Thomason) designs. Heat storage is in a shallow water tank beneath the floor of the house. (Description in G. Crouch, The Autonomous Servicing of Dwellings - Design Proposals, part of dissertation submitted for 5th Year Diploma in Architecture, University of Cambridge 1972)

Technical Research Division, Cambridge University Department of Architecture

A house which is entirely independent of centralised network services is planned by the Autonomous Housing Study at the University of Cambridge Department of Architecture's Technical Research Division. The project is under the direction of Alexander Pike, and the house is to be built on land owned by the University, in Cambridge. Solar water and space heating will be incorporated, as well as means of exploiting direct solar gain where this is desirable. A variety of possible designs and system configurations are under study.

Note added October 1974. If my list of existing solar buildings has become out of date during 1974 since the time of writing, then this list of projects is also in need of some revision – although in fact most of the proposals described here remain still in the planning or construction stages.

The GSA office building in Manchester, New Hampshire is expected to be built by 1976. The collector area is now planned to be 6,000 ft^2, and heat storage will be in three water tanks totalling 30,000 gal. capacity.

The Cary Arboretum building in Millbrook, New York is scheduled to start construction in late 1974. The solar collector will be in seven elongated panels on a horizontal roof, totalling 5,000 ft^2 in area. Heat pumps will be used.

The engineering building for NASA's Langley Center at Hampton, Virginia will have a collector area of 15,000 ft^2. Installation is scheduled for 1975.

The Dimetrodon Condominium in East Warren, Vermont, using Thomason-type roof collectors, will be completed in 1975.

The plans for Grassy Brook Village have been somewhat revised, and new details and drawings are given on pp. 271 and 272. Construction was under way in 1974 and completion is expected in 1975.

The Wilson house in Shanghai, West Virginia, will be completed in 1975. The same architects, Burt, Hill and Associates, are currently designing a 10,000 ft^2 collector array and 100 ton solar air-conditioning system for an elementary school in Atlanta, Ga.

The Meinel house in Tucson is now solar heated (see p. 120).

E.M. Barber is to build a house, for himself, starting 1974, in Guilford, Connecticut (architects Charles W. Moore Associates), with 450 ft^2 of collector set at 57°, and heat storage in a tank in the main space of the house.

E.A. Farber and others are consulting on the design of a solar heating system for a house at Land o' Lakes in Florida.

In England an experimental solar heating system is to be installed in a house of standard design at the new city of Milton Keynes. The collector will be 40 m^2, at a 30° tilt, with heat storage in a 5 m^3 water tank. Reported in S.V. Szokolay, 'Design of an Experimental Solar Heated House at Milton Keynes', International Solar Energy Society, UK Section, Conference on Low Temperature Thermal Collection of Solar Energy in the UK, Polytechnic of Central London April 1974, paper 3.

Solar energy bibliography

Many of the important papers in the literature of solar energy have been contributions to the various solar energy conferences and symposia which have taken place since 1950, and are published in the transactions or proceedings of those conferences. To sort out which of these proceedings and symposia are which is sometimes tricky, and so a chronological listing of both meetings and publications is presented here. To avoid repetition in the bibliography proper, abbreviations are used (in brackets) to indicate which volume of proceedings any individual paper is published in.

Journals

Two journals are entirely devoted to the subject of solar energy. The Journal of Solar Energy Science and Engineering was first published in 1957 by the Association for Applied Solar Energy in Phoenix, Arizona. The title of the journal was changed to Solar Energy in 1958. It is currently published by Pergamon, Oxford. Applied Solar Energy is an English translation of a Russian journal, published in America by Allerton Press Inc.

Coverage

Because of the very extensive nature of the literature of solar energy, this bibliography does not attempt to cover the following subjects: solar distillation, focussing collectors, industrial and commercial solar power applications, selective surfaces, solar engines, thermoelectric and thermoionic conversion. The concentration is on solar heating and cooling of buildings, and heat storage methods for these purposes; with a somewhat restricted coverage of solar water heating and photovoltaic conversion.

Dates of conferences, and abbreviations

Full bibliographical details of proceedings or transactions of conferences or symposia, with dates of publication, are as follows:

(MIT) 1950

R. Hamilton, ed., Space Heating with Solar Energy, M.I.T. Press 1954; proceedings of Space Heating Symposium held at Massachusetts Institute of Technology under auspices of Space Heating Committee, Cabot Solar Energy Research program, August 20–26 1950

1951

'Sun in the Service of Man', American Academy of Arts and Sciences, Vol.79, 1951 pp.181–326

1953

W.C. MacNevin, 'The Trapping of Solar Energy', Ohio Journal of Science, Vol.53 No.5, 1953, pp.257–319; report of Symposium sponsored by Ohio Academy of Sciences

(Solar Energy Research) 1953

F. Daniels and J.A. Duffie, eds., Solar Energy Research, University of Wisconsin Press, Madison 1955; also Thames and Hudson, London 1955; report of NSF-sponsored Symposium at University of Wisconsin 1953

(New Delhi) 1954

Wind Power and Solar Energy: Proceedings of the New Delhi Symposium, UNESCO, Paris 1956

(Phoenix) 1955

Proceedings of the World Symposium on Applied Solar Energy, Phoenix, Arizona 1955, Stanford Research Institute, Menlo Park, California 1956

(Scientific Basis) 1955	Transactions of the Conference on the Use of Solar Energy: The Scientific Basis, University of Arizona Press, Tucson 1958
1958	J.H. Fisher, An Analysis of Solar Energy Utilization, WADC Technical Report 59-17, Vols 1 and 2, Wright Air Development Center, ASTIA Document No.AD 214611, 1959; report of a conference held in Los Angeles, 1958
(Mont-Louis) 1958	Applications Thermiques de l'Energie Solaire dans le Domaine de la Recherche et de l'Industrie, Centre National de la Recherche Scientifique, Paris 1961; report of a Symposium held at Mont-Louis, France, 1958
1961	'Research Frontiers in the Utilization of Solar Energy', Proceedings of the National Academy of Science, Vol.47, 1961, pp.1245-1306; also special issue of Solar Energy, Vol.5, Sept.1961; report of a Symposium held in April 1961
(UN: Rome) 1961	United Nations Department of Economic and Social Affairs, New Sources of Energy and Energy Development, United Nations, New York 1964; proceedings of U.N. Conference on New Sources of Energy, Rome 1961
(Sounion) 1961	A.G. Spanides and A.D. Hatzikakidis, Solar and Aeolian Energy, Plenum Press, New York 1964; Proceedings of Advanced Study Institute for Solar and Aeolian Energy, Sounion, Greece, Greek Atomic Energy Commission and the Hellenic Scientific Society of Solar and Aeolian Energy, 1961
1970	International Solar Energy Conference, Melbourne, Australia, March 1970
1971	International Solar Energy Society Conference, Greenbelt and College Park, Maryland, May 10-14 1971
(Paris) 1973	'The Sun in the Service of Mankind', International Congress sponsored jointly by the International Solar Energy Society, the Coopération Méditerranéenne pour l'Energie Solaire and the Association Française pour l'Etude et le Développement des Applications de l'Energie Solaire, Paris, July 2-6 1973
	Note: proceedings of the 1973 Paris Congress have not been published at the time of writing, but because of the importance of this meeting, the titles of certain relevant papers as announced in the Congress program are listed here, although these may or may not correspond to the papers as given or as published in due course.

C.G. Abbott, The Sun and the Welfare of Man, Smithsonian Institution Series Inc., Vol.2, New York 1929

C.G. Abbott, Solar Radiation as a Power Source, Smithsonian Institution Report 1943

A.E. Al-Hadithi, 'Solar Air Heating for Space Heating' (Paris) B 21

Manfred Altman (principal investigator), Conservation and Better Utilization of Electric Power by means of Thermal Energy Storage and Solar Heating, Phase II Progress Report No. NSF/RANN/SE/GI27976/72/4, University of Pennsylvania Dec.31 1972

Bruce Anderson, Solar Energy and Shelter Design, M.Arch. thesis, Massachusetts Institute of Technology, Department of Architecture 1973

L.B. Anderson, 'Architectural Problems' (MIT)

L.B. Anderson, J.M. Hunter, R.H. Dietz and W.A. Close, 'The Architectural Problems of Solar Collectors, a Round Table Discussion' (Phoenix) pp.201-14

L.B. Anderson, H.C. Hottel and A. Whillier, 'Solar Heating Design Problems' (Solar Energy Research) pp.47-56

S. Andrassy, 'Solar Water Heaters' (UN: Rome) E 35-S96

Architectural Forum, 'Water Cooled Roofs' in issue of June 1946 pp.165-9

Architectural Forum, report on Löf's solar house work at Denver, Colorado in Vol.86, No.2 Feb.1947 p.126

Architectural Record, 'MIT Builds Solar House' in issue of April 1949, Vol.105 No.4 pp.135-138

William F. Arnold, 'Will Solar Cells Shine on Earth?', Electronics May 22 1972

N.G. Ashar and A.R. Reti, 'Engineering and Economic Study of the Use of Solar Energy Especially for Space Cooling in Inida and Pakistan' (UN: Rome) E 35-S37

D. Ashbel, New World Maps of Global Solar Radiation During IGY (International Geo-Physical Year 1957-58), The Hebrew University Department of Climatology and Meteorology, Jerusalem 1961

Association for Applied Solar Energy, Living with the Sun, Phoenix 1958 (AFASE solar house competition designs)

Association for Applied Solar Energy, Dictionary of World Activities and Bibliography of Significant Literature, Phoenix 1959

E. Ayres, 'Power from the Sun', Scientific American Vol.183 No.2, August 1950 pp.16-21

Steve Baer, 'Solar House', Alternative Sources of Energy No.10, March 1973 p.8

V. Baum, A. Karabaev, A. Handurdiev, 'Utilisation de l'Energie Solaire et des Particularités Climatiques dans un Climat Torride et Aride pour la Réfrigération Estivale' (Paris) B 21

W.A. Beckman, G.O.G. Löf, J.A. Duffie, 'Simulation of Solar Air Conditioning' (Paris) B 21

Jerome Belanger, 'How to Use the Sun around Home', Organic Gardening and Farming, Jan. 1972

I. Bennett, 'Monthly Maps of Mean Daily Insolation for the United States', Solar Energy Vol.9 No.3, July-Sept. 1965 pp.145-58

J.N. Black, 'The Distribution of Solar Radiation over the Earth's Surface', Arch. Met. Geoph. Biokl. B. Bd., Vol.7, H.2, 1956 p.165

J.N. Black, 'Some Aspects of the Climatology of Solar Radiation' (UN: Rome) E 35-S13

P.M.S. Blackett et al., 'Utilization of Solar Energy', Research Applied in Industry, Vol.5, 1952 p.527

P. Blanco, 'Solar Energy Availability and Instruments for Measurements' (UN: Rome) E 135-GrS11

R.W. Bliss Jr., 'Design and Performance of the Nation's Only Fully Solar-Heated House', Air Cond. Heat. Vent., Oct.1955

R.W. Bliss Jr., 'The Derivations of Several Plate Efficiency Factors Useful in the Design of Flat-Plate Solar Heat Collectors', Solar Energy, Vol.3 No.4, 1958 pp.55-64

R.W. Bliss Jr., 'Performance of an Experimental System Using Solar Energy for Heating and Night Radiation for Cooling a Building' (UN: Rome) E 35-S30

H.A. Blum, J.M. Estes and E.E. Kerlin, 'Design and Feasibility of Flat Plate Collectors to Operate at 100-150C', Department fo Mechanical Engineering, Southern Methodist University, Dallas, July 1973; 'Feasibility of Practical Flat Plate Solar Collectors at the 250-300F Level' (Paris) B 21

K.W. Böer, 'A Description of the Energy Conversion System of the University of Delaware Solar House', Institute of Energy Conversion, University of Delaware, July 20 1973

K.W. Böer, 'The Solar House and its Portent', Chemtech July 1973 pp.394-400

K.W. Böer, Direct Solar Energy Conversion for Terrestrial Use, Publication No.165, Institute of Energy Conversion, University of Delaware, n.d.

K.W. Böer, A Solar House System Providing Supplemental Energy for Consumers and Peak-Shaving with Power-on-Demand Capability for Utilities, Publication No.166, Institute of Energy Conversion, University of Delaware, n.d.

K. Bogus and S. Mattes, 'High Efficiency Cu_2S-CdS Solar Cells with Improved Stability', Proceedings of the 9th IEEE Photovoltaic Specialists Conference, Silver Spring, Maryland, May 2-4 1972

Brace Research Institute, How to Heat Your Swimming Pool using Solar Energy, Leaflet No. L-3, Brace Research Institute, Quebec, Canada, revised edn. Feb.1973

Brace Research Institute, How to Build a Solar Water Heater, Leaflet No.L-4, Brace Research Institute, Quebec, Canada, revised edn. Feb.1973

David Brand, 'Catching Sunbeams: Old Dream of Putting Sun's Power to Work Gets Renewed Attention', Wall Street Journal, Vol.CLXXXI No.74, 16 April 1973

Franklin M. Branley, Solar Energy, Crowell, New York 1957

F.H. Bridgers, D.D. Paxton and R.W. Haines, 'Performance of a Solar Heated Building', Heating, Piping and Air-Conditioning Vol.27, Nov.1957 p.165

B.J. Brinkworth, Solar Energy for Man, Compton Press, Wiltshire, England 1973

F.A. Brooks, Solar Energy and its Use for Heating Water in California, U.C. Agricultural Experiment Station Bulletin 602, University of California, Berkeley Nov.1936

F.A. Brooks, Use of Solar Energy for Heating Water, Publication 3557, Smithsonian Institution, Washington DC 1939

F.A. Brooks, 'Notes on Spectral Quality and Measurement of Solar Radiation' (Solar Energy Research) pp.19-29

H. Buchberg and J.R. Roulet, 'Simulation and Optimization of Solar Collection and Storage for House Heating', Solar Energy Vol.12, 1968 pp.31-50

E.J. Burda, ed., Applied Solar Energy Research: A Directory of World Activities and Bibliography of Significant Literature, Stanford Research Institute, Menlo Park, California 1955

Burt, Hill and Associates, The Technological and Economic Feasibility of Solar Assisted Heating and Cooling Systems, report prepared for Congressman Mike McCormack, House Energy Sub-Committee of the Committee on Science and Astronautics, Butler, Pennsylvania, 15 August 1973

Business Week, 'French Switch on to Sun Power' in issue of May 9, 1970 p.126

<u>Business Week</u>, 'The Sun Breaks Through as an Energy Source' in issue of May 19, 1973 pp. 68D–68H

Everett Carlson Jr., 'Sunshine Power', <u>Mother Earth News</u> No.9, May 1971 pp.19–23

D.M. Chapin, 'The Direct Conversion of Solar Energy to Electrical Energy' in <u>Introduction to the Utilization of Solar Energy</u> (A.M. Zarem and D.D. Enway eds.), McGraw-Hill, New York 1963 pp.153–89

Day Chahroudi, 'Solar Energy' in <u>Domebook Two</u>, Pacific Domes, Bolinas, California

Graham Chedd, 'Brighter Outlook for Solar Power', <u>New Scientist</u>, 5 April 1973 pp.36–7

<u>Chemical and Engineering News</u>, 'Solar Energy may Achieve Wide Use by 1980's' in issue of 29 Jan.1973 pp.12–13

<u>Chemical and Engineering News</u>, 'Chance for Solar Energy Conversion' in issue of 20 Dec. 1971 p.39

J.C.V. Chinnappa, 'Performance of an Intermittent Refrigerator Operated by a Flat-Plate Collector', <u>Solar Energy</u> Vol.6, 1962 pp.143–50

R. Chung, G.O.G.Löf and J.A. Duffie, 'Solar Space Cooling', <u>Chem. Eng. Progr.</u>, Vol.55 No.4, April 1959 p.74

R. Chung and J.A. Duffie, 'Cooling with Solar Energy' (UN: Rome) E 35–S82

Congressional Committee on Science and Astronautics, Staff Report: <u>Solar Energy Research, A Multidisciplinary Approach</u>, U.S. House of Representatives, 92nd Congress, 2nd Session, Serial Z, December 1972; U.S. Government Printing Office, Washington DC 1973

Andrew P. Corty, 'Solar Homes: The "Clan" is Growing', <u>Environmental Action Bulletin</u> Vol.4 No.38, 22 Sept. 1973 pp.4–6 (Delaware Solar One and Project Ouroboros)

John-Robertson Cox, <u>Architectural Planning and Design Analysis of Energy Conservation in Housing through Thermal Energy Storage and Solar Heating</u>, Report No. NSF/RANN/SE/GI27976/TR72/2, National Center for Energy Management and Power, University of Pennsylvania, Sept.1970

E. Crausse and H. Gachan, 'The Study of a Saharan Solar House' (UN: Rome) E 35–S76

R.L. Cummeron, 'The Theory of Energy Conversion in P-N Junctions' (Scientific Basis) Vol. 5 pp.57–64

C.G. Currin, K.S. Ling, E.L. Ralph, W.A. Smith and R.J. Stirn, 'Feasibility of Low Cost Silicon Solar Cells', Proceedings of the 9th IEEE Photovoltaic Specialists Conference, Silver Spring, Maryland, 2–4 May 1972

J.T. Czarnecki, 'A Method of Heating Swimming Pools by Solar Energy', <u>Solar Energy</u> Vol.7 1963 pp.3–7

Farrington Daniels, <u>Direct Use of the Sun's Energy</u>, Yale University Press 1964

J.H. Dannies, 'Solar Air Conditioning and Solar Refrigeration', <u>Solar Energy</u> Vol.3 No.1, Jan.1959 pp.34–9

D. Dawes and J. Weingart, 'Urban Sun Rights. Socio-Legal Implications for Large Scale Use of Solar Energy for Space Conditioning' (Paris) C 21

John C. Devlin, 'Energy from the Sun will Heat and Cool an Office Building', <u>New York Times</u>, 12 August 1973 (Massachusetts Audubon Society)

Albert G.H. Dietz, 'Large Enclosures and Solar Energy', <u>AD</u> No.4, 1971 pp.239–40

Albert G.H. Dietz and E.L. Czapek, 'Solar Heating of Houses by Vertical Wall Storage Panels', reprint ASHVE Journal Section, <u>Heating, Piping and Air-Conditioning</u>

M.D.C. Doyle, 'Climatisation d'une Salle de Conférences par l'Energie Solaire' (Paris) B 21

John Dreyfuss, 'Unique Dome Home Harnesses Sun and Wind: New Mexico House is First Totally Heated, Powered by Elements', <u>Los Angeles Times</u> Jan.1 1973

A.J. Drummond, 'Sky Radiation, Its Importance in Solar Energy Problems' (Scientific Basis) Vol.1 pp.113-31

A.J. Drummond, 'Instrumentation for the Measurement of Solar Radiation – A Survey of Modern Techniques and Recent Developments' (UN: Rome) Vol.4 p.335

James C. Dudley, Thermal Energy Storage Unit for Air Conditioning Systems Using Phase Change Material, Report No. NSF/RANN/SE/GI27976/TR72/8, National Center for Energy Management and Power, University of Pennsylvania August 1972

Fred S. Dubin, 'GSA's Energy Conservation Test Building – A Report', Actual Specifying Engineer, August 1973 pp.84-92

Murray Dubin, 'International Touch for Solar House', Philadelphia Inquirer, Sunday July 22 1973 p.6-B (Delaware Solar One)

J.A. Duffie, 'New Materials in Solar Energy Utilization' (UN: Rome) E 35 Gr-S12

J.A. Duffie, G.O.G. Löf and E.M.A. Salam, 'Solar Heat Exchangers', Chem. Eng. Progr. Vol.56 No.7, July 1960 p.63

J.A. Duffie, C. Smith and G.O.G. Löf, Analysis of World Wide Distribution of Solar Radiation, Bulletin 21, Engineering Experiment Station, University of Wisconsin, Madison 1964

F.E. Edlin and D.E. Willauer, 'Plastic Films for Solar Energy Applications' (UN: Rome) E 35-S33

M.M. Eisenstadt, F.M. Flanigan and E.A. Farber, 'Solar Air Conditioning with an Ammonia-Water Absorption Refrigeration System', Am.Soc. Mech. Eng., Paper 59-A-276, 1959

Encyclopedia of Science and Technology, article on 'Solar Energy' in Vol.12, McGraw-Hill, New York 1960 p.467

Energy Digest, 'NSF to Fund Cadmium Sulfide Project in Search for "Cheap" Solar Cell', in issue of 31 May 1972

C.D. Engebretson, 'Use of Solar Energy for Space Heating, M.I.T. House IV' (UN: Rome) E 35-S67

C.D. Engebretson and N.G. Ashar, 'Progress in Space Heating with Solar Energy', Paper No. 60-WA-88, Winter ASME Meeting, December 1960

E.A. Farber, 'Solar Water Heating and Space Heating in Florida', Solar Energy Vol.3 No.3 October 1959 pp.21-25

E.A. Farber, 'The Florida Program in Solar Refrigeration and Air Conditioning', Solar Energy Vol.3 No.3, October 1959 pp.33-4

E.A. Farber, 'The Use of Solar Energy for Heating Water' (UN: Rome) E 35-S1

E.A. Farber, 'Solar Energy Conversion and Utilization', Paper No.439, Engineering Progress at the University of Florida, Vol.XXIII No.7, July 1969

E.A. Farber, 'Design and Performance of a Compact Solar Refrigeration System', Paper No. 6/58, International Solar Energy Conference, Melbourne, Australia, March 1970

E.A. Farber, 'Solar Energy, Its Conversion and Utilization', Solar Energy Vol.14 1973 pp. 243-52

E.A. Farber, F.M. Flanigan, L. Lopez and R.W. Polifka, 'University of Florida Solar Air-Conditioning System', Solar Energy Vol.10 No.2, 1966 pp.91-5

E.A. Farber, C.A. Morrison and J. Triandafyllis, 'The University of Florida Solar House' (Paris) C 11

S. Fritz, 'Solar Radiation during Cloudless Days', Heating and Ventilating Vol.46 No.1, 1949

S. Fritz, 'Transmission of Solar Energy through the Earth's Clear and Cloudy Atmosphere' (Scientific Basis) Vol.1 pp.17-36

S. Fritz and T.H. MacDonald, 'Average Solar Radiation in the United States', Heating and Ventilating, Vol.46 No.7, July 1949

S. Fritz et al., 'Some Solar Radiation Data Presentations for use in Applied Solar Energy Programs' (by international group of authors including S. Fritz, E. Barry, H. Hinzpeter, K.J. Kondratyev, M.P. Manolova and T.H. MacDonald), Solar Energy, Vol.4 No.1, 1960 pp.1-22

N. Fukuo et al., 'Installations for Solar Space Heating in Gerin' (UN: Rome) E 35-S112

H.P. Garg, 'Conception et Etude du Rendement d'un Système de Chauffage des Habitations au Moyen de l'Energie Solaire' (Paris) B 21

J. Geoffroy, 'Use of Solar Energy for Water Heating' (UN: Rome) E 35-S58

C.P. Gilmore, 'On the Way: Plentiful Energy from the Sun', Popular Science Dec.1972, pp.86-9, 112-5

P.E. Glaser and J.E. Murphy, A New View of Solar Energy, paper presented at Intersociety Energy Conversion Engineering Conference, Boston Mass., August 3-6, 1971; Arthur D. Little, Cambridge 1971

E.W. Golding, 'The Combination of Local Sources of Energy for Isolated Communities', Solar Energy, Vol.2 No.1, Jan. 1958 pp.7-12

M. Goldstein, 'Some Physical-Chemical Aspects of Heat Storage' (UN: Rome) E 35-S7

A.J.B. Goodwin, The Performance of the Brisbane Solar House, M.Eng.Sc. thesis, University of Queensland, Australia 1969

P.J. Grillo, 'Sun-Heated Ski Lodge Slit into Mountain Slope', Interiors, Jan. 1951, pp.114-5

J.P. Gupta and R.K. Chopra, 'Solar Space Heating at High Altitude Conditions' (Paris) B 21

D.S. Halacy, Power from the Sun , Murray 1962

D.S. Halacy, The Coming Age of Solar Energy, Harper and Row, New York 1964

A.L. Hammond, 'Solar Energy: The Largest Resource', Science Vol.177, 22 Sept. 1972, pp.1089-90

I.F. Hand, 'Solar Energy for House Heating', Heating and Ventilating, Dec. 1947 pp.80-94

I.F. Hand, 'Insolation on Clear Days at the Time of Solstice and Equinoxes for Lat. 42°N', Heating and Ventilating, Vol.47, 1950 p.92

H.R. Hay, 'Improved Natural Air Conditioning for the Tropics', Symp. Environmental Physics, Central Building Research Institute, Roorkee, India, Feb.1969

H.R. Hay, 'New Roofs for Hot Dry Regions', Ekistics No.183, Feb.1971 pp.158-64

H.R. Hay, 'The Solar Era, Part 3: Some Solar Radiation Implications and Adaptations', Mechanical Engineering Oct.1972

H.R. Hay, 'Natural Air Conditioning in the California Solarchitecture House' (Paris) B 12

H.R. Hay, 'Solar Energy, Solar Power and Pollution' (Paris) B 12

H.R. Hay and J.I. Yellott, 'Construction and Operation of a Naturally Air-Conditioned Building', Winter Annual Meeting of the Am.Soc.Mech.Engrs., New York Dec.1968

H.R. Hay and J.I. Yellott, 'Natural Air Conditioning with Roof Ponds and Movable Insulation' Semi-Annual Meeting of ASHRAE, Chicago Jan.1969; ASHRAE Transactions Vol.75 Part 1, 1969 pp.165-77

H.R. Hay and J.I. Yellott, 'International Aspects of Air Conditioning with Movable Insulation', Solar Energy Vol.12 1969 pp.427-38

H.R. Hay and J.I. Yellott, 'A Naturally Air-Conditioned Building', Mechanical Engineering, Vol.92 No.1, 1970 pp.19-25

L.J. Heidt, 'Converting Solar to Chemical Energy' (Phoenix)

A.L. Hesselschwerdt, 'Performance of the M.I.T. Solar House (MIT)

A.L. Hesselschwerdt, 'Heating by Sunpower: A Progress Report', Heating and Air Conditioning Contractor Oct.1956 p.44

H. Heywood, 'Solar Energy for Water and Space Heating', J. Inst. of Fuel, July 1954

H. Heywood, 'Solar Water Heating in Great Britain', Solar Energy Vol.3 No.3, Oct.1959
        pp.29-30

H. Heywood, 'Simple Instruments for the Assessment of Daily Solar Radiation Intensity'
        (UN: Rome) E 35-S9

T. Hisada and I. Oshida, 'Use of Solar Energy for Water Heating' (UN: Rome) E 35 Gr-S13

F.N. Hollingsworth, 'Solar Heat Test Structure at MIT' Heating and Ventilating May 1947
        pp.76-77

H.C. Hottel, 'Residential Uses of Solar Energy' (Phoenix); also Publication 60, Cabot Solar
        Energy Research Program, M.I.T.

H.C. Hottel, 'Solar Energy for Heating', in Mechanical Engineers' Handbook (L.S. Marks, ed.)
        McGraw-Hill, 5th edn. pp.1636-8

H.C. Hottel, H. Heywood, A. Whillier, G.O.G. Löf, M. Telkes and R.W. Bliss Jr., 'Panel
        on Solar House Heating' (Phoenix) pp.103-58

H.C. Hottel and J.B. Howard, New Energy Technology - Some Facts and Assessments, M.I.T.
        Press 1971. (Chapter 7, 'Special Energy Conversion Systems of
        Secondary Importance' largely devoted to solar energy)

H.C. Hottel and T.A. Unger, 'The Properties of a Copper Oxide-Aluminum Selective Black
        Surface Absorber of Solar Energy', Solar Energy Vol.3, 1959
        pp.410-15; and Colloq. Internatl. du Centre Natl. de la Res.Sc.,
        Vol.85, 1961 pp.523-38

H.C. Hottel and A. Whillier, 'Evaluation of Solar Collector Performance' (Scientific Basis)
        Vol.2 pp.74-104

H.C. Hottel and B.B. Woertz, 'The Performance of Flat-Plate Solar Heat Collectors', Trans.
        Am. Soc. Mech. Eng., Vol.64, 1942 pp.91-104

F.C. Houghten, H.T. Olson and C. Gutberlet, 'Summer Cooling Load as Affected by Heat
        Gain through Dry, Sprinkled and Water Covered Roofs', Am. Soc.
        Heating, Vent. Engrs. Trans. Vol.46, 1940 p.231

F.W. Hutchinson, 'The Solar House', Progressive Architecture May 1947

International Solar Energy Society, Proceedings, U.S. Section Annual Meeting, NASA-Lewis
        Research Center, Cleveland, Ohio, Oct.3-4 1973

S.R. Jagadish, 'The Prospects of Utilization of Solar and Wind Power for Generation of Power,
        Air-Conditioning and Refrigeration in Climatic Conditions Similar
        to India's' (Paris) B 12

R.C. Jordan, ed., Low Temperature Engineering Application of Solar Energy, ASHRAE,
        New York 1973

R.C. Jordan and J.L. Threlkeld, 'Solar Energy Availability for Heating in the United States',
        Heating, Piping and Air Conditioning Vol.25, Dec.1953 p.111

J.C. Kapur, 'A Report on the Utilization of Solar Energy for Refrigeration and Air- Cond-
        itioning Applications', Solar Energy Vol.4, 1960 pp.39-47

J.C. Kapur, 'Socio-economic Considerations in the Utilization of Solar Energy in Under-
        developed Areas (UN: Rome) Gen.8

Ken-Ichi Kimura, H. Ishino, M. Udagawa, M. Sanbe, G. Ohmura and H. Ueno, 'Exploring
        in House Cooling with Solar Energy' (Paris) B 21

M. Kobayoshi, 'Utilization of Silicon Solar Batteries' (UN: Rome) E 35-S11

M.V. Krpichev and V.A. Baum, 'Exploitation of Sun's Rays', Privoda Vol.43, 1954 p.45

E. Laloy, The Sun, Prentice-Hall 1963

H.E. Landsberg, 'Solar Radiation at the Earth's Surface', Solar Energy Vol.5 No.3, 1961
        p.95

B.Y.H. Liu and R.C. Jordan, 'The Interrelationship and Characteristic Distribution of

Direct, Diffuse and Total Solar Radiation', Solar Energy Vol.4
No.3, 1960 pp.1-19; and Solar Energy Vol.7, 1963 pp.71-4

B.Y.H. Liu and R.C. Jordan, 'Daily Insolation on Surfaces Tilted Toward the Equator',
ASHRAE Journal Vol.3 No.10, 1961 p.53

B.Y.H. Liu and R.C. Jordan, 'The Long-Term Performance of Flat-Plate Solar Energy
Collectors', Solar Energy Vol.7 No.2, 1963 p.53

G.O.G. Löf, 'House Heating and Cooling with Solar Energy' (Solar Energy Research) pp.33-45

G.O.G. Löf, 'Cooling with Solar Energy' (Phoenix) pp.171-89

G.O.G. Löf, 'The Use of Solar Energy for Space Heating, General Report' (UN: Rome) E 35
Gr-S14

G.O.G. Löf, 'The Heating and Cooling of Buildings with Solar Energy' in Introduction to the
Utilization of Solar Energy (A.M. Zarem and D.D. Enway, eds.),
McGraw-Hill 1963

G.O.G. Löf, J.A. Duffie and C.O. Smith, World Distribution of Solar Radiation, Report No.
21, Solar Energy Laboratory, College of Engineering, University
of Wisconsin, Madison, July 1966

G.O.G. Löf, M. El-Wakil and J. Chiou, 'Design and Performance of Domestic Heating
System Employing Solar-Heated Air, The Colorado Solar House'
(UN: Rome) E 35-S114

G.O.G. Löf and R.A. Tybout, 'Cost of House Heating with Solar Energy', Solar Energy Vol.
14, 1973 pp.258-78 (revised version of R.A. Tybout and G.O.G.
Löf, 'Solar House Heating', Natural Resources Journal Vol.10 No.
2, April 1970 pp.268-326)

G.O.G. Löf and R.A. Tybout, 'The Design and Cost of Optimized Systems for Cooling
Dwellings by Solar Energy' (Paris) B 21

Harold G. Lorsch, Solar Heating Systems Analysis, Report No. NSF/RANN/SE/GI27976/
TR72/19, National Center for Energy Management and Power,
University of Pennsylvania, Nov.1972

Harold G. Lorsch, 'The Use of Solar Energy for Residential Space Heating', Energy Conversion
Vol.13 No.1, Jan.1973 pp.1-5

H.G. Lorsch and B. Niyogi, Influence of Azimuthal Orientation on Collectible Energy in
Vertical Solar Collector Building Walls, Report No. NSF/RANN/
SE/GI27976/TR72/18, National Center for Energy Management and
Power, University of Pennsylvania, August 1971

The Martinsburg Journal, 'Environmental Harmony in Sylvan Setting: Solar Energy Home
Planned in County', issue of Wed. June 13, 1973 (Mrs A.N.
Wilson house)

H. Masson, 'Les Insolateurs à Bas Potential' (Scientific Basis) Vol.3 pp.47-66

K.N. Mathur, 'Use of Solar Energy for Heating Purposes, Heat Storage' (UN: Rome) E 35
Gr-S17

K.N. Mathur, 'Heat Storage for Solar Energy Space Heating', Solar Energy Vol.6 No.3, 1962
pp.110-2

K.N. Mathur et al., 'Domestic Solar Water Heater', Journal of Scientific Industrial Research,
18A, Feb.1959

K.N. Mathur and M.L. Khanna, 'Solar Water Heaters' (UN: Rome) E 35-S102

A.B. Meinel with M.P. Meinel, B.O. Seraphin and D.B. McKenney, Report on Progress in
Solar Photothermal Power Conversion presented to the Sub-
committee on Environment, Committee for Interior and Insular
Affairs, House of Representatives, Washington DC, 13 June 1973

Jacques Michel, 'Chauffage par Rayonnement Solaire', Architecture d'Aujourdhui No.167,
pp.88-93

Colin Moorcraft, 'Solar Energy in Housing', AD October 1973 pp.634-61

R.A. Morgen, 'The Heat Pump' (Solar Energy Research) pp.69-70

R.N. Morse, 'Solar Water Heaters' (Phoenix) pp.191-200

R.N. Morse, Solar Water Heaters for Domestic and Farm Use, Commonwealth Scientific and Industrial Research Organisation, Engineering Section Report ED 5, Melbourne, Australia 1957

R.N. Morse, Installing Solar Water Heaters, Commonwealth Scientific and Industrial Research Organisation, Circular 1, Melbourne, Australia 1959

R.N. Morse, 'Solar Energy Research: Some Australian Investigations', Solar Energy Vol.3 No.3, Oct.1959 pp.26-8

R.N. Morse, 'Water Heating by Solar Energy' (UN: Rome) E 35-S38

A. Mouchot, L'Energie Solaire et ses Applications Industrielles, Gauthier-Villars, Paris 1869

G.R. Mowry, 'Solar Energy Supplemented Rural-Home Heat Pump', Solar Energy Vol.8 No.1, 1964

H.E. Nastelin, J.M. Smith III and A.L. Gombach, CdS Solar Cell Development, Final Report, NASA Contract NAS3-13467, June 16 1971

National Academy of Sciences, Solar Energy in Developing Countries: Perspectives and Prospects, National Academy of Sciences PB 208 550, March 1972

National Science Foundation/ National Aeronautics and Space Administration Solar Energy Panel, Solar Energy as a National Energy Resource, University of Maryland, Dec.1972

National Research Council, Ad Hoc Panel on Solar Cell Efficiency, Solar Cells; Outlook for Improved Efficiency, National Academy of Sciences, Washington DC 1972

Newsweek, 'Turning on the Sunpower' in issue of 16 July 1973 pp.78-9

A. Olgyay, 'Design Criteria of Solar Heated House' (UN: Rome) E 35-S93

A. Olgyay and M. Telkes, 'Solar Heating for Houses', Progressive Architecture March 1959 pp.195-203

Optical Sciences Center Newsletter, 'Solar Energy at OSC' in issue No.3, Vol.6, Optical Sciences Center, University of Arizona, Tucson, Dec.1972

Optical Spectra, report on Delaware Solar One house in issue of Jan.1973

J.K. Page, 'The Estimation of Monthly Mean Values of Daily Total Short Wave Radiation on Vertical and Inclined Surfaces from Sunshine Records for Latitudes 40°N-40°S' (UN: Rome) Vol.4 p.387

J.K. Page, 'The Concept of "Town-Country" or Integrated Human-Botanical Energy Process for Habitat' (Paris) C 21

W. Palz, J. Besson, J. Fremy, T. Nguyen Duy and J. Vedel, 'Analysis of the Performance and Stability of CdS Solar Cells', Proceedings of the 9th IEEE Photovoltaic Specialists Conference, Silver Spring, Maryland, May 2-4 1972

G.L. Pearson, 'Electricity from the Sun' (Phoenix) pp.281-88

M. Perrot, L'Energie Solaire, Fayard Bilandela Science, Paris 1963

B.V. Petukhov, Solar Water Heating Installations, U.S.S.R. Academy of Sciences, Moscow 1953

I. Peyches, 'Special Glasses and Mountings for the Utilization of Solar Energy' (UN: Rome) E S91

C. Pfeiffer, P. Schoffer, B.G. Spars and J.A. Duffie, 'Performance of Silicon Solar Cells at High Levels of Solar Radiation', Trans. Am. Soc. Mech. Eng., 84A: 33, 1962

C. Pisoni, 'Examination of Some Heat Storage Systems for Solar Collectors in Building Heating Applications' (Paris) B 21

G.V. Pleijel and B.I. Lindström, 'Stazione Astrofisica Svedese - A Swedish Solar-Heated House at Capri' (UN: Rome) E 35-S49

Popular Mechanics, 'The House that Stores the Sun' in issue No.4, Vol.108, Oct.1957 p.158 (about MIT House IV)

Popular Mechanics, 'Will Your Next House Get its Heat from the Sun?' in issue of Feb.1958 p.110

M.B. Prince, 'Latest Developments in the Field of Photovoltaic Conversion of Solar Energy' (UN: Rome) E 35-S65

Progressive Architecture, 'Roundup: Recent Solar Heating Installations' in issue of March 1959

E.L. Ralph, 'A Plan to Utilize Solar Energy as an Electric Power Source', 8th Photovoltaic Specialists Conference, Seattle, Washington, August 1970

E.L. Ralph, 'A Commercial Solar Cell Array Design', Heliotek Division of Textron, Sylmar, California; presentation to Solar Energy Society Conference at Greenbelt, Maryland, May 1971

P. Rappaport, 'Photoelectricity', Proc. Nat. Acad. Sci., Vol.47, 1961 pp.1303-6; also in Solar Energy (special issue) Vol.5, Sept. 1961 pp.59-62

P. Rappaport and H.I. Moss, 'Low Cost Photovoltaic Conversion of Solar Energy' (UN: Rome) E 35-S106

Hans Rau, Sonnenenergie, Athenäum-Verlag Junker and Dünnhaupt K G, Bonn 1958; English edition Solar Energy (trans. M. Schur, ed. D.J. Duffin), Macmillan, New York 1964

L.E. Ravich, 'Thin Film Photovoltaic Devices for Solar Energy Conversion' (UN: Rome) E 35-S56

R. Reines, 'Ecocompatible Life Support Systems for Spaceship Earth. A Working Prototype', (Paris) C 11

D.C. Reynolds, 'The Photovoltaic Effect in Cadmium Sulfide Crystals' (Scientific Basis) Vol.5 pp.102-16

R.K. Riel, 'Large Area Solar Cells Prepared on Silicon Sheet', Proceedings of the 17th Annual Power Sources Conference, Atlantic City N.J. May 1963

G.E. Roberts and N.R. Sheridan, Air Conditioned Housing for Northern Australia, Solar Research Note No.3, University of Queensland, Australia 1969

N. Robinson, A Brief History of Utilization of the Sun's Radiation, Actes de Septième Congrès, International d'Histoire des Sciences, Jerusalem 1953

N. Robinson, Solar Radiation, Elsevier, New York and Amsterdam 1962

N. Robinson and E. Neeman, 'The Solar Switch, An Automatic Device for Economizing Auxiliary Heating of Solar Water Heaters' (UN: Rome) E 35-S31

Douglass E. Root Jr., 'Practical Aspects of Solar Swimming Pool Heating', Solar Energy Vol.4 No.1, Jan.1960 pp.23-4

H.H. Safwat and A.F. Souka, 'Design of a New Solar-Heated House Using Double Exposure Flat-Plate Collectors', Technical Note, Solar Energy Vol.13 No.1, April 1970 pp.105-119

Dominic Sama, 'Sunlight to Power Home', Philadelphia Inquirer, July 14 1973 p.1 (Delaware Solar One)

Alan P. Saunders, Test Facility for Experimental Solar Collectors, Report No. NSF/RANN/ SE/GI27976/TR72/12, National Center for Energy Management and Power, University of Pennsylvania, Oct.1972

J. Savornin, 'Study of Solar Water Heating in Algeria' (UN: Rome) E 35-S72

R. Schoen, 'Solar Energy for Industrialized Housing Systems' (Paris) C 11

R. Schoen and A. Hirshberg, 'An Overview of Failure and Success in Technological Innovation in the U.S. Housing Industry: Implications for Widespread Residential Use of Solar Energy (Paris) D 22

E. Schönholzer, 'Hygienic Clean Winter Space Heating with Solar and Hydro-electric Energy Accumulated during the Summer and Stored in Insulated Reservoirs', Solar Energy Vol.12 No.3, May 1969 pp.379-85

M.K. Selcuk, 'Flat Plate Solar Collector Performance at High Temperatures', Solar Energy Vol. 8, 1964 pp.57-62

M.K. Selcuk and J.I. Yellott, 'Measurement of Direct, Diffuse and Total Radiation with Silicon Photovoltaic Cells', Solar Energy Vol.6, 1962 pp.155-63

S. Selkowitz and J. Weingart, 'Ecosystemic Design and the Emerging Role of Solar Energy Conversion' (Paris) B 11

R. Seybold, 'Fusible Salts and Nitrogen Dioxide Adsorption for Utilizing Solar Energy', B.S. thesis, University of Wisconsin, Madison 1956

N.R. Sheridan, 'Prospects for Solar Air Conditioning in Australia' (UN: Rome) E 35-S39

N.R. Sheridan, Solar Water Heaters, Solar Research Notes 1, University of Queensland, Australia 1969

N.R. Sheridan, On the Solar Operation of Absorption Air Conditioners, Ph.D. thesis, University of Queensland, Australia 1969

N.R. Sheridan, 'Performance of the Brisbane Solar House', Solar Energy Vol.13 No.4, July 1972 pp.395-401

N.R. Sheridan and W.H. Carr, A Solar Air Conditioned House in Brisbane, Solar Research Notes 2, University of Queensland, Australia 1967

C.H. Shinbrot and A.D. Tonelli, 'Advance Deployable Solar Cell Battery Power System Development', Proceedings of Intersociety Energy Conversion Engineering Conference, 1971 pp.152-62

P.A. Siple, 'Climatic Considerations of Solar Energy for Space Heating' (MIT)

Gerry E. Smith, Economics of Solar Collectors, Heat Pumps and Wind Generators, Working Paper 3, Technical Research Division, Cambridge University Department of Architecture, 1972

R. Sobotka, 'Solar Water Heaters' (UN: Rome) E 35-S26

Sol Shot 1 (wallsheet describing 'solar chimney' collector and heat storage system), Cookbook Fund - Lama Foundation, Corrales, New Mexico 1973

Southern Illinois University Department of Design, A Design Approach for Application of a Solar Energy System to a Geodesic Structure, 1971

E. Speyer, 'Solar Buildings in Temperate and Tropical Climates' (UN: Rome) E 35-S8

P. Sporn and E.R. Ambrose, 'The Heat Pump and Solar Energy' (Phoenix) pp.159-70

Carol Sterkin, Solar Energy Utilization, California Institute of Technology, Pasadena 1971 (bibliography)

Sun at Work, 'Economic Feasibility Reached in Solar Home' in issue of First Quarter, 1960 pp.6-7

S. Szokolay and R. Hobbs, 'Using Solar Energy in Housing', Royal Institute of British Architects' Journal April 1973 pp.177-9

H. Tabor, 'Selective Radiation I. Wavelength Discrimination' (Scientific Basis) 2A p.24; also in Bull. Res. Council Israel Vol.5A Nos.2 and 3, April 1956

H. Tabor, 'Solar Energy Collector Design' (Scientific Basis) Vol.2 pp.1-24

H. Tabor, 'Use of Solar Energy for Cooling Purposes' (UN: Rome) E 35 Gr-S18; also in Solar Energy Vol.6 No.4, 1962 pp.136-42

I. Tanishita, 'Recent Development of Solar Water Heaters in Japan' (UN: Rome) E 35-S68

W.P. Teagan, 'A Solar Powered Combined Heating/Cooling System with the Air Conditioning Unit Driven by an Organic Rankine-Cycle Engine' (Paris) B 21

M. Telkes, 'Solar House Heating, A Problem of Heat Storage', Heating and Ventilating Vol.44, 1947 p.68

M. Telkes, 'A Review of Solar House Heating', Heating and Ventilating, Sept.1949 pp.68-74

M. Telkes, 'Space Heating with Solar Energy', The Scientific Monthly, LXIX No.6, Dec.1949

M. Telkes, 'Low-Cost Solar Heated House', Heating and Ventilating, Vol.47, Aug.1950 p.72

M. Telkes, 'Future Uses of Solar Energy', Bulletin of the Atomic Scientists Vol.II No.7-8, Aug.1951; reprinted in Tech. Engineering News, May 1952, pp. 12-13, 40

M. Telkes, 'Nucleation of Supersaturated Salt Solutions', Ind. Eng. Chem., Vol.44, 1952 p.1308

M. Telkes, 'Solar Heat Storage' (Solar Energy Research) pp.57-62

M. Telkes, 'Thermal Storage of Solar Energy' (Paris) B 21

M. Telkes and E. Raymond, 'Storing Solar Heat in Chemicals: A Report on the Dover House', Heating and Ventilating Nov.1949 pp.80-5

Irving E. Thomas, 'Let the Sunshine In!', Survival Times, Santa Barbara Vol.2 No.5

H.E. Thomason, six miscellaneous articles in Sun at Work magazine 1960-3

H.E. Thomason, 'Solar Space Heating, Water Heating, Cooling in the Thomason Home' (UN: Rome) E 35-S3; also in Solar Energy Vol.4 No.4, Oct.1960 pp.11-19 under title 'Solar Space Heating and Air Conditioning in the Thomason Home'

H.E. Thomason, 'Solar-Heated House Uses $\frac{3}{4}$ hp for Air Conditioning', ASHRAE Journal Vol.4 No.11, 1962 pp.58-62

H.E. Thomason, 'House with Sunshine in the Basement', Popular Mechanics, Feb.1965 pp.89-92

H.E. Thomason, 'Three Solar Houses', American Society of Mechanical Engineers Paper No. 65-WA/-SOL-3, 1965

H.E. Thomason, 'Experience with Solar Houses', Solar Energy, Vol.10 No.1, Jan./March 1966 pp.17-22

H.E. Thomason, Solar Houses and Solar House Models, Publication 9069, Edmond Scientific Co., Berrington N.J., 2nd edn. 1972

H.E. Thomason and H.J.L. Thomason Jr., 'Solar Houses/ Heating and Cooling Progress Report', Solar Energy Vol.15 No.1, May 1973 pp.27-39

J.L. Threlkeld and R.C. Jordan, 'Solar Collector Studies at the University of Minnesota' (Scientific Basis) Vol.2 pp.105-14

D. Trivich, 'Photovoltaic Cells and Their Possible Use as Power Converters for Solar Energy', Ohio Journal of Science, Vol.53, 1953 pp.310-14

D. Trivich, P.A. Flinn and H.J. Bowlden, 'Photovoltaic Cells in Solar Energy Conversion' (Solar Energy Research) pp.149-54

F. Trombe and C.H. La Blanchetais, 'Principles of Air Conditioning in Countries with a Clear Sky' (UN: Rome) E 35-S111

F. Trombe, A. Le Phat Vinh and Mme Le Phat Vinh, 'Etude sur le Chauffage des Habitations par Utilisation du Rayonnement Solaire', Revue Générale de Thermique Vol.IV No.48, Dec.1965

F. Trombe et al., 'Le Chauffage des Habitations par Captage du Rayonnement Solaire' (Paris) B 21

F. Trombe et al., 'Le Refroidissement Naturel des Habitations' (Paris) B 21

R.A. Tybout and G.O.G. Löf, 'Solar House Heating', Natural Resources Journal Vol.10 No.2, April 1970 pp.268-326

United Nations Department of Economic and Social Affairs, New Sources of Energy and Economic Development, United Nations, New York 1957

United Nations Department of Economic and Social Affairs, 'Solar Energy Availability and Instruments for Measurements: Radiation Data, Networks and Instrumentation' (UN: Rome)

United States Department of Commerce, Office of Technical Services of Library and Reports Division, Solar House Research at University of Denver, Report PE-25375, Washington DC

R.J.D. Vale, Results of Solar Collector Study, Working Paper 12, Technical Research Division, University of Cambridge Department of Architecture 1973

S.S. Visher, Climatic Atlas of the United States, Harvard University Press 1954

Volunteers for International Technical Assistance (VITA), Glass Plate Solar Water Heater, Village Technology Plan 5513.2, Mt. Rainier, Maryland, n.d.

G.T. Ward, Possibilities for the Utilization of Solar Energy in Under-developed Rural Areas, Bulletin 16, Agricultural Engineering Branch, Food and Agricultural Organization of the United Nations, Rome 1961

Washington Post, report on Mrs. A.N. Wilson house in 'Style' section, People/The Arts/Leisure, Saturday May 19 1973, pp.D1, D3

Jerome Weingart, 'Solar Energy Technology Options and the Energy Requirements of Structures and Communities', unpubl. ms., May 24 1972

Jerome Weingart, 'Everything You've Always Wanted to Know about Solar Energy, but Were Never Charged up Enough to Ask', Environmental Quality Dec. 1972

Ron Weintraub, 'A Review of a Possible Scheme of Power Generation on a Local Level', Alternative Sources of Energy No.4, Jan.1972 pp.4-8

A. Whillier, 'Principles of Solar House Design', Progressive Architecture May 1955 pp.122-6

A. Whillier, 'The Determination of Hourly Values of Total Solar Radiation from Daily Summations', Arch. Met. Geoph. and Bioklim., Vol.7 No.2, 1956 p.14

A. Whillier, 'Plastic Covers for Solar Collectors', Solar Energy Vol.7, 1963 pp.148-51

A. Whillier, 'Performance of Black-Painted Solar Air Heaters of Conventional Design', Solar Energy Vol.8 No.1, 1964 pp.31-7

D.A. Williams, G.O.G. Löf, D.A. Fester and J.A. Duffie, 'Intermittent Absorption Cooling Systems with Solar Regeneration', Refrigeration Engineering Vol.66, Nov.1958 p.33

M. Wolf, 'Developments in Photovoltaic Solar Energy Conversion for Earth Surface Applications' (UN: Rome) E 35-S44

M. Wolf, 'Cost Goals for Silicon Solar Arrays for Large Scale Terrestrial Applications', Proceedings of the 9th IEEE Photovoltaic Specialists Conference, Silver Spring, Maryland, May 2-4 1972

M. Wolf, 'Historical Development of Solar Cells', 25th Power Sources Conference, Atlantic City, May 23-25 1972

M. Yanagimachi, 'How to Combine Solar Energy, Nocturnal Radiation Cooling, Radiant Panel System of Heating and Cooling, and Heat Pump to Make a Complete Year Round Air-Conditioning System' (Scientific Basis) Vol.3 pp.21-31

M. Yanagimachi, 'Report on Two and One-half Years Experimental Living in Yanagimachi Solar House II' (UN: Rome) E 35-S94

Hsuan Yeh (principal investigator), Conservation and Better Utilization of Electric Power by Means of Thermal Energy Storage and Solar Heating, Phase III Progress Report No. NSF/RANN/SE/GI27976/PR73/1, National Center for Energy Management and Power, University of Pennsylvania, March 31 1973

J.I. Yellott, 'Thin Film Water Heater' (Sounion) pp.112-23

J.I. Yellott and H.R. Hay, 'Thermal Analysis of a Building with Natural Air Conditioning', Semi-Annual Meeting of ASHRAE, Chicago Jan.1969; ASHRAE Transactions Vol.75 Part 1, 1969 pp.178-89

A.M. Zarem and D.D. Enway eds., Introduction to the Utilization of Solar Energy, McGraw-Hill, New York 1963

Wind power

The wind, like the sun, is an effectively inexhaustible, if
fickle source of energy. In fact it can be regarded as an
indirect form of solar energy, the movements of the atmosphere
resulting as they do from the intermittent heating effects of the
sun's radiation on the air itself and on the earth and the sea.
The wind has provided mechanical power for pumping water and
for milling grain through many centuries of course; and in this
century wind-powered generators have served, and continue to
serve, the electrical power requirements of many thousands of
homesteads and farms in the remoter rural areas of America,
Russia, Australia and throughout the world.

History

It is hardly necessary to describe the most familiar design of windmill,
consisting of some kind of wheel or rotor, made up of a number of
separate blades, mounted in the vertical plane; together with some
device, generally a tail fin or secondary rotor, to steer the main
rotor always into the wind. Passing references to windmills built
on this principle occur in ancient Chinese and Classical literature,
although the first known technical description appears to have
been given by Hero of Alexandria. It was only in the 12th century
that the windmill was introduced to Western Europe. Of the small
mass-produced windmills which may still be seen in their thousands
all over rural America, the machines with many-vaned wheels are
used generally for pumping water, and run at low speeds, while the
– now much rarer - machines for generating electricity have
aeroplane-type propellers with usually either two or three blades,
and operate at relatively higher speeds. But although the vertical
wind wheel or propeller is the most usual and best-tried form of
wind power device, it is by no means the only possibility.

Horizontal
mills

Instead of being set vertically, the plane of rotation of the mill
may be set horizontally; and some arrangement devised with stops
or cranks whereby the vertical blades or sails on one side of the
mill are set to catch the wind, while on the other they are allowed
to spill the air. With a horizontal rotation there is no problem of
steering the machine as a whole to face the direction of the wind.
Remains of mills built on this plan and using cloth sails have been
found in Persia, dating from the 5th century A.D. One of the
more modern versions, using an ingenious crank mechanism for
aligning its three vertical aerofoil section blades, was the machine
invented and built by J.C. Donaldson in Florida during the 1940s.

The Darrieus
rotor

The efficiency of sail-type horizontal wind machines is limited by
the fact that the peripheral speed of the rotor cannot exceed the
speed of the wind. In a type of horizontal windmill first invented
by the Frenchman Darrieus in 1927, this problem is overcome by
using thin aerofoil section blades, so that the rotor is driven by the
aerodynamic lift on these blades, rather than being pushed directly
by the force of the wind itself. Recent work by P. South and

R.S. Rangi at the National Aeronautical Establishment of Canada has demonstrated that machines on the Darrieus principle show promise of proving both efficient and cheap to construct. Their prototypes are built with either two or three blades, of extruded metal formed into a constant aerofoil section, and each bent into a catenary curve, connected top and bottom to a central axis.

The Flettner rotor

A totally new type of wind power machine was pioneered by the German inventor Anton Flettner during the 1920s. This was the 'Flettner rotor', which makes use of the so-called Magnus effect. If a cylinder is spun on its axis at high speed, then the drag or friction between the cylinder's surface and the surrounding air results in the creation of an effective sail or blade. If the spinning rotor is set vertically in the wind, there will be a lateral force set up on the rotor at an angle to the wind's direction. Flettner used his rotor originally as a form of sail for sailing ships.

Rotor ships

His rotor-powered ship the Baden Baden crossed the Atlantic in 1926, to the amazed disbelief apparently of most who saw it. A converted schooner, it carried two tall slim metal cylinders on its deck, spun by small motors, in place of the usual masts and sheet sails. The virtues of the rotor for this purpose are that it requires no setting to face the wind's direction, as conventional sails do, since it presents the same aspect from all sides; indeed Flettner's ship could sail backwards as easily as forwards (by reversing the direction of spin of the rotors). And since the solid surface area presented to the wind by the rotor is much less than that of normal sails, and its effective 'sail' area is dependent on the relative speeds of the wind and of the rotation of the rotor itself, there is little danger of capsizing in high winds or gusts,

Horizontal wind motor built by J.C. Donaldson in Cocoa, Florida in the 1940s.

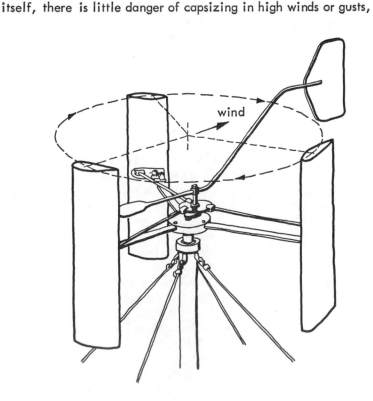

wind

and the rotor ship is able to weather heavier conditions, and to sail much closer to the wind, than conventional sailing craft. For the Magnus effect to be useful, the rotor should have a circumferential speed of at least $3\frac{1}{2}$ times the velocity of the wind.

Flettner
windwheel

A number of applications of the Flettner rotor for generating electricity were suggested and a few machines built. Flettner himself founded a Windturbine Company in 1925, and built a 'windwheel' with rotors on four arms, and an overall diameter of 66 feet, in Benrath, Germany. This wheel was mounted in the vertical plane, on a tower, in the same manner as normal propeller windmills. His company had plans for giant wheels of 300 foot diameter and more. At the same time an American inventor C.E. Sargent of Elgin, Illinois, produced designs for a small wind motor using the Flettner principle, but with four cylindrical rotors mounted vertically on a revolving horizontal circular frame. In the early '30s the Public Service Corporation of New Jersey made some experiments with Flettner rotors for possible use in the generation of electricity on a large scale. Their very grandiose

Wind machine with Flettner rotor blades, built by the Flettner Windturbine Company in Benrath, Germany in 1925. The diameter of the whole wheel was 66 ft, the individual rotors 16 ft long, made of aluminum alloy and spun by AC motors mounted inside the rotor shells. From Anton Flettner, The Story of the Rotor, New York 1926 p.98 fig.59

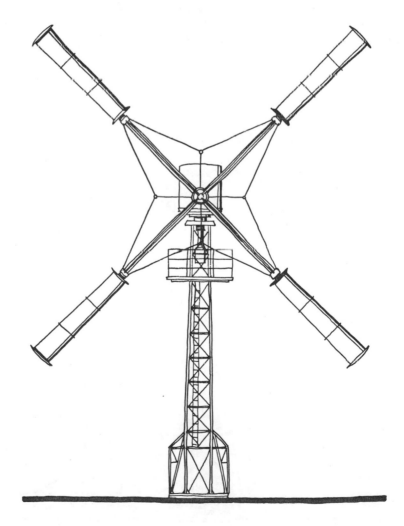

proposal was to build a circular railway track of very broad gauge some 3000 feet in diameter, with a series of twenty flat-cars running on this track, joined by cables, and carrying aluminum rotors ninety feet high and twentytwo feet in diameter. Each car was to carry an electrical generator it seems, driven presumably off the wheels. The rotors would reverse their direction of spin with every half circuit that each car made of the track. The scheme was never carried out. A number of projects for generating electrical power from the wind on a commercial scale using the more usual propeller type of machine have been carried into successful operation however, from the beginning of this century onwards, and some of these will be described shortly.

The Savonius rotor

Meanwhile to conclude this brief occount of other types of wind machine, mention should be made here of the horizontal motor designed by Captain Sigurd Savonius in Finland during the 1920s which combines some features of the sail type of mill with a partial use of the Magnus effect. The design may be understood by imagining a hollow vertical cylinder split into two halves in the vertical plane, and these two halves offset somewhat. Air is caught in the half that presents its open, concave face in the direction of the wind; while the opposite, convex half presents less wind resistance. It is essential that the wind be allowed free passage between the two halves; in passing through the air creates pressures on the two wings in opposite directions about the central axis. At the same time the Magnus effect acts on the outer edges of the whole spinning assembly.

Captain Savonius' wind motor built in Helsinki in 1924; with diagrammatic plan of the rotor arrangement. Adapted from G. Bathe, Horizontal Windmills, Draft Mills and Similar Airflow Engines, Allen, Lane and Scott, Philadelphia 1948 Plate XVII

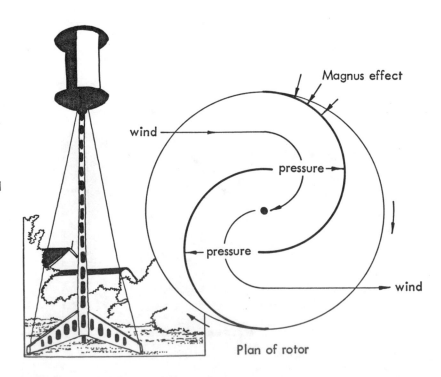

Plan of rotor

Other wind devices	Other suggestions for ways of harnessing wind power, of a rather extreme or eccentric character, have involved the use of kites, 'diaphragm pumps' to exploit the differences in pressure on the windward and leeward sides of large obstructions, and methods for converting the movements of trees in the wind into useful mechanical form – either by using bilge type pumps connected between the branches, or else by triangulating with cables and feeding the relative movements into a central ratchet-driven motor or dynamo.

Large scale wind-electric machines **Danish work**	Some of the earliest work on the generation of electricity using windmills was done in Denmark under the direction of Professor P. La Cour, beginning around the turn of the century. Machines of up to 30kW capacity were built at this time (for comparison, the small machines formerly in wide use on American farms have capacities of the order of 1 to 3kW), and Denmark has continued to make use of wind powered generators, in particular during the two World Wars when coal and fuel oil were in short supply. During World War 2 there were some 88 large wind-driven generating plants in operation, with capacities of up to 70kW. A 75 foot diameter, 200kW aero-generator put into commission at Gedser, Denmark in 1957 and supplying power for the Danish public power system, is probably the largest working machine in the world today.
Russian work	The Russians were early pioneers in this field also, and an experimental windmill of 100 feet diameter, driving a 100 kW generator, was built at Balaclava on the Black Sea in 1931. The power from the machine supplemented the output of a conventional steam-turbine plant at Sevastopol, twenty miles away. The project was sponsored by the Moscow Central Wind Power Institute which was set up after the Revolution in connection with the drive towards rural electrification, and which produced plans for a number of much larger units, to varying designs, none of which were apparently ever constructed.
The Smith-Putnam machine	The largest machine ever built and operated in America – and indeed in the world – was the so-called 'Grandpa's Knob' windmill, named after the hill on which it stood near Rutland, Vermont – a gigantic 1,250kW machine whose two stainless steel blades swept a circle 175 feet in diameter, and were visible from a distance of 25 miles. The inventive genius behind the Grandpa's Knob project was the engineer Palmer C. Putnam, who became interested in wind-driven generators in the middle '30s, and subsequently after his experience with the giant machine was to write one of the principal books on the subject, Power from the Wind. The Vermont project was financed, and the machine itself built, by a Pennsylvania manufacturer of hydraulic turbines, the S. Morgan Smith Company (hence the name by which it was alternatively known, the Smith-Putnam windmill). The two propeller blades were designed and made in Philadelphia by the

75 ft wind turbine at Gedser, Denmark, in operation since 1957. The 200 kW machine generates about 400,000 kWh/year, roughly one third of the output of the Smith-Putnam turbine. From J.McCaull, 'Windmills', Environment, Jan/Feb 1973 p.8

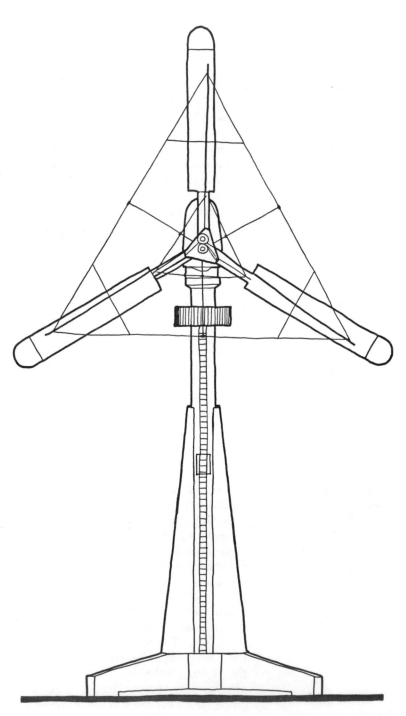

Budd Company, and the 110-foot tower at Ambridge, Pa. by the American Bridge Company. The machine was assembled at the Vermont site during 1941, and began supplying power to the Central Vermont Public Service Corporation network in October of that year. It continued working for the following three and a half years, generating a maximum of 1,500kW and withstanding winds of up to 115mph. From 1943 to 1945 it was shut down for repairs, but in March 1945 was put back in operation. There had been worries from the start of the project about the structural design of the spars supporting the blades, but the problems were impossible to remedy, and it was decided to run the machine at a calculated risk of structural failure. On March 26th 1945 one of the two spars broke, the blade flew off, and the Grandpa's Knob experiment came to an end.

P.H. Thomas

During the fuel shortages of the Second World War engineers in a number of countries turned their attention to the possibilities of wind power. Besides Putnam's work in America, some feasibility and cost studies for large machines were carried out by P.H.Thomas under the auspices of the Federal Power Commission towards the end of the War. In Hitler's Germany some designs for aero-generators of up to 20,000kW capacity were put forward (schemes which E.W. Golding dismisses however as 'fanciful'). In 1949 an institute devoted to the study of wind power, the 'Studiengesell-schaft Windkraft', was set up in Stuttgart, with the purpose of making wind surveys in Germany, and of designing and constructing a prototype 100kW machine. One of the leading figures associated with these developments was Dr. U. Hütter. In France at this same period a very complete wind survey was made throughout the country, and 140 or so potential wind power sites investigated.

British work

In Britain, interest in large scale wind machines also continued on into the 1950s. A 100kW unit was built in the Orkney Islands, where the average annual wind speed is close to 30mph. A second wind-driven generator was built at St. Albans, Hertfordshire during the early 1950s. Also producing 100kW, this machine, the Enfield-Andréau generator, constructed to an ingenious design by the French inventor Andréau, used its hollow-bladed propeller to draw air up through a tubular supporting tower, and to drive a turbine with this air flow inside the tower at ground level. A scheme for a 3,670kW machine was commissioned by the British Ministry of Fuel and Power from the Folland Aircraft Company also in the early '50s. This was to have had a rotor 225 feet in diameter supported on a steerable tripod structure; and the cost studies, for a wind regime similar to that of the Orkneys, estimated a cost per kW hour less than half that using coal-fired plants.

Current American research

Energy and environmental problems have resulted in a recent revival of interest, in America and elsewhere, in use of the wind as a source of power. At least five university groups are currently involved in theoretical studies and in the testing of prototype

1,250 kW Smith-Putnam
windmill, built at Grandpa's
Knob, Rutland, Vermont
in 1941. Note the scale of
the human figures at the
base of the tower.

University of
Oklahoma

designs. At the University of Oklahoma at Norman, work is going
on under the direction of Karl. H. Bergey, Associate Dean of the
College of Engineering, in connection with the development of
a 'hybrid' electric and propane driven car for urban and suburban
use. A windmill is being used for recharging the car's batteries
overnight; the machine has a 12' rotor with variable pitch blades,
connected to a standard automobile alternator rated at 40amps
at 12 volts. Bergey has also designed a much larger wind-powered
generator for power production on a commercial scale.

Princeton
windmill

At the Forrestal Campus of Princeton University, Thomas Sweeney,
director of the Advanced Flight Concepts Laboratory, has built a
25' diameter windmill with a generating capacity of about 7kW in
a 20mph wind. The novel feature of Sweeney's design is the light-
weight construction of the 'sail-wing' blades, each of which is
made from two sheets of Dacron, a fabric used for boat sails,
stretched over a shaped leading-edge spar, the trailing edge being
held taut by a stretched cable. At rest, the 'sail-wings' are flat,
but in the wind they assume an efficient aerofoil contour.

The Heronemus
proposal

At the University of Oregon at Corvallis, a number of
utility companies are sponsoring a three-year $132,000 study
of the possibility of using Oregon's powerful coastal winds for
power generation. Another research program is going on at
Montana State University in Bozeman. The most ambitious
large scale wind power project presently being advanced, is
the scheme by Professor W. Heronemus of the Department of
Engineering at the University of Massachusetts in Amherst.
The Heronemus proposal involves the use of windmills with
rotors of the order of 80' or so diameter, but with twenty such
rotors mounted together on single structures up to 850'tall.
These colossal towers with their clusters of propellers would
be dotted across the Great Plains in a path from Dallas, Texas
in the south up to North Dakota in the north. Other studies by
Heronemus have looked at the possibility of offshore sites along
the New England coast; and a list of locations prepared by an
NSF/NASA study panel includes also the Texas gulf coast, the

NSF/NASA
recommendations

Great Lakes and the Aleutian Chain. This same NSF/NASA
report recommends a 10-year research and development program
for wind power studies at an estimated cost of $610 million,
with emphasis placed on storage techniques and in particular on
fuel cell design, as well as on meteorological, aerodynamic and
engineering aspects. A recently held (June 1973) Wind Energy
Conversion Systems Workshop in Washington and jointly sponsored
by NASA and NSF brought together wind power experts and
veterans of pre-War and World War 2 experiments from all over
the country and abroad.

Windworks

On a smaller scale, and outside the universities, research
work is going on at Windworks, a Wisconsin commune headed
by Hans Meyer, who among other activities has collaborated with
Buckminster Fuller in the installation of a machine on an island
owned by Fuller off the coast of Maine. Also in Maine is the site

College of the Atlantic	of one building project in which it is proposed to use wind power for electricity generation, the College of the Atlantic. The designer is Ed Barnes, the engineering consultants Lehr Associates.
Solar Wind Co.	The Solar Wind Co. in East Holden, Maine, run by Henry Clews, is the U.S. agent for machines produced by the Swiss firm Elektro, and by the Australian company Quirk's. Clews has erected a new 2kW windplant manufactured by Quirk's to power his own homestead, as described in his useful booklet, Electric Power from the Wind.
VITA windmills	Plans have been published by Volunteers in Technical Assistance of Mount Rainier, Maryland, for a variety of small windmills, for use in pumping water and in generating mechanical or electrical power. The designs are intended to be cheaply and easily constructed by unskilled labour, using readily available materials and parts. They include a machine with helical canvas sails (the 'Bicol' windmill) and a Savonius rotor type, as well as more conventional multi-vane designs.
Reines house	The dome house designed and built by Bob Reines in Tijeras, New Mexico, draws its electrical power exclusively from wind generators, with no backup systems; and its battery storage provides for running up to a week at full power without wind. Windmills will also be used to power tools in a machine shop presently being completed on the same site by Reines' group, Integrated Life Support Systems Laboratories. The wind-electric machines are all old ones, rebuilt and reconditioned.
Project Ouroboros	Project Ouroboros, a student-built energy conservation house at the University of Minnesota in Minneapolis, will have a 15' diameter 3kW windmill on a 60' tower, constructed to an original design by Allan Sondak, a student from the School of Architecture.
Brace Institute	In Canada the Brace Institute at McGill University in Quebec has very considerable experience in small scale wind power applications, going back some number of years. Experts from the Institute recently provided help with the installation of a wind-powered generator of commercial (Lübing) design in the 'Ecol Operation' house, a student project at McGill. Brace Institute windmills have been installed and tested in various parts of the world; in Barbados and in Nevis, as well as in Canada. The Institute now has an agreement with the firm of Budgen and Associates whereby Budgen will manufacture and act as agents for the Institute's engineering developments including wind power apparatus.

Theoretical considerations

This is not the place to discuss any of the theoretical or engineering problems arising in the use of wind power for electricity generation on a large scale. It will be appropriate here however to look at some considerations entering into the design or choice of wind-electric machines with small and medium capacity, suitable for use in supplying power to home-steads, farms or to single larger buildings.

The two fundamental factors determining the amount of power which can be generated by any size of windmill are, first, the speed of the wind, and second, the diameter of the propeller. The amount of power produced varies - other things being equal - with the cube of the wind speed and with the square of the diameter of the rotor. These relationships may be expressed by the formula

Power formula

$$P_c \propto V^3 d^2$$

(assuming a fixed value for the air density, or for barometric pressure and temperature).

> where $\quad$ P_c is the rated power capacity
> $\quad\quad\quad$ V is the wind speed
> and $\quad\quad$ d is the diameter of the rotor

It is not possible for a windmill to extract <u>all</u> the power from the stream of wind which meets it, at any speed, since in the nature of the situation the air is not stripped of all its kinetic energy (if so it would be brought to a complete stop), but must pass through the rotor, to emerge at reduced velocity. It has been shown (by Betz) that the theoretical upper limit on the amount of energy which may be extracted is 59% of the total.

Efficiency

Furthermore there is another consideration which limits in practice the total amount of energy which may be collected, even within this theoretical fraction, and that is the variability of the speed of the wind. While the above equation describes the power produced at any given wind speed, and it is possible to design a machine for optimum efficiency at some given speed, it is however not practical to design machines which can operate efficiently over the <u>whole range</u> of wind speeds which may be experienced. In general it is accepted that at very low and very high wind speeds, wind machines will not collect all of the energy that is in principle available. What is usually done is to have the machine cut in at some low wind speed, say 6 or 8mph, and to generate no power below this speed (in any case the power produced would be very little). At the 'rated speed', chosen to be some 5 or 10mph faster than the average annual wind speed for the site, the machine is designed to produce its full power (this is the explanation of the term 'rated power capacity'); and for all higher wind speeds, the output is controlled to this maximum rated value. Control is effected by limiting the maximum speed of the rotor, either by varying the pitch of the blades automatically

Rated power capacity

Governors

or alternatively with some form of governor. The governor may be either of an air brake type, or else act to turn the rotor as a whole either vertically or horizontally through some angle away from the wind, and thus effectively reduce the rotor area. In order to protect the machine from possible damage, it is also general practice to incorporate some furling mechanism which turns the rotor completely out of the wind when the wind speed rises dangerously high.

Taking into account mechanical losses, and losses in the generator and control gear, Golding suggests that the 'overall power coefficient' of wind-electric machines 'may not greatly exceed 40%'. With small fixed-blade rotors, the maximum value for the aerodynamic efficiency may be of the order of 35% he estimates, while taking into account the low efficiency of small-power, low-voltage DC generators, the overall coefficient could be as little as 20%. Clews has prepared a table showing the relationship of propeller diameter, wind velocity and rated power capacity,

Multi-vane water pump-ing type windmill, familiar to the agri-cultural middle West. Adapted from VITA, 'Two Plans for a Fan Bladed Turbine Type Windmill, with Applic-ations', Plan 11133.3, Mt. Rainier, Maryland, fig.25

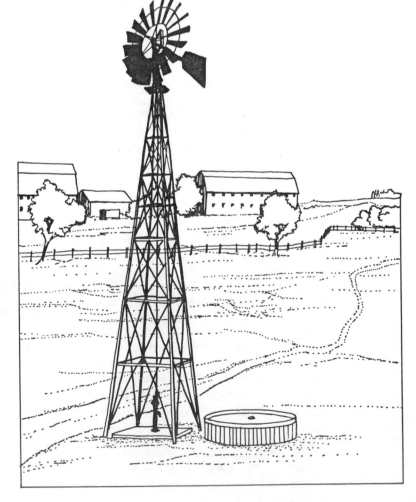

reproduced below, for which he has assumed an efficiency of
70%; that is to say 70% of the theoretical maximum, i.e. 70%
of 50%, or roughly 41% overall. This is for efficient high-speed
propellers and relatively large capacity generators, but the
figure is still perhaps optimistic.

Windmill Power Output in Watts (assuming 70% efficiency),
from H. Clews, Electric Power from the Wind, Solar Wind Co.,
Maine 1973 p.4.

Propeller diameter in feet	Wind velocity in mph					
	5	10	15	20	25	30
2	0.6	5	16	38	73	130
4	2	19	64	150	300	520
6	5	42	140	340	660	1150
8	10	75	260	610	1180	2020
10	15	120	400	950	1840	3180
12	21	170	540	1360	2660	4600
14	29	230	735	1850	3620	6250
16	40	300	1040	2440	4740	8150
18	51	375	1320	3060	6000	10350
20	60	475	1600	3600	7360	12760
22	73	580	1940	4350	8900	15420
24	86	685	2300	5180	10650	18380

To take an example, to show the use of the table; for a site
where the average annual wind speed is 15mph say, and it is
decided that maximum generating capacity should be reached at
25mph wind speeds, then a propeller diameter of 8' would produce
at this maximum something over 1kW of power.

Height of tower

Besides propeller diameter, two other significant variables in the
design of windmills, are the height of the tower, and the maximum
speed of rotation of the propeller. On the question of the height
of the tower: as a general rule, the mean wind speed is slower
nearer the ground, and increases with increasing height. This
'vertical wind speed gradient' is more marked over flat terrain
than it is at the summits of hills. It follows that for flat sites
especially, the higher the tower the better; the limiting factors
being structural and economic. The behaviour of the wind on a
very local scale is affected considerably by trees, buildings and
other obstructions. It is usually necessary to mount the rotor at
least 30' or 40' above ground and in the most exposed part of the
site to achieve good results. It is not very satisfactory to mount
the windmill on a rooftop, since the flow of wind immediately
above the roof's surface is turbulent; and there may also be
dangerous stresses imposed on the roof structure by the machine
in high winds.

Speed of rotation of propeller	The speed of propeller rotation is related to the design of generator. Most electrical generators of small size are designed to run at relatively high speeds, up to 5,000rpm., while the speed of rotation of windmills is rather low, seldom more than 300rpm. In the medium size commercially produced wind-electric machines a compromise is reached by using a fairly low-speed generator, running at perhaps 1,000rpm., and gearing up the drive from the rotor appropriately by a factor of four or five.
Tip speed ratio	The speed of rotation of windmill propellers is usually given as a 'tip speed ratio', that is the ratio of the peripheral speed of the propeller tips to the wind velocity. The more efficient modern high-speed propeller designs run at tip speed ratios of around 5 or 6, and going as high as 8 (in the Swiss Elektro machines). For comparison the slow multivane waterpumping mills run at tip speed ratios typically of between 1 and 3, which is much less efficient but which suits the requirements for pumping application quite adequately.
Electricity storage	The fact that the speed of the wind is variable and unpredictable, at least from hour to hour and from day to day (although the wind's behaviour on average measured over longer periods is surprisingly regular) means that to exploit its power usefully, some method of energy storage must be found. Many of the larger scale machines, such as the Smith-Putnam windmill, were intended simply to provide supplementary generating capacity to a network supplied principally by fossil fuel powered stations. As such there was no call for electricity storage associated with these machines. In the current discussions of windmill application for commercial scale power production, there is talk of the use of wind-generated electricity to electrolyse water, producing hydrogen - i.e. storing chemical energy - this hydrogen either to be burned directly as fuel, or else to be used in fuel cells.
Hydrogen as a fuel	Hydrogen has been promoted widely in recent discussions of energy problems as the 'ideal fuel of the future' to replace oil products and natural gas. As long ago as 1932 there was a scheme in Germany to produce hydrogen by electrolysis of water, using cheap night power, and then to use the gas, stored at high pressure in metal cylinders, to power road vehicles with modified internal combustion engines. Piped hydrogen could have application in total energy systems, much as natural gas does today; and could be used to power fuel cells in a similar manner for example to the Pratt and Whitney 'Project Target' in which a design of natural gas fuel cell, intended for domestic use, is currently being tested.
Fuel cells	The fuel cell is essentially a device for generating electricity from gaseous or liquid fuel by an electrochemical oxidation reaction, using oxygen from the air. Briefly, although the prospects are very promising, the present cost seems too high for general application in buildings or for domestic electricity

supply; although where the requirement is for a very light-weight, maintenance-free source of electrical power with less emphasis on cost, e.g. in remote mountain locations, or on navigational buoys, fuel cells are already in practical use. A short history or fuel cell developments and an account of the chemical and engineering principles involved, is given by F.T. Bacon – the man with whose name the fuel cell is primarily associated – in 'Fuel Cells, Past, Present and Future' in Electrochimica Acta Vol.14 1969,p.p.569-85. A recent review article on the use of hydrogen as a fuel is F.T. Bacon and Tom Fry, 'When there's no more oil and gas...', New Scientist 10 August 1972 pp.285-7.

Another possibility proposed for energy storage involves using windmills to augment the output of, or supply the head of water for hydro-electric plants, by pumping water from the lower level to the higher level, i.e. storing potential energy. Both this and the electrolysis of water are however only really appropriate for large scale use. Two possibilities which have been raised for energy storage in conjunction with small independent wind machines, involve using mechanical power direct to drive a heat pump, or else using wind-generated electricity to run electrical resistance heating, and storing the heat (destined for space and water heating purposes) in either case in some form of thermal storage reservoir (as discussed in the chapter on solar heating). Meanwhile the possibilities for electricity storage come down at present in effect to the conventional lead-acid accumulator, or else some other form of electrical battery, which is charged when the wind is blowing, and which provides a reserve of power when the weather is calm.

Electrical generators (as powered by small windmills) are of two kinds, the brush type generator which produce direct current, and the alternator, giving alternating current. Batteries must be charged using direct current, and this is simply done with a DC generator, which can quite practically be run at varying speeds depending on the strength of the wind and the speed of the rotor. When the wind machine is used to drive an alternator, then the speed must generally be kept constant, and the AC current must be passed through a rectifier for the purposes of battery charging. Some machines have combined both DC generator and alternator driven off the same shaft.

Types of electricity storage battery

The most common and presently the cheapest form of battery available (both in terms of capital and running costs) is the familiar lead-acid type, which has been well-tried in its application in the automobile. It is capable of giving a high voltage on discharge, and can operate over a wide range of temperatures. It is however damaged by overcharging, and by being discharged too far. Ideally lead-acid accumulators should not be discharged below half-way, to preserve their life- although this practice of course increases the total capacity needed. Under good conditions they will be capable of undergoing

2,000 or so charge/discharge cycles. Reserve lead-acid batteries in telephone exchanges and power stations can have a life of up to twenty years, though a more normal working life is five or six years.

Between 1950 and 1965 advances in battery design resulted in a reduction of weight and volume for given output of 20%. The size and weight of a lead-acid battery storage system are given by typical figures of 44 watt hours/kilogramme and 0.08 watt hours/cc. For use with windmills there are not the same restrictions on size and weight as there are with automobile accumulators, and special purpose 'stationary' batteries are sold (e.g. by the Australian firm Quirk's), which come in sizes from 10 Ah to 8,000 Ah. The small sizes come as three-cell 6-volt batteries, and the larger sizes as single-cell 2-volt batteries. All of the Quirk's batteries are equipped with built-in 'pilot ball' indicators which give a visible index of their state of charge.

Alkaline batteries

In principle it would be possible to use as an alternative the alkaline battery, either a nickel-iron or a nickel-cadmium type. These batteries are more efficient than the lead-acid, longer-lasting, not liable to damage from overcharging or complete discharge, and capable of a greater number of cycles; but they are also more bulky and more expensive. Other more marginal future possibilities are the silver-zinc battery, with a very high energy density but also a very high cost; and the zinc-air type of cell which is still under development.

Battery storage capacity

The capacity of battery to be installed depends on the capacity of the generator and on its voltage, as well as on the maximum anticipated number of consecutive hours or days of calm weather Most systems will need storage capacity to cover at least three days without wind; and where there is no alternative back-up power supply - such as a gas-driven generator - for calm periods, capacity for probably as much as seven days. To determine the required size of generator and battery storage, needs a calculation of the average total rate of power consumption expressed in say kWh/month, and some estimate of the maximum current to be drawn at any one time. The total anticipated rate of power consumption can be worked out if necessary by taking all the appliances to be used, determining their rated power use in each case in watts, and estimating the amount of hours per month each is likely to be operated. Tables of statistics for the average power consumption of various domestic appliances are available (some figures are given by Clews, Electric Power from the Wind, p.25). The resulting monthly consumption gives an indication of the size of generator required. This relation-

Size of generator

ship is a complicated one, since the monthly output in kWh of a generator of some given rated power capacity, is a factor of the wind regime obtaining at the particular site, as well as the efficiency of the machine and the range of wind speeds over which power is produced. Clews has prepared a table based on a composite of his own actual experience and figures supplied by manufacturers, which in an approximate way relates average monthly output in kWh to rated power capacity and average windspeed (assuming typical modern machines with tip speed ratios of around 5 and efficiencies of 70%, operating between 6 and 25mph at the limits).

Average monthly output in Kilowatt-hours
from H. Clews, Electric Power from the Wind, Solar Wind Co., Maine 1973 p.7

Nominal output rating of generator in watts	Average monthly wind speed in mph					
	6	8	10	12	14	16
50	1.5	3	5	7	9	10
100	3	5	8	11	13	15
250	6	12	18	24	29	32
500	12	24	35	46	55	62
1,000	22	45	65	86	104	120
2,000	40	80	120	160	200	235
4,000	75	150	230	310	390	460
6,000	115	230	350	470	590	710
8,000	150	300	450	600	750	900
10,000	185	370	550	730	910	1090
12,000	215	430	650	870	1090	1310

Once it is established that the average monthly output of the generator is sufficient to supply the anticipated monthly power demand, then the next step is to determine the required battery storage capacity. If the maximum period of calm to be covered is say three days, then the storage must be sufficient to cover one tenth of the monthly consumption. The design of battery storage is also affected by the peak current expected to be drawn at one time. The type of stationary battery used typically for these purposes is designed to supply only low currents and is generally limited to some maximum discharge rate. This maximum rate is much lower than that of the usual automobile accumulator, which must produce large currents for short periods as for example when used to drive the starter motor. It is this limitation on the rate of discharge which gives the stationary battery its relatively much longer life.

Generator voltage

The generator voltage on very small windmills, up to 500W capacity, might be 6-12v, while with the larger machines the voltages might be 24, 32, 48 or 115v. The standard mains supply in the United States is AC at 60 cycles/sec and 115 volts, and most domestic and other electric appliances are designed accordingly; so a wind-electric system running on 115 volts will be particularly appropriate for this reason, and will avoid the need for transformers. Some appliances and circuits, such as lights, heating devices and power tools can be run off direct current. Most electronic apparatus however is designed specifically for AC, such as stereo or television sets, and for these it will be necessary to use some type of inverter. The available types comprise the 'motor-generator' or 'rotary inverter', powered by a DC motor and which produces the sine-wave AC demanded by electronic equipment. Its average efficiency, however, is only 60%, and at low loads it is particularly inefficient. Otherwise a solid state inverter may be used, which is more expensive, but has an efficiency of 80%. It is sensible to split the power coming from the windmill or batteries, using the greater part

Elektro wind
electric generator

Automatic switching

directly in the DC circuits, while confining the use of the inverter only to that equipment for which it is essential. A wind-electric system will have some means for the automatic switching of loads from generator output to storage and vice-versa, for channelling unused current from the generator to the batteries, and for cutting off the generator output when the batteries are fully charged and no current is being drawn.

Costs

A very rough figure for the overall capital cost of medium size wind-electric systems including machine, tower, battery storage and controls, seems to be around $800 - $1,300/ kilowatt. Smith gives an approximate formula in sterling for the cost of blading and generator assembly, with controls but without tower or batteries, based on a survey of manufacturers, of £260 + £130/kW. In dollar equivalents this is $624 + $312/kW. Some more precise details of the actual current costs of commercially available machines are given in the list of windmill manufacturers which follows, including in some cases also the costs of towers and control equipment.

Costs of batteries and inverters

Some prices of stationary battery sets produced by the Australian manufacturer Quirk's and available through their U.S. agent Solar Wind Co. of Maine are :

12 volt, 130Ah set (2x6 volt units)	$60.00
12 volt, 270Ah set (6x2 volt units)	$138.00
12 volt, 540Ah set (12x2 volt units)	$265.00
32 volt, 270Ah set (16x2 volt units)	$375.00
115 volt, 130Ah set (19x6 volt units)	$545.00
115 volt, 270Ah set (56x2 volt units)	$1,295.00
115 volt, 540Ah set (112x2 volt units)	$2,495.00

Some designs of inverters are sold for the purposes of camping, at a cost of around $50.00, which will invert the 12v DC current from an automobile battery to 115v AC. Small combination inverters and battery chargers are sold by Sears Roebuck Co. Rotary inverters are available from Electro Sales Co. Inc., 100 Fellsway West, Somerville, Mass. 02145. Electronic DC to AC inverters are sold by the Nova Manufacturing Co., 263 Hillside Avenue, Nutley, N.J. 07110. A design of electronic inverter marketed under the name of The Power Plug is available from Creative Electronics, 7060 N. Lawndale Ave., Chicago, Ill. 60645. Prices are as follows :

Model D12A1	12v DC to 115v AC	1,000W	$489.95
Model D12A2	12v DC to 115v AC	2,000W	$589.95
Model D24A3	24v DC to 115v AC	3,000W	$689.95

Windmill manufacturers

This list covers windmill manufacturers and related companies
and agents; and gives details of windmill cost, performance etc.
where known. Much of the information is drawn from G.Smith's
list of windmill manufacturers, prepared in the University of
Cambridge Department of Architecture's Technical Research
Division. Prices are 1973, exclusive of shipment charges or
(on foreign machines) customs duty.

America

Aermotor Division

Braden Industries, 800 E. Dallas St., Broken Arrow, Oklahoma
74012

Multivane waterpumping, 'reportedly all manufacturing done by
Argentine licensee' (Smith). Sizes 6', 8', 10', 12', 14', 16'.

Dempster Industries

711 S. 6, Beatrice, Nebraska 68310
Tel.: (402) 223 4026

Multivane waterpumping

Model	Size	Stroke	Price (without tower)
No. 12	6'	5"	$264
No. 12A	8'	5" or $7\frac{1}{2}$"	$365
No. 12	10'	$5\frac{1}{2}$" or $7\frac{1}{2}$"	$620

Towers available, heights from 22' to 39'

Dyna Technology

Ecological Science Corp., Sioux City, Iowa 51102
Tel.: (712) 252 1821
Eastern sales : 1561 Lister Rd., Box 7407, Baltimore Md.21227
Tel.: (301) 242 4700

'Wincharger' electric machine Model 1222H is only design still
in production, 12 volt DC, 200W generator, 6' two-bladed
propeller, air-brake governor. Cost with 10', 4-leg tower but
without batteries, $395.

| Heller-Aller Co. | Corner Perry & Oakwood, Napoleon, Ohio 43545 |
| | Tel.: (419) 592 1856 |

Multivane waterpumping only: 'Baker Run-in-Oil' models

Size	Stroke	Price (without tower)
6'	$4\frac{1}{4}$"	$234
8'	$5\frac{1}{4}$"	$317
10'	$6\frac{1}{2}$"	$434
12'	8"	$697

Towers available from 15' to 80'

| Solar Wind Co. | R.F.D. 2, Happytown Rd., East Holden, Maine 04429 |
| | (Henry Clews) |

Not manufacturer, but U.S. agent for Quirk's of Australia, and Elektro GmbH of Switzerland (q.v.). Also selling plans of 500W, 12 volt DC or (with inverter) 115 volt AC design, the 'Sencenbaugh 0_2 Powered Delight' by Jim Sencenbaugh of Palo Alto, Ca. described in Mother Earth News No. 20 pp. 32-36

| VIIA | (Volunteers in Technical Assistance) |
| | 3706 Rhode Island Ave., Mt. Rainier, Maryland 20822 |

Not manufacturers; plans available at nominal charge for 'VITA-Essex' 10' multivane windmill, 'Bicol' 10' machine with helical canvas sails for waterpumping, Savonius rotor built from 45 gal. oil drums also for waterpumping, and two designs for 6' 6-blade and 10' 8-blade machines for generating either mechanical or electrical power.

| Windworks | Box 329, Route 3, Mukwanago, Wisconsin 53149 |
| | (Hans Meyer, Ben Wolff) |

Research and development only, no products. Design for home-built machine by Hans Meyer, 3-bladed rotor, 12' tower, rotor blades formed from expanded paper, d.i.y. cost about $200, published in Popular Science Nov. 1972 pp.103-5, 142

Other American windmill manufacturers in business at one time, or about whom no further information has been obtained:

| Baker Mfg. Co. | 133 Enterprise, Evansville, Wisconsin |

| Bucknell Engineering | 10717 Rush St., S. El Monte, California 91733 |
| | (Electric 220W machine to order) |

Fairbury Co.

Fairbury, Nebraska

Howard Smith Co.

1201 Sawyer, Houston, Texas

Jacobs Corp.

2714 Fowler Street, Fort Meyers, Florida
(Made wind electric machines, no longer in business)

M.J. Kestin Co.,

225 Lafayette, New York, New York

Foreign manufacturers

The following are manufacturers or organisations presently
producing or selling wind-electric equipment, abroad.

Aerowatt S.A.

37 Rue Chanzy, 75 Paris 11^e, France

'Electric, elegant, efficient, expensive, 30W to 4kW' (Smith)

Brace Institute

Ste. Anne de Bellevue 800, Quebec, Canada

Not manufacturers, plans only for 10kW 3-blade fixed pitch
machine. 32' prototype in operation tested both for waterpumping
and electricity generation.

Dunlite Co.

Divn. of Pye Industries, 21 Frome St., Adelaide 5000, Australia

1kW model L, 3-blade variable pitch, voltages from 12 to 50
2kW model W, 3-blade variable pitch, voltages from 12 to 110

Elektro GmbH

Winterthur, St. Gallerstrasse 27, Switzerland
(U.S. agent Solar Wind Co., Maine, q.v.)

World's largest manufacturer of modern wind electric generators.
Four main models:

Model		Voltage DC	Propeller	Blades	Price
KSV 300	300W	12	7'7"	2	$575
WV 15 G	1.2kW	12,115	9'10"	2	$1045
WV 25/3G	2.5kW	115	12'6"	3	$1435
WV G 5	6kW	115	16'6"	3	$1785

Other sizes and voltages, including 50W to 250W panemone
type also available. Prices cover complete windplant (but not
tower) including voltage regulator, control panel and packing
for ocean shipment. Automatic high wind cut-off controls extra.
'In a recent survey by the Government of India, the Elektro model
WVG 5 proved to be the most economical source of wind-generated

power in the world, even compared to units many times larger.' In general Electro appears to offer some of the best value for size machines available.

Enag S.A.

Rue de Pont-l'Abbe, Quimper, Finisterre, France

'180W to 2kW, 2-blade variable pitched, average prices' (Smith)

Harber Ventus Ltd.

Bridge Approach, Hamworthy, Poole, Dorset, England

Yachting use, 5W

Lübing

Ludwig Bening, 2847 Barnstorf, P.O. Box 171, Germany

Manufacturers of M022-3 G024-400 400W 3-blade machine producing 24 volts AC (and other models ?)

Quirk's Victory Light Co.

33 Fairweather St., Bellevue Hill, New South Wales, Australia (U.S. agent Solar Wind Co., Maine, q.v.)

Model L	1kW	32 volt	12'	3-bladed	$1,145
Model M	2kW	24, 32, 48 or	12'	3-bladed	$1,675
		115 volts			

Prices include tower cap, Diotran solid state voltage regulator and control panel. (These are the same machines as the Dunlite but rather more highly priced). 3-leg towers available, 10' to 70', prices $148 to $695.

Wind power bibliography

Aerowatt S.A., Wind-Blown Generators, publication of Aerowatt S.A., 37 rue Chanzy, 75 Paris 11e, France

P.Ailleret, 'L'Energie Eolienne; Sa Valeur et la Prospection des Sites', Revue Générale d'Electricité, Paris 1946

Alternative Sources of Energy, wind power feature in No. 8, Jan 1973, reprinted in Lifestyle' No. 3 Feb. 1973

Aviation Week and Space Technology, 'Windmill Turbine Developed at Princeton' issue of Nov. 13 1972 p.47

T.H. Barton, A Simple Electric Transmission for a Free Running Windmill, Brace Research Institute, Ste. Anne de Bellevue, 800, Quebec, Canada

Greville Bathe, Horizontal Windmills, Draft Mills and Similar Air-flow Engines, Allen, Lane and Scott, Philadelphia 1948

Arnold Benson, Plans for the Construction of a Small Wind Electric Plant, pubn. No. 33 Oklahoma State University, Sillwater, Ok. 74079

Hartmut Bossel, 'Low-cost Windmill for Developing Nations' in VITA Handbook, VITA 3706 Rhode Island Ave., Mt. Rainier, Maryland 20822

C.A. Cameron Brown, Windmills for the Generation of Electricity, Institute for Research in Agricultural Engineering, Oxford 1933

N. Carruthers, 'Variations in Wind Velocity near the Ground', Quarterly Journal of the Royal Meteorological Society Oct. 1943

R.E. Chilcott, 'Notes on the Development of the Brace Airscrew Windmill as a Prime Mover', technical note in The Aeronautical Journal of the Royal Aeronautical Society Vol. 73, April 1969 p.334

Henry Clews, 'Solar Windmill', Alternative Sources of Energy No. 8, Jan. 1973 p.14

Henry Clews, Electric Power from the Wind, Solar Wind Co., Maine 1973

Dick Coon, 'Giant Wind Machine for Generating Electricity gets Federal Scrutiny', The National Observer June 24th 1972 (Montana State University project)

Albert E. De Le Rue, Man and the Winds, Hutchinson 1955

Engineering, 'Putting the Wind to Work', issue of Nov.22, 1968 pp.760-1 (Brace Research Institute work)

R. Fardin, 'Windpower: Its Advantages and Possibilities', Proceedings, U.N. Scientific Conference on the Conservation and Utilisation of Resources Vol. III p.322, Lake Success 1949

Lanny Fasching, 'Whirlwind', Mechanix Illustrated April 1941 pp.102-3

Anton Flettner, The Story of the Rotor, trans from the German by F.O. Willhofft, published by the translator, New York 1926

Kendall Ford, 'Wind Driven Generator', Popular Science Monthly Aug. 1938

J. Frankiel, 'Wind Power Research in Israel', Wind and Solar Energy, UNESCO 1956 (q.v.)

Stanley Freese, Windmills and Millwrighting, Cambridge University 1957

Bill Gibbons, 'Rebuilt Windchargers', Alternative Sources of Energy No. 8 Jan. 1973 p.14

M.A. Giblett, The Structure of the Wind over Level Country, Meteorological Memoir No. 54

E.W. Golding, The Electrification of Agriculture and Rural Districts, English Universities Press 1937

E.W. Golding, Large Scale Generation of Electricity by Wind Power,
Electrical Research Association Technical Report C/T101,
Cranfield 1949

E.W. Golding, 'Wind Generated Electricity and its Possible Use on the Farm',
Farm Mechanization March 1953

E.W. Golding, 'Harnessing the Wind', Discovery Dec. 1953

E.W. Golding, The Generation of Electricity by Wind Power, Spon, London;
Philosophical Library, New York, 1955

E.W. Golding, 'Electrical Energy from the Wind', Proceedings of the Institute
of Electrical Engineers Vol. 102 Part A No. 6, Dec. 1955

E.W. Golding, 'The Economic Utilization of Wind Energy in Arid Areas', Wind
and Solar Energy, UNESCO 1956 (q.v.)

E.W. Golding, 'The Combination of Local Sources of Energy for Isolated Communities',
Solar Energy Vol. II No. 1 pp.7-12, Jan 1958

E.W. Golding, 'The Influence of Aerodynamics in Wind Power Development'
Report 401, NATO Advisory Group for Aeronautical
Research and Development, NASA, Langley Field,
Va. 23365

E.W. Golding, 'Windmills for Water Lifting and the Generation of Electricity
on the Farm', Informal Working Bulletin 17 of Agricultural
Engineering Branch, Land and Water Development Division,
Food and Agriculture Organization of the United Nations

E.W. Golding and A.H. Stodhart, 'The Potentialities of Wind Power for Electricity
Generation with Special Reference to Small Scale Operation',
Electrical Research Association Technical Report W/T16,
Cranfield 1949

E.W. Golding and A.H. Stodhart, 'The Selection and Characteristics of Wind Power
Sites', Electrical Research Association Technical Report
C/T108, Cranfield 1952

E.W. Golding and A.H. Stodhart, 'The Use of Wind Power in Denmark',
Electrical Research Association Technical Report C/T112,
Cranfield 1954

Senator Mike Gravel, 'Clean Energy via the Wind', Congressional Record Washington
D.C. Dec. 7 1971 Vol. 117 No. 190

Senator Mike Gravel, 'Gentle Solutions for Our Energy Needs', Congressional
Record, Washington D.C. Feb.9 1972 Vol. 118 No. 17-11

Lyman E. Greenlee, 'Electric Power from the Wind', Alternative Sources of Energy
No. 4 Jan. 1972 pp. 1-3

T.G.N. Haldane, 'Power from the Wind', The Times Review of Industry, Oct 1949

T.G.N. Haldane and E.W. Golding, 'Recent Developments in Large-Scale Wind
Power Generation in Great Britain', Fourth World Power
Conference, Section K, London 1950

Her Majesty's Stationery Office, Wind Power, Technical Paper No. 17
pp.129-131, H.M.S.O. London

E.W. Heronemus, 'Power from the Offshore Winds', Proceedings of the 8th
Annual Marine Technology Society Conference, Washington
D.C. 1972

E.W. Heronemus, The U.S. Energy Crisis : Some Proposed Gentle Solutions,
paper presented to local sections of American Society
of Mechanical Engineers and Institute of Electrical
and Electronic Engineers, Jan. 12 1972, West Springfield,
Mass.

U. Hütter, 'Plans and Balancing of Energy of Small Output Wind Power-Plant',
    Wind and Solar Energy, UNESCO 1956 (q.v.)

J.Juul, 'Investigation of the Possibilities of Utilisation of Wind Power',
    Elektroteknikeren Vol. 45 pp. 607-635 No. 20, 22
    Oct 1949

J. Juul, 'Wind Machines', Wind and Solar Energy, UNESCO 1956 (q.v.)

Stephen Kidd, 'Windmills and Other Things', Princeton Alumni Weekly, April 24
    1973 pp.12-13

S. Kidd and D. Garr, 'Can We Harness Pollution-Free Electric Power from Windmills ?'
    Popular Science Nov. 1972 pp.70-72

Narciso Levy, 'Current State of Windpower Research in the Soviet Union',
    Technical Report No. T56 of Brace Research Institute
    Ste. Anne de Bellevue 800, Quebec, Canada

G.M. Lilley and W.T. Rainbird, 'Investigation into the Potentialities of Ducted
    Windmills', Electrical Research Association Technical
    Report C/T119, Cranfield 1957

Julian McCaull, 'Windmills', Environment Vol. 15 No. 1, Jan./Feb. 1973
    pp.6-17

Marshall F. Merriam, 'Is There a Place for the Windmill in the Less Developed
    Countries ?', Working Paper No. 20, Technology and
    Development Institute, East-West Center, March 1972

Hans Meyer, 'Wind Generators: Here's an Advanced Design You Can Build',
    Popular Science Nov.1972 pp.103-5, 142

Mother Earth News, 'Windmills' in issue No. 7, Jan.1971 p.14; 'Free Power from the
    Wind' in issue No. 17, p.60; 'Henry Clews' Wind-
    Powered Homestead' in issue No. 18, p.25; Jim
    Sencenbaugh, 'I Built a Windcharger for $400' in issue
    No. 20 pp.32-36

NSF/NASA Solar Energy Panel, An Assessment of Solar Energy as a National Energy
    Resource, College of Engineering, University of Maryland,
    Dec. 1972 (includes coverage of wind power)

H.E. Parsons, 'Wind Power -History and Present Status', paper presented to 66th
    Annual General and Professional Meeting of Engineering
    Institute of Canada, Vancouver, 9th May 1952, published
    in The Engineering Journal Jan. 1953

F.D. Pigeaud and R. Wailes, 'Power in the Wind', New Scientist May 1965

F.E. Powell, Windmills and Wind Motors : How to Build and Run Them,
    Spon and Chamberlain, New York 1910

P.C. Putnam, Power from the Wind, Van Nostrand, New York 1948

Winnie Redrocker, 'Build a Wind Generator', Alternative Sources of Energy
    No. 8 Jan. 1973 pp.12-13

J. Reynolds, Windmills and Watermills, Praeger, New York 1970

H.H. Rosenbrock, 'An Extension of the Momentum Theory of Wind Turbines',
    Technical Report C/T105, Electrical Research
    Association, Cranfield 1951

S.J. Savonius, 'The S-Rotor and its Application', Mechanical Engineering
    Vol. 53 No. 5 May 1931

Sierra Club Bulletin, 'Windpower' in issue of Sept. 1971

J.M. Sil, 'Windmill Power', The Indian Journal of Meteorology and Geophysics
    Vol. 3 No. 2 1952

M.H. Simonds, B.E. and A. Bodek, 'Performance Test of a Savonias Rotor',
    Technical Report No. T10 of Brace Research Institute,
    Ste. Anne de Bellevue 800, Quebec, Canada

C.P. Skilton, British Windmills and Watermills, Collins, London 1947

A.G. Spanides and A. Hatzikakidis eds., Solar and Aeolian Energy
Plenum Press, New York 1964

David Stabb, 'Wind', Architectural Design April 1972 pp.253-4

Frederick Stokhuyzen, The Dutch Windmill, Universe Books, New York 1967

P.H. Thomas, Electric Power from the Wind, U.S. Federal Power Commission 1945

P.H. Thomas, 'Harnessing the Wind for Electric Power', Proceedings, U.N.
Scientific Conference on the Conservation and
Utilization of Resources Vol.III p.130, Lake Success 1949

United Nations, Proceedings of the U.N. Conference on New Sources of Energy,
Rome 1961; Vol. 7 devoted to Wind Power. U.N.
Publications, New York 1964

United Power News, 'Power from the Wind' in issue of Jan. 1972, United Power
Association, Elk River, Minnesota 55330

UNESCO, Symposium on Wind and Solar Energy, New Delhi 1954. Proceedings
published by UNESCO, Paris 1956

John Venters, 'The Orkney Windmill and Wind Power in Scotland', Engineer
No. 189 July 27 1959 p.106

Volunteers in Technical Assistance (VITA); 'Two Plans for a Fan-Bladed Turbine-
Type Windmill with Applications'; 'The Bicol Windmill'
No. 11131.1; 'Savonius Rotor for Water Pumping' No.
11132.1; 'VITA-Essex Windmill' No.11133.1. 3706
Rhode Island Ave., Mt. Rainier, Maryland 20822

Rex Wailes, Windmills in England, Architectural Press, London 1948

J.G. Walker, 'The Automatic Operation of a Medium-Sized Wind Driven
Generator Running in Isolation', Technical Report C/T122
(160), Electrical Research Association, Cranfield

Hans Witte, Windkraftwerke, Rudolf A. Lang, Possneck 1950

World Meteorological Organisation, Energy from the Wind: Assessment of Suitable
Winds and Sites, Technical Note No. 4, Geneva 1954
(contains bibliography)

A bibliography of wind energy literature has been published by
the Windworks organisation:

Windworks, Wind Energy Bibliography, October 1973. Available from Box 329, Route 3,
Mukwonago, Wisconsin 53149

Small scale water power

Power available

The kinetic energy of water flowing from a higher to a lower level can be harnessed to produce useful mechanical or electrical power. Traditionally mechanical power for milling, pumping or sawing was generated with the use of water wheels, turned by the flow of streams or small rivers. The normal arrangement with water wheels involves damming the stream so as to produce a head of water ('head' being the difference in height between the upper and lower levels), and diverting usually only a part of the flow along a channel or 'headrace' to the wheel. Once through the wheel the water returns to the main stream via a lower channel or 'tailrace'. The maximum amount of power available in theory from the flow of water is related to the speed of flow, and the head, and may be expressed by the following formula: gross power (horsepower) =

$$\frac{\text{Minimum water flow (ft}^3/\text{sec) x gross head (ft)}}{8.8}$$

This figure must be reduced to take account of losses through inefficiencies in the various parts of the machinery, the arrangement of water flow, and the power transmission. The water flow in a stream is variable with the seasons, and so it is usual to size the machine appropriately for the <u>minimum</u> rate of flow, as measured during the driest part of the year.

Water wheels

Water wheels run at between 2 and 12 revolutions per minute, and are particularly appropriate where the rate of water flow is fluctuating. It is not practicable to control their speed to a fixed rate; and because of their slow speed it is generally necessary to gear up the drive to any machinery. One advantage of water wheels over water-driven turbines (described below) is that they are robust and self-cleaning, and do not need to be protected from debris, branches etc. carried down by the water.

Overshot wheels

There are two distinct types of water wheel, the 'overshot' in which, as the name indicates, the water passes over the top of the circumference of the wheel; and the 'undershot' where the water passes below. The overshot type is suitable for heads of water of between 10 and 30 feet, and for flow rates from 1 to 30ft^3/sec. The undershot wheel is appropriate for smaller heads of water –1.5 to 10 feet – and flow rates from 10 to 100 ft^3/sec. In the overshot type or wheel a flow of water of one to two foot depth is directed onto the wheel through a wooden or metal channel or 'flume', at a velocity of about 3 ft/sec. At the end of the flume is a gate, adjustable so that the issuing jet of water strikes the wheel at a speed of between 6 and 10 ft/sec. The width of the wheel is greater than that of the flume by about one foot, and is dependent on the

Undershot water
wheel; adapted
from H.W. Hamm,
'Low-Cost Develop-
ment of Small
Water-Power Sites',
VITA, Schenectady,
New York 1971
p.35 fig.32

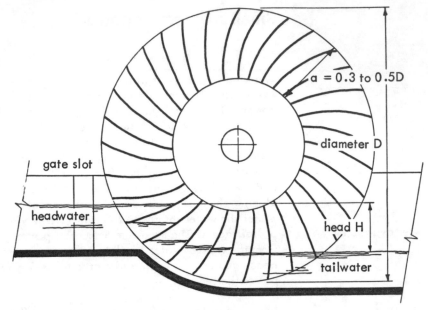

gate slot

headwater

a = 0.3 to 0.5D

diameter D

head H

tailwater

Overshot water
wheel; adapted
from H.W.Hamm,
'Low-Cost
Development of
Small Water-Power
Sites', VITA,
Schenectady,
New York 1971
p.34 fig.31

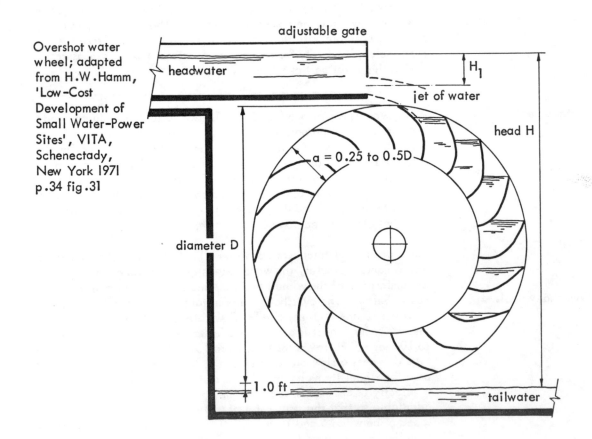

adjustable gate

headwater

H_1

jet of water

head H

diameter D

a = 0.25 to 0.5D

1.0 ft

tailwater

amount of water used. The diameter of the wheel is about two foot less than the head dimension, and the depth of the blades or buckets is from a quarter to a half of the wheel's diameter. The efficiency of a good overshot water wheel may be from 60% to 80%.

Undershot wheels

With undershot wheels the diameter should be three to four times the head, so that the actual size may vary from 6 to 30 feet. The wheel dips between one and three feet into the water, and the flow rate should be from 3 to 10 ft^3/sec for each foot of wheel width. The depth of the blades is from a third to a half of the wheel diameter. The efficiency of well-designed undershot wheels can vary from 60% to 75%.

Hydraulic turbines

Because of the higher speeds of rotation required than are possible with traditional water wheels, the generation of electricity from water power requires the use of turbines. In general the efficiency of turbines is greater than that of water wheels, usually around 80%.

As a simpler and more economical expedient than special-purpose turbines it is possible to use water pumps in reverse rotation to generate electricity (though the efficiencies of these will be much lower). The pumps may be either of propeller or centrifugal types. Since the speed of rotation tends to be variable, the use of pumps run backwards as turbines is generally more suitable for generating direct current – though A.C. can be generated if the flow of water is controlled by a valve and the rotational speed of the pump by a governor.

Pelton turbines

Michell or Banki turbines

Water turbines proper for small-scale power generation are of two types; the 'impulse' or Pelton type, where a jet of water from a nozzle is directed at a rotating runner carrying a series of cupped blades or buckets on its circumference; and the Michell or Banki type; where the water is led from the nozzle onto the surface of a bladed runner and passes into the centre and out through the further side of the runner before discharging into the tailrace. The impulse type turbines are suitable for use with high heads and low flow rates. They run at high speeds and are simple and economical. Michell or Banki type turbines are very flexible in their range or applications, for use both with high or low heads, the speed of rotation being dependent on this head dimension. Differences in the rate of flow can be accommodated by varying the width of the nozzle and the width of the runner, between dimensions from 2 to 14 inches. Nozzle and runner widths (in inches) are given by the following formulae:

Nozzle width

$$\frac{210 \times \text{flow (ft}^3\text{sec)}}{\text{Runner outside diam. (inches)} \times \text{head (feet)}}$$

Runner width

$$= \text{Nozzle width} + 1''$$

Rotational speed

$$\frac{862 \times \text{head (feet)}}{\text{Runner outside diam. (inches)}} \quad \text{(rpm)}$$

Small impulse
turbine runner,
from H.W. Hamm,
'Low-Cost Develop-
ment of Small
Water-Power Sites',
VITA, Schenectady,
New York 1971
p.25 fig.24

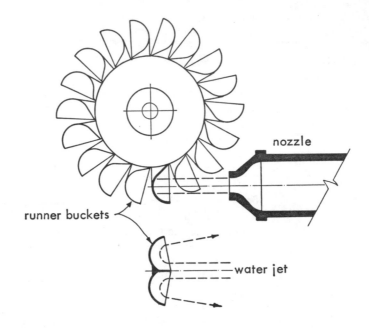

nozzle

runner buckets

water jet

Detail of nozzle
for 12" Michell
runner, from W.H.
Hamm, 'Low-Cost
Development of
Small Water-
Power Sites', VITA
Schenectady, New
York 1971 p.30
fig.28

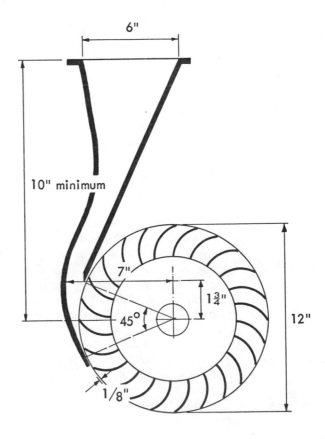

6"

10" minimum

7"

$1\frac{3}{4}$"

45°

12"

1/8"

The efficiency of a Michell turbine can be 80% or more. It is possible to regulate the water flow and rotational speed by means of a gate in the nozzle, and a governor, so as to give constant speed for generating alternating current – although this is expensive.

Measuring head and flow of water

Detailed instructions are given by Hans Hamm in his paper 'Low-Cost Development of Small Water-Power Sites', and also in pamphlets prepared by the James Leffel & Co., for methods of measuring the available head of water at any given site, and for measuring the rate of water flow. The methods of measuring flow are simple in principle; either by channelling the flow (for very small streams) through a pipe and measuring the time taken to fill a container of known volume; by constructing a temporary weir with a rectangular opening and measuring the depth of water flowing over this opening (the width being known); or finally by the 'float' method. This last method, though less accurate, is more convenient for larger streams. The cross-sectional area of the stream is measured approximately by taking the depth at a series of intervals across its width, and using these figures to construct the cross-sectional shape of the stream bed. The speed of flow is measured by timing floats carried below the surface of the water between two fixed points. Together these measurements can give the stream flow in ft^3 per unit time.

Losses in efficiency

Hamm also gives methods of calculating the losses in efficiency from the theoretical power available, resulting from friction in the headrace channel – dependent on its 'hydraulic radius' (a function of the channel cross-section), and the particular material of construction of the channel wall. Additional power losses occur where the water flows from the headrace, through the trash rack, a grating of bars designed to prevent leaves, branches and other floating objects from entering the turbine, and down the penstock or tubular pipe which directs the water flow onto the turbine itself.

Dams

The available head of water may be augmented by the construction of a dam, and Hamm gives details again of the construction of a number of simple types of dam, either of earth, timber, masonry or concrete. With a pond contained behind the dam of sufficient area it is possible to build up an effective power reservoir, so that if the turbine is run intermittently, say during the day-time only, it may operate with a faster rate of water flow than would otherwise be possible, this water being replaced as the pond refills during the night-time. This was the practice with many of the old wheel-driven flour mills; and for electricity generation means that higher peak loads can be carried than with an undammed stream where the flow is constant.

Other types of water driven device

Designs for a novel type of water driven generator have been published by Volunteers in Technical Assistance. The proposed machine consists of a submerged wooden float anchored to the river bottom and carrying four five foot diameter propellers connected by belt drives to a generator. The power capacity for a water speed of

5 or 6 ft/sec is calculated at 1 kW. At the time of publication (1971) a full-size version of the machine had not yet however been built.

Manufacturers of small hydraulic turbines

The principal manufacturers of small-scale water power equipment in the United States are the James Leffel and Co. of Springfield, Ohio whose Hoppes Hydro-Electric Units in particular – complete turbine, generator and control gear assemblies for generating either A.C. or D.C. made in 1 to 10 kW capacities – have been in widespread use on farms and estates since the 1920s. The Leffel Company's small vertical Samson turbine is available in 3 to 29 horsepower sizes.

European manufacturers of small hydraulic turbines include Drees and Co. of Werl, Germany; Officine Bühler, Taverne, Canton Ticino, Switzerland; and Ossberger-Turbinenfabrik, 8832 Weissenburg, Bayern, Germany (the sole manufacturers of Banki type turbines).

Other firms (listed by MacKillop) are :
Gilbert Gilkes and Gordon, Kendal, Westmoreland, England
Armfield Ltd., Ringwood, Hampshire, England
Woodward Governor Co., Rockford, Illinois 61101
Irons Bros., The Forge, Sticklepath, Cornwall, England

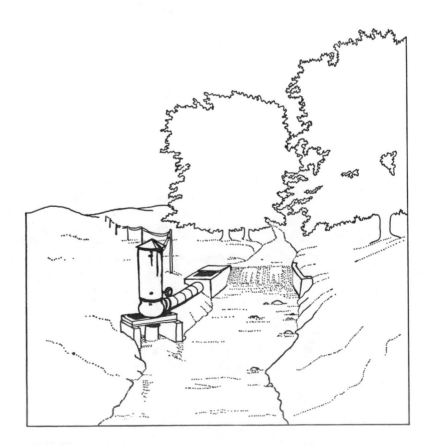

Hoppes Hydro-Electric Unit: small hydraulic turbine generating up to 10 kW, manufactured by the James Leffel & Co., Springfield Ohio. Drawing adapted from pamphlet 'Hoppes 56-1'

The table below summarising data on commercially available turbines is adapted from Hamm:

	Impulse or Pelton	Michell or Banki
Head range (feet)	50 to 1,000	3 to 650
Flow range (ft^3/sec)	0.1 to 10	0.5 to 250
Application	high head	medium head
Power (horsepower)	1 to 500	1 to 1,000
Manufacturers	James Leffel & Co Drees & Co Officine Bühler	Ossberger-Turbinenfabrik

Small scale water power bibliography

Access Catalog, 'The Owner Built Hydro-Electric Plant' in Vol. 1, No. 7 pp.12-15

C.D. Bassett, series on water power published in Popular Science: 'Your Own Water-
Power Plant', April 1947 pp.186-9; 'Your Own Water-Power
Plant, Part II', May 1947 pp 180-4; 'Dams Turn Water into
Kilowatts', June 1947 pp. 202-3; 'Water Wheel Delivers Over
3 H.P.', July 1947 pp.194-7; 'Building an Overshot Wheel',
August 1947 (Series reprinted in Mother Earth News March 1972)

J. Guthrie Brown ed., Hydro Electric Engineering Practice, 3 vols., Gordon and Breach,
New York 1958, Blackie and Sons, London 1958.

W.P. Creager and J.D. Justin, Hydro Electric Handbook, 2nd edn., Wiley New York 1950

C.A. Crowley, 'Power from Small Streams, Part I', Popular Mechanics Sept.1940 p.466- ;
'Power from Small Streams, Part II', Popular Mechanics Oct 1940
pp. 626-30

A.M. Daniels, 'Electric Light and Power from Small Streams', U.S.D.A. Yearbook 1920 (?)
pp. 221-223

A.M. Daniels, Power for the Farm from Small Streams, U.S.D.A., Washington D.C. January
1925

Calvin V. Davis, Handbook of Applied Hydraulics, 2nd edn. McGraw-Hill, New York 1952

L.A. Haimerl, 'The Cross Flow Turbine', Water Power (London), Jan. 1960 (reprints available
from Ossberger-Turbinenfabrik, 8832 Weissenburg, Bayern, Germany)

Hans W. Hamm, Low-Cost Development of Small Water-Power Sites, Volunteers in
Technical Assistance, Schenectady, New York 1967

Harris and Rice, Power Development of Small Streams, Rodney Hunt Machine Co., Orange,
Mass. 1920

James Leffel & Co., Hints on the Development of Small Water Powers, Pamphlet 'A'
Springfield Ohio, n.d.

James Leffel & Co., Hydro-Electric Power from a Hoppes Hydro-Electric Unit, Bulletin H-49,
Springfield, Ohio, n.d.

Don Marier, 'Measuring Water Flow', Alternative Sources of Energy No. 1 July 1971 pp.8-10

C.A. Mockmore and F. Merryfield, The Banki Water Turbine, Oregon State College Engineering
Experiment Station Bulletin No. 25, Corvallis, Ore., Feb 1949

Emil Mosonyi, Water-Power Development, Akademiai Kiado, Budapest 1967

T.A.L. Paton, Power from Water, Leonard Hill, London 1961

John Reynolds, Windmills and Watermills, Praeger, New York 1970

L. Syson, British Watermills, Batsford, London 1965

J.N.T. Vince, Discovering Watermills, Shire Publications 1970

VITA (Volunteers in Technical Assistance), 1 kW River Generator, Village Technology
Plan 11000.1, Mt. Rainier, Md., 1971

A.H. Zerban and E.P. Nye, Power Plants, 2nd edn., International Textbook Co., Scranton Pa.
1952 (chapter 12 discusses hydraulic power plants)

Composting, waste treatment and methane gas as a fuel

The types and amounts of waste materials that accumulate in any building, and which must be disposed of or otherwise treated, will vary of course with the use of that building and the habits of its occupants. In general however the types of waste which would be produced in and around large buildings would include most or all of the following :

Food wastes and food preparation wastes
Food wrappings
Cans, bottles and other containers
Dust, sweepings
Ash
Waste paper

(Where there is gardening and planting :)
Grass clippings, dead plants, leaves, fallen branches

Waste (dirty) water

Human wastes : faeces and urine
(Where animals are kept :)
Animal wastes: faeces, urine and bedding

In addition there will be the occasional disposal of items of furniture, utensils, worn-out appliances etc.

The subject of waste water treatment is discussed in another chapter. In the specialised terminology of the literature of solid waste treatment, the remainder of the materials in this list can be classified under three headings : sewage, 'garbage' (which covers principally food wastes and vegetable trimmings) and 'rubbish' (which describes most of the remaining non-food material) - these last two, 'garbage' and 'rubbish', being referred to together as 'refuse'.

There are special reasons why it is appropriate here to look at both the problems of sewage treatment and refuse disposal together; although it would be more usual to treat the subjects separately. The typical means of transporting the two categories of waste in advanced urban societies is different, sewage being water-borne as a rule, and refuse carried in trucks. The special problem of sewage disposal is the danger of infectious disease, and it is the great achievement of the sanitary engineering profession, following in the footsteps of the great Victorian pioneers, that this danger has been largely abolished with the introduction of modern plumbing, sewer systems and centralised treatment plants or remote disposal points. But these achievements have been won at the expense of certain penalties.

Centralised
sewage
treatment

Though potentially dangerous to health when untreated, sewage nonetheless contains valuable nutrients which in rural societies were and are returned to the soil. When sewage sludge containing these nutrients in a highly concentrated form is discharged into waterways and lakes, it causes excessive growth of weeds and algae which can disturb the balance in the natural ecosystem (eutrophication), and can eventually cause the biological death of these bodies of water. Where the sewage is discharged untreated there is the danger to human health in addition. In neither case do the plant nutrients get back to the agricultural land where their fertilising properties would be of value. This has been true only of human sewage up to recently, but the introduction of intensive methods of livestock rearing, feed-lots and battery or factory farming has resulted in the concentration of hugh quantities of animal wastes too, and a problem with their disposal; where previously, when animals were grazed on the open range, their wastes were returned immediately to the land.

Finally the use of water-borne systems of sewage transport, introduced at a time when water was in more plentiful supply, is now a major factor in the problem of water shortages. The water supplied for domestic purposes is all of a purity fit for drinking, but in typical patterns of domestic use only 3% of this water actually goes for cooking and drinking, while up to one third is used for flushing toilets and in sinks for flushing away food wastes.

Inorganic and
organic wastes

Instead of drawing the usual distinction within solid wastes between sewage and refuse, one might draw another kind of distinction which would divide these wastes in a different way: into organic and inorganic materials. The organic materials - sewage, food wastes, garden wastes - are all subject to the natural processes of putrefaction and decomposition, and for the most part decay rapidly. Inorganic wastes on the other hand are more stable and long-lived. They are for the most part in a condition to be dumped as such, or, much better, the materials which are of potential value can be recovered and recycled - in particular aluminum and steel (largely from cans), and glass. Some organic materials, in addition, especially paper and more marginally rags and bones, have scrap value as such - though all these can equally be decomposed along with other organic wastes. We shall return to the question of resource recovery from refuse later. Meanwhile let us look first at the processes of decay of organic material, and the useful purposes to which they can be put.

Composting

When the decomposition of organic waste materials is carried on under controlled conditions, the process is referred to as composting. The word 'compost' conjures up the image perhaps of a decaying heap of grass clippings and old leaves in some discreetly hidden corner of a suburban garden. But composting as a modern method of municipal refuse treatment is practised widely in Europe, and in recent years a number of urban composting plants have been built by private enterprise in the Unites States, though the commercial success which these undertakings have met with has been mixed. Composting is defined by Clarence Golueke, one of the world's experts on the subject, as 'a biological process for converting solid wastes into a stable, humus-like product whose chief use is as a soil conditioner.'

Aerobic and anaerobic decomposition

There are two ways in which the decay of organic materials can take place, aerobically (in the presence of oxygen), and anaerobically (in the absence of oxygen). The difference is due to the activities of different types of bacteria, which are the main agent in decomposition, some of which thrive in oxygen, and others which do not. As a rule 'composting', and especially in the gardener's sense, is taken to mean specifically aerobic decomposition, where the wastes are piled in open containers or in the open air, and turned at intervals so as to allow the air access to all parts of the compost heap. Aerobic decomposition generates heat, and the whole process goes on at higher temperatures than does anaerobic decomposition. Anaerobic processes are also characterised by the emission of foul odours, which proper aerobic composting is not. The term 'composting' in a general sense can be applied to both aerobic and anaerobic decomposition however; and in fact there will tend to be a degree of anaerobic decomposition going on even in open, largely aerobic composting, at the centre of the stacks in parts which the air cannot easily reach.

Aerobic decay goes on naturally all the time, in the decomposition of animal wastes deposited on the ground, fallen leaves and limbs of trees, dead plants, dead animal bodies. The products of this decay are humus, a rich generally blackish or dark-coloured material whose principal constituents of fertiliser value are nitrogen, phosphorus and potassium compounds; together with gases, ammonia and carbon dioxide, which are given off to the atmosphere. Anaerobic decomposition occurs in nature both as digestion in the guts of animals, as well as under water in swamps or ponds, where organic matter- dead waterplants and suchlike - putrefies in the absence of oxygen. In this case the solid products are respectively manure, and peat; while in both cases the gaseous products consist of a mixture of methane and carbon dioxide, together with small quantities of hydrogen sulphide which is responsible for the characteristic rotten smell.

History of composting

Sir Albert Howard

It is apparently the time-honoured custom to begin historical works on composting with the remark that it is one of the most ancient of agricultural arts; and so that tradition will not be broken here. Modern research in aerobic composting begins with the work of Sir Albert Howard in India in the 1930s. Howard's purpose was to refine and systematise the traditional Indian and Chinese methods of composting, and to study the biological mechanisms involved. It was customary in rural India to mix human wastes along with animal manure and agricultural wastes in the material for composting, there being no other means for sewage disposal and treatment. And so the interest in composting was as much as a sanitary measure, as it was as a means of soil nutrient conservation. Howard's procedure involved piling layers of sewage, manure and garbage alternately with layers of relatively drier, more stable material such as leaves

End products of organic
decay, from New
Alchemy Institute West,
Newsletter No.3,
Methane Digesters for
Fuel Gas and Fertilizer,
(available from PO Box
376, Pescadero, Cali-
fornia 94060 price $3.00)
1973, p.2

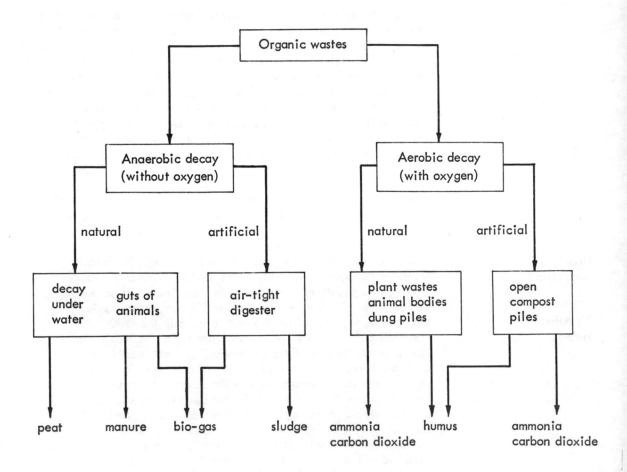

or straw, to a depth of about five feet – either on flat ground, or in pits. The composting period was about six months, during which time the material was turned twice; and so it is likely that for a great part of the time the decomposition in the centre of the stack was anaerobic. The length of the period allowed for decomposition was probably advisable in view of the health dangers of composting human sewage. The process was known as the 'Indore method', after the region of India in which it was developed. Organic gardeners today mostly use some variation on the Indore method, for home composting of kitchen garbage and garden refuse.

Indore method

Howard's work was carried on by several Indian workers, while a modified version of the Indore method known as the Bangalore process was devised and promoted widely by the Indian Council of Agricultural Research at Bangalore. The Indore method with modifications was studied in Malaya, in East Africa and elsewhere. And in South Africa Van Vuren carried out studies on the composting of human wastes, with special attention to the problems of public health, and to the use of compost as a fertiliser. Work was done in Northern China by Scott and others from 1935 onwards, on these same subjects, rural sanitation and agricultural composting; the results of their work were reported in Scott's Health and Agriculture in China, published in 1952. One important development from the Indore method through this period was in the practise of turning the composted material more frequently so as to aerate it more effectively, to ensure that decomposition was truly aerobic, and to reduce the composting period to a matter of weeks or days rather than months.

Scott's work in China

Some of the fundamental microbiological work on aerobic decomposition, on the influence of temperature, and the roles of different microorganisms, was carried out by Waksman and his colleagues between the years 1926 and 1941. Since the 1950s the majority of the significant work on composting in this country has been done at the University of California at Berkeley in the Sanitary Engineering Laboratory, and under the direction of H.B. Gotaas, C.G. Golueke and P.H. McGauhey. Of these the first two are both authors of books with the title Composting. The California group studied in detail the effects of a whole range of variables in aerobic decomposition: temperature, moisture, aeration by turning and by other means, the carbon/nitrogen ratio of the organic materials (a proper balance being important to the dynamics and duration of the composting process), the use of special biological inocula to initiate the decomposition (though sold commercially and their virtues extolled by their promoters, these are quite unnecessary); and grinding or shredding the material. Other studies by the Berkeley investigators, according to Gotaas 'also yielded data on the types of organisms present in composting, techniques for judging the condition of the compost during and after the operation, the insulating and heat-retention characteristics . of compost materials, and process-design considerations.'

Composting research at Berkeley

Cycle of nitrogen and
carbon in aerobic de-
composition, adapted
from K. Imhoff and G.M.
Fair, Sewage Treatment,
(copyright (c) 1940 by
John Wiley and Sons, Inc.)
New York 1940, fig.2
p.26. By permission of
John Wiley and Sons, Inc.

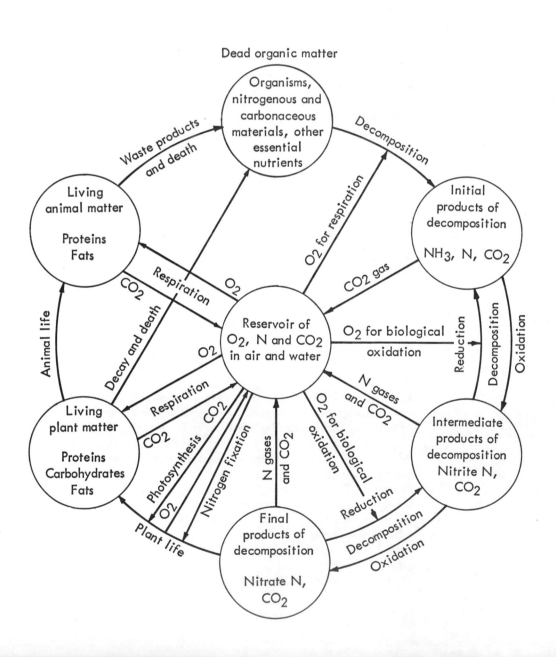

Dead organic matter

Cycle of nitrogen and
carbon in anaerobic
decomposition, adapted
from K. Imhoff and G.M.
Fair, Sewage Treatment,
(copyright (c) 1940 by
John Wiley and Sons, Inc.)
New York 1940, fig.3
p.27. By permission of
John Wiley and Sons, Inc.

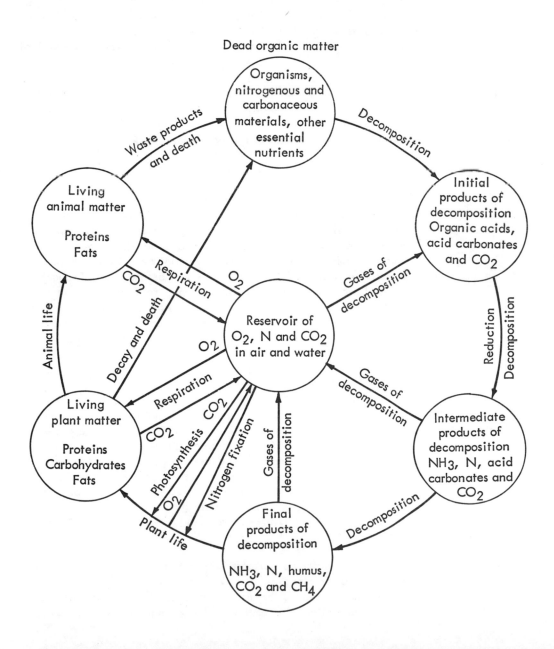

Technology of large scale composting	In parallel with this progress in the scientific theoretical understanding of aerobic decomposition, was running a series of developments in the mechanics of the operation of composting, with applications in the processing of urban wastes on an industrial scale and by semi-automated methods of handling. One of the first patented composting techniques was that developed by Beccari in Florence, which consisted simply in piling the material in enclosed cells for an initial period of anaerobic decomposition, and then opening air vents so that the final stages of decay were partially aerobic. Several Beccari-type plants were built in America during the 1920s and '30s, but all have since been closed. An improvement on Beccari's method was made by Verdier in France, who sought to increase the aeration and recirculation of drained liquors and gases. Subsequent developments were all largely concerned with the question of increasing aeration through different techniques of agitation of the material, passing it over grids set at successive levels in silos, or else along sloping rotating cylindrical containers.
Beccari process	
Dano process	One system which has been widely used throughout the world and which was originally developed in Denmark is the Dano process. This consists in the first place of a method of mechanically sorting, shredding and aerating raw refuse. Metal scrap is removed magnetically and other salvageable materials are picked out by hand. The remainder then passes to a rotary grinding device called the Egsetor. The shredded product can be composted in 'windrows' - that is, in long piles in the open air. Alternatively, a mechanical digester developed by the Dano Corporation in the middle 1950s and called the Bio-stabilizer, provides an enclosed and continuous means of composting. This consists of a large tilted slowly rotating drum with a capacity of about 100 tons, in which the material is retained for three to five days before being discharged at the lower end. Numerous Dano plants are in operation in several European countries. The first in America was installed at Sacramento, California; the second in Phoenix, Arizona, which had four Bio-stabilizers in operation before the plant closed in 1963.
VAM process	Another type of mechanical refuse grinding device has been produced by VAM, a Dutch non-profit refuse disposal company set up by the Netherlands government. Once again the materials with salvage value are removed first, and the shredded product coming from the grinder is composted in windrows. The Fairfield Hardy digester, produced during the 1960s, introduced a new method of aeration. Whereas previous techniques and devices had relied on tumbling or turning the material for aeration, the Fairfield Hardy system incorporates a series of hollow perforated augurs which rotate in and are rotated through the composting mass. Air is blown along the augurs, and enters the decomposing material through the perforations.
Fairfield Hardy digester	
Compost Corp. of America	In the early 1950s the Compost Corporation of America carried out extensive pilot-plant and economic studies. A full-scale operational plant was planned for the city of Oakland, Ca., using what amounted to a modern automation of the old Indore method, with the windrow

**1965 Solid
Wastes Act**

**Failure of
commercial
operations**

piles turned mechanically. American research in composting was
stimulated in the middle '60s as a result of financial support
following on the passage of the 1965 Solid Wastes Act; although
in the opinion of Golueke very little new of worth was produced,
beyond the rediscovery of findings by earlier workers. Public
interest in compost revived and grew as a result of increasing
concern for the environment. A number of commercial composting
operations were established, most of these ending however in
financial failure. The reasons for this lack of success appear to be
that composting mechanisation had gone too far. And more importantly, that there was a double standard by which the economics of
solid waste treatment were judged, whereby disposal of refuse in
landfills and by incineration was seen as a public service and
supported by taxation, while composting of these same materials
was expected to yield a profit to private enterprise on the sale of
the recoverable scrap and composted products alone. Account was
not taken of the real environmental and long-term benefits to society
of composting, in reducing pollution, restoring agricultural
fertility and waste land, slowing the growth of unsightly
municipal dumps and recovering valuable non-renewable
materials - in particular metals - for reuse. The commercial
value of compost as a soil conditioner measured by the increase
in crop yields resulting from its application is certainly small by
comparison with inorganic fertilisers; and as a consequence it
may not be worthwhile economically to transport compost long
distances from where it is produced. But the comparison is an
unreal one since the long-term benefits of the application of
compost to the soil are undeniable; and especially by contrast
with the problems of water contamination which result from the
washing out of inorganic nitrogen fertilisers from the soil, when
these are used to excess.

According to Golueke there is today a renewed optimism, tempered
by a new realism, amongst composting advocates, about the
prospects for composting of municipal wastes as a non-profit
undertaking, especially for medium-sized cities; not as a
universal answer to the solid waste disposal problem, but as a
complementary method of treatment alongside incineration and
landfilling. Some of the most promising applications of compost,
besides those in agriculture, are in the reclamation of waste land
such as the land laid bare by strip-mining, or land scorched by
fire. Experiments have shown how by spraying a liquid slurry of
compost mixed with grass seeds on denuded hillsides, a temporary
sun-dried crust can be formed which stabilises the land, prevents
erosion, and, in time, as the grass grows, forms a new vegetation
cover and top soil layer.

The composting cause is keenly promoted by the Rodale Press
periodical Compost Science, as well as in their Organic Gardening
and Farming magazine. The executive editor of both magazines is
Jerome Goldstein; his messianic forecast of the coming of the new
golden age of composting, Garbage As You Like It, is also published
by Rodale.

Anaerobic decomposition and the production of methane gas

One of the chief gaseous products of anaerobic decomposition is methane gas, CH_4. Methane is the main constituent (95%) of the so-called 'natural gas' which is recovered along with oil and petroleum liquids, and whose origin was in the same decomposition process, but taking place during the prehistoric periods over which the fossil fuels were laid down. From either present-day or fossil sources, methane is a readily combustible gas with a high fuel value, which can be burned for such purposes as cooking, heating, lighting and even for powering automobiles. In fact when methane is produced naturally in the decay of organic matter beneath stagnant water (as 'marsh gas'), it sometimes ignites spontaneously as it escapes from the surface, this being the explanation of the ghostly phenomenon of the 'Will-o'-the-Wisp'.

Methane digesters for waste treatment, fuel gas and fertiliser production

It is possible therefore to combine the sanitary treatment of sewage, animal manure and organic wastes, with the production of useful fuel gas (known variously as 'sewage gas', 'dungas' or 'bio-gas'), into a single operation; and numerous plants for this purpose have been developed since the beginning of the century. Besides the gas yield, the process also produces a liquid effluent or sludge which can be returned to the soil, as a conditioner and fertiliser. Historically, the greatest interest in this type of 'methane digester' for waste treatment and gas production has been in India, where it can fill the combined functions of improving rural sanitation and the return of nutrients to agriculture, with a cheap and local source of fuel. One of the principal present sources of fuel in India continues to be cattle dung, burned for cooking and heating. This is an unsatisfactory material as a fuel in any case, being hard to light; but worse, its combustion means that the growing properties of the soil are not enriched and replenished as they might otherwise be. It is calculated that about 350 million tons of cattle dung are burned in India every year.

History of methane digesters

Pasteur made reference to the fuel possibilities of methane from organic decay, writing in the 19th century. It is known that the Chinese collect methane for power uses from covered sewage lagoons, and it is possible that this practice is an old one. In London at one time a number of the street lamps were run on gas from the sewers below.

It seems that the first specially built plant for producing methane for manure, was in Bombay in 1900. Experimental studies have been carried on in several countries including India, France, Germany, Algeria, England and the United States from the '30s onwards. In 1939 experiments were made at the Indian Agricultural Research Institute in New Delhi, and small prototype gas plants were installed for testing in ten villages around Delhi. During World War II there was interest, in several European countries, and particularly in Germany, in methane as a fuel to substitute for gasoline which was then of course in short supply. One small type of unit produced in Germany, the Kronseder, was intended to supply gas for domestic purposes as for example cooking. In the post-war period a number of European farmers set up methane digesters; and in France there

German work during World War II

were, by 1952, around 1,000 installations in operation.

The process is particularly useful and succesful in warmer regions, because the digesting material must be maintained at temperatures in the 90° to 140°F range, and because health problems are often more serious and the decay of organic matter more rapid in these climates. During the late 1950s in India designs were tested by the Planning Research and Action Institute; and one important centre of activity has been the Gobar Gas Research Station ('gobar' is Hindi for cowdung) at Ajitmal, Etawah, Uttar Pradesh in Northern India, where Ram Bux Singh, author of the book Bio-Gas Plant, has been director since 1961. At a farm near Lucknow a 225 ft^3 bio-gas plant was installed in 1961 which used the gas produced for heating, lighting, refrigeration, water-pumping and for running other machinery. By 1971 there were over 2,500 gas plants working throughout India.

Indian work of the '50s and '60s

Work of L.J. Fry

One very succesful plant was built in South Africa in the early '60s by L. John Fry, who is now continuing his studies of methane digesters in Santa Barbara, California. Fry ran a hog farm near Johannesburg, and the two tons of manure which the 1,000 animals produced daily posed a serious disposal problem. Fry first tried out the principles of methane production with a series of digesters made from 50-gallon oil drums, during the years 1956-7; and then went on to build a large digester with twin tanks, which yielded 8,000 ft^3 of gas per day on average. The total cost, including a gas-driven 13 hp converted diesel engine, was $10,000. The plant ran for six years virtually uninterrupted, and without problems. Another pig farmer, Dr G.W. Groth Jr, has a gas plant on his farm at San Diego, from which he runs a 10kW generator which provides light and power for the farm buildings.

Biochemistry of anaerobic decomposition

The method for decomposing organic matter under controlled conditions to yield methane, consists, in its simplest essentials, in loading the material into a closed tank – the 'digester' – and allowing it to remain there for a period of weeks or months, during which, given favourable environmental and chemical conditions, the biological processes involved will take their course. Since anaerobic digestion can only take place in the absence of oxygen, there will be an initial period of decomposition during which aerobic processes will occur, and all traces of oxygen will be used up, with the production of CO_2. The anaerobic processes themselves will then commence.

Phases of liquefaction and gasification

There are two stages or phases of decomposition – characterised by the activity of different types of bacteria – which in general succeed each other but which may be going on simultaneously in different parts of the digester: a phase of liquefaction, and a phase of gasification. With a newly started digester, it will be necessary to 'seed' the process with a 'starter brew', cultivated from a small quantity of fresh manure or supernatant from a sewage works, so that the necessary bacteria are present. With a digester once in

'Seeding' the digester

operation, then each batch can be 'seeded' from the last, and one digester from another. Without the presence of the methane-producing bacteria, the result will be that only liquefaction will occur.

In the first, liquefaction phase, large complex organic molecules (fats, proteins, starches) are broken down into simpler substances such as sugars, alcohol, glycerol, peptides and amino acids. One of the principal organic acid products at this stage is acetic acid. In the second, gasification stage, a second population of bacteria take over from the first, and convert organic acids into methane. The methane-producing bacteria multiply less rapidly than do the bacteria involved in liquefaction, and are more sensitive to variations in the environmental conditions within the digester.

Temperature

The most important factors affecting the success of the digestion process are temperature, pH (or acidity), and the chemical composition of the materials being digested, in particular the ratio of solids to liquids, and the ratio of carbon to nitrogen present. Some digestion will occur over a very wide range of temperatures, from about 32° to 156°F at the extremes; but the rate of decomposition and gas production is rather sensitive to temperature, and in general the process goes faster at higher temperatures. Much below 60°F the process slows to a virtual standstill. There are two ranges of temperature within which digestion proceeds best, from 85° to 105°F, and from 120° to 140°F. In this latter range a different group, of 'thermophilic' bacteria are active; but these are very sensitive to environmental changes, their action results in the production of a sludge of rather low fertiliser value, and in general it seems preferable to run a digester at a temperature around 90 to 95°F; this being easier to maintain without elaborate heating arrangements, in any case.

Acidity and alkalinity

As for pH, digestion is inhibited by excessive acidity, and it is best (according to Merrill and Fry) to keep the pH in the range 7·5 to 8·5 – that is, just above neutrality (7·0). During the early stages of decomposition, when much CO_2 is produced, forming carbonic acid in solution, and later when organic acids are produced, the pH can drop to 6 or below. But as these acids are consumed in the production of methane, so the pH rises again, and the mixture becomes less sensitive to the addition of acid or alkali – that is to say it becomes self-stabilising, or 'well-buffered'. In the initial phases the mixture is likely to become too acidic if new material is fed in too fast, and if this occurs then the supply rate should be slowed. If the pH rises too high, because of excessive alkalinity of the raw material, then there is little to be done except to wait for the build-up of CO_2 to bring the pH down again.

Proportion of solids to liquids

The recommended percentage of solids in the digesting mixture is between 7% and 9%. This is rather higher than the average proportion in municipal sewage (5% solids) which is heavily diluted with flushing water; but lower than that in animal manure and vegetable wastes (18% solids in fresh cow dung, maybe 30 to 40%

in vegetable material), which must therefore be mixed with water in appropriate quantities, prior to feeding to the digester. The 'solids' referred to include only those organic 'volatile' solids which will undergo digestion; and are calculated as weights of <u>dry</u> material. (There will in addition be some proportion of 'fixed', inorganic or inert solids which will remain in the sludge or scum unchanged throughout.)

Ratio of carbon to nitrogen

The bacteria in the digestion process use up the carbon present 30 to 35 times faster than the rate at which they convert nitrogen. It follows that a ratio of the elements of around 30:1 in the raw material is optimal. If the amount of carbon is excessive, then the digestion slows. If on the other hand there is too much nitrogen present, this is lost from the process in gaseous form (as ammonia, NH_3), which much reduces the nutrient value of the resulting effluent. A mass of data is available on the carbon to nitrogen ratio, and on the volatile solids to liquid ratio, of a great variety of organic materials – animal manure including faeces and urine, human sewage, and plant matter of all sorts. No detailed statistics will be given here, but instead the reader is referred to the composite tables presented by Singh (<u>Bio-Gas Plant</u>, 1971, p.33), by Merrill and Fry (New Alchemy Institute Newsletter No.3, <u>Methane Digesters for Fuel Gas and Fertilizer</u>, 1973 p.14 and p.16), and by Moorcraft ('Plant Power', <u>AD 2/74</u> p.74), where data from a variety of sources is brought together. Figures for C/N ratios calculated from laboratory analysis can be misleading however, as Merrill and Fry point out, since these may not correspond to the actual ratios available to, and digestible by the decomposing bacteria; and the ratios for particular plant materials or animal wastes can vary very much with age or growing conditions of the plant, and with the age and diet of the animal – so that published figures must be regarded as rough averages only.

Composition of 'bio-gas'

The gas itself which is produced by anaerobic digestion, is a mixture, with the chief constituent being methane, CH_4, varying as a proportion from about 54% to 70%. The next largest fraction is CO_2, varying between about 27% and 45%; and in small amounts, nitrogen, hydrogen, carbon monoxide, and traces of mercaptans and hydrogen sulfide. These last mentioned, in particular H_2S with its classic 'rotten eggs' smell familiar from elementary chemistry lessons, are responsible for the gas's odour.

Fuel value of 'bio-gas'

The fuel value of the gas is dependent on the methane content. Pure methane itself has a higher fuel value than does ordinary 'town gas'; and 'bio-gas' can have a calorific value varying between 580 and 750 Btu/ft^3. This compares with values for propane and butane of 2,400 $Btus/ft^3$ and 3,100 $Btus/ft^3$ respectively. 'Bio-gas' has a low toxicity, containing only small quantities of carbon monoxide. It burns with a violet flame, and will burn continuously when the proportion of methane to air is 1:20 or less. The mixture of methane with air is explosive though at concentrations less than about 1:7 (between 5% and 14% methane); and it is important therefore to take precautions that air is not trapped in pipes or gasholders, and that any gas leaks are traced and plugged. One particular problem to be watched for is the possible build-up of gas in porous insulation materials around the digester chamber.

The presence of hydrogen sulfide in the gas may cause corrosion, as for example to iron pipes, and can be removed by passing the gas over iron filings. The non-combustible CO_2 can be removed by scrubbing with lime water (calcium hydroxide). When the gas leaves the warm digester it is liable to be saturated with water vapour, which could also cause corrosion in metal pipes and gasholders, and could be removed by absorption methods.

Amounts of gas produced

The total amount of gas produced from a given quantity of material can vary with temperature and total period of digestion, as well as with the composition and type of materials themselves. Singh gives figures for the volume of gas produced from different materials, per lb of dry weight, which vary between $7 \cdot 0$ and $15 \cdot 0$ ft^3. Merrill and Fry quote figures from various sources also derived from experience with actual working digesters, again in terms of ft^3 of gas per lb of dry matter (total solids). These are: $6 \cdot 0$ to $8 \cdot 0$ ft^3 for pig manure, $3 \cdot 1$ to $4 \cdot 7$ ft^3 for cow manure (India), $6 \cdot 0$ to $13 \cdot 2$ ft^3 for chicken manure and $6 \cdot 0$ to $9 \cdot 0$ ft^3 for sewage in conventional treatment plants. Singh's higher figures relate to straw from cereal and other crops, which yield more gas than do these various manures. It seems likely however that the proportion of CO_2 to CH_4 is higher also in gas from vegetable materials, and so the net fuel value may not be any higher.

Types of digester

The simplest type of methane digester is just a closed container such as a drum, tank or pit in the ground, into which the digestible material is loaded. The container is then sealed to the air. Some means must be found for trapping the gas which is given off. This can be done most readily by floating an inverted container over the digesting mixture. This gasholder rises vertically as the gas accumulates inside it; and the gas can be drawn off by means of a tap and a tube.

Batch-fed digesters

Despite its simplicity, and the fact that it requires little attention once digestion is started, this 'batch-fed' type of digester has some drawbacks. A great deal of labour is required for loading it, and for removing the sludge when digestion is complete. And during the weeks over which digestion takes place, the rate of gas production varies, rising to a peak after perhaps ten days, and then dropping again to a lower level which might be maintained for two or three months more. In order to ensure a continuous steady level of gas production with batch-fed digesters, it is necessary to have at least two units, and ideally five or six, operating simultaneously and out of phase with each other, so that while one say is emptied and re-loaded, another is at the peak of production.

Continuous-feed digesters

The alternative is to have a digester which is fed continuously with small amounts of new material, while spent sludge is withdrawn or displaced continuously from the opposite end or side of the tank.

The digester may be arranged as a single vertical chamber, and the new material introduced and the spent sludge withdrawn by means of pipes. This can mean however that partially digested material may be withdrawn prematurely; that digestion takes place unevenly; and also that stirring currents may be set up in the material which also disrupt the smooth process of digestion. A further development, which partially avoids these difficulties, is to have a single tank divided into two chambers by a central wall, such that material undergoes preliminary digestion in one half, and then spills over to the second section. Thus material at the two stages of decomposition is kept separate, and new material is added only to the one section, spent sludge withdrawn only from the other.

One design of this kind by Singh, popular in the village units widespread throughout India, and adapted by him here for colder climates, is illustrated below. The digester chamber is a vertical cylinder sunk into the ground, with a gasholder which rises vertically on a central locating column. The material is pre-mixed in a separate small tank and piped to the lower part of the digester proper. The chamber is divided into two halves by a wall, and digesting material spills over this wall as more material is added. The effluent passes to a discharge tank through a second pipe. The whole digester is surrounded by an insulating jacket to maintain the temperatures required.

Single tank vertical type bio-gas plant with two-section digester chamber, designed by R.B. Singh for cold climatic areas. From R.B. Singh, Bio-Gas Plant, Ajitmal, U.P., India, 1971

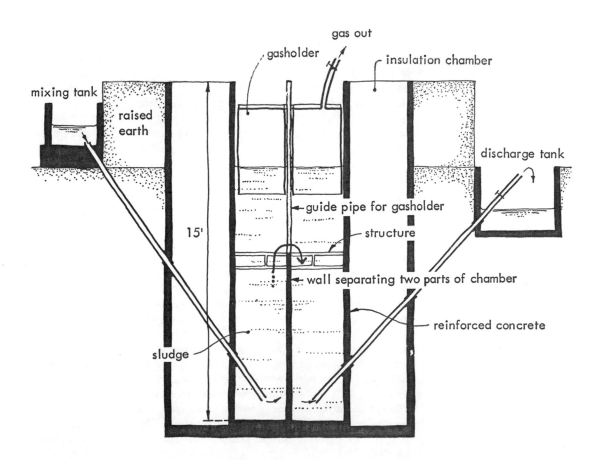

The separate sections of a two-chamber digester may be formed from separate tanks, linked by a siphon passage. One arrangement which is sometimes adopted is to use a first, smaller tank to hold the material during the first ten or fifteen days during which gas production is greatest; and a secondary tank, perhaps five or six times larger, where material is retained for the much longer period over which gas production is slower.

Displacement
digesters

Perhaps the most satisfactory system altogether is the displacement type of digester. Here the tank is horizontal rather than vertical, and the material is pushed along the tank during the retention period, from one end to the other. The displacement digester is a type pioneered by Fry in South Africa and Santa Barbara. According to Fry, it avoids the problems of vertical digester types as used widely in India, while offering several extra advantages. First, if the digesting mixture at the input end begins to sour, the flow along the digester can be reversed so that strongly buffered material from the further end is recirculated. Second, the surface area of digesting material is greater than that with a vertical tank; and so it takes longer for the layer of scum which forms on this surface to reach a point at which it inhibits digestion. The displacement digester is also more easily cleaned of this scum and of the sediment of undigested inorganic material, than is a vertical type, when the time for washing the tank out arrives.

Scum

The formation of scum is a general problem in digester operation, in particular with continuous-feed types. In the displacement digester it may be possible to remove scum via a pipe at the top of the tank. Both gas and scum are forced up through this pipe, to a chamber where the scum is trapped and from which it may be removed periodically, while the gas passes on to the gasholder.

Fry inner tube
digester

One very cheap and simple small design of continuous-feed digester has been produced by Fry, in which the digestion chamber is an inner tube from a truck tyre, filled through a pipe from a bucket by a gravity feed; and connected via a second pipe to a gasholder made from several more inner tubes. Full details on how to make this digester, at an approximate cost of $20.00 or less, are given in the New Alchemy Institute Newsletter No.3, Methane Digesters for Fuel Gas and Fertilizer, 1973, pp.31-9.

Preparation and
pre-mixing of materials

It is convenient to have a separate tank for the pre-mixing of materials, as in the design by Singh illustrated, since in most cases they will require some dilution with water. Also vegetable material, particularly for continuous-feed digesters, should be chopped into small pieces, generally no bigger than 1" cubes. The smaller the pieces, as a rule, the faster the speed of digestion. There is a quite large component of lignin and other indigestible substances in vegetable wastes, which can form scum and slow digestion. This problem does not arise with plants which are low in fibrous material such as algae or seaweed; and these are therefore particularly suitable for gas production. There is also the possibility of digesting juices pressed from succulent plants such as cactus, or making use of the gelatinous wastes left from the industrial processing of such crops as jute – in both cases all the fibrous parts of the plant being thus removed before digestion.

Heating of digesters

In order that the temperature of digesters be maintained at or around the optimal 95°F, it is usual to have some form of insulation surrounding the tank – either of natural materials such as straw or sawdust, or possibly of polystyrene foam. In hot climates the tank may be heated directly by exposure to the sun, and ambient temperatures may be sufficiently high for succesful digestion without any supplementary heating being necessary. In some small rural installations the tank is surrounded with an aerobic compost pile whose heat is conducted partly to the digester. The most satisfactory arrangement, guaranteeing constant and even warming, is to pass heated water (or steam) through a set of coils immersed within the digester. The circulating water might be heated by a solar heater, or in a boiler heated by burning some of the methane produced. The temperature should be controlled thermostatically. An electric or propane-fired heater might be used to raise the temperature initially, to get digestion started.

Toxic materials

Digestion can be inhibited by the presence of certain toxic heavy metals – such as copper, chromium, nickel, zinc or mercury – which might be found in small quantities in urban wastes. The same is true of synthetic detergents, which can present problems where household wastes are to be digested.

Efficiency of digesters

The overall efficiency of anaerobic digestion is quite widely variable depending on materials and conditions. A range of figures are given by Merrill and Fry, from different sources, from which they conclude that a conversion rate of 60% to 70% is average – that is the ratio of the energy content of the methane produced to the energy content of the input materials. Account must be taken of the energy required to maintain the temperature of the digestion process however, and this brings the net efficiency to something more like 50%. Even this does not allow for energy expended in collecting materials and in feeding or maintaining the digesters.

Applications of digesters

There are a variety of applications for anaerobic digesters and for the methane and sludge effluent which they produce. In rural areas and in underdeveloped countries they may serve, as we have seen, the joint purposes of sewage and other waste disposal, and return of nutrients to the soil, as well as providing fuel for cooking, lighting, heating or running agricultural machinery. The centralised type of water-borne sewage system requires a dense concentration of population for it to be economically feasible; and even then demands a very great capital investment in the network and plant. In rural and dispersed situations some other means of waste disposal may be more sensible, and not necessarily any the less hygienic.

Use of methane in sewage works

This certainly does not mean however that it is impossible in large centralised sewage systems, to recover methane by anaerobic digestion; and it has proved worthwhile to do just this in many large European sewage works, where the gas produced is burned to power the machinery of the works themselves. For example the three biggest plants serving the population of London, about six million people between them, together generate nearly six million ft^3 of gas per day. The gas in municipal works in Britain is used for heating digesters and for running diesel and gas-turbine engines for power and electricity generation. The same is true in some American plants; although no great efforts appear to have been made to maximise gas production, or to use the gas for purposes outside the waste processing installations themselves.

Methane digesters on the farm

In the large-scale farming typical of developed countries, there are promising applications for methane digesters, especially where livestock is raised intensively, as in hog farms, cattle feed-lots and battery poultry farming. The problems of disposing of the large amounts of manure which are accumulated in these operations, are themselves serious. It is calculated that the total quantity of animal wastes produced annually in the U.S. is 1·3 billion tons, which is seven times the total quantity of urban solid wastes. The NSF/NASA Solar Energy Panel estimate that, of this, about 20 million tons of dry material could practicably be recovered and processed annually. When animals were kept on the open range, or on small dispersed farms, then there were no problems of waste disposal, and manure was returned directly to the land. But with the livestock concentrated together in the great feed-lots such as those near Omaha and Los Angeles, and in the Middle West, the situation is very different. There are many cases in the industrial processing of foodstuffs, as in the dairy, sugar refining, wine-making and tanning industries, where organic wastes suitable for anaerobic digestion are also produced.

The installations on hog farms built by Fry and Groth have already been referred to; and another interesting and advanced design of digester for animal manure by Coulthard of Victoria, Australia is illustrated by Bell et al. (Methane, Fuel of the Future, Singer 1973, pp. 33-4). Coulthard's system has a large preformed butyl rubber bag for the digester, and also makes use of the output sludge to grow a crop of algae (chlorella), which is in turn processed into animal feed.

Methane-powered vehicles

On the farm the methane can be used for the various purposes of powering machinery, for heating and for lighting as mentioned. It may also be used to power vehicles, as for example tractors or automobiles. One of the properties of methane which limits its usefulness in this application though, as well as making it less convenient generally than other comparable gaseous fuels such as propane or butane, is the fact that it cannot be liquefied by compression, at least at the sort of pressures achievable in normal practice; and so it is rather bulky to transport. At the relatively high pressure of 2,800 psi, the equivalent of 420 ft^3 of methane at atmospheric pressure can be compressed to around 2 ft^3, giving the fuel equivalent of roughly 3½ gallons of gasoline (Merrill and Fry).

Such vehicles as have been converted to run on methane have carried cylinders of compressed gas of this order of size. (This has meant that their range has been rather limited.) One far-famed example is the aging Hillman car converted to methane by Harold Bate, a chicken farmer from Devon, England, now one of the folk-heroes of alternative technology.

The conversion of the engine is a relatively simple matter, requiring, besides the gas tank, a special injector, gas regulator, and either adjustments to the existing carburettor, or a special separate carburettor. Some sewage works used to run their vehicles off methane; and it is quite common practice to burn natural gas in taxis and fork-lift trucks. There is less exhaust pollution than from petrol-engined vehicles, and a lowered consumption of oil. Because of the bulk and difficulty of transporting methane however, it has probably greater application in stationary engines. Here there is an added opportunity for energy conservation, in that the otherwise waste heat from exhaust and cooling water can be recirculated to heat the digester.

Domestic scale methane digesters

It has been proposed, particularly by those designers working on the concept of the 'autonomous house', that small anaerobic digesters might be developed at the scale of the single building, to treat sewage, kitchen and possibly garden wastes, and to provide a small supply of fuel gas for cooking or other purposes. Designs of combination privies with anaerobic digesters, intended for rural and outdoor use, have been published by Gotaas (Composting, WHO, Geneva 1956 chapter 9 pp.171-93); and one domestic system has been actually installed, in the experimental 'Street Farmhouse' designed and built by Grahame Caine in London. These installations will be described shortly.

Problems with domestic digesters

Amounts of material

There are two main drawbacks to the domestic or single-building digester. The first concerns the amounts of digestible material available, and the resulting quantities of gas to be expected. Considering sewage alone; the average weight of faeces (depending on diet and other factors) excreted by one adult per day is $0 \cdot 4$ to $0 \cdot 5$ lbs, the average quantity of urine two pints, and the combined weight of both together about $2 \cdot 7$ lbs. These are total figures for the complete day. There would clearly be differences between the amounts and composition of material to be treated in different buildings - for example as between dwellings, and central urban buildings occupied only during working hours - depending on patterns of occupation and people's hygienic habits. On average the total amount of sewage processed in central plants, from British statistics, yields about $1 \cdot 2$ ft^3 of gas per person served, per day. This is to be compared with the domestic consumption of gas solely for cooking purposes (again going by U.K. figures), of the fuel equivalent of roughly 32 ft^3 of methane per day, for a three-person household. It is obvious immediately that the gap between this demand, and the potential supply, is wide.

There might be a possibility of increasing this efficiency of gas production; and the inclusion of organic food wastes and appropriate garden refuse would much increase the yield, perhaps to somewhere nearer 3 or 4 ft^3 of gas per person per day. Even so it seems quite out of the question to supply domestic gas needs from this source alone, even just for cooking, and even assuming some fairly drastic energy conservation measures through the design of the cooker and by changes perhaps in cooking habits.

Augmenting input to domestic digesters

For domestic scale methane digesters which will provide any appreciable output of fuel, some means must be found for increasing the amount of material available for digestion. This might be animal manure - and if the household or smallholding is planned to be self-sufficient in food as well as energy supplies, then the cows, goats, pigs or chickens which are kept for this purpose will provide the manure necessary to supply the digester. Detailed figures are available in the agricultural literature for the average production and chemical composition of manure, for a variety of types of farm animals and birds. Otherwise the alternative is to cultivate some special vegetable crop as raw material for digestion. The

Algae/methane systems

most appropriate species are algae, which can be grown in tanks and require no great effort in harvesting; whose photosynthetic efficiency is very high; which contain little indigestible fibrous matter which might block the digester; and which being microscopic in size have a high surface to volume ratio and can be grown in a homogenous culture which is very readily digestible.

Several designs of combined algae/methane systems have been proposed, and some built. These are described briefly below. Meanwhile the second problem, besides quantities of material, with the small-scale local treatment of human sewage - either by

Dangers of disease

aerobic or anaerobic means - is the grave danger of disease. It is this danger of course which was the principal reason for the development of centralised water-borne sewage systems during the last century. The main hazards to health are those presented by faecal-borne diseases, of which the most common are cholera and the various forms of typhoid, dysentery, enteritis and diarrhoea. Few or no public health problems arise by contrast in the treatment and disposal of urine.

Destruction of pathogens

Most of the bacteria and other pathogenic organisms, as well as the eggs of flies which play an important role in the transmission of such diseases, are destroyed by temperatures in the 110° - 130°F range. It is usual for temperatures at the centre of a reasonably sized aerobic compost pile to reach 150°F or so. Temperature is the most important agent in the destruction of pathogens; but there are also synthesised in composting material a number of antibiotic substances, such as actinomycetes and fungi, which play an additional part in pathogen destruction. Aerobic composting can thus be effective as a sanitary measure; and it was in part as a means of treating human sewage that the practice of composting was introduced in India, South Africa, China and in Europe. The observations of many workers in these countries, in particular those of Van Vuren in South Africa, indicate that in properly managed

composting operations, pathogens and fly eggs are satisfactorily
destroyed, so long as adequate time is allowed for the process.
There can nevertheless still be dangers resulting from sloppy
handling of the material, or if the composting piles are not turned
thoroughly so that all material is exposed to the high temperatures
at the piles' centres.

In view of these problems, and the difficulty of maintaining
perfect control of composting operations at all times, Golueke
warns that 'the composting of night-soil or of raw sewage sludge
with refuse should be undertaken with great reluctance. The
resulting compost product should be subjected to heat sterilization.
If not sterilized, its use should be restricted to applications that
involve no human contact, directly or indirectly.' It would
obviously be foolish not to heed these warnings. Nevertheless
composting is widely and succesfully practised as a means of sewage
treatment; and there is on the market at least one design of composting toilet, the Swedish- manufactured 'Clivus' (described and
illustrated below), in which sewage and kitchen wastes are composted together with grass, leaves, earth and peat mould, to
yield a humus which is removed at intervals of about a year or
longer. It is probably this very long period for which the composted material is allowed to rest before use that ensures the free-
dom from dangers to health, in this case.

As for anaerobic decomposition, this as we have seen proceeds
usually at temperatures up to and around 95°F, and so the thermal
destruction of pathogens is not ensured as it is with aerobic composting. In the designs for combination latrines with anaerobic
digesters which have been put forward by Gotaas, he recommends
that since human sewage is digested along with other wastes, a
period of three months at a minimum should be allowed for
digestion so that pathogens shall be destroyed. It would probably
be wise to allow much greater periods, quite as long as those
allowed in the Clivus aerobic system for instance.

Composting toilets

**Latrine/digesters
designed by Gotaas**

The privies illustrated by Gotaas are designed to serve either one
family or to be shared between several. The digester tank is placed
below ground level, and the gas-holder is central over the tank,
and rises vertically. Manholes are provided for loading and un-
loading the digester, and these are sealed while the plant is in
operation. The manure and digesting material is covered by an
overlying layer of water. The latrine pits themselves connect
directly with the digestion tank, but the water layer, together with
a baffle between tank and pit, ensure cleanliness in operation and
prevent the escape of gas.

'Street Farmhouse'

At Eltham in South London, on the playing fields of the Thames
Polytechnic, Grahame Caine and other members of the 'Street
Farm' group have built an 'Eco-house', otherwise 'Street Farmhouse',
which has a methane digester for the treatment of sewage and
household organic wastes, together with an algal cultivation
system. This arrangement seems to be the first of its kind ever

built, and is still in the stages of testing and development. The
sewage and waste water from toilet and sink pass directly into a
primary digester tank. The tank is insulated, and is heated by
means of solar water heating panels. The heat from waste washing
water also help maintain the temperature, and flushing water is
warmed also. Flushing water is reduced to two pints per flush
only, and the toilet unit is a bidet water-jet type, so that there
is no paper introduced into the digester. The small quantity of
water used for flushing means that the digesting material is not
excessively diluted, and also helps with water conservation at the
same time.

Some digestion, with breakdown of solids and production of methane,
takes place in this primary tank. The material then passes to a
second tank - by displacement and without the need for pumps -
where algae are cultivated on the partly-digested sludge. The
tank has a perspex panel on the outside of the house through which
the algae are exposed to sunlight. The exposure to ultra-violet
light at this stage is intended to destroy pathogenic organisms. In
winter the algal tank will be lit and warmed partly by fluorescent
lighting from the inside of the house. Finally the sludge and
algae mixture is passed to a third tank where further anaerobic
digestion goes on, and more methane is generated. The cultivation
of algae, since it effectively increases the quantity of digestible
material, should result in a higher gas yield. Even so, Caine has
doubts as to whether sufficient gas will be produced to meet his
own cooking needs. The final sludge effluent is to be used by
Caine for hydroponic gardening and for growing vegetables in a
conservatory which forms part of the house (see p.276 for further
details and drawings).

'Streetfarmhouse 2'

A group associated with Caine and including Colin Moorcraft are
planning a second experiment, 'Streetfarmhouse 2', which will
apply a similar approach in a converted existing house in central
London. (C. Moorcraft, 'Plant Power', AD 1/74 pp.27-9). Here
the proposal is to combine both aerobic composting and anaerobic
digestion for methane production; and to grow special crops such
as radish and beet expressly as raw material for the digester.
These crops could be grown hydroponically and in a limited space,
in racks, on the roof, even on vertical surfaces.

Although both of the Street Farmhouse systems are designed for
single dwellings, it would probably make more sense -as the Street
Farmers themselves argue - to share sewage systems, waste treatment and digesters on a small community basis, especially in the
urban situation. The Grassy Brook Village condominium project
in Vermont, described in detail on pp.269-73 is planned to have
such a shared system, serving jointly a group of ten houses.

Golueke and Oswald
algae/methane system
and autonomous house

One more proposal which should be mentioned is the autonomous
house design by C. G. Golueke and W. J. Oswald of the University of California at Berkeley, described in Compost Science
('An Algal Regenerative System for Single-Family Farms and

Villages', in issue of May/June 1973 pp.12-15). Golueke and Oswald have worked on the treatment of, and reclamation of nutrients from, agricultural and animal wastes; and have also worked on the problems of biological life-support systems for spacecraft. They have put this experience together into the design of an autonomous house which involves the combination of anaerobic digester with algal growth ponds; and assumes that animals are kept, both to supply food and to supply manure to the digester.

The design illustrated is for a cylindrical structure, 10m in diameter and 3m high. The digester is a vertical cylindrical tank placed centrally in the plan. It is supplied with all manure and urine, waste wash water, and kitchen wastes, loaded in once a day, and introduced below the level of the material already in the tank to avoid the possibility of air entering or gas escaping. The gas generated is used for cooking, lighting and for running a gas refrigerator. Through the effects of introducing new material, supernatant from the digester tank is displaced into a series of shallow tanks 36cm deep on the flat roof of the building. There are three of these ponds arranged concentrically; and here algae are cultivated. The algal slurry progresses from the inner ring out towards the outer tank, and is there collected in a sump. With a pond surface area of 64 m^2, Golueke and Oswald calculate that in warm, sunny conditions a production of 1 to 2·5 kg dry weight of algal protein could be expected each day.

Carbon dioxide which is given off when the bio-gas is burned in cooking and other uses, is convected to the ponds on the roof where it acts partly as an extra carbon source for the growing algae. As the roof ponds are exposed to sunlight, all pathogens are destroyed, and the gradual progression from pond to pond helps to ensure this. The final algal slurry, which is very largely water, is drawn off and given to the cow for drinking. The algae in the water provide an extra source of food for the cow. Any slurry which the cow does not drink is piped to beds of sand where the algae are allowed to dry. The dried product is then fed either to the chickens, to the cow, or is sold. To ensure maximum growth of algae in the ponds, these are stirred daily either with a pump, or manually with brooms or paddles. Since the digester is in the centre of the house, the warmth of the interior serves to maintain its temperature. The animals – cow and chickens – are also penned in the house, and constitute a source of (body) heat. The depth of the pond on the roof acts as insulation or as a thermal buffer against excess heat.

Other features of this house are a surface for collecting rain on the roof, and a roof-mounted solar distillation apparatus. The house is designed mainly for use in hot climates and tropical areas, and depends on a good deal of sunlight for the algal cultivation process – although it would be workable in other parts of the world, at least in summer. One resulting problem of hot climates is the possible loss of water by evaporation from the roof ponds, and it would probably be necessary to import water into the system, since the supply from rainwater would be insufficient. The algal ponds might be covered with transparent materials, but this might result in rather high temperatures in the ponds. It is possible that strains of algae could be employed which are specially resistant to heat.

The house is small and hardly luxurious; and would demand a certain amount of labour from the occupants for maintenance of the system, besides the labour involved in looking after the necessary animals. Nevertheless the authors believe that the house and farming operation could be economically self-supporting, and with the sale of surplus milk, eggs, vegetables and algae could actually bring a profit of between $250 and $1,000 a year. The operating costs would be between $50 and $100 a year.

Applications of sludge effluent in horticulture, aquaculture

Various other applications of the sludge effluent from anaerobic digestion are possible, not so directly integrated with the dwelling; and have been described by Merrill and Fry in the publication quoted as well as in other Newsletters from the New Alchemy Institute. The sludge is rich in nitrogen in the form of ammonium (NH_4), and also in phosphorus, potassium and metallic salts, all of which are important in plant growth and nutrition. It may be used in hydroponic horticulture; that is the growing of plants in a nutrient solution without the presence of soil. It may be used for growing algae, which may be fed to livestock, or used to augment the input to digesters, as described; or the algae may be fed to insects or small invertebrates for fish food, or fed directly to fish, in 'aquaculture' systems for the intensive raising of such species as carp and tilapia, after the model of Chinese, Israeli and medieval European fish-farming methods. Some experiments with the culture of tilapia by members of the New Alchemy Institute East are described briefly at the end of this report on p. 274.

To conclude this discussion of the treatment of sewage, some reference should be made to the variety of designs of toilet which have been published and some of which are now on the market – besides the anaerobic digestion types described so far – which have the virtues both of providing means for local waste treatment without connection to a network, and of conserving water in **Low water use toilets** flushing. A whole number of types are listed in a compendious publication by the Minimum Cost Housing group at McGill University School of Architecture, with the rousing title Stop the Five Gallon Flush! (1973). They vary from the old-fashioned earth closet, and the simple 'put a brick in the tank' expedient, to complicated and costly electric, freezer and chemical systems.

The authors of the booklet have adopted a classification of waste disposal systems made by Winblad (Evaluation of Waste Disposal Systems for Urban Low Income Communities in Africa, Scan Plan Report No.3, Copenhagen 1972), into five categories, according to the method of disposal in each case: by infiltration into the ground, by manual removal, by mechanical removal, destruction **Infiltration** or decomposition. The infiltration type systems would include the traditional pit latrine, the septic tank and the so-called 'aqua privy', in which the toilet is placed over a tank of static water, where anaerobic digestion goes on. The resulting gases are vented to the exterior, and the overflow from the tank is channelled to soakaway pits. Infiltration methods can only be used where the absorptive capacity of the ground is good, and are not suitable obviously for urban situations or for high densities of population.

Manual removal

Where the ground is not capable of absorbing the wastes - being non-porous or frozen, or where the density of population is too great - then the traditional solution has been the bucket type of toilet, which is the simplest form of 'manual removal'. Other more modern and sanitary versions include chemical toilets, the freeze toilet where wastes are frozen in plastic bags for removal and treatment elsewhere, 'packaging' toilets where a similar principle is used but without refrigerating the bags, and the recirculating type of chemical toilet, where the liquid contents of the waste holding tank are treated and recirculated for flushing. In all cases water is conserved, but the cost in chemicals and (with the freeze and electric-driven flushing types) in energy use, can be appreciable; and with chemical treatment the potential fertiliser value of the processed wastes is lost.

Mechanical removal

Under 'mechanical removal' would be the type of system where a holding tank or 'privy vault' is pumped out at intervals by a vacuum truck. The wastes might or might not be treated chemically in the tank. Under this category too would come the normal type of centralised water-borne system, with variations such as the vacuum-driven type of network developed in Sweden, which conserves water, though involving a greater energy input than does the normal method of depending on gravity for the flow in the network. Various designs of toilet have been introduced, of the usual water closet type, but in which the amounts of water used in flushing are much reduced from the five gallons or more which is the average quantity per flush usually. Examples are the dual flush cistern which will flush either one gallon or two according to how long the handle is depressed, manufactured by Ideal Standard Ltd of Hull, England. Another similar type, which flushes only for as long as pressure is applied to the flexible plastic cistern, is the Nibo, produced by Nibo Plast of Montevideo, Uruguay.

One new development not yet in commercial production, is for use with conventional flush toilets, but employs a special white fluid instead of water for flushing, which is immiscible with urine and faeces, and can thus be readily separated and recirculated indefinitely. This is the 'magic flush' manufactured by Monogram Industries, 1165 East 230th Street, Carson, California 90745. Another similar system is the 'Aqua Sans' produced by Chrysler in which a mineral oil flushing fluid is used in conjunction with an incinerator for destruction of wastes.

One ingenious method of water conservation has been devised by the McGill University group themselves, by combining together a wash-basin and toilet, the basin being placed on top of the cistern, and the dirty waste wash water being used for flushing the toilet. The unit is manufactured commercially by Toto Ltd., 458 Shinozaki, Kokura-Ku, Kitakyushu, 802 Japan. Some of the designs of autonomous house listed in a later chapter have also proposed a similar reuse of 'grey' waste water from basins, baths and sinks, for flushing purposes.

Destruction

Under the category of destruction as a means of disposal would be included incinerating toilets, where the wastes are destroyed completely by combustion using an electrical or gas burner. There is a small residue of harmless ash. Though water is conserved, there is again an appreciable use of energy to outweigh this saving.

Decomposition

As for composting methods for the treatment of sewage, these have been already discussed earlier. The principle has been applied in the design of a mass-produced unit manufactured in Sweden and intended originally for remote holiday houses. This is the 'Clivus' which is made of fiberglass and consists of a large tank beneath the toilet and kitchen garbage disposal chute, into which the sewage and food wastes are deposited. A layer of straw, leaves or sawdust is placed in the container first, to absorb the liquids and give a balanced composting mixture. The resulting humus product can be removed - after a suitably long composting period to ensure destruction of pathogens - by means of a trap door at the bottom of the tank. Air is drawn through the unit mechanically to ensure proper aeration of the compost, and in cold climates the container can be heated electrically to maintain the temperature. The unit is illustrated in the accompanying diagram. Other aerobic composting toilets are the 'Microphor', made in California, which has a digester chamber containing redwood bark fibre which serves to increase the exposed surface area; and the 'Biodynamics' unit made in Dublin, Ireland, which has a gravel layer to act as the digesting surface in the holding tank, a layer of activated charcoal which filters the water reused for flushing; and which requires the weekly addition of a specially supplied enzyme and bacteria mixture to maintain the digestion process.

One further possibility is to combine water for flushing, with aerobic decomposition of wastes, this being done by carrying the water and wastes to a holding tank where they are aerated continuously with the type of pump used for example to aerate aquariums. The aerated liquid is recirculated for flushing, and must be changed at intervals. A system of this type has been constructed for the 'Ecol' house at McGill University by the Minimum Cost Housing group (see next chapter); although so far it has not apparently proved entirely satisfactory in operation (the system tends to develop smells both when overused and when left unused), and also requires electricity continuously to run the pump.

Finally there are the methane/algae kinds of anaerobic decom-

Clivus unit, manu-
factured by AB Clivus,
Tonstigen 6, 135 00
Tyresö, Sweden, for
aerobic composting of
sewage and organic
kitchen wastes. Made
from fiberglass. Cost
$678-$875 (inc. tax)

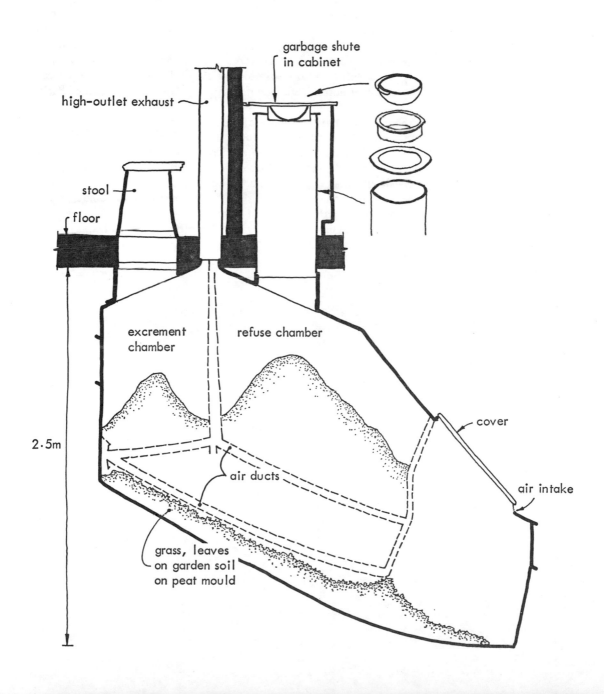

Single building
sewage treatment
plants

position system mentioned already, and as proposed for the
Golueke/Oswald house, and installed in the 'Street Farmhouse'.
And there are some systems commercially available in the United
States which amount to conventional sewage treatment plants at
the scale of the single home or building (where septic tanks or
connection to network services are not possible for any reason)
which are expensive but which do make some contribution to
water conservation. Manufacturers of such plants include
Cromaglass Corporation, Williamsport, Pennsylvania 17701 (who
produce units suitable for a single household, and others to handle
wastes from up to 25 people a day), Waltec Industries Ltd.,
Wallaceburg, Ontario, Canada (the 'Aquarobic' system, for up
to eight persons), and Associated Naval Architects, 1861 SE 17th
Street, Fort Lauderdale, Florida 33316. Self-contained sewage
treatment plants which will serve populations of between 30 and
1,200 people, and are suitable for single large buildings such as
hospitals or hotels, are manufactured by Société Vivaqua of Paris.

There are 52 types of waste disposal system, most of them commercially produced, listed in Stop the Five Gallon Flush!, with
details of costs, water use and addresses of manufacturers given in
most cases. Numerous types of low water use, electrical and
chemical toilet are produced for camping, and also for boats (some
of these use sea-water in flushing). A considerable number are
listed, again with details, in a report by D. and P. Fisk, Sweet 'n
Sour, or the Unsweetened Sweet's Catalog, from the Department
of Architecture, University of Texas, Austin, Texas.

Composting and methane bibliography

C.N. Acharya, 'Preparation of Compost Manure from Town Wastes', Indian Council of Agricultural Research, Ministry of Agriculture Bulletin No.60, Calcutta 1950

C.N. Acharya, Organic Manures, Indian Council of Agricultural Research, Research Revision Series, Bulletin 2, New Delhi 1952

C.N. Acharya, 'Cow-dung Gas Plants', Indian Farming, December 1953

C.N. Acharya, 'Preparation of Fuel Gas and Manure', Indian Council of Agricultural Research, Ministry of Agriculture 1955

C.N. Acharya, Preparation of Fuel Gas and Manure by Anaerobic Fermentation of Organic Materials, Indian Council of Agricultural Research, ICAR Research Series No.15, New Delhi 1958

C.N. Acharya and V. Subrahmanyan, 'Hot Fermentation Process for Composting Town Refuse and other Waste Material. I. Introductory', Indian J. Agric. Sci. 9, 741, 1939

Agricultural Research Council (Great Britain), The Agricultural Use of Sewage Sludge and Composts, Technical Communication No.7, ARC, London 1948

L. Anderson, Energy Potential from Organic Wastes: A Review of the Quantities and Sources, Bureau of Mines Information Circular 8549, U.S. Department of the Interior 1972

M.S. Anderson, Sewage Sludge for Soil Improvement, U.S. Department of Agriculture Circular No.972, Washington DC 1955

Associated Naval Architects of Fort Lauderdale, Waste Treatment Module for a Private Dwelling, Booklet No.21, Fort Lauderdale Fla., n.d.

Associated Naval Architects of Fort Lauderdale, Animal Waste Treatment and Disposal, Advanced Systems, Booklet No.22, Fort Lauderdale Fla., n.d.

Associated Naval Architects of Fort Lauderdale, The Digester System of Waste Treatment and Disposal, Fort Lauderdale, Fla.

K.S.V. Ayyar, 'Symposium on the Utilization of Waste Products: Utilization of Farm Wastes', Madras Agric. J. 21, 335, 1933

J. Bailey and H. Wallman, 'A Survey of Household Waste Treatment Systems', J. Water Poll. Control Fed., Vol.43, No.12 pp.2349-60, 1971

T. Ballu, 'Le Gaz de Fumier', Machinis. Agric. July 1946

H.J. Banse, G. Farkasdi, K.H. Knoll and D. Strauch, Composting of Urban Refuse, Information Bulletin No.38, International Research Group on Refuse Disposal, May 1968

G. Beccari, Apparatus for Fermenting Garbage, U.S. Patent No. 1,329,105, 27th Jan.1920. Re-issue No. 15,417, 25th July 1922

C. Bell, S. Boulter, D. Dunlop and P. Keiller, Methane, Fuel of the Future, Andrew Singer, Bottisham, Cambs., England 1973

H.L. Bohn, 'A Clean New Gas', Environment Vol.13, No.10, Dec.1971, pp.4-9

W.H. Boshoff, 'Methane Gas Production by Batch and Continuous Fermentation Methods', Tropical Science Vol.V, No.3, pp.155-165

W.H. Boshoff, 'Reaction Velocity Constants for Batch Methane Fermentation on Farms, Notably in the Tropics', J. Agric. Sci. Camb., Vol.68, pp.347-9

W.H. Boshoff, 'The Application of Methane Installations in the Tropics', Tunnel Co. Ltd. (Hutchinson Metharfe Plants), Fort Terhan, Kenya

A.M. Boswell, 'Microbiology and Theory of Anaerobic Digestion', Sewage Works Journal 19, 28, 1947

250

L. P. Brunt, Municipal Composting, Albert Howard Foundation of Organic Husbandry, Publication No.2a, 1949

J.S. Burlew, ed., Algal Culture from Laboratory to Pilot Plant, Carnegie Institution of
Washington Publication 600, Washington DC 1964

C.E. Burr, 'Solution to Pollution', Mother Earth News No.3, May 1970 pp.41-3

G. Caine, 'A Revolutionary Structure', Street Farmer No.2, London 1973

Chemical Engineering News, 'Process Converts Animal Wastes into Oil', in issue of Aug.16,
1971, p.43

G.G. Cillie, M.R. Henzen, G.J. Stander and R.D. Baillie, 'Anaerobic Digestion - IV. The
Application of the Process in Waste Purification', Water Research,
Vol.3, 1969 pp.623-43

Dano Corporation, The Dano-method Dano Bio-stabilizer, Copenhagen 1955

G.L. Dugan, C.G. Golueke and W.J. Oswald, 'Recycling System for Poultry Wastes', J.
Water Poll. Control Fed. Vol.44 No.3, March 1972 pp.432-440

Environmental Sciences and Technology, 'Converting Solid Wastes to Electricity' in issue of
Aug. 1970, 4, 8, pp.631-3

E. Eweson, A Digester with Superposed Chambers for Conversion of Organic Wastes such as
Garbage, Etc. by Bacterial Action, U.S. Patent No.2,178,818,
November 7, 1939

E. Eweson, Profitable Garbage Disposal by Composting, University of Kansas Bulletin of
Engineering and Architecture No.29, 1953

Farm Journal, 'Now... Electricity from Manure Gases', in issue of May 1963 (Groth hog farm,
San Diego)

L.J. Fry, 'Power and Electric Light from Pig Manure', Farm and Country (London), April 1960

L.J. Fry, 'Farmer Turns Pig Manure into Horse-Power', Farmers' Weekly (S. Africa), Feb.22,
1961

L.J. Fry, 'Methane Gas Power for this Farm is Fuelled by 900 Pigs', Farmers' Weekly (S. Africa),
Nov.3, 1961

Gas and Oil Power, 'Profitable Combination of Sewage Treatment and Refuse Composting' in
issue of Sept./Oct. 1970

K.D. Gilbert, 'How to Generate Power from Garbage', Mother Earth News No.3, May 1970,
pp.45-53

J. Goldstein, Garbage As You Like It, Rodale Press, Emmaus, Pa., 1970

C.G. Golueke, 'Temperature Effects on Anaerobic Digestion of Raw Sewage Sludge', Sewage
and Industrial Wastes, 30, 1225, Oct.1958

C.G. Golueke, 'The Biological Conversion of Light Energy to the Chemical Energy of Methane',
in Transactions of the Conference on the Use of Solar Energy: The
Scientific Basis, University of Arizona Press, Tucson 1958

C.G. Golueke, Composting: A Study of the Process and its Principles, Rodale Press, Emmaus, Pa.,
1972

C.G. Golueke and H.B. Gotaas, 'Public Health Aspects of Waste Disposal by Composting',
Amer. J. Publ. Hlth. 44, 339, March 1954

C.G. Golueke and W.J. Oswald, 'Biological Conversion of Light Energy to the Chemical
Energy of Methane', Applied Microbiology 7, 1959, pp.219-27

C.G. Golueke and W.J. Oswald, 'Power from Solar Energy via Algae-Produced Methane',
Solar Energy 7, 3, 1963, pp.86-92

C.G. Golueke and W.J. Oswald, 'Harvesting and Processing Sewage-Grown Planktonic Algae',
J. Water Poll. Control Fed. 1965

C.G. Golueke and W.J. Oswald, The Photosynthetic Reclamation of Agricultural Solid and
Liquid Wastes, Second Progress Report (Sanitary Engineering Research
Laboratory Report No.70-1), University of California 1970

C.G. Golueke and W.J. Oswald, 'Recycling System for Poultry Wastes', J. Water Poll.
Control Fed., 44, 3, March 1972 pp.432-40

C. G. Golueke and W. J. Oswald, 'An Algal Regenerative System for Single-Family Farms and Villages', Compost Science May/June 1973, pp.12-15

C. G. Golueke and W. J. Oswald, 'A Recycling System for Single-Family Farms and Villages', Organic Gardening and Farming August 1973, pp.64-66 (abbreviated version of article in Compost Science May/June 1973 q.v.)

H.B. Gotaas, Composting: Sanitary Disposal and Reclamation of Organic Wastes, World Health Organization, Monograph Series No.31, Geneva 1956

K. Gray, 'Research on Composting in British Universities', Compost Science 11, 5, 1970 p.12

Gray, Sherman and Biddlestone, 'A Review of Composting', Process Biochemistry June 1971

S. Greeley and C.R. Velzy, 'Operation of Sludge Gas Engines', Sewage Works Journal 8, 1, 1936 pp.57-62

S. Haman and G.A. Shastry, 'Design of Egg-Shaped Digesters', Environmental Health Vol.7

C.E. Harding, 'Recycling and Utilization', Compost Science 9, 4, Spring 1968

S.A. Hart, Solid Wastes Management – European Activities and American Potential, Final Report U.S.P.H.S., Dept.H.E.W., Dec.1967

L. Hills, 'The Clivus Toilet – Sanitation without Pollution', Compost Science, May/June 1972

A. Hollaender et al., An Inquiry into Biological Energy Conversion, report on Workshop held Oct.12-14, 1972 at University of Tennessee, Knoxville

A. Howard, 'The Waste Products of Agriculture: Their Utilization as Humus', J. Roy. Soc. Arts, 82, 84, 1933

A. Howard, 'The Waste Products of Horticulture and Their Utilization as Humus', Sci. Horticulture, 3, 213, 1935

A. Howard, 'The Manufacture of Humus by the Indore Process', J. Roy. Soc. Arts, 84, 25, 1935

A. Howard, 'The Manufacture of Humus from the Wastes of the Town and Village', J. Roy. Sanit. Inst., 59, 279, 1938

A. Howard and Y.D. Wad, The Waste Products of Agriculture; Their Utilization as Humus, London 1931

C. G. Hyde, 'The Thermophilic Digestion of Municipal Garbage and Sewage Sludge, with Analogies', Sewage Wks. J., 4, 993, 1932

M.A. Idnani and C.N. Acharya, Bio-Gas Plants: Their Installation, Operation, Maintenance and Use, Indian Council of Agricultural Research, New Delhi, n.d.; also available as Village Technology Plan 11300.1, Volunteers for International Technical Assistance, Mt.Rainier, Md.

K. Imhoff, 'Digester Gas for Automobiles', Sewage Wks. J., 18, 17, 1946

K. Imhoff and G.M. Fair, Sewage Treatment, Wiley, New York 1940

K. Imhoff and C. Keefer, 'Sludge Gas as Fuel for Motor Vehicles', Wat. Sewage Wks., 99, 284, 1952

K. Imhoff, W. Müller and D. Thistlethwayle, Disposal of Sewage and Other Water-Borne Wastes, Ann Arbor Science Publishers, Ann Arbor, Mich., 1971

Indian Farming, 'Cow Dung Gas Plants', in issue No.3, 1953

Indian Farming, 'The Cow Gas Plant is in the News Again', in issue No.9, 1959

Indian Ministry of Agriculture, Proceedings of the Second All-India Compost Conference and Second Meeting of the Central Manure (Compost) Development Committee held at Jaipur, 16-17 December, 1948, Calcutta 1949

M. Isman, 'Une Etude sur les Modes d'Utilisation Pratique des Appareils à "Gaz de Fumier"', Elevage et Culture, No.21, Oct.1950

F.K. Jackson and Y.D. Wad, 'The Sanitary Disposal and Agricultural Utilization of Habitation Wastes by the Indore Process', Indian Med. Gaz., 69, 93, 1934

F.K. Jackson, Y.D. Wad and V.G. Panse, The Supply of Humus to Soils, Bureau of Plant Industry, Central India, Bulletin No.2, 1934

S.H. Jenkins, Organic Manures, Harpenden, England 1935

J.E. Johnson, 'The Production of Methane by the Anaerobic Decomposition of Garbage and Waste', U.S. Bureau of Mines

W. Joppich, 'German Farms too Use Fuel Gas Plants', Indian Farming, Vol.6 No.2

C.B. Kenahan, 'Solid Waste: Resources out of Place', Envir. Sci. Tech., 5, 1971, 594-600

F.H. King, Farmers of Forty Centuries: Permanent Agriculture in China, Korea and Japan, Jonathan Cape, London 1911

S. Klein, 'Anaerobic Digestion of Solid Wastes', Compost Science, Feb.1972

K.H. Knoll, Composting from the Hygienic Viewpoint, Information Bulletin No.7, International Research Group on Refuse Disposal, July 1959

J.P. Kotze, P.G. Thiel and W.H.J. Hattingh, 'Anaerobic Digestion - II. The Characterization and Control of Anaerobic Digestion', Water Research Vol.3 No.7, pp.459-93, 1969

F. Kudrna, 'Putting Sewage Solids Back to Work', Compost Science, Jan/Feb. 1972 pp.12-14

G. Kupchick, 'The Economics of Composting Municipal Refuse', Public Works, 97, 127, Sept.1966

J.P. Law, Nutrient Removal from Enriched Waste Effluent by the Hydroponic Culture of Cool Season Grasses, Federal Water Quality Administration, Dept. of the Interior, Washington DC 1969

J.N. Loots, 'Diseases Liable to be Spread by Present Methods of Disposal of Municipal Night Soil, Refuse and Abattoir Wastes', Publ. Hlth. (Johannesburg), April 1943

R.D. Lossin, 'Compost Studies', Compost Science, 11, 16, Nov/Dec.1970

H. Martin-Leake, How Can We Use our Sewage and our Refuse?, Albert Howard Foundation of Organic Husbandry, Publication No.2, London 1949

H. Martin-Leake and L.E. Howard, Methane Gas from Farm Manure, Albert Howard Foundation of Organic Husbandry, Publication No.9, London 1952

P.H. McGauhey, American Composting Concepts, Publication No.SW-2r, Bureau of Solid Waste Management, U.S. Dept. H.E.W., 1969

P.H. McGauhey and H.B. Gotaas, 'Stabilization of Municipal Wastes by Composting', Trans. Amer. Soc. Civ. Engrs., 120, 1955, 897

W. McLarney, 'An Introduction to Aquaculture on the Organic Farm and Homestead, Organic Gardening and Farming, Aug.1971 pp.71-6

W. McLarney, The Backyard Fish Farm, Organic Gardening and Farming Magazine Readers Research Project No.1, New Alchemy Institute, Rodale Press, Emmaus, Pa. 1973

F. Mignotte, Gaz de Fumier à la Ferme, la Maison Rustique, Agricole Horticole, Paris 1952

Minimum Cost Housing Group, School of Architecture, McGill University, The Ecol Operation, ('The Problem Is' No.2), Montreal 1972

S. Mishihara, 'Digestion of Human Fecal Matter', Sewage Works Journal 7, 5, 1935 pp.798-809

C. Moorcraft, 'Methane Power', AD No.2, 1972, p.131

C. Moorcraft, 'Plant Power', AD No.1, 1974 pp.18-29; cont'd in AD No.2, 1974 pp.73-4

F.E. Mossey, J.D. Stanwick and D.A. Hughes, 'Factors Affecting the Ability of Heavy Metals to Inhibit Anaerobic Digestion', Water Poll. Control Vol. 70, No.6, 1971

Mother Earth News, 'The Marvellous Chicken-Powered Motorcar', in issue No.10, July 1971 pp.14-19

Mother Earth News, 'Plowboy Interview with Ram Bux Singh', in issue No.18, 1972

National Science Foundation/ National Aeronautics and Space Administration Solar Energy Panel, Solar Energy as a National Energy Resource, University of Maryland, Dec.1972

Natural Resources (Technical) Committee, (Great Britain), The Use of Town's Wastes in Agriculture, London 1954

New Alchemy Institute, Methane Digesters for Fuel Gas and Fertilizer, Newsletter No.3, New Alchemy Institute West, Pescadero, Calif., Spring 1973

Organic Gardening and Farming, 'Methane Gas - An Overlooked Energy Source' in issue of June 1972 pp.98-101

W.J. Oswald, 'Productivity of Algae in Sewage Disposal', Solar Energy Vol.15 No.1, 1973 pp.107-117

W.J. Oswald and C.G. Golueke, 'Biological Transformation of Solar Energy', Advances in Applied Microbiology, 2, 1960, 223-262

W.J. Oswald and C.G. Golueke, 'Solar Power via a Botanical Process', Mechanical Engineer Feb.1964 pp.40-43

F.D. Pohland, General Review of the Literature on Anaerobic Sewage Sludge Digestion, Engineering Extension Division of Purdue University, Lafayette, Ind., 1962

R. Poincelot, The Biochemistry and Methodology of Composting, Bulletin 727, Connecticut Agricultural Experiment Station, New Haven, Conn., March 1972

W.A. Pretorius, 'Anaerobic Digestion - III. Kinetics of Anaerobic Fermentation', Water Research, Vol.3, No.8, 1969 pp.545-58

W.A. Pretorius, 'Anaerobic Digestion of Raw Sewage', Water Research, Vol.5, No.9, 1971 pp.681-7

C. Proujon, 'The Bio-Battery: Electricity from Bacteria', Science World, April 3 1965 pp.11-13

Public Cleansing, 'Accelerated Composting of Organic Wastes with Digestion' in issue of July 1970

J.H. Quastel, 'Influence of Organic Matter on Aeration and Structure of Soil', Soil Sci. 73, 419, 1952

R. Rodale, 'Goodbye to the Flush Toilet', Environmental Action Bulletin, Nov.13, 1971 (Clivus system)

G. Rosenberg, 'Methane Production from Farm Wastes as a Source of Tractor Fuel', Agriculture (London) Vol.58, 1952 pp.487-94

F.A. Sanders and D. Bloodgood, 'The Effect of Nitrogen to Carbon Ratio on Anaerobic Decomposition, J. Water Poll. Control Fed., 37, 1965, 1741

C.W. Savery and D.C. Cruzan, 'Methane Recovery from Chicken Manure Digestion', J. Water Poll. Control Fed., Vol.44 No.12, Dec.1972 pp.2349-54

J.W. Scharff, 'Composting: the Safe Conversion of Village Refuse and Night Soil into Valuable Manure', J. Malaya Br. Brit. Med. Ass., 4, 1926, 1940

F. Schmidt and W. Eggersgluess, 'Gas from Agricultural Waste', Gas Journal 279, 2861, 1954

T.R. Schneider, 'Substitute Natural Gas from Organic Materials', paper presented to American Society of Mechanical Engineers Winter Annual Meeting, Nov. 27-30 1972, New York

K.L. Schulze, Aerobic Decomposition of Organic Waste Materials (Continuous Thermophyllic Composting) Final Report, Michigan State University, Lansing, Mich., April 1961

Science and Culture, 'Power Gas from Sewage Sludge' in Vol.20 No.7

C.S. Seabrook, 'Composting of Organic Municipal Wastes', in Proceedings of the 6th Pacific N.W. Industrial Waste Conference, University of Washington, Seattle, Wash. 1954

J.L. Setser and E.P. Schneider Jr., Combined Wastewater Treatment and Power Generator, U.S. Patent No.3,635,764, Jan.18, 1972

R.B. Singh, Bio-Gas Plant: Generating Methane from Organic Wastes, Gobar Gas Research Station, Ajitmal, Etawah (U.P.), India, 1971

R.B. Singh, 'The Bio-Gas Plant', Compost Science Vol.13 No.1, 1972

R.B. Singh, 'Building a Bio-Gas Plant', Compost Science, Vol.13 No.2, 1972

G.E. Smith, Economics of Water Collection and Waste Recycling, Working Paper 6, Technical Research Division, Cambridge University Department of Architecture, 1973

W. Sopper et al., 'Revegetation of Strip Mine Spoil Banks through Irrigation with Municipal

Sewage Effluent and Sludge', Compost Science Nov/Dec.1970

J.D. Stanwick and M. Foulkes, 'Inhibition of Anaerobic Digestion of Sewage Sludge by Chlorinated Hydrocarbons', Water Poll. Control, Vol.70 No.1, 1971

E.J. Stokes et al., 'Effect of Drying and Digestion of Sewage Sludge on Certain Pathogenic Organisms', J. Inst. Sewage Purif., Part 1, p.36, 1945

R.H. Stoughton, 'The Uses of Habitation Wastes in Agriculture and Horticulture', paper read at the 48th Annual Conference, Institute of Public Cleansing, Great Britain, 3 June 1946

R.P. Stovroff, 'Composting: A New Look at Municipal Refuse Disposal', in Proceedings of the 1953 Congress of the American Public Works Association, Chicago 1954

C.L.W. Swanson, 'Preparation and Use of Night Soil, Green Manure and Unusual Fertilising Material', Agronomy J., July 1949

D.F. Toerien and W.H.J. Hattingh, 'Anaerobic Digestion - 1. The Microbiology of Anaerobic Digestion', Water Research, Vol.3, No.6, 1969 pp.385-416

Undercurrents, 'Methane Power' in issue No.2, 1972

United States Environmental Protection Agency, Composting of Municipal Solid Wastes in the United States, Publication SW-47r, EPA, Cincinnati, Ohio 1971

University of California, Sanitary Engineering Laboratory, Composting for Disposal of Organic Refuse, Technical Bulletin No.1, Berkeley, Ca. 1950

University of California, Sanitary Engineering Laboratory, Bibliography on the Disposal of Organic Wastes by Composting, Technical Bulletin No.2, Berkeley, Ca., 1950

University of California, Sanitary Engineering Laboratory, Reclamation of Municipal Refuse by Composting, Technical Bulletin No.9, Berkeley, Ca., 1952

University of Pennsylvania, National Center for Energy Management and Power, Technology for the Conversion of Solar Energy to Fuel Gas, Quarterly Report No.NSF/RANN/SE/GI34991/73/1, April 1973; and Semi-Annual Report No.NSF/RANN/SE/GI27976/PR/73/2, July 1973

F.G. Viets Jr., 'The Mounting Problem of Cattle Feedlot Pollution', Agr. Sci. Rev., 9, 1970 1-8

J. Vlamis and D.E. Williams, 'Utilization of Municipal Organic Wastes as Agricultural Fertilizers', Calif. Agriculture 25, 7, 1971, 7

VITA (Volunteers in Technical Assistance), How to Build a Latrine, Village Technology Plan No.5515.2, Mt. Rainier, Md., n.d.

J.P.J. van Vuren, Soil Fertility and Sewage, Faber, London 1949

E.G. Wagner and J.N. Lanoix, Excreta Disposal for Rural Areas and Small Communities, WHO Monograph No.39, 1958

S. Waksman, Humus: Origin, Chemical Composition and Importance in Nature, Williams and Wilkins Co., Baltimore 1938

S.A. Waksman, Soil Microbiology, New York 1952

E.F. Watson, 'A Boon to Smaller Municipalities: The Disposal of House Refuse and Night-Soil by the Indore Method', Comm. Techn. J., Calcutta, October 1936

W.A.G. Westrate, The Processing of City Wastes into Composts in the Netherlands, Amsterdam 1953

J.S. Wiley, 'Composting Studies II. Progress Report on High-Rate Composting Studies', Purdue University Engineering Bulletin, Proceedings of the 12th Industrial Waste Conference, Lafayette, Ind., 1957

Wiley and Westerberg, 'Survival of Pathogens in Composted Sewage', Applied Microbiology, Dec.1969 pp.994-1001

F.B. Wilson, 'A System of Composting Farm and Village Waste', E. Afr. Agric. J., 14, 2, 1948

J.C. Wylie, 'Composting', Public Cleansing and Salvage, 41, 495, Nov.1951

J.C. Wylie, 'The Value of Sewage and Refuse in Promoting Food Production', J. Roy. Soc.
        Arts, 100, 489, 1952

J.C. Wylie, Fertility from Town Wastes, Faber, London 1955

J.C. Wylie, The Wastes of Civilisation, Faber, London 1959

J.C. Wylie, 'An Approach to Municipal Composting', Compost Science, 2, 6, Summer 1961

Journals

Compost Science, Journal of Waste Recycling, Emmaus, Pa. 18049

Environmental Science and Technology, American Chemical Society, 1155 16th NW,
        Washington DC 20036

Solid Waste Report, Business Publishers Inc., P.O.Box 1067, Blair Station, Silver Spring,
        Md. 20910

Water and Wastes Engineering, 666 Fifth Avenue, New York 10019

Notes on water conservation, and local water collection

The annual consumption of water by an average north American family is 88,000 gallons. This is very roughly half as much again as water use by European families; and is perhaps (at a complete guess) about two or three times the rate of use which might be achieved with the introduction of various conservation measures and without any significant reductions in standards of convenience or hygiene. About 40% of this water, all of it of a standard fit for drinking, goes for flushing toilets. In some parts of the world fresh water is in plentiful supply, and there is less need for conservation; but in many parts of America, and elsewhere, water is a valuable commodity for which demand is constantly growing, both with growth in population, and in use per capita. This growth in demand must be met either by the exploitation of ever more sources, requiring large new reservoirs and extensive systems of supply; or else might be slowed through the conservation of water by different means, and by reliance on local supplies where these are available.

G. Smith gives a table, reproduced here, in which he has brought together figures on current average rates of water consumption per person per day (in litres) from several surveys, both American and British. As Smith points out, the principal differences in consumption between the two countries are in the uses in personal hygiene and in flush toilets, which he suggests might be accounted for by the different climates of the two countries in the one case, and in the other by the larger standard toilet cistern in America (between 5 and 7 gallons per flush). In an experimental trial at McGill University, two people making a conscious effort to save water, used 200 gallons for cooking and washing in one month; and 780 gallons for flushing toilets over the same period.

Average per capita water use in litres per person per day, from G.E. Smith, Economics of Water Collection and Waste Recycling, Working Paper 6, Technical Research Division, University of Cambridge Department of Architecture, July 1973 p.1 table 1

Item	UK ave	UK: all	hot	cold	US ave	UK:	small flats	large flats
Toilet	50	43		43	78			
Personal hygiene	45	55	40	15	70	cold:	68	62
Laundry	15	21	7	14	8	hot:	50	53
Dishes	15	6	5	1	17			
Drinking and cooking	5	4		4	10		17	22
Garden and car	10	2		2	7			
Losses	20	-			30			
Total	160	131	52	79	220		135	137
Data from:	Sharp (1967)	Marsh (1971)		Fair (1966)		Webster (1972)		

(These studies are referenced in the bibliography on p.264)

Conservation of
water

There are different ways in which the conservation of water might
be effected. In the first place fittings and appliances might be
redesigned so that the amounts used for the same functions are
reduced. Examples here are the kind of high-pressure atomiser
spray or 'fog gun' for personal washing and showers pioneered by

Fuller 'fog gun'

Buckminster Fuller in early experiments in the '30s and '40s. A
complete bath with the fog gun could be had using only one pint of
water, although the process occupied as much as an hour. (There
was no run-off water either, since all the atomised spray was simply
evaporated - so no plumbing or disposal problems.) Other possibilities in bathing are the Finnish sauna (which saves water but

Finnish sauna,
Japanese tub

perhaps not energy for heating); and the Japanese system, where
a small wooden tub serves as the bath and is used only for soaking.
The Japanese take a shower before the bath and so bath-water is
not dirtied and is used in turn by several people. The bath is also
kept continuously warm and covered with a lid when not in use;
and so the whole process saves heat as well as water. It is usual
for bath water in Japan to be solar heated (see pp.96-7).

Spray taps, waterless
toilets

Other opportunities for reduced use of water are offered by spray taps,
pressure cookers, and the numerous types of toilet mentioned in
the last chapter, in which the amount of water used in flushing is
reduced drastically, to perhaps one gallon or in some instances
to nothing. Use of water in gardening and for car washing might
be reduced through public campaigns designed to encourage
water-saving habits.

Recycling of waste
water

A second area in which conservation of water resources can be
effectively achieved, may be through recycling some of the water
within the individual building or home, either with or without
intermediate treatment. It is useful in this connection to class
the grades of purity of water required for different purposes.
Typically the distinction might be made between the 'white' water
of high purity, fit for drinking, cooking and dishwashing; the
slightly less stringent requirements on water quality for such uses
as showers, bathing, washing and laundry; the 'grey' waste water
coming from these operations and which might well be used in
flushing toilets, or for watering gardens (though it might be
necessary to filter out soap and detergent residues for this purpose);
and the 'black' waste water which is contaminated with sewage.

Some systems for water recycling, and some methods of filtering
water, will be described shortly. Meanwhile, one further way in
which to relieve demand on mains water supplies is to make use
instead of local water sources, either underground water or rainwater. 'Autonomy' in water supply is nothing new of course, and
many farms or rural houses depend either on supplies from wells,
pumped or raised by hand; or else on supplies of rainwater,
collected from roofs or off other surfaces and stored in cisterns.
Many traditional Mediterranean houses have this latter arrangement.
The cistern is placed below the house, and so long as it remains
structurally sound and without cracks, and since it is kept always
in the dark, the water remains pure and fresh throughout the year

and quite free from animal or plant growth. The present day practice is to treat the water in these cisterns chemically, by chlorination; but presumably they were quite workable in the past without such treatment (though probably not safe for drinking).

Wells

A number of methods of drilling wells simply and cheaply are discussed in the VITA Village Technology Handbook (1970). The type of multivane windmill used widely for pumping water has been described here in the wind energy chapter (see p. 196); and various designs of waterpumping mill have been described also by VITA ('Village Technology Plans' - see wind power bibliography p. 212). Water supplies might be drawn from a local

Streams and rivers

stream or river, especially if near the source or if fast-flowing, shallow and gravel-bottomed - though care must obviously be taken to avoid polluted waters in this case, and the problem of cleaning out mud and debris will be more complicated than with say rainwater.

Rainwater

The calculation of the quantities of rainwater which may be collected from the roof of a building or from some equivalent hard surface (e.g. a solar collector or rainwater pond at ground level) is a simple matter given the average monthly or annual rainfall and the effective (horizontal) area of the surface. The roofs of greenhouses might be used as additional collecting surfaces (much water is required in the greenhouses themselves of course, for watering). According to VITA, an allowance of 10% should be made for losses in collection. Ideally the best collecting surfaces are hard smooth ones such as glass, galvanised iron or asbestos cement; and collection off lead roofs (and the use of lead in plumbing) should be avoided because of the danger of dissolved lead salts.

Filtering water

Water which is supplied from a stream, or collected from the roof, will require cleaning especially if used in drinking and cooking, both to remove biological or disease-carrying contaminants, and suspended solids, and to rid the water of impurities which may affect its taste. There are four separate progressive stages in cleaning and filtering water. The first is a screening stage, where large particles and debris are removed with a series of wire meshes of increasingly finer gauge. At the second stage, that of sedimentation, the speed of flow of the water is slowed and the larger suspended particles of mud or clay are allowed to settle out by gravity. If the suspended particles are very small, almost colloidal, then they may need to be coagulated together artificially in order for them to settle. This can be done by adding small quantities of aluminum sulfate (alum).

The third stage is that of filtration, and this has traditionally and most satisfactorily been done by a process of slow percolation through beds of sand and gravel. The gravel is graded by size into successive layers of increasing fineness, with the top layer, through which the water passes first, consisting of sand. Slow sand filters are effective in removing almost all impurities, including

Combined cistern and
sand filter, from VITA,
Village Technology
Handbook, Mt. Rainier,
Md., 1970

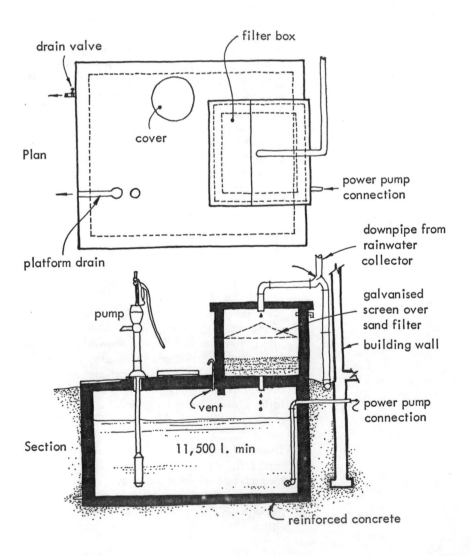

Plan

drain valve

filter box

cover

power pump
connection

platform drain

downpipe from
rainwater
collector

galvanised
screen over
sand filter

building wall

pump

vent

power pump
connection

Section

11,500 l. min

reinforced concrete

Slow sand filters	those organisms by which water-borne diseases are transmitted. The action of the filter is in part mechanical and in part biological, since a layer of filtered material builds up on the sand surface (the 'schmutzdecke') which acts as a fine sieve, but below which biological and bacterial activity goes on to decompose all organic matter. As the filter becomes clogged periodically, it must be cleaned by removing the top sand or by back-flushing. A design of combined slow sand filter and cistern for rainwater illustrated by VITA is shown in the accompanying drawing.
Sterilisation	Finally a stage of sterilisation may be introduced to ensure absolute purity; either by chlorination, by exposure to ultra-violet light, or by using a special ceramic 'candle' filter which is made from unglazed earthenware baked from diatomaceous earth and impregnated with silver. The silver is very effective as a sterilising medium. The water may either be trickled through the filter by gravity, or forced through under pressure. Small filter candles for local and domestic use are manufactured in Britain by British Berkefeld Filters of Tonbridge, Kent (under the trade name 'Sterasyl'); and also by Stella-Meta Filters of Whitchurch, Hants.
Distillation	An alternative method of water purification is by distillation, though this is generally expensive in energy. The stills might either be solar heated or might use some other fuel-burning heat source. One special problem in collecting rainwater for human consumption in urban areas, is that the levels of pollution in the atmosphere
Lead pollution in water	may be sufficiently high to render for example the lead content of the water dangerous. It seems that distillation might be the best way to counter this problem. If waste water from laundry or
Cleaning waste soapy water	from bathing or dishwashing is to be cleansed for recycling in secondary uses, there may be special problems in removing liquid detergent and soap wastes. One method for this involves the addition of dilute sulfuric acid, which has the effect of coagulating the detergent and soap particles together and causing them to form a scum which can then be removed. The problem is less serious where rain is the original source of the water, since this is very soft and only small amounts of soap are needed anyway.
'Ecol' Operation bathroom unit	A number of integrated water collection, treatment and recycling systems have been designed, some of which are in the process of commercial development. In the 'Ecol' house at McGill University, the Minimum Cost Housing group have designed a free-standing self-contained bathroom unit which is illustrated diagrammatically here. The roof is a combination rainwater collection surface and solar still. The rainwater which is collected is used untreated for showers, laundry, handwashing and hairwashing. The waste water from the wash-basin is used to flush the toilet, as explained in the previous chapter. Waste water from the shower can also be used for flushing, and is distilled to produce first quality pure water for drinking, cooking and washing dishes.
Vale Autonomous House water system	In the system designed for her autonomous house by Brenda Vale, of which a schematic diagram is reproduced here, the collected

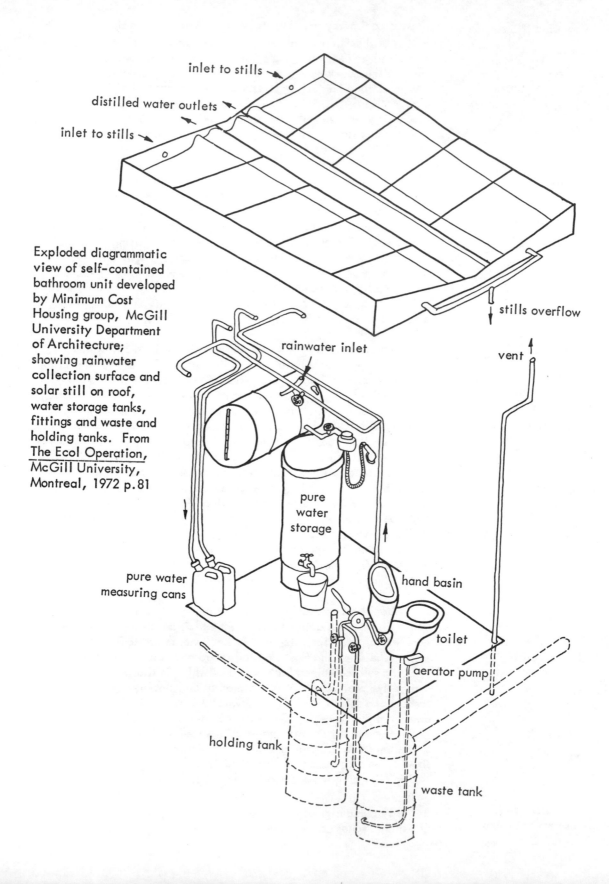

inlet to stills

distilled water outlets

inlet to stills

stills overflow

Exploded diagrammatic
view of self-contained
bathroom unit developed
by Minimum Cost
Housing group, McGill
University Department
of Architecture;
showing rainwater
collection surface and
solar still on roof,
water storage tanks,
fittings and waste and
holding tanks. From
The Ecol Operation,
McGill University,
Montreal, 1972 p.81

rainwater inlet

vent

pure
water
storage

pure water
measuring cans

hand basin

toilet

aerator pump

holding tank

waste tank

Diagrammatic scheme
of water system for
Vale Autonomous
House, showing mini-
mum tank capacities
and estimated daily
flows. From B. Vale,
The Autonomous House,
Cambridge 1972

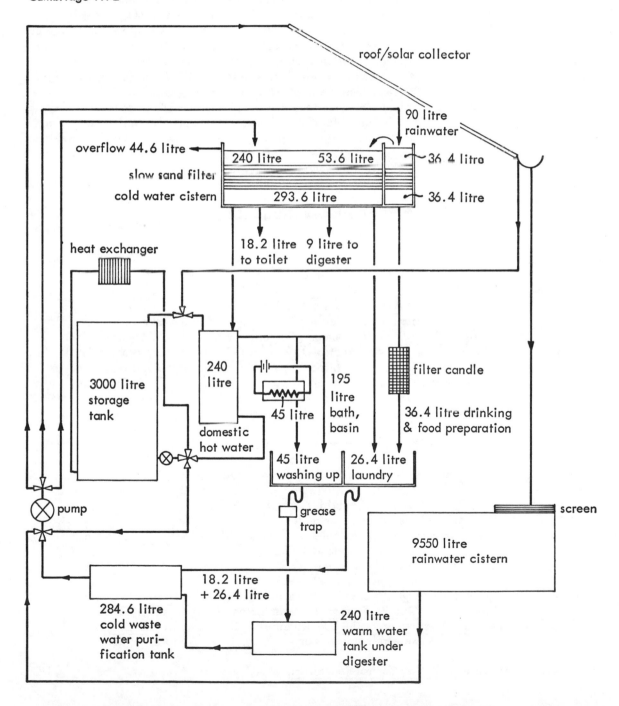

rainwater is passed through a slow sand filter for washing, bathing and laundry purposes, through a further ceramic candle filter for drinking and cooking – while waste laundry and washing water are cleaned of soap and other impurities by coagulation and precipitation with sulfuric acid and alum. The manufacturers of the Clivus composting toilet unit (see p.247) have developed a parallel treatment unit for grey waste water from baths, sinks and laundry, again using flocculation and precipitation with alum. Integrated systems for water and waste treatment at the domestic scale are under development by Westinghouse at their Research and Development Center in Pittsburgh. The whole project is called the 'Homelab', and in the system grey waste water is treated by a reverse osmosis process, and recycled fifteen times. Another equivalent system proposed by the Grumman Corporation uses distillation to reclaim waste water. Both Grumman and Westinghouse systems are inspired from these companies' work in equivalent closed waste and water treatment systems for spacecraft; but their adaptations to domestic requirements are still costly, and in all probability in their consumption of res ources and energy are not yet justified by the resulting savings in water or in connections to the network services.

Water conservation bibliography

G.M. Fair, J.C. Geyer, D.A. Okun, Water Supply and Waste Water Removal, Wiley 1966

G.M. Fair, J.C. Geyer, D.A. Okun, Water and Wastewater Engineering, Wiley 1968

C.G. Golueke, W.J. Oswald, H.J. Gee, Waste Water Reclamation through the Production of Algae, Technical Bulletin No.22, University of California Sanitary Engineering Laboratory, Berkeley 1959

G.J.W. Marsh, Water for Six, Marley Plumbing Technical Publication 5, Lenham, Kent 1971

Minimum Cost Housing group (A. Ortega et al.), The Ecol Operation ('The Problem Is' No.2) School of Architecture, McGill University, Montreal, Canada 1972

Minimum Cost Housing group (A. Ortega et al.), Stop the Five Gallon Flush! ('The Problem Is' No.3), School of Architecture, McGill University, Montreal 1973

J. Prat and A. Giraud, Pollution of Water by Detergents, Organisation for Economic Cooperation and Development, Paris 1964

R.G. Sharp, 'Estimation of Future Demands on Water Resources in Britain', J. Inst. Water Engineers, London 1967

G.E. Smith, Economics of Water Collection and Waste Recycling, Working Paper 6, Technical Research Division, University of Cambridge Department of Architecture, Cambridge, England 1973

A.C. Twort, A Textbook of Water Supply, Arnold 1963

VITA (Volunteers for International Technical Assistance), Village Technology Handbook, Mt. Rainier, Maryland 1970

E.G. Wagner and J.N. Lanoix, Water Supply for Rural Areas and Small Communities, WHO Monograph No.42, 1959

H. Wallman, 'Should We Recycle/Conserve Household Water?', 6th International Water Quality Symposium, Washington, April 18–19, 1972

C.J.D. Webster, An Investigation of the Use of Water Outlets in Multi-Story Flats, Building Research Station Current Paper 4/72, Watford, England 1972

Journal of the Water Pollution Control Federation, 2900 Wisconsin Ave, NW, Washington DC

Some autonomous, energy-conserving and ecological buildings and projects

The purpose of this chapter is to list and describe some of the buildings, existing or planned, in which the attempt has been made to integrate into one design a whole variety of energy-conserving measures, systems for the exploitation of ambient or local energy sources, and other 'ecological' features (such as local waste processing, water collection and treatment, integration of food production with the dwelling and so on.) Several of these projects go very far along the road towards complete autonomy, that is to say independence from centralised network service systems. Some have been mentioned already in other contexts, as for instance in the specific discussions of solar heating, wind energy and methane digesters; and the same information will not be repeated here.

Though many of the systems and devices described so far in this report may be installed and used quite independently, there are quite new possibilities which emerge when the design of a building is considered as an integrated whole; for bringing together these separate items such that their combination amounts to very much more than just the sum of their parts. In some instances the same piece of mechanical apparatus may serve two or more functions, as in the combined solar thermal and solar electric collector devised for the University of Delaware Solar One house, or the single wind machine with generator and alternator, or with electrical and mechanical power taken off the same shaft (the latter arrangement as in the Cambridge autonomous house scheme). The roofs of buildings or of greenhouses may serve many purposes - doubling as solar collectors, solar stills, rainwater collection surfaces, and radiators or evaporative surfaces for space cooling on summer nights.

In other circumstances the same equipment may serve two functions at different times, for example during the day and night; as with the design of solar collectors for water heating in the Cambridge autonomous house which when emptied slide up to act as insulating shutters over the south-facing windows at night. Other examples are the insulating shutters on the Baer house in Corrales, N.M., which form reflectors for the solar heating system during the winter days; or the Thomason and Hay types of solar collector which double as radiators for cooling to the night sky. A variety of possibilities for the multiple use of heat storage tanks have been referred to earlier. The use of heat from waste bath and laundry water, for pre-heating the incoming water supply, and for maintaining the temperature of anaerobic digesters, are two more suggested means for the integration of systems.

In several of the projects and buildings described here, the plan is to include food production as an integral part of the lifestyle of the building's (or smallholding's) occupants. This is all part of a

Apparatus with double function

Food production integrated with dwelling

general move towards self-sufficiency in terms of commodities as well as energy supplies. At the same time it offers possibilities for integration of the biological processes involved, with the design of the dwelling itself.

Animal dung and horticultural wastes can be used to augment the output of methane digesters. 'Grey' waste water can be used for irrigation. Horticulture can be brought inside the house itself, with an integrated greenhouse or conservatory. This has the additional function of acting as a form of solar heat collector, since the heated air from a south-facing conservatory can be passed to the living spaces of the house proper - or, if the back wall of the greenhouse is glazed also, there will be some direct solar radiation passing right through to the rooms behind. What is more, since through their metabolic processes the plants in a greenhouse absorb carbon dioxide and release oxygen, they constitute a kind of natural air-conditioning system, to balance the converse effects of human respiration; so reducing the requirements for air change in the dwelling, which can be an appreciable factor in heat loss. Warm waste water or solar heated water may be used in algal culture (for waste treatment, to supplement the input to a digester, or as food for livestock), or in aquaculture. The nutrients in digested sewage sludge may also be used for the same purposes, as well as in horticulture. In some of the schemes listed, one very traditional biological source of energy is exploited, and that is timber, burned for cooking and heating. Studies have been made of the acreage required and of appropriate techniques of silviculture for given rates of consumption of wood.

One final general point: there may be ways in which different energy systems can complement each other on a seasonal basis, the most obvious being the combination of solar heating and solar cooling systems (using the same collectors and storage reservoirs), and the combination of solar with wind power installations, in those climates where the one energy source is the most plentiful in summer, the other in winter.

Several more detailed aspects of the integration of energy, waste and water treatment and agricultural systems are mentioned in the pages which follow. A system diagram by Brenda Vale for her Autonomous House proposal (see p.281) which is illustrated here, shows features and interrelationships common to a number of current projects.

Integration of
greenhouse with
dwelling

System diagram for Vale
Autonomous House, show-
ing components and inter-
relationships. From B.
Vale, The Autonomous
House, part of a 5th year
thesis submitted to the
University of Cambridge
Department of Archi-
tecture, 1972

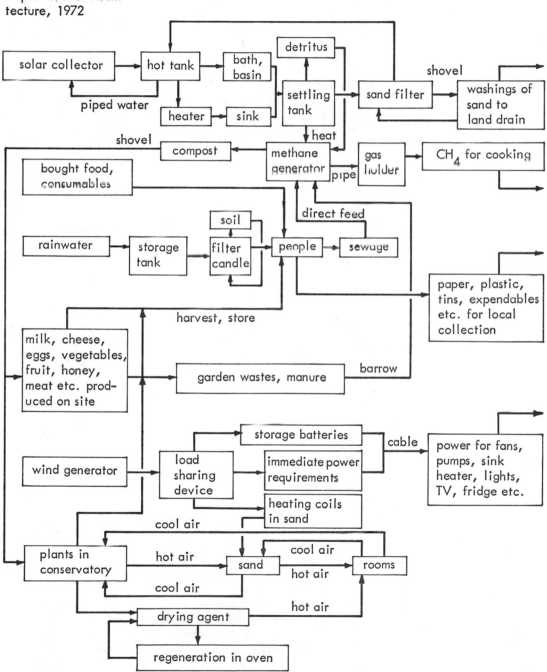

Integrated Life
Support Systems
Laboratories

Details of the Prototype 1 dome house built by Robert Reines and Integrated Life Support Systems Laboratories at Tijeras near Albuquerque, N.M., have been already given in the solar energy chapter (pp. 149-50). The wind-electric system for the house is described there under the 'Remarks' section. The ILS Labs are continuing to design, build and experiment with further energy-conserving systems, as well as carrying out an extensive program of instrumentation and evaluation of performance on the first prototype dwelling. Current projects include the construction of three more domes of various sizes, one as a wind and solar powered machine shop (where yet more prototypes will be made) and with solar collectors built into the surface of the dome itself.

In the preliminary design stage is a scheme for a mass-production version of the ILS dwelling which could be erected by unskilled labour and would be competitive in price with mobile homes; also energy conservation schemes and solar and wind powered systems at the scale of multiple dwellings and of whole communities. Studies are being made of the redesign of household appliances, in particular refrigerators and cookers, with a view to energy conservation. ILS Labs are an approved project of the John Muir Institute for Environmental Studies in San Francisco.

Project Ouroboros

Project Ouroboros in Minneapolis has been already described in the chapter on solar energy also (p.145). A plan drawing and sectional diagram appear on p.146. Project Ouroboros is a house built during 1973 by 160 students from the University of Minnesota School of Architecture and Landscape Architecture, under the direction of Professors Dennis Holloway and Tom Bender. The name 'Ouroboros' is a reference to the mythical snake which swallows its own tail - 'Now the dragon, while it bites itself in its tail and devours for the most part itself, becomes food for itself' - so a classic image of recycling, of the closure of systems. Besides the Thomason type solar heating, the auxiliary wood-burning and electric immersion heating systems, and the special insulating earth berm and sod roof, the house features a design of wind-electric generator developed by Allan Sondak (a student at the School) with a 15', two-bladed propeller on a 60' tower. The output is expected to vary from 500W in a 15 mph wind to 4kW in 25 mph, at 110v DC. Three parallel electrical systems will be installed, one DC for heating, some lighting and motors, one AC inverted from the wind generator output for electronic apparatus, and a supplementary AC mains circuit. Electricity storage is in a 250 Amp-hour house lighting battery set.

The water supply is from the mains, but conservation of water is helped by the use of a Japanese-style cedar tub for bathing, and a high pressure shower. There are future plans to install a waste water filtration and recycling system. Sewage and kitchen wastes are digested aerobically in a 'Clivus' composting unit (so saving water otherwise used for flushing). A room in the basement will be used as a cold store in winter and a root cellar during the rest of the year. It is suggested that a design of refrigerator might be possible which would exchange heat automatically with the outside air in cold weather, without any expenditure of electrical energy; though this idea remains to be explored. It is planned that the performance of the house be monitored in detail, using special instruments and statistical analysis by computer.

Other projects envisaged for the future include construction of an anaerobic sewage digester to produce methane: a second house whose design would build on the experience gained from the first; and the redesign and conversion of existing central city houses in St. Paul (see p.120) to cut heat losses, conserve water and conserve energy (e.g. by appliance design, solar water heating etc.).

Ecol Operation

'Ecol' is the name given by Buckminster Fuller to a house built by the Minimum Cost Housing group at the McGill University School of Architecture, in Montreal, when he visited the School and the house in October 1972. (Described in A. Ortega et al., The Ecol Operation ('The Problem Is', No.2), Montreal 1972.) Although erected in Montreal, the design is intended as a prototype for low cost, self-built housing for hot climates and underdeveloped countries.

The walls of the house are made of hand-cast sulfur blocks, and from a proprietary design of prefabricated 'log cabin' type timber system. The roof is of asbestos sewer pipes cut lengthwise to form giant elongated pantiles. The water collection and recycling, solar distillation and waste treatment systems in the freestanding bathroom unit alongside the house, have been described in the last chapter. The Brace Research Institute have advised on the installation of a 400W Lübing wind-electric generator which powers the lights in the house and powers the aerator motor for the waste treatment tank. The group has built a simple solar cooker for use by the occupants of the house. Total cost of the materials for the structure and the sanitary and electrical systems (but not including the Lübing windmill) was $1,900.

Grassy Brook Village

One of the few current attempts at 'autonomous' housing on a scale larger than the single dwelling, is the condominium called Grassy Brook Village planned by the developed Richard Blazej for a site near Brookline, Vermont. ('Grassy Brook Village... An Ecologically Sound Community in the Works', Lifestyle! No.2, Dec.1972 pp.76-81.) Two clusters each of ten houses are planned, together with communal workshops, laundry and central green or common, on a small part of a plot totalling 43 acres. The remainder will be left wooded. The architects are People/Space Company of Boston. The engineering consultants are Dubin-Mindell-Bloome of New York.

It is particularly interesting that Blazej is developing Grassy Brook Village as a speculative venture, and will thus be obliged to work broadly within the financial constraints of the existing housing

'Ecol' house, Montreal, designed and built by the Minimum Cost Housing Group, School of Architecture, McGill University. The left-hand section is built from sulfur blocks, the right-hand from the 'Pan-Abode' cedar log prefabrication system. The center section is a covered porch. The windmill is a Lübing 400W machine installed by members of the Brace Research Institute.

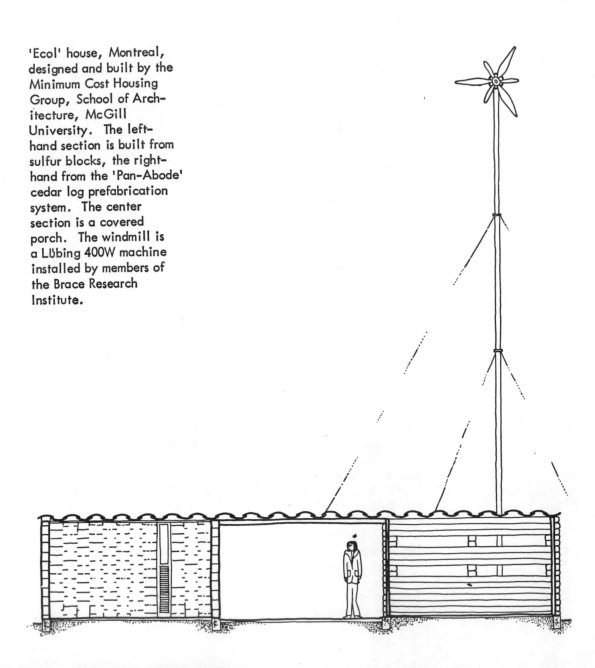

market. (Although the prices of the house units could be expected to take account of the lowered running costs which will offset any higher capital cost, as well of course as the less tangible attractions of the proposed community – its philosophy and purpose.)

The accompanying drawings show the site plan of one ten-unit cluster with the communal spaces, and a perspective view. The scheme is of particular interest because of the possibilities which it introduces for shared service systems on a scale intermediate between that of a single building and the very highly centralised large scale network typical of current practice. A single solar collector will be installed for each group of ten houses, for instance. (This collector will be 4,500 ft^2 in area, at a tilt of 57° and arranged in saw-tooth form to reduce height and wind loads.) This brings intrinsic economies in construction, over the cost of ten separate collectors; and what is more the combined peak load for ten houses will not be equal to the sum of the ten separate peak loads, since these would not be expected to coincide exactly in time. The fact of separating collector from houses – though this could lead to heat losses possibly, from the heat transfer systems and from the collector itself – does mean that the severe constraints on architectural form imposed by the requirements of integrated collectors, are relaxed. Instead the houses will have their south faces free to be opened up with large windows to allow the passage of direct solar heat – these windows being covered up with insulating shutters at night and in the hotter parts of the summer.

Communal living can in general bring savings both in energy and in resources – as for example in the communal laundry and other services at Grassy Brook Village, or say in communal cooking (which is not planned in this case). (See, in this context, the article by M. Corr and D. MacLeod, 'Getting it Together' in Environment, Nov.1972.) Indeed there is a sense in which one might argue that the move towards the isolated single-family 'autonomous' house could involve a duplication of equipment and systems, and a waste of resources as a result, by comparison with the opportunities for conservation, where systems are shared at the community or group level as in Blazej's scheme.

It is proposed that a single large heat storage reservoir of 20,000 gals capacity be employed at Grassy Brook Village. Here again the fact of using one large reservoir instead of ten smaller ones, will tend to cut heat losses because of the higher resulting volume to surface ratio. Heat transfer to the houses is via circulating hot water to standard fan coil units. The output will be boosted with the use of heat pumps. Auxiliary heating is with an oil-fired burner to boost the temperature of the central heat storage reservoir; as well as by wood-burning stoves in each individual house. The wood for these stoves will be collected from the surrounding forest; and fallen branches, fallen trees and the products of necessary clearing and trimming should provide enough for this occasional need.

Grassy Brook Village, Brookline, Vermont: plan of ten-unit condominium with common facilities, and, <u>below</u>, perspective view showing shared solar collector at left. Scheme as revised August 1974.

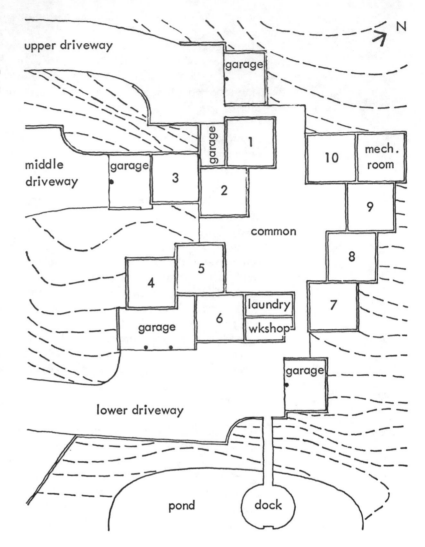

Various waste treatment and water conservation schemes are planned for later stages. Sewage may be treated by means of an anaerobic digester, along the lines of those designed by Singh, to yield methane and humus. The digester may be warmed with waste bath, sink and laundry water circulated through a water jacket. Some of this waste water may be cleaned, using a sand filter, and recycled for such uses as flushing and laundry. For electricity supply, two possibilities are under consideration; methane-powered fuel cells, and a wind-electric generator. There are certain economies of scale operating in the use of a single wind machine, of large size, rather than several small ones, as already explained. In the short term and for emergencies the development will be wired into the central utility supply.

Cary Arboretum, New York Botanical Gardens

At the Cary Arboretum of the New York Botanical Gardens, in Millbrook, N.Y., besides the projected solar water heating, space heating and cooling systems for the new administration and research building designed by architect Malcolm Wells and engineers Dubin-Mindell-Bloome (see p. 164), ecological and energy concerns are emphasised in other ways – through the use of deep earth-covered, planted roofs; the use of rainwater, sub-surface water and recycled drain water in flushing and irrigation; and the use of a waterless, composting organic waste treatment system. Other possibilities being investigated are wind power, methane digesters, and various means for reduction of power use, e.g. in lighting and through heat recovery devices.

College of the Atlantic

Edward L. Barnes and Valentine Lehr (of Lehr Associates), both of New York, are the architect and engineer respectively for the new College of the Atlantic buildings to be put up at the College's site at Bar Harbor, Mount Desert Island, off the coast of Maine. The College of the Atlantic was founded in 1969 as an undergraduate liberal arts college placing special emphasis on such subjects as ecology and the relation of man to the environment. Rene Dubos is one of the College's trustees. New buildings are planned, to house classrooms, laboratories, a library, dormitories and common rooms.

The site is on a saddle between two hills, and the development plan takes account of the findings of an ecological analysis, and of the climate, terrain and plant life of the area. A variety of alternatives for energy conservation and environmentally sound systems and features in the building were reviewed, divided into those thought to be practical and economic immediately, those whose function would be as demonstrations and which could serve a teaching purpose, and those which were considered experimental only, and might be developed further at a later date. Most appropriate for the climate of the Maine coast would seem to be the exploitation of wind power, both for water pumping and to generate electricity. A report on the feasibility of a wind power system has been submitted to the College by the Windworks organisation. It proposes that the complete installation for the College should comprise two groups each of fifty 20' diameter machines ('windmill farms') on the crests of the two neighbouring hills. The type of energy storage which is suggested is a hydrogen system using electrolysis of water together with a hydrogen fuel cell.

Other features of the plans are solar water heating; use of the 'Kalwall' translucent fibreglas panel system for skylights with high thermal insulation value in top-lit rooms, and heavy insulation of the wall construction to U-values of 0·05 or 0·06; a rainwater collection and storage system (though fresh water is not in fact in short supply in this area); waste heat recovery from exhaust air with thermal wheels; and provision for a future localised sewage treatment system. (Report in E.L. Barnes and Lehr Associates, College of the Atlantic Master Plan and Supplement, July 1973).

| Mrs A. N. Wilson House, Shanghai, West Virginia | The solar heating system and general arrangement of the house designed for Mrs A. N. Wilson by Burt, Hill and Associates of Butler, Pennsylvania have already been extensively described (pp. 165-6). This house is to be erected at Shanghai near Martinsburg in West Virginia. Besides solar water and space heating, and possibly solar electric and solar cooling systems, the house will also have a wind-powered electrical system and a 'Clivus' composting toilet and waste disposal unit. Living areas are disposed on the southern side of the house, while the bedrooms, staircase and bathroom have a northern exposure, since a lower design temperature may be accepted in these spaces. The wood-burning fireplace is located centrally so as best to supplement the solar heating system. In several places storage units are incorporated into the outside wall so that the enclosed air space has an insulating effect. Elsewhere the special design of triple-glazed window (cf. p.166), and the greenhouse airlock to the main entrance will also act to cut heat losses. |

| Golueke and Oswald house system | The design for an autonomous house with anaerobic digester and algal ponds by C.G. Golueke and W.J. Oswald of the University of California at Berkeley ('An Algal Regenerative System for Single-Family Farms and Villages', published in Compost Science May/June 1973 pp.12-15) has been fully described in a previous chapter (pp.242-4) and the reader is referred back to that description for details. |

| New Alchemy Institute, Cape Cod | Most of the activities of the New Alchemy Institute, which has branches in Cape Cod, Massachusetts, and Santa Barbara, California, are to do with organic gardening and farming, aquaculture and biological research. At the Cape Cod farm the Institute has made a start on the design of appropriate farm buildings, with the help of Malcolm Wells among others. A proposed 'Ecobarn' which will be used for animal husbandry, for raising fish and for horticulture, is intended to be solar heated, and will possibly use wind power for heating also. The upper floor of the building will contain a greenhouse and aquaculture installation, together with algal tanks; some effective heat storage will be constituted by the water in these tanks themselves. The animals penned in the |

lower story will provide another source of (body) heat (as in many medieval and traditional farmhouses, where animals and people shared the space together; and stored hay often provided insulation too).

During 1973 the New Alchemists built two 16' aquaculture ponds covered by 25' geodesic domes. The principal species raised was tilapia. Some use is made of solar water heating for the ponds (where the fish flourish in warmer water), and in raising insects as fish food. An experimental 'insectary' uses household wastes and sewage for growing algae and aquatic plants, as well as for the culture of insects of several kinds, clams and small fish. These are all in turn fed to the larger, edible fish; and the liquid residues from the tanks are used for irrigating crops. Other New Alchemy centers for experimental agriculture and aquaculture are planned in New Mexico and Costa Rica.

Chahroudi 'Biosphere'

A proposed 'Biosphere' house by Day Chahroudi is described in a broadsheet published by the Biotechnic Press, Albuquerque, N.M., April 1973. The 'Biosphere' is a freeform fibercement shell structure with glass wool insulation. Living areas are on the north side, where fruit and vegetables are to be raised. It is intended that the glass wall of the greenhouse be covered with plastic foam, aluminum-faced insulating shutters (or else that the Zomeworks 'Beadwall' principle be used) at night, and also during the hottest part of the summer when solar gain may otherwise be excessive.

The proposed solar heating system has already been described (p. 167). Waste water from sinks, bath and shower is used to water the greenhouse plants, and kitchen wastes for compost. It is suggested that the sloping roof of the greenhouse might be used for solar distillation of waste water. 'By making a living area more self-sustaining, a lot of long distorted communications loops are replaced by short accurate loops. Instead of working at a job unrelated to tomatoes, getting paid and buying tomatoes from someone who never met the people who grow the tomatoes, if you live in a biosphere and you want to eat a tomato, you grow a tomato... It's no fun spending your life picking other people's tomatoes.'

Haenke proposal

Proposals for another 'biospheric house' by David Haenke, with solar heating on the Baer house model, greenhouse and methane digester, are published in Alternative Sources of Energy No.12 Oct/Nov 1973 pp.27-8.

Nearhoof house

A design for a house by Stephen Nearhoof, of State College, Pennsylvania, incorporates substantial foam insulation in the structure, a system for the cleaning of grey waste water by flocculation, precipitation and chemical treatment before release to the ground, and a Swedish 'Multrum' converter for sewage and garbage disposal. Water supply is from a well, and electricity and space heat are provided from a propane-fired generator.

Mother Earth News
and Lifestyle.
Research Center

The twin magazines Lifestyle and Mother Earth News have jointly
launched a scheme for an Ecological Research Center (see Lifestyle.
No.1, October 1972 pp.22-23 in particular), where it is envisaged
that experiments would be carried out on alternative power sources,
organic gardening and farming, aquaculture, 'low technology',
forms of construction using local materials, alternative forms of
transport, and craft industry. Funds for this Center are being
raised by subscription from readers of the magazines.

'Ecology House',
New Paltz, N.Y.

Eugene Eccli and others are reported as working on an 'Ecology
House' in the Experimental Studies Department of the State
University College at New Paltz, N.Y. The architect is Landis
Gore, and the energy consultant Paul Sturges. (see p.120)

British work

Street Farmhouse

In the earlier discussion of anaerobic digesters and methane as a
fuel, some space has been devoted (pp.241-2) to the system
developed by Grahame Caine for the 'Street Farmhouse', built
during 1972/3 in Eltham, South London, on the playing fields of
the Thames Polytechnic. A plan of the whole house, and a sketch
view looking north are reproduced here. Descriptions of the project
are to be found in G. Caine, A Revolutionary Structure, broadsheet
1973; F.P. Hughes, 'The Eco-House', Mother Earth News No.20
pp.62-5; Architectural Design March 1972; and G. Leach,
'Living off the Sun in South London', Observer, 27 August 1972.

'Street Farmhouse', Eltham,
South London, England:
plan, and general view
looking north, showing
greenhouse at right and
solar water heating panels
and algal tank exposed
to sunlight, at left.

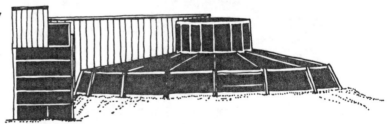

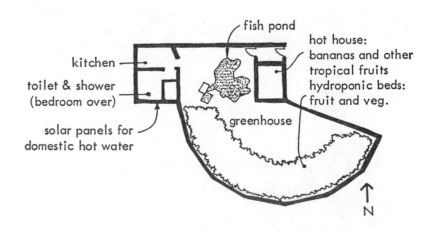

Caine's house is a fifth year examination project at the Architectural Association school. The house is built of timber, and the greenhouse of plastic sheet, and the size is 40' by 37'. Total cost of materials was about £700. The house has the methane/algae system already mentioned, a solar water heating system and a conservatory with hydroponic horticulture (Caine is growing some exotic plants such as bananas and tobacco, and is also experimenting with growing plants 'vertically' (to save space), that is to say rooted into the sides of earth walls which are retained by wire mesh.

The solar collectors are black-painted central heating radiators. Rainwater for washing, drinking and cooking is collected from the roof, whose area is 600 ft^2, and which with an annual rainfall of 25", should give about 20 gallons per day, according to Caine. The water is cleaned with a sand filter. Since the London rainwater is heavily polluted with lead from vehicle exhausts, Caine is investigating devices for filtering out heavy metals also. The house is connected to mains water supplies in case of drought and to mains electricity for standby heating. The intention is that electricity might be generated with a windmill in future. The solar heat accumulated in the greenhouse will provide some space heating to the house.

There is a strong anarchist and revolutionary philosophy at the basis of Caine's design. The purpose is to demonstrate a visible working example of a house that can be built cheaply, by anyone without special skills (Caine: 'As someone who knows my carpentry skill, or lack of, said, "If you can build it, anyone can."'), and which is independent of centralised service and food distribution systems. 'I consider the project', says Caine, 'not to contain a romantic attitude but a revolutionary one in that it indicates both a possible means to revolution, and the stimuli, in that it exhibits a realistic alternative to the exploitational vision of the environment.'

Low Impact
Technology House

Andrew MacKillop, Ian Hogan and Low Impact Technology are building a low-cost energy-conserving house in Wadebridge, Cornwall, England, with the name Chybant-an-sul, Cornish for 'The Small House on the Slope under the Sun'. The house is a mixture of primitive techniques of construction with elements of 'junk technology' - car windscreens for skylights, egg boxes for insulation - as well as some systems for exploiting ambient energy sources. The basic structure is an earth/cement dome reinforced with hazel and withy rods, and supported on a base of local stone. The dome is set into the hillside, and the surrounding earth, which is carried over the dome roof, provides extra insulation. On the south-facing front of the dome is a greenhouse through which the house is entered, by a glass door with an insulating shutter. Water heating is by solar heat in summer, and space heat and winter water heating by a central wood burning stove with back boiler. A wind generator will be used to produce electricity. The cost is expected to be £2,500, and construction is scheduled to start in March 1974. (Reported by Nigel Hawkes, 'House of the Warming Sun', Observer, 23 Dec. 1973 p.4)

BRAD Community

The BRAD Community (Biotechnic Research and Development), founded by Robin Clarke and others in the hills of Montgomeryshire in Wales, is an ecologically-based research organization, in which theoretical work will be combined with practical experiment in alternative technologies, self-supporting agriculture and small-scale manufacture. The group have purchased a 42 acre farm with existing house and outbuildings. This will be occupied jointly by four families, totalling 15 people. This figure relates to a calculation of 1·5 acres of pasture, 1 acre of crops and 0·5 acres of timber (the new growth being burned for heating) per person.

Clarke's philosophy in setting up BRAD is expounded in a paper entitled 'The Third Alternative' (1970) and two articles, 'Soft Technology: Blueprint for a Research Community' in Undercurrents No.2, May 1972, and 'Technology for an Alternative Society', New Scientist, Jan.11 1973 pp.66-8. A further description of BRAD's work is to be found in M. Kenward, 'Alternative Technology – Politics and Yogurt?, New Scientist, Jan.11 1973 pp.68-70; and a very full discussion of the service systems and of some technical aspects, in particular water and house heating, and silviculture, in Robert Vale, Services for an Autonomous Research Community in Wales, Working Paper 5, Technical Research Division, University of Cambridge Department of Architecture, June 1973.

Clarke sees as common features of the new technologies – soft, intermediate, alternative, biotechnic, whatever they might be called – that they '... seek to put men before machines, people before governments, practice before theory, student before teacher, the country before the city, smallness before bigness, wholeness before reductionism, organic materials before synthetic ones, plants before animals, craftmanship before expertise, and quality before quantity.' He does not see this movement however as a soft option intellectually, nor as a return necessarily to lower standards of convenience, comfort or quality of life. 'It should be noted', he says, 'that a new technology is far from the easy way out and certainly requires fiendish scientific ingenuity.'

The kind of broader movement of which BRAD see themselves as part, is one which concerns itself with means for reversing the flight from the country to the city, with the problems of the real development of the third world, with the restoration of a proper perspective on science and technology, and with the resolution of the ecological crisis by the reintegration of man into natural systems. Clarke has a vision of a future Utopian landscape, for which the BRAD community is a first prototype, that is curiously reminiscent of Morris's News from Nowhere: '... a countryside dotted with windmills and solar houses, studded with intensively but organically worked plots of land; food production systems dependent on the integration of many different species, with timber, fish, animals and plants playing mutually dependent roles, with wilderness areas plentifully available where perhaps even our vicious distinction between hunting and domestication was partially broken down; a lifestyle for men and women which involved hard physical work but not over-excessively long hours or in a tediously repetitive way; an architecture which sought to free men from external services and which brought them into contact with one another, rather than separated them into cubicles where the goggle box and bed were the only possible diversions; a political system so decentralized that individuals – all individuals – could play more than a formal, once every five years role; a philosophy of change that viewed the microsystem as the operative unit; and a city-scape conceived on a human scale and as a centre for recreation. Whoever conceived the idea that the country was best suited to become a human dormitory, and the city best suited to provide space for people to sit at desks, has much to answer for.'

The specific proposals for the Wales farm and buildings are described in the paper by Vale. The farm itself is to support a diversified agriculture, on organic principles, with vegetables, wheat, fish and livestock, from which the community hope to be self-supporting for their food needs. The timber crop will be coppiced hazel, and Vale discusses the finer points of this ancient craft, as well as various designs of wood-burning stove, such as are made in Scandinavia, whose efficiency is much higher than that of the open log fire. BRAD's objections to current methods of large-scale agriculture, and their espousal of organic methods, are on grounds of greater biological efficiency and ecological soundness in decreased pesticide, chemical fertiliser and energy use, rather than any crankiness or sentimental consideration.

An extension to the existing farmhouse, designed by Peter Bynon, will have 150 mm of polystyrene insulation in the walls and roof, and double glazing. At one time a solar heating system of the Trombe/Michel type was planned (see p.168). Water will be solar heated in the summer, and a conservatory will be built to form part of the south wall of the house itself. A water-to-air heat pump will be installed, using a local stream as heat source. The house drainage will be to a septic tank, and warm waste water to a holding tank, with an immersed heat pump evaporator coil. A digester is to be built at some later date, to take animal dung and bedding, and to produce methane for cooking.

Cambridge Autonomous House

A group at the School of Architecture (Technical Research Division) at the University of Cambridge, are working on the design of an 'autonomous' family house which will be independent of all centralised network services. This 'autonomous housing study' is financed by the Science Research Council and the Department of the Environment, and is directed by Alexander Pike. The staff include J. Thring, G. Smith and J. Littler, architect, engineer and chemist respectively. To date much of the work has been theoretical, and a number of publications (referred to here extensively in previous chapters and bibliographies) have been issued. These have reviewed previous work in the field, and report economic analyses of the comparative costs of ambient energy systems and local water and waste treatment, as against network systems.

A site has been provided by the University for a prototype building, which will be erected during 1974/5. Several schemes are under study, using computer modelling techniques for the analysis of heat flow and solar system performance. In one preliminary design, the various features proposed are as follows.

The general form of the house, approximating to a hemisphere, is designed to minimise heat loss. The north walls are of heavy construction, using local chalk or resin-stabilised compacted earth, to create thermal mass. The south side carries movable solar collector panels, which slide vertically. During the day these are filled with water and occupy a position at ground level below the windows to the main living areas on the first floor; the rooms thus receive direct solar radiation and have a view of the outside. At night the collector panels are emptied, and are raised to cover and insulate the first floor windows. The windows on the north face of the house are triple glazed.

There is a very large (25,000 litre) basement water tank beneath the house which stores solar heat from summer to winter. The heat from this tank is upgraded with a heat pump driven directly from a Savonius rotor mounted centrally on the roof. Part of the south side of the building forms a conservatory, which gives additional insulation, solar heating and exchange of oxygen and carbon dioxide with the air from the rooms of the house itself, thus reducing requirements for air changes.

Besides providing mechanical power directly for the heat pump, the 2 kW Savonius rotor, made from resin-bonded fiberglass - supplies electrical power for lighting, pumps and some appliances. Economies in electricity consumption will be achieved by the use of fluorescent lamps, and by redesign of appliances. The design of roof and of overhanging eaves is calculated to increase windspeeds and reduce turbulence around the rotor. Rainwater is collected from the roof (whose surface area is extended by the deep eaves) and is filtered through sand and diatomaceous earth for drinking, cooking and clothes washing. Water conservation will be helped by the use of such devices as atomiser sprays for washing. Waste water will be used for flushing and for the irrigation of crops. The roof carries a solar still for water purification.

Organic wastes from sewage, food preparation, horticulture and animal dung will be treated in an anaerobic digester, to yield methane for cooking purposes. Liquid effluent from the digester will be filtered through a sand bed and then passed to a tank at roof level for exposure to the ultra-violet radiation in sunlight to ensure destruction of pathogens, and for use in the cultivation of algae, which will supplement the digester input. Sludge from the digester will be dried in open beds, and worked into the garden soil. It is anticipated that most of the food supply for the house will be raised on two acres, part of it under glass. Goats and chickens may also be kept to provide a source of animal protein and carbohydrates.

Vale Autonomous House

The general plan, solar heating system and conservatory of the autonomous house designed by Brenda Vale at the University of Cambridge Department of Architecture, have been described in the solar energy chapter on pp.168-9. The rainwater collection and waste water treatment systems have been referred to and illustrated on pp.263-4. The design is described, with supporting drawings and calculations, in B. Vale, The Autonomous House, part of a 5th year thesis submitted for the Diploma in Architecture, Cambridge 1972. (Copies are available from the Technical Research Division, University of Cambridge Department of Architecture, Cambridge, England.) A system diagram from that report is reproduced here, showing the relationship of the various parts and processes. (p.267)

The house is intended for a family of four who will be interested in raising much of their own food. It will be autonomous so far as power and heating go, with the possible exception of occasional demands for heating fuel (e.g. propane or oil) in severe winters. The wind generator, providing 10 kWhr/day in the Cambridge area wind regime, is a Quirk's machine. Any excess of electrical power over that taken by lights, pumps and appliances is used to raise the temperature of the supplementary heat storage reservoir of damp sand beneath the floor of the house, by means of embedded resistance coils. A methane digester is supplied with human sewage, pig and goat manure and green wastes from the cultivation of vegetables. The digester chamber itself is heavily insulated, and below ground; and there are separate mixing and discharge tanks. Vale also gives details of the expected food yield from livestock - goats, rabbits, chickens and pigs - and from a proposed layout of fruit, vegetables and pasture crops, on a plot of 0·4 acres.

Crouch Autonomous House

Another design of autonomous house, by Gerrard Crouch, was also submitted for the same 5th year Architecture Diploma at Cambridge in 1972. (G. Crouch, The Autonomous Servicing of Dwellings - Design Proposals). A brief description of the solar heating system for this house has been given on p.169. Other features are a rainwater collection system off the roof, with purification by primary screening and a slow sand filter, and then through a silver impregnated ceramic candle filter; a wind-electric generator; anaerobic digestion of sewage and organic wastes; and insulating window shutters.

Girardet Radial House

Herbert Girardet has described a scheme for a house of dodecagonal plan form and with a conical roof, which he calls The Radial House (in Resurgence Vol.4 No.5 Nov/Dec 1973 pp.13-16). The plan is concentric in arrangement, with a central chimney, living areas in an inner ring, and, on the outside of the plan a greenhouse on the southern side, and work and other rooms with lower demands for heating, on the north. The overall shape of the house is intended to reduce heat loss by reduction of the surface area to volume ratio and by reducing exposure to wind. Water heating and part of the space heating is by solar heat, electricity supply from a centrally mounted wind generator, a waste digester system supplies methane for cooking, and rainwater is collected from the roof. The house is to be set in something over one acre of vegetable garden.

Futures Centre   The Futures Centre runs a farm at Ickenshaw near Bradford, where experiments are under way with methane, hydro-, wind and solar power, with recycling and with organic horticulture.

Periodicals, books, papers and consultants

Periodicals

The following periodicals devote much space on a regular basis to the general subjects of alternative sources of energy, energy conservation, environmental protection, recycling, organic gardening and farming, alternative (soft, low, radical, intermediate etc.) technology, owner-built housing, small-scale industry and crafts, and related topics.

AD (Architectural Design), monthly from The Standard Catalogue Co Ltd., 26 Bloomsbury Way, London WC1A 2SS, England

Alternative Sources of Energy, approximately bimonthly from Donald Marier, Route 1, Box 36B, Minong, Wisconsin 54859

Compost Science, Journal of Waste Recycling, bimonthly from Rodale Press, 33 E. Minor Street, Emmaus, Pa. 18049

Ecologist, monthly from 73 Molesworth Street, Wadebridge, Cornwall PL27 7DS, England

Environment, published monthly by the Scientists' Institute for Public Information, distributed by Hackett Publishing Co., 4047 North Pennsylvania Street, Indianapolis, Ind. 46205

Environment Action Bulletin, weekly from Rodale Press, 33 E. Minor Street, Emmaus, Pa. 18049

Lifestyle!, bimonthly from P.O. Box 1, Unionville, Ohio 44088

Mike Gravel (U.S. Senator - Alaska) Newsletter, U.S. Senate, Washington DC 20510

The Mother Earth News, bimonthly from P.O. Box 38, Madison, Ohio 44057

New Alchemy Newsletter, occasionally from The New Alchemy Institute, Box 342, Woods Hole, Mass. 02543

Organic Gardening and Farming, monthly from Rodale Press, 33 E. Minor Street, Emmaus, Pa. 18049

Undercurrents, bimonthly from 275 Finchley Road, London NW3, England (now incorporates what was previously a more frequently published newsletter, Eddies)

Organisations

The following organisations have published numerous papers and other documents relating to alternative energy sources and intermediate technology:

Brace Research Institute, Macdonald Campus of McGill University, Ste. Anne de Bellevue 800, Quebec, Canada

VITA (Volunteers in Technical Assistance), 3706 Rhode Island Avenue, Mt. Rainier, Maryland 20822 ('Village Technology Plans' and Village Technology
Handbook)

Autonomous Housing Study, Technical Research Division, University of Cambridge Department
of Architecture, 1 Scroope Terrace, Cambridge CB2 1PX, England

Lists of publications are available from all of the above three
organisations.

Books and papers

Much relevant information on these subjects, especially on do-
it-yourself house building and alternative technology and energy
sources, is to be found in:

Domebook Two (Lloyd Kahn ed.), Pacific Domes, Bolinas, California 1971
Shelter, Shelter Publications, P O Box 279, Bolinas, California 1973
Ken Kern, The Owner-Built Home, Ken Kern Drafting, P.O.Box 550, Oakhurst, California 1961
The Last Whole Earth Catalog, Portola Institute, Menlo Park, California 1971

Despite the finality of the above title, there is to be a further
Whole Earth Epilog published by POINT during 1974, containing
much new material on the energy and building fields.
Two comprehensive reports already mentioned in previous chapters
should be listed here:

Bruce Anderson, Solar Energy and Shelter Design, M.Arch. thesis, Massachusetts Institute of
Technology Department of Architecture 1973

R. Church, G. Crouch and B. Vale, The Autonomous Servicing of Dwellings, Cambridge 1972,
available from Technical Research Division, Cambridge University
Department of Architecture (see above)
A more political and philosophical analysis is provided by:

David Dickson, Alternative Technology and the Politics of Technical Change, Fontana 1974

Two recent articles by Donald Watson and Everett Barber provide
an excellent brief review of the subject:

Donald Watson, 'Energy Conservation in Architecture, Part 1: Adapting Design to Climate',
Connecticut Architect, March/April 1974

Donald Watson and Everett Barber Jr., 'Energy Conservation in Architecture, Part 2:
Alternative Energy Sources', Connecticut Architect, May/June 1974
Many aspects are covered in a short space in:

Fred S. Dubin, 'Energy for Architects', Architecture Plus, July 1973 pp.38-49, 74
Some papers and publications by the architect Malcolm Wells
should be mentioned:

'The Absolutely Constant Incontestably Stable Architectural Value Scale', Progressive
Architecture, March 1971 pp.92-7

'An Ecologically Sound Architecture is Possible', Architectural Design 7/72, pp.433-4
Not the least relevant of Wells' writings to the interests of the
Academy of Natural Sciences is a paper which he contributed to
Museums and the Environment: A Handbook for Education,
published by the Environmental Committee, American Association
of Museums, New York 1971. Wells' chapter (pp.177-82) is
entitled 'Museums and the Ecological Imperative', and in it he
shows how the museum of the future will exercise 'environmental
self-control', through the use of solar energy, proper waste
management, preservation of the local landscape and natural

environment, and in general expressing a 'new American land conscience'.

Organic gardening, and aquaculture

The subjects of organic gardening, farming and aquaculture are well beyond the scope of this report, and to try to give even any very abbreviated bibliography would be quite out of the question. Two indispensable 'leads' for anyone pursuing this literature however would undoubtedly be Rodale's Organic Gardening and Farming magazine (see above), as well as Rodale's books and other publications; and, on the subject of fish farming, the Aquaculture Bibliography prepared by William O. McLarney of New Alchemy Institute East, P.O. Box 432, Woods Hole, Mass. 02543. A highly praised beginner's guide to organic farming is Richard W. Langer, Grow It!, Avon, New York 1972. Another book which promises to contain much interesting material is Radical Agriculture, edited by Richard Merrill of New Alchemy West, forthcoming from Harper and Row.

Consultancies

One consultancy company in this field, offering advice on solar, wind and water power, and acting as agents for the marketing of various pieces of equipment including solar collectors, the 'Clivus' system, waterpumping and aerogenerator windmills, waterwheels, turbines etc. is Low Impact Technology Ltd., 'Catesby', Molesworth Street, Wadebridge, Cornwall, England (contact Andrew MacKillop or Peter Bunyard).

Low Impact Technology

Pliny and Daria Fisk, University of Texas

At the University of Texas in Austin (School of Architecture and Planning) Pliny and Daria Fisk run a 'Laboratory for Maximum Potential Building Systems' which has made experiments with methane digesters, solar collectors, wind generators (including a version of the Hans Meyer design) and sulfur block production. They also run an information service and have compiled a list of commercially available products:

Sweet 'n Sour, or the Unsweetened Sweet's Catalog, a Home Growin' Resource Book (compiled by D. and P. Fisk), Department of Architecture, University of Texas, Austin, Texas

Zomeworks Corporation

The Zomeworks Corporation, Box 712, 1212 Edith Boulevard NE, Albuquerque N.M. 87103, under the direction of Steve Baer, is carrying out experimental and consultancy work on solar heating, dome and 'zome' construction, and is developing Baer's design of 'Skylid' shutter and Dave Harrison's 'Beadwall' system.

Intermediate Technology Group

The Intermediate Technology Group, 9 King St, London WC2E 8HN, England, is an organisation devoted to helping development in third world countries through the introduction of small-scale, rural-based, labour-intensive industry. Some of the Group's work is on the design of tools and simple agricultural machines; other parts of their work concern building technology and methods.

A note on transport

The subject of transport is strictly outside the scope of this report, but it seems appropriate to make some brief mention; if only for the fact that architecture, through city planning, is inextricably involved with systems of transport - and at the most mundane level there will be in the majority of modern buildings requirements for vehicular access and car parking space.   The environmental problems arising out of the unlimited use of the petrol-engined automobile do not need to be re-emphasised: problems of photo-chemical smog generation, tetraethyl lead pollution, and the rapid exhaustion of oil supplies hastened by the extreme inefficiency of the average over-powered American car, carrying often only a single occupant. What is perhaps less well known is how the average automobile compares quantitatively in energy consumption with other transport modes.

Comparisons can be made between all modes in terms of a net propulsion efficiency, calculated as the number of passenger-miles moved per gallon of fuel (or equivalent). Figures here are from Richard A. Rice, 'System Energy and Future Transportation' published in Technology Review January 1972. For an average American-type automobile, carrying two persons on the open road, Rice gives an efficiency of approximately 32. This compares with efficiencies for an urban bus (12 passengers) of 40; for a Volkswagen 'beetle' (2 persons) nearly 60 (with three occupants this figure rises to 100); for high-speed and well-filled passenger trains upwards of 110, for a 2 hp motorcycle (1 person) 180; and as the most efficient vehicle listed - way above trains, planes, ships and other road vehicles - the Volkswagen 'microbus', which with an occupancy of 7 has an efficiency according to Rice of around 200.

Quite apart from their wastefulness in fuel consumption, many Detroit cars are very large in physical size. This, together with the low average rate of occupancy, of course increases the areas required for parking, thus involving extra costs for parking structures, the covering of additional land area with tarmac, and the rainwater runoff problems so created.

Small electric-powered vehicles for urban travel have often been proposed as an alternative to the petrol-engined car, and indeed there have been electric-driven delivery vans in use in many countries, particularly England, for some years. The world land speed record (65.8 mph) was held in 1899 by an electric car (later by steam cars), and in 1936 an English design of electric car was produced capable of 32 mph, with a range of 60 miles. Performance since then has not improved greatly, and the most recent model of electric car to be announced will have the same range, with a top speed of 40 mph. It is this short range, resulting from the great weight of batteries to be carried, that is the principal disadvantage of electric vehicles; but on the positive side, they are certainly less noisy, and have a somewhat higher efficiency than conventional gasoline-powered cars, especially in heavy traffic, since energy is not consumed while the vehicle is stationary, as it is in idling petrol engines. As regards pollution, while the vehicles themselves are cleaner, they depend on electricity being generated somewhere, and so their pollution is in effect transferred to the generating stations. Their batteries can be charged at night however, thus avoiding any extra load on daytime peaks. Professor Karl Bergey at the University of Oklahoma is directing a group working on the design of an electric powered car whose batteries are to be recharged at night with the use of a windmill - completely non-polluting.

To take energy conservation in transport to its extreme, one can always not travel at all; just as the extreme method of energy conservation in building would be not to build. The President's Office of Emergency Preparedness make some proposals in their report on energy conservation, for measures designed to discourage some less essential car travel. But assuming journeys will be made, then for short distances at least there is always the possibility of walking rather than driving - and the value of more walking to the general health might not be negligible. The energy efficiency of walking on a comparative basis with the figures given earlier is about 1,000; or roughly one hundred and forty times more efficient than center city driving, alone, in a large car.

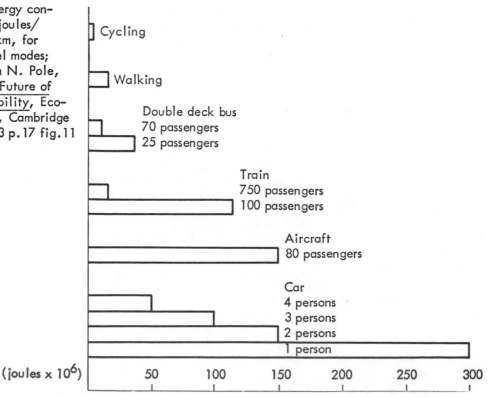

Transport energy consumption in joules/person/100 km, for various travel modes; adapted from N. Pole, Oil and the Future of Personal Mobility, Eco-Publications, Cambridge England 1973 p. 17 fig. 11

Cycling

Walking

Double deck bus
70 passengers
25 passengers

Train
750 passengers
100 passengers

Aircraft
80 passengers

Car
4 persons
3 persons
2 persons
1 person

(joules x 10^6)   50   100   150   200   250   300

More efficient still, if this is imaginable, is travel by bicycle.
Recently developed designs for lightweight pedal-powered cars
offer some prospect of getting over the traditional disadvantages
of riding a bicycle; the fact of being exposed to the weather, that
it is difficult to carry baggage, and the bicycling is a solitary
pastime without the social joys of travelling in company which can
redeem other modes. The PPV (people-powered vehicle) being
manufactured by Environmental Vehicles Inc. of Sterling Heights,
Michigan, is a two-seater, three-wheeled boat-shaped plastic car,
in which the occupants sit side by side and both pedal. It is
capable of 20 mph without too much effort, so the makers claim,
and can touch 30 mph if the pedallers go flat out. The cost is
$389. The chief discomfort of bicycle travel, that it is very hard
work going uphill, still undeniably applies; and for the weak-thighed,
EVI are planning an electric-powered version of the same vehicle.
Meanwhile one other design of pedal-driven car is to be produced
by the Environmental Tran-Sport Corporation of Windsor, Connecticut,
a four-wheel two-seat machine called the Pedicar, selling for about
$500.

PPV (people-powered
vehicle), manufactured
by Environmental
Vehicles Inc., of
Sterling Heights, Mich.